The Center for South and Southeast Asia Studies of the University of California is the unifying organization for faculty members and students interested in South and Southeast Asia Studies, bringing together scholars from numerous disciplines. The Center's major aims are the development and support of research and the language study. As part of this program the Center sponsors a publication series of books concerned with South and Southeast Asia. Manuscripts are considered from all campuses of the University of California as well as from any other individuals and institutions doing research in these areas.

PUBLICATIONS OF THE
CENTER FOR SOUTH AND SOUTHEAST ASIA STUDIES

EUGENE F. IRSCHICK
Politics and Social Conflict in South India: The Non-Brahman Movement and Tamil Separatism, 1916-1929 (1969)

ROBERT L. HARDGRAVE, JR.
The Nadars of Tamilnad: The Political Culture of a Community in Change (1969)

ANGELA S. BURGER
Opposition in a Dominant-Party System: A Study of the Jan Sangh, the Praja Socialist Party, and the Socialist Party in Uttar Pradesh, India (1969)

JAMES T. SIEGEL
The Rope of God (1969)

NEW INDIA
1885

This volume is sponsored by the
CENTER FOR SOUTH AND SOUTHEAST ASIA STUDIES
University of California, Berkeley

The First Indian National Congress, 1885

New India, 1885

British Official Policy
and the Emergence of the
Indian National Congress

by

BRITON MARTIN, JR.

UNIVERSITY OF CALIFORNIA PRESS

Berkeley and Los Angeles

1969

University of California Press
Berkeley and Los Angeles, California
University of California Press, Ltd.
London, England
Copyright © 1969, by
The Regents of the University of California
SBN: 520-01580-0
Library of Congress Catalog Card Number: 70-98140
Printed in the United States of America

Foreword

No one approaches the study of history without a profound sense of the impossibility of recapturing for the present *all* that has happened in the past. Whether his proposed work is to range over centuries or concentrate on a few hours of human experience, the historian must be selective. Hence, perhaps only the most significant of happenings deserve the most thorough analysis—that which seeks out every circumstance, however remote, impinging upon them. The first meeting of the Indian National Congress in 1885 may be regarded as such a happening for it set in motion a train of events which was to lead to the establishment of India and Pakistan as independent nations. It is given to few to have the opportunity to make such an analysis. During six years in London devoted to the study of the beginnings of the Congress, Briton Martin, Jr., had this opportunity. Then within two and a half years death overtook him at Poona in January 1967, just after he had begun his academic career but not before he had seen much of the India which had been constantly in his thoughts as he wrote the following pages. Revised with great courage, devotion, and skill by his wife, Dr. Yan-kit Martin, they stand as an enduring monument to his memory.

HOLDEN FURBER

University of Pennsylvania
June 1968

Preface

I have undertaken this study to examine the relationship between British official policy and the emergence of the Indian National Congress in 1885 and the significance of that relationship for the development of an official policy toward the Congress by 1888. From the large quantity of source material, chiefly reports and secondary sources, that has been available for some time, numerous studies have been written on the formation of the Congress. Even so, with regard to this aspect of the subject, pertinent facts and details have been missing for some years, with the result that our understanding of the setting, of such key personalities as Allan Hume, and of the events leading up to the Congress and to its final form and purpose has not been entirely free of contradictions and erroneous conclusions. Concerning the attitudes of officials toward this new phase of Indian political development, the influence of the imperial policy of the Home Government and of the fiscal policy of the Indian government upon these attitudes, the role of various of the officials, in particular Lord Dufferin, in shaping the Congress, and official policy toward the Congress movement from 1885 to 1888, we have had to rely principally upon partial explanations culled from limited materials, primarily biographical in character. The result has been an incomplete and insufficient picture, historically speaking. Thus, on both accounts, I thought it of some value and interest to examine the subject as a whole, using primary source materials now available at the India Office Library, the British Museum, and the Public Record Offices of Northern Ireland and of London. I hope that the study will supply a few of the missing links and fill some of the gaps wherever necessary.

It is very difficult to know where to begin to express my gratitude to those who have assisted me in one way or another in the preparation of this work. Mr. Stanley Sutton, the Librarian at the India Office Library, and his staff have been most cooperative and helpful at every stage. I also wish to thank various librarians, in particular Mr. Douglas Matthews, formerly of the India Office Library and now Librarian at the Home Office. Others who were most helpful were Mr. James Hutton, the Deputy Keeper of the Public Record Office, Northern Ireland; Miss Coates of the Manuscript Section of the Public Record Office, London; Mr. Awdry and Miss Bettina Wadia, the Keeper of Manuscripts and the Keeper of the State Paper Room at the British Museum, respectively, who gladly advised me and provided me with facilities during my research. I am most grateful to Mrs. R. A. Lyall not only for permitting me to use Sir Alfred Lyall's private papers for the study, but also for her interest, hospitality, and friendship. Lady Ragnor Colvin's assistance was also valuable. I would like to record my appreciation to Mrs. Camella Wilson of the Department of South Asia Regional Studies, University of Pennsylvania, for her advice on various points.

Likewise, I extend many thanks to Dr. Sarvepalli Gopal, who very kindly lent me his Kimberley notes when the Kimberley papers were no longer open for research. I must also thank Mrs. Holden Furber, and Mr. Hugo Brunner of the Oxford University Press, both of whom read various sections of the original manuscript and made most helpful suggestions. I wish to thank Professor Norman Brown of the Department of South Asia Regional Studies, University of Pennsylvania, for having read some of the later chapters of the work. I am indebted to Professor Holden Furber, Department of History and Department of South Asia Regional Studies, University of Pennsylvania, for his advice, criticisms, and suggestions at every stage of the research and the writing.

Finally, I wish to thank my wife, Yan-kit, who has been of invaluable assistance at every stage of this study. By her own work on the Dufferin papers in a related field, she brought much understanding and interest to the work at hand.

BRITON MARTIN, JR.

London
June 1964

I would like to thank Professor Joseph E. Schwartzberg and his colleagues of the South Asia Historical Atlas Project, University of Minnesota, for designing the map.

Y.K.M

Philadelphia
September 1969

Contents

Abbreviations

C.   Lord Randolph Churchill
D.   Lord Dufferin
G.   William Ewart Gladstone
H.   Allan Octavian Hume
K.   Lord Kimberley
L.   Lord Lytton
R.   Lord Ripon
S.   Lord Salisbury
BM Add. MSS   British Museum Additional Manuscripts
CRO   (India Office Library) Commonwealth Relations Office
DP   Dufferin Papers, Public Record Office, Northern Ireland,
    D.1071H/M
RP   Ripon Papers, BM Add. MSS
DVP, R.   Dufferin Viceregal Papers, CRO, Reel
LVP   Lytton Viceregal Papers, CRO, Eur. E. 218
RVP   Ripon Viceregal Papers, BM, I.S. 290
B.G.O.S.   The Bombay Gazette Overland Summary
I.N.C.   Report 1885 (and subsequent years). *Report of the First
    Indian National Congress* (and succeeding congresses, publish-
    ed annually).
*M.M.S. Annual Report   The Madras Mahajana Sabha: Annual
    Report for 1885-1886* (Madras, 1886).
P.P., Com.   *Parliamentary Papers,* Command Paper
P.P., Ret.   *Parliamentary Papers,* Return Paper
V. of I.   The Voice of India
Abstract, Gov.-Gen.   Abstract of the Proceedings of the Council
    of the Governor-General of India for Making Laws and Reg-
    ulations
Abstract, Lt-Gov.   Abstract of the Proceedings of the Council of
    the Lieutenant-Governor of Bengal for Making Laws and
    Regulations
Bengal Milit. Let.   Bengal Military Letters and Enclosures
Fin. Let.   Indian Financial Letters and Enclosures

Home Corr.   Political and Secret Records (Home Correspondence)
Milit. Procs.   Government of India Military Proceedings, Abstracts
Pub. Let.   Public Letters from India and General Letters from Bengal, Judicial and Public
Selections from Disp.   Selections from Dispatches Addressed to the Several Governments in India by the Secretary of State in Council

NEW INDIA

1885

INDIA - 1885

0   500
          Miles

Balkh
Herat
Kabul   KHYBER
         PASS   KASHMIR
AFGHANISTAN Peshawar Srinagar
Kandahar   TIBET   CHINA
        ASSIGNED   Lahore
Quetta BRIT.DISTS PUNJAB   Lhasa
BOLAN
PASS   BAHAWALPUR   NEPAL   SIKKIM
PERSIA Indus R.   Delhi   Brahmaputra R.
                N.W.PROVINCES   OUDH   SIKKIM
BALUCHISTAN RAJPUTANA Agra   Lucknow   MANIPUR
        AJMERE   Jumna R.   Patna   Irrawaddy R.
        MERWARA   Benares Ganges R.
BOMBAY   CENTRAL INDIA AGENCY   Chittagong Mandalay
                Narmada R.   BENGAL   Calcutta   BURMA
        Tapti R.   CENTRAL
PRESIDENCY   PROVINCES
        BERAR Nagpur   BRITISH
Bombay   Godavari R.   BURMA
ARABIAN   HYDERABAD   Rangoon   SIAM
  SEA   Hyderabad   PRESIDENCY
        Kistna R.
GOA   MADRAS   BAY
(PORT.)   OF
        MYSORE   BENGAL   Andaman Is.
COORG Mysore Madras
TRAVANCORE
                                        Nicobar Is.
            CEYLON
Colombo (CROWN COLONY)
      INDIAN   OCEAN   ACHIN

☐ British India and Ceylon
▨ Dependent and Subordinate
   Indian States
▥ Independent States

Introduction

In the spring of 1884, shortly before his viceroyalty ended, Lord Ripon wrote urgently to Lord Kimberley,[1] then Secretary of State for India, about a critical question of policy confronting the government of India: "You may rely upon it that there are few Indian questions of greater importance in the present day than those which relate to the mode in which we are to deal with the growing body of Natives educated by ourselves in Western learning and Western ideas."[2] Ripon was pointing to the existence of a new class of English-educated Indians within British-Indian society and to the failure of the government of India to acknowledge this class and absorb its talents and influence within the structure of British-Indian administration. That this problem begged for a realistic solution by 1884, he had no doubt; it had been left too long to fester in a mode damaging to the class itself and dangerous to British rule.

No other socio-political problem of the post-Mutiny era was as thorny as this one. When the Mutiny occurred, this class had been in existence for some twenty years. It was the product of the Anglicized higher-educational scheme instituted by Bentinck, Macaulay, Trevelyan, Adam, Mill, and Grant in response to the gusts of Utilitarianism and Evangelicalism that were buffeting the East India Company.[3] With smug English middle-class pride and practicality, it had been agreed during the debates on the Charter Renewal Act of 1833 that India could never advance as a nation unless it imbibed

---

[1] Kimberley, John Wodehouse, first Earl: b. 1826; Eton and Oxford; B.A., 1847; succeeded to Baronetcy, 1847; Under-Secretary of State for Foreign Affairs, 1852-1856, 1857-1861; for India, 1864; Lord-Lieutenant of Ireland, 1864-1866, dealt resolutely with Fenian Movement; Earl of Kimberley, Norfolk, 1866; Lord Privy Seal in Gladstone's first cabinet, 1868-1870, also Colonial Secretary, 1870-1874; in Gladstone's second cabinet as Colonial Secretary, 1880-1882; Secretary of State for India, 1882-1885.

[2] R. to K., Apr. 4, 1884, RVP, I.S. 290/5, No. 18.

[3] J. Cumming ed., *Political India 1832-1932* (London, 1932), Ch. II; B. T. McCully, *English Education and the Origins of Indian Nationalism* (New York, 1940), chs. I-II; L. S. S. O'Malley, ed., *Modern India and the West* (London, 1941), chs. II, IV; B. B. Misra, *The Indian Middle Classes* (London, 1961), pts. I, II.

English morality, enlightenment, and material progress.[4] To meet this end, Bentinck had called for extensive use of the English language throughout Indian administration,[5] Macaulay had advocated advancement of English-speaking Indians into the more responsible positions of the Company, and together they had recast the Indian colleges and high schools in an English mold[6] so as to produce a new class "who may be interpreters between us and the millions whom we govern—a class of persons Indian in colour and blood, but English in tastes, in opinions, in morals and in interests."[7] By 1857, the scheme was producing its graduates, especially in Bengal where annually some 500 were seeking employment in the Company's service.[8] But with realities such as Cornwallis' Regulation of 1793, the politics of patronage at home, and the racial superiority complex rife in official thinking from the 1820s onward, all the senior positions paying annually over £800 were reserved for men appointed in England under Covenant and hence not open to Indians. Good positions in the subordinate, or Uncovenanted, service were few and not readily available to the graduates unless they had strong official patronage.[9] Hence arose the difficulty of a growing body of educated Indians with limited opportunities.[10]

Leaders of the new class such as Prosunna Kumar Tagore, Ram Gopal Ghose, and Hurish Chunder Mukherji at Calcutta, Raghunath Rao and Madhava Rao at Madras, and Naoroji Furdunji, Dadabhai Naoroji, and Sorabji Bengali at Bombay, speaking through journals such as *The Hindu Intelligencer, The Crescent,* and *Rast Goftar,* and associations such as the British Indian Association, the Madras Native Association, and the Bombay Association, called for an improved system of higher education in universities, increased employment of educated Indians in responsible official posts, and representation in the governors' councils; but these de-

---

[4] Parliamentary Debates, 3 *Hansard,* 18, 19 (1832).

[5] P. Spear, "Bentinck and Education," *Cambridge Historical Journal,* 6 (1938), 83.

[6] G. M. Young, ed., *Speeches by Lord Macaulay* (London, 1935), pp. 116-155; C. E. Trevelyan, *On the Education of the People of India* (London, 1838); A. Mayhew, *The Education of India* (London, 1926), chs. I, II, V, VIII; Spear, pp. 83-101; K. A. Ballhatchet, "The Home Government and Bentinck's Educational Policy," *Cambridge Historical Journal,* 10 (1951), 224-229.

[7] Young, p. 359.

[8] *P.P.,* 1847-48, Vol. 48, Ret. 20, pp. 137 ff.; for statistics 1845-1857, see *The Report of the Indian Education Commission* (Calcutta, 1883), CRO, Record Dept., Parl. Branch, pp. 269, 274.

[9] *P.P.,* 1857-58, Vol. 42, Ret. 201-VI, pp. 155 ff.

[10] Delhi College Report, 1850, and statements by Principal, Benares College, and President, Council of Education, Bengal, see J. W. Kaye, *The Administration of the East India Company,* 2nd ed. (London, 1853), pp. 605-607.

mands were not met.[11] The Act of 1853, renewing the Company's charter, neither opened the Supreme Council to educated Indians nor restored the councils in Madras and Bombay,[12] although the Covenanted Civil Service was opened to public competitive examination held annually in England for all British subjects between the ages of 18 and 23.[13] However, the benefit thus extended to educated Indians was illusory: few could meet the financial and social pressures involved in going to England to compete; the first Indian entered ten years later. Wood's educational scheme of 1854,[14] which raised standards of higher education by an examination system at the matriculation, First Arts, Bachelor, and Master levels and shifted Company support from higher to lower education, only served as a momentary check upon the annual output of graduates. Employment in the public service still remained the chief goal of higher education.

Finally, the Mutiny intervened. In the reassessment which followed the assumption of government by the Crown, the grievances of the educated Indians were overshadowed by more momentous issues and, if not ignored, were treated in a reactionary manner by the successive viceroys and secretaries of state. The Mutiny led both Canning and Wood to believe that the Indian princely and aristocratic class had the wealth, influence, and power to support or undermine British rule and that domestic policy should concentrate upon this class and be shaped to ensure its loyalty.[15] John Lawrence opposed the interests of educated Indians. Almost as much preoccupied with the interests and grievances of the peasants as Canning had been with those of the rajahs,[16] Lawrence did not want to interpose any Indian officials, particularly Bengalis, between the English

[11] Petitions of 1852 and 1853 of the Bombay Association, see P. Griffiths, *The British Impact on India* (London, 1952), pp. 257-259.

[12] 16, 17 Vic., c. 95.

[13] *Ibid.*, ss. 36-42. Sir Charles Wood, then Secretary of State, successfully opposed competitive examination in India in 1853 and after the Mutiny on the grounds that it would facilitate entry of educated Indians into the Civil Service. See Wood to C. Trevelyan, Apr. 9, 1860, CRO, Wood Papers, Eur. F. 78, Let. Bk., Vol. 3.

[14] Dispatch No. 49, July 19, 1854. See H. H. Dodwell, ed., *The Cambridge History of India*, VI (Cambridge, 1932), 118-119.

[15] T. R. Metcalf, "The Influence of the Mutiny of 1857 on Land Policy in India," *Historical Journal*, 4 (1961), 152-163; M. Maclagan, *"Clemency" Canning* (London, 1962), pp. 269, 271, 297-301. See also Canning to Wood, Feb. 4, June 8, with minute, Sept. 18, 1861, Wood Papers, Eur. F. 78, Corr. India, Box 2 (A); Wood to Canning, Aug. 27, 1860, June 3, 1861, Let. Bks., vols. 4, 8.

[16] D. Pal, *The Administration of Sir John Lawrence in India 1864-1869* (Simla, 1952), pp. 45-60; G. R. G. Hambly, "Richard Temple and the Punjab Tenancy Act of 1868," *English Historical Review*, 79 (1964), 47-66.

district officer and the ryot.[17] He replied to Secretary of State Northcote's concern over the employment of educated Indians with a
Resolution relegating Indians to subordinate judicial service in
non-Regulation provinces, and with a vague proposal whereby the
Indian government could select intermittently a few Indians—not
Bengali—for advanced study in England leading to public or professional employment.[18] Northcote's successor, the Duke of Argyll,
infused with Lawrence's prejudices, saw a threat to British rule in
Indian, especially Bengali, entry into the Covenanted Service by
open competition in England (four had passed the examinations in
1869). He proposed to restrict it by having the Indian government
select candidates annually on the basis of merit and social standing
instead of "mere intellectual acuteness."[19] This stipulation, in addition to others reserving the majority of Covenanted posts for Englishmen and limiting Indians to the judicial branch with lower
rank and pay, was embodied in the Act of 1870,[20] which marked
the beginning of a reactionary policy directed against the new class.
Only Northbrook, who in 1872 had become Viceroy on Mayo's
assassination, saw the shortsightedness of such a policy and en-
deavored to give official recognition to this new class as well as to
the rajahs and ryots. In framing rules to implement Argyll's Act,
he sought to give Indians selected for Covenanted Service executive
as well as judicial posts, with pay and rank equal to those of Englishmen; moreover, for the Covenanted competition, he advised a
return to the age limit of 1853 because the reduction in 1870 from
23 to 21 seriously interrupted the university preparation of Indians.[21] But the Bengal-Bihar famine and growing differences with
Salisbury over Central Asian policy and the reduction of cotton
duties seriously handicapped his efforts.[22] When Northbrook resigned in early 1876, Salisbury, acting in the teeth of all official
opinion, lowered the Covenanted examination age to 19 and thus
put the finishing touches on the reactionary policy.[23]

From 1870 to 1885, the thorny problem of English-educated Indians was intensified. Indian higher education, having adapted to

[17] Lawrence to Northcote, Aug. 17, 1867, see Misra, p. 372.
[18] Pal, pp. 113-118; *P. P.*, 1867-68, Vol. 50, Ret. 178, Vol. 51, Ret. 108; 1878-79, Vol.
55, Com. 2376, pp. 1-8.
[19] Dispatch of Secretary of State, No. 3, Pub., Apr. 8, 1869, P. P., 1878-79, Vol. 55,
Com. 2376, pp. 8-12.
[20] 33 Vic., c. 3.
[21] Note by L., Oct. 16, 1876, LVP, Eur. E. 218/520/1, pp. 444-445.
[22] B. Mallet, *Thomas George Earl of Northbrook G.C.S.I.* (London, 1908), Ch. II.
[23] Dispatch of Secretary of State, No. 19, Pub., Feb. 24, 1876, CRO, Selections from
Disp., 1876.

Wood's reforms during the previous decade, began to expand rapidly, especially in Bengal and Madras. For the first time since 1854, the enrollment figures in government-supported and -aided colleges exceeded those of the late 1840s.[24] Likewise the annual output of B.A. and M.A. graduates increased; in 1870, there were 175; by 1880, the figure had risen to 404, and, by 1884, to 470.[25] The increasing number of unsuccessful First Arts and B.A. students who left the colleges posed another problem.[26] Having received a good secondary school education up to the matriculation level and having attended a university, these men were educated and, compared to the town-dweller or village ryot, very well educated. What were these men to do if, under the new system, better official and unofficial employment required B.A. and M.A. degrees?

Their difficulty in securing employment commensurate with their education can best be gauged by considering the plight of graduates with B.A. or postgraduate degrees. Of these, during the 1870s, only one-fifth entered law, mostly in Bengal and Madras, where changes in High Court procedure and practice had given qualified Indian barristers and pleaders greater opportunity; only one-tenth entered medicine and enginering, because senior appointments in both fields were closely geared to Government and hence dominated by English appointees; the majority, some three-quarters, entered public service.[27] Of those entering public service, only eleven passed the Covenanted examination from 1870 to 1880, and all but one of these did so before Salisbury in 1876 lowered the age limit.[28] Thereafter (until 1885) only one Indian entered the Covenanted Service by examination, and all those appointed in 1879 and 1880 under Argyll's Act were drawn from the upper classes. Opportunity was no more promising for the B.A. graduate

[24] *Education Report*, Table I, p. 274.

[25] Statement III, *Report of the Public Service Commission 1886-87* (Calcutta, 1888), CRO, Record Dept., Parl. Branch, No. 241a, App. M, p. 81. J. Strachey, in *India* (London, 1888), p. 187, stated that there were 4,526 B.A. and M.A. graduates from 1853 to 1884, but the figures for 1870 through 1884 alone in the *Public Service Report* were 4,532, while those for 1857 through 1870 in the *Education Report* (p. 269) were 1,001, making a total for 1857 through 1884 of 5,533.

[26] Statement IV, *Public Service Report*, App. M, p. 82. Failures of First Arts in 1870 were 570, in 1880, 1,110, and in 1884, 1,289. To get the figures for the English-educated class, the total number of unsuccessful First Arts and B.A. candidates would have to be tallied for 1857 through 1884 and added to the successful final candidates. Sir Henry Maine estimated five times 5,000 B.A.-M.A. for 1853 through 1883, or 25,000 out of an estimated population of 250,000,000. See J. Strachey, p. 187.

[27] Of 3,311 total, 1,244 entered public service, 684 law, 255 medicine, and 53 engineering. See *Education Report*, Table IX, p. 281.

[28] Statistics by J. K. Cross (Parliamentary Under-Secretary), enclosed in K. to R., May 22, 1884, RP, BM Add. MSS 43525, pp. 78-79.

in the Uncovenanted Service, into which all but eleven graduates passed. Available openings had decreased sharply by 1870, especially in the revenue and judicial branches, and continued to do so thereafter owing to retrenchment and financial decentralization.[29] Furthermore, many of the middling appointments had already been filled in the 1840s by Indians who now were poised to fill any of the more senior Uncovenanted posts made available to them. Thus, opportunities in the public services were limited to inferior posts, which were, perforce, accepted by many talented, well-educated Indians.

The nascent difficulty of the 1840s had become the mature problem of the 1870s: there were too many English-educated graduates and far too few opportunities for employment. It led to frustration and discontent.[30] It cast into sharp relief the question of the role and purpose of the English-educated Indian in post-Mutiny India. Affected by this situation and aggravating it was a new generation of leaders.[31] Born in the 1840s and 1850s, these men were educated under Wood's system just before and after the Mutiny. Many by ability and tenacity overcame racial prejudice to rise to the fore in their respective provinces and to join their mentors among the older, English-educated leaders. Finding the doors to the higher Civil Service closed to them, they turned to the "orthodox" alternatives of law and teaching or to the "unorthodox" ones of journalism and politics, or to a combination of both. For instance, dismissal from the Uncovenanted Service in 1857 on questionable grounds alienated Kristo Das Pal, who became editor of *The Hindoo Patriot,* and in 1861 Assistant Secretary to the British Indian Association. Surendranath Banerjea, summarily dismissed from the Covenanted Service in 1874, turned to college teaching in Calcutta while editing *The Bengalee* and founding the Indian Association between 1876 and 1878. Lack of prospects for advancement in official service led the Ghose brothers, Motilal and Shishir, in 1869 and G. Subramania Iyer and Viraghava Chariar in 1878 to establish two of the leading Indian journals, *Amrita Bazar Patrika* of Cal-

[29] Statistics for 1857, *P.P.*, 1857-58, Vol. 42, Ret. 210-VI; for 1870, 1881, *P.P.*, 1894, Vol. 60, Com. 7378, pp. 65-94.

[30] *Report of the Director of Public Instruction in the Bombay Presidency for the Year 1877-78,* see S. A. Wolpert, *Tilak and Gokhale: Revolution and Reform in the Making of Modern India* (Berkeley, 1962), p. 18, n. 28.

[31] For these new leaders, see G. P. Pillai, *Representative Indians* (London, 1897); C. E. Buckland, *Dictionary of Indian Biography* (London, 1906); H. P. Mody, *Sir Pherozeshah Mehta* (Bombay, 1921), Vol. I; S. Banerjea, *A Nation in Making* (London, 1925); M. Barns, *The Indian Press* (London, 1940); H. B. Tyabji, *Badruddin Tyabji* (Bombay, 1952); J. Natarajan, *History of Indian Journalism,* Republic of India, Report of the Press Commission, Pt. II (New Delhi, 1954).

cutta and *The Hindu* of Madras City, respectively. Failure in the Covenanted examinations in 1864 and 1865 caused Man Mohan Ghose to read for the London Bar. As the first Indian barrister, he returned home to become a searching critic of the iniquity of the Covenanted examination system. Mahadev Ranade, an Uncovenanted servant in the Bombay Educational Department, taught at Elphinstone College but devoted his real energies to supervising the journal *Indu Prakash* and to furthering social and educational reform by establishing the Prarthana Samaj of Bombay and the Sarvajanik Sabha in Poona during the 1870s. Kashinath Telang, after teaching at Elphinstone, switched to law and became an important young Bombay barrister interested in political and Civil Service reform.

Indeed, it was to the law, not the Civil Service, that many younger leaders looked for advancement. Romesh Chunder Mitter, Piari Mohan Mukherji, Womesh Chandra Bonnerjee, and Lal Mohan Ghose at Calcutta, Badruddin Tyabji, Pherozeshah Mehta, and Hormusji Wadia at Bombay, Syed Mahmud at Allahabad, and Rangiah Naidu and Ramaswami Mudaliar at Madras—each, during or after his college career, studied law in England or India and joined the Bar as barristers, attorneys, or pleaders *(vakils)*. Others followed the same pattern of legal training but branched out into journalism: Ajudhia Nath developed *The Indian Herald* (1879-1889) at Allahabad; Narendra Nath Sen became in 1879 the sole proprietor and editor of the principal Indian daily, *The Indian Mirror;* Syed Ameer Ali controlled and edited the influential *Mahomedan Observer* of Calcutta; Narayan Ganesh Chandarvarkar under Ranade's guidance edited the Anglo-Marathi journal, *Indu Prakash,* during the 1870s and 1880s; Ananda Mohan Bose, after a brilliant legal career at Cambridge, assisted Banerjea with *The Bengalee* and the Indian Association; and Ananda Charlu published *The People's Magazine* in the early 1880s.

Within the field of journalism itself, a new generation of editors and owners was coming to the fore in these decades. Minocher-Homji of *Bombay Samachar,* N. N. Gupta of *The Sind Times* of Karachi, Gangaprasad Varma of *The Hindustani* of Lucknow, Sitala Chatterjee and Sitalchandra Mukherji of *The Tribune* of Lahore, Guru Prasad Sen of *The Behar Herald* of Patna, Bal Tilak and Ganesh Agarkar of the *Mahratta* and *Kesari* of Poona, respectively, and Jogendra Bose of the *Suravi* of Calcutta—these and nonuniversity men, such as Behramji Malabari of *The Indian Spectator* and Kaikhusru Naoroji Kabraji of *Rast Goftar* in Bombay, wrote forcefully on behalf of educated Indians when little was being done by new political associations. Only Banerjea's Indian Association in Calcutta, the Poona Sarvajanik Sabha led by Ranade, Sitaram Hari Chiplonkar, and Krishnaji Nulkar, and the Triplicane Literary Society guided by Iyer and Chariar in Madras arose during the late 1870s to espouse the cause of educated Indians. These organizations, however, only partially replaced the older associations of the fifties—the British Indian, Madras Native, and Bombay associations—each of which by the seventies had grown conservative, were represented in the official councils, and were either zemindari or mercantile in interest with only secondary concern for the grievances of educated Indians. On the new leaders of the Indian press, therefore, and not upon the new associations, fell responsibility for the continued presentation of Indian claims.

Such was the new generation of educated Indian leadership. The complex problems of its role and purpose in British-Indian society pressed for solution. Lytton on the one hand and Ripon on the other proposed alternative solutions, contrary in spirit and conflicting in nature. Lytton advocated a solution which was even more repressive than Argyll's. Taking his cue from the mission on which he had been sent to India by Disraeli and Salisbury, namely to bring Indian external policy into line with British foreign policy in its attempts to counter Russian designs against Turkey, he strove to make the "Russian question" "an imperial, not an Indian one" in the minds of Indian officials,[32] and it was this imperial perspective with its portent of British-Indian military activity against the Russians in Afghanistan and Central Asia that led him to give priority to Indian external policy and to shape domestic policy so as to subserve external policy. In domestic policy, he concentrated upon those classes which he considered vital to the success of the imperial mission: upon the Indian chiefs, princes, and traditional landholders, who formed "a powerful aristocracy"[33] that could lead the inert peasant millions, and upon the British senior services, the Covenanted Civil and commissioned military, both of which, in his opinion, personified British rule to Indian princes, landlords, and ryots alike.[34] To ensure their allegiance and active support, he devoted much of his domestic policy—ranging from suggestions for an aristocratic Privy Council and plans for the magnificent "feudal" Delhi Durbar in

[32] L. to S., July 2, 1876 (priv.), LVP, Eur. E. 218/518/1, p. 262.

[33] L. to S., May 11, 1876 (priv.), LVP, Eur. E. 218/518/1, p. 149.

[34] Note by Viceroy on Admission of Natives to Covenanted Service, Oct. 16, 1876, LVP, Eur. E. 218/520/1, p. 449.

honor of the Queen Empress, to uniforms for the Covenanted Service, pensions, and remission of taxes in 1878 and 1879—to keeping
these classes docile. His principal concern was to check any mischief emanating from inferior classes that might agitate the upper
strata. Thus he was brought face to face with the English-educated
class. Prone to evaluate the latter on the basis of his exposure to
"Baboodom" with its outspoken Bengali editors, he readily adopted
Salisbury's anti-Bengali prejudices and John Strachey's and Ashley
Eden's despotic ideas and concluded that the new class was an
unfortunate "social anomaly,"[35] the product of "very shallow English education," which turned out nothing more than graduates
who for a livelihood "spout and scribble English with a fatal
facility."[36] Contemptuous of the graduates, fearing that they would
upset the influential classes, Lytton chose to ignore the graduates'
grievances, discriminate against their interests, and repress their
talents.

Aware that the Covenanted officials disliked Northbrook's proposed rules for implementing Argyll's Act, because of the partial-
ity of those rules toward educated Indians, Lytton set them aside[37]
and proposed instead a plan for two distinct services: the Covenanted, to consist of all senior posts that would be restricted to
Englishmen who entered by competitive examination, and the
"native service," to consist of Indians appointed in India from
the aristocratic classes who would fill the senior and middling Uncovenanted posts.[38] Undaunted by the fact that neither Salisbury
nor his successor, Cranbrook, fearful of the difficulties of introducing new legislation in Parliament, encouraged the plan, Lytton
nevertheless succeded in incorporating "all the characteristics and
features" of the plan into his rules of 1879 for implementing Argyll's Act.[39] The result was the Statutory Service.

Lytton applied the same discriminatory and repressive principles
to the Indian vernacular press and the possession of arms by Indians. Claiming that Indian princes were being blackmailed, Cove-

[35] L. to S., May 11, 1876 (priv.), LVP, Eur. E. 218/518/1, pp. 149-150. In Salisbury's
words, "a deadly legacy from Metcalfe and Macaulay" (S. to L., June 3, 1876 [priv.],
LVP, Eur. E. 218/516/1, Let. 25).

[36] L. to Cranbrook, May 12, 1879 (priv.), LVP, Eur. E. 218/518/4, p. 347.

[37] See n. 34 above, Note by Viceroy, pp. 445-449; L. to S., Feb. 9, Mar. 16, 1877, LVP,
Eur. E. 218/518/2, pp. 113-114, 208-209.

[38] Note by Viceroy, May 30, 1877, LVP, Eur. E. 218/520/1, pp. 554-589; L. to S.,
May 10, 1877, LVP, Eur. E. 218/518/2, pp. 357-359.

[39] L. to Cranbrook, Sept. 10, 1878 (priv.), LVP, Eur. E. 218/518/3, pp. 647-648;
Dispatch of Governor-General-in-Council, No. 31, Pub. (Home), May 1, 1879, *P.P.*,
1878-79, Vol. 55, Com. 2376, pp. 24-25.

nanted officials maliciously attacked, and Her Majesty's government's policy in Turkey publicly maligned by Indian vernacular
editors,[40] he lost no time in securing Salisbury's permission to
pass an executive act controlling the Indian press[41] but exempting
journals in English, the majority of which were English-controlled.
Similarly, when he sensed serious dissatisfaction among district
officials and European planters over the fact that increasing numbers of Indians were acquiring pistols and rifles through the va-
garies of the Arms Act of 1860, he immediately had a new Arms
Act passed,[42] compelling Indians to pay a license fee in order to
possess a weapon but conspicuously exempting Europeans and
Eurasians and giving special privileges to large Indian landholders.

The results anticipated by Lytton from these measures were
only in part realized, whereas much that he did not expect came
to pass. True, the vernacular editors remained muffled and polite,
the Arms Act yielded numerous prosecutions, and five young scions
of aristocratic houses were appointed to the Covenanted Service
under the rules of 1879, which, nevertheless, left the Covenanted
officials as disgruntled as ever, while the aristocratic class remained
largely indifferent. The educated class, in turn, was goaded into
political agitation. Banerjea and his colleagues in the Indian Association carried the issue of the Covenanted Service to other
educated groups in the chief towns and cities during 1877, 1878,
and 1879, and also led protest meetings against the Press and Arms
acts.[43] More fuel was thrown on this fire when the British Indian
Association in Calcutta and the wealthy merchants of the Bombay
Association came out in strong protest against Lytton's discriminatory reduction of Indian import duties on Lancashire and Manchester cotton goods.[44] The petition embodying these and other
protests carried by L. M. Ghose to Bright, Fawcett, and other
radical Liberals in England figured in the campaigns of 1879 and
1880 through which Gladstone toppled the Beaconfield government and forced Lytton to resign. Thus the aggrieved voice of
educated India, dismissed by Lytton as unimportant, was heard
and answered. Lytton, in pursuing his imperial mission, had not

[40] Minute by Viceroy on Vernacular Press, Oct. 22, 1877, LVP, Eur. E. 218/520/1,
pp. 769 ff.
[41] L. to S., Mar. 8, 1878 (priv.), LVP, Eur. E. 218/518/3, p. 162; Act IX, Mar. 1878.
[42] Act X, June 1878.
[43] Banerjea, pp.44-67. John Bright and petition from India, Parliamentary Debates,
3 *Hansard*, 246 (June 12, 1879), 1723.
[44] Mody, pp. 93-107; Parliamentary Debates, 3 *Hansard*, 247, (May 23, 1879), 1142-
1146, (May 23, 26, 1879), 1226.

produced a solution to the problem of the educated Indian but had merely aggravated it and left it pending.

If Lytton's solution was prompted by the Disraeli-Salisbury imperial mission, then his successor, Lord Ripon, took his cue from Gladstone's Midlothian denunciations of Lytton's actions in India.[45] The emphasis was to be reversed: the good governmnt of India and the material and moral progress of her peoples were to take precedence over ambitious imperial schemes in Central Asia: the true defense of India rested in the former.[46] "The whole effect of Lytton's administration," Ripon concluded, "was to give an impression, right or wrong, that in all ways—in foreign policy, in finance, in such matters as the Vernacular Press Act and the Arms Act—the interests of the natives of India were sacrificed to those of England."[47] One of his principal objects, therefore, was to remove this impression from the minds of the Indian people and to restore their confidence in British rule. To do so, Ripon turned to Indian public opinion, more particularly to "the elements" of such opinion, which he considerd already in existence and exerting "a distinct and appreciable influence."[48]

These consisted of "the small class of highly educated natives"[49] which, in Ripon's opinion, was well-schooled in the English language and in English political thought under the system of Indian higher education and which was increasing annually in the chief urban centers.[50] Its education and talents, not its social standing, gave this class significance. This was true especially of the better products of this class: those who competed in England for the Covenanted examination, or the more influential and skilled of "the writers in the press, the speakers at the public meetings, the pleaders before the Courts, and not infrequently the officials of Native States."[51] Mature, competent, moderate, and loyal, these men were not to be distrusted, ordered about like infants, or deluded by Delhi durbars, imperial titles, and "rubbish of that sort."[52] In Ripon's view, they possessed legitimate ambitions and aspirations in keeping with their education and the pledges of Parliament over the past fifty-odd years. They were no longer to be disregarded or dallied

[45] S. Gopal, *The Viceroyalty of Lord Ripon* 1880-1884 (London, 1953), pp. 1-5.
[46] Dispatch of Secretary of State, Dec. 3, 1880, *P.P.*, 1881, Vol. 70, Com. 2852, p. 237.
[47] R. to G., Oct. 22, 1881 (priv.), RVP, I.S. 290/7, No. 112.
[48] R. to Hartington, Dec. 10, 1881 (priv.), RVP, I.S. 290/5, No. 65.
[49] Note by Viceroy on Local Self-Government, Apr. 27, enclosed in R. to Hartington, May 25, 1882 (priv.), RVP, I.S. 290/5, No. 33.
[50] R. to K., May 4, 1883, RVP, I.S., 290/5, No. 38.
[51] R. to J. K. Cross, Apr. 3, 1884 (priv.), RVP, I.S. 290/5, No. 17.
[52] R. to K., May 4, 1883, RVP, I.S., 290/5, No. 38.

with; for if they became convinced that such was the government's intention, they would turn against Government and excite in the minds of the masses the same discontent which seethed in their own. He did not intend this to happen: he wished loyalty and support for British rule from educated Indians, not disaffection and enmity. It was better to acknowledge the new class as a political reality in British-Indian society and ascertain its grievances, to trust its leaders and encourage them, and "by timely foresight, take steps to supply the legitimate outlets for those aspirations and to satisfy those ambitions consistent with the maintenance of authority."[53]

This philosophy guided Ripon's domestic policy throughout his viceroyalty (1880-1884). To ascertain educated Indian opinion, he consulted those persons he considered most intimately informed. With the assistance of Courtnay Peregrine Ilbert, his Legal Member, he enlisted the counsels of such men as Ali, Mahmud, Bonnerjee, M. M. Ghose, Banerjea, Iyer, Tyabji, Naoroji, Javerilal Umiashankar Yajnik, Telang, Mehta, and others. He consulted Professor William Wordsworth, Principal of Elphinstone College, and Sir William Wedderburn, the radical, aristocratic Scot of the Bombay Covenanted Service, about grievances of educated Indians and needed reforms, while Allan Octavian Hume, a senior official in the Northbrook and Lytton administrations until his radical and petulant personality led to his downfall and retirement to Allahabad, became a chief link with educated Indian circles in Bombay, Calcutta, and Allahabad.

Then, too, Ripon met the grievances expressed by the educated Indian leaders and tried to provide increased outlets within the administrative system for their political talents. These endeavors were tantamount to a complete reversal of Lytton's discriminatory measures. Ripon settled the Afghan question, withdrew British-Indian troops by 1881, and saw to it that the English Exchequer paid most of the costs for Lytton's "imperial" war.[54] Likewise, he resolutely opposed Gladstone and his ministers when they wanted India to pay the entire costs of the British-Indian troops sent to Suez in 1882 to help repress Arabi Pasha's uprising,[55] and when they wished to revert to Lytton's forward strategy in Afghanistan to counter the Russians' renewed advance in Central Asia during 1882 and 1883.[56]

[53] R. to K., May 4, July 10, 1883, RVP, I.S. 290/5, nos. 38, 53.

[54] R. to G., Oct. 22, 1881 (priv.), RVP, I.S. 290/7, No. 112.

[55] R. to Hartington, July 26, 1882, RVP, I.S. 290/5, No. 45; R. to G., Oct. 6, 1882 (priv.), I.S. 290/7, No. 118.

[56] R. to Hartington, Apr. 29, 1882 (priv.), R. to K., June 14, 1883 (priv.), Apr. 4-5, 1884, RVP, I.S. 290/5, nos. 27, 47, 18.

Antijingoism and noninterference were the axioms of this external policy based on India's need for peace and economic stability. He held rigidly to Northbrook's tenets of light taxation,[57] repealed the "detestable" Vernacular Press Act in 1882,[58] an action acclaimed by Indian editors,[59] drafted a new Arms Act without the clauses favoring Europeans and Eurasians,[60] and initiated an inquiry into the progress of education since 1857, aimed at linking primary education to higher education and strengthening its new class of graduates.[61]

His efforts to provide outlets for the political expression of "educated India" were singular. He proposed further reforms in local self-government which would convert the scheme laid down by Mayo and Strachey in 1870 for administrative economy into one of "political education" for the Indian leaders and the people and which would give Indians elected to District Boards responsibility for administering their own "parish affairs" with the District Officer standing by in a nonparticipating yet supervisory capacity.[62] He planned broad reforms in the Uncovenanted Service,[63] particularly in the Public Work Department and the Roorkee Engineering School, to provide Indians entering or already in the service with greater opportunity. He gave the Covenanted Indian civilian, Justice R. C. Mitter, a temporary appointment in the Bengal High Court after his claims had been deliberately overlooked by the Bengal government;[64] and he called for reform of the Criminal Procedure Act so that Indians with responsible positions in the Covenanted Judicial Service would have the same rights as their English colleagues to try Europeans in criminal cases.[65] Finally, he pressed

[57] R. to Northbrook, Sept. 23, 1881 (priv.) , RVP, I.S. 290/7, No. 102; Confidential Note by Viceroy Opposing Increased Taxation, June 10, 1884, I.S., 290/8-II, No. 172.

[58] Note by Viceroy on Repeal of Vernacular Press Act, enclosed in R. to Hartington, Feb. 12, 1881 (priv.), RVP, I.S. 290/5, No. 9; Dispatch of Governor-General-in-Council, No. 12, Pub., Feb. 21, 1881, *P.P.*, 1881, Vol. 68, Ret. 160, p. 741.

[59] Address from Editors of Vernacular Press, Feb. 28, 1882, RVP, I.S. 290/8-I, No. 149.

[60] Note by Viceroy on Arms Act, Apr. 11, 1881, RVP, I.S. 290/5, pp. 74-77; R. to Hartington, May 19, 1882 (priv.), I.S., 290/5, No. 32.

[61] Minute by Viceroy on Education, May 9, 1881, RVP, I.S. 290/5, pp. 118-120.

[62] R. to Hartington, Jan. 26, 1881, Note by Viceroy on Local Self-Government, Apr. 27, enclosed in R. to Hartington, May 25, 1882 (priv.), Memo. on Policy of Government of India in Regard to Local Self-Government, enclosed in R. to K., Dec. 26, 1882 (priv.), RVP, I.S. 290/5, nos. 5, 33, 78.

[63] R. to Hartington, Dec. 17, 1881 (priv.), Feb. 17, 1882 (priv.), RVP, I.S. 290/5, nos. 67, 10.

[64] R. to Hartington, June 29, 1882 (priv.), RVP, I.S. 290/5, No. 39.

[65] Dispatch of Governor-General-in-Council, No. 33, Jud., Sept. 9, 1882, *P.P.*, 1883, Vol. 51, Com. 3512, pp. 649-651; R. to Northbrook, Feb. 5 (priv.), R. to Halifax, Feb. 26, 1883, RVP, I.S. 290/7, nos. 14, 21.

for broad reforms of the Covenanted Civil Service, with revision of Lytton's rules to allow for provincial competitive examinations in place of nomination, and with the age limits of 18-23, established in 1854, restored for the Covenanted examinations in England.[66]

Such were Ripon's comprehensive proposals for the solution of the problem of the educated Indian. Yet his policy proved no more sucessful than Lytton's. As Lytton had disregarded the educated Indians and their friends in Parliament, so Ripon overlooked the Anglo-Indians,[67] official and nonofficial, and their spokesmen in England. He moved too far and too fast with his reformist schemes for the Cabinet at home, for the Council at the India Office, and for the senior officials and the European community in India, especially in Bengal.[68] At every phase he was thwarted by one group or the other, except in the repeal of the Vernacular Press Act. By 1883, the undercurrent of anxiety and opposition within the Anglo-Indian community of lawyers, editors, merchants, and planters in Bengal and Bihar, and among the Covenanted officials of the Bengal government over Mitter's appointment and the proposed reforms in the Uncovenanted Service, local self-government, and criminal procedure, erupted into bitter agitation, ostensibly over the Criminal Procedure Amendment, the so-called Ilbert Bill.[69] Lasting a year in intensity but longer in feeling, and centered in Calcutta but debated throughout India and in Parliament, this feverish agitation was directed solely at Ripon and his pro-Indian policy. In the end, Ripon, apprehensive lest counteragitation begin in the educated Indian community and hence cause irreparable damage to the scheme of local self-government and to the ultimate working of the Ilbert Bill itself, chose to compromise with his Anglo-Indian critics and granted them special jury privileges denied to Indians.[70]

But the conflagration, with its Parliamentary overtones, damaged his reputation more than the outcome. Northbrook and Halifax, Forster and even Gladstone questioned his judgment in introducing the Ilbert Bill at a time when he had introduced so many reforms.[71] It also paralyzed what remained of his domestic policy.

[66] R. to K., Apr. 13, June 11, 1883 (priv.), Feb. 19, Mar. 16, Apr. 4, 1884, RVP, I.S. 290/5, nos. 28, 46, 9, 14, 18.

[67] "Anglo-Indian" is used throughout in its earlier sense as referring to Europeans, preponderantly British, whose lives and careers were chiefly associated with India.

[68] Northbrook to R., Feb. 9 (priv.), C. E. Bernard to R., May 4, 1883, RVP, I.S. 290/7, nos. 21, 57d.

[69] Gopal, Ch. IX, "The Ilbert Bill."

[70] R. to K., June 8, 1883, RVP, I.S. 290/5, No. 45; R. to G., Dec. 23, 1883 (priv.), I.S. 290/7, No. 150.

[71] Halifax to R., Mar. 2, G. to R., Apr. 17, W. E. Forster to R., Apr. 27, 1883, RVP, I.S. 290/7, nos. 27, 50a, 56.

Kimberley, still smarting from public criticism of his Majuba Hill policy in South Africa when he was at the Colonial Office, had no intention of receiving more of the same and made common cause with the cautious, critical India Council which had refused to proceed with Ripon's policy.[72] More serious still, Ripon's fight for the Ilbert Bill awoke educated Indian leaders to the fact that no amount of goodwill and effort by Ripon or any other viceroy could secure for them a place in the sun and that they too would have to organize and fight. Banerjea, A. M. Bose, and others drew this conclusion at the end of 1883 when they held the Indian National Conference at Calcutta, ostensibly all-Indian but with members drawn principally from Bengal, Bihar, and the Northwest Provinces, and organized to increase Indian participation in the provincial councils and to ensure reform of the rules of 1879 for the Covenanted Civil Service and of the age limit for the Covenanted examination.[73] This was a first step toward independent political action, or the very result which Ripon had aimed to prevent by his domestic policy. His efforts, aside from stimulating Indian political consciousness and aspirations, proved devoid of substance. His misjudgment over the Ilbert Bill brought about the failure of his solution to the problem of the educated Indian.

Thus, by the spring of 1884, when Ripon wrote to Kimberley about it, the problem posed by the emergence of the English-educated Indian class remained more complicated and more in need of a solution than ever before. Clearly, a dilemma confronted the Indian government concerning the solution to this problem. Was it to be Lytton's or Ripon's? The decision rested upon an essential question: Was this educated class one which the government could afford to ignore, alienate, and allow to become detached in its search for responsibility and representation?[74]

Kimberley answered in the affirmative. Like his predecessors, Argyll and Salisbury, and like Maine and Eden then serving with him on the India Council, Kimberley looked upon the educated Indians less as a class and more as "a small clique" which was Bengali in voice and numbers.[75] To make concessions to such a clique and hence exacerbate the feelings of the European class was, in his

[72] Bernard to R., May 4, J. Gibbs to R., May 25, Aug. 10, 1883, RVP, I.S. 290/7, nos. 57d, 61, 89a. On K.'s South African policy, see R. Robinson and J. Gallagher, *Africa and the Victorians* (London, 1961), pp. 65-72.

[73] Circular for meeting of Dec. 29, 30, *Bengalee,* Dec. 22, 1883; for the conference, see *Bengalee,* Dec. 29, 1883, Jan. 5, 1884; W. S. Blunt, *India under Ripon: A Private Diary* (London, 1909), pp. 114, 116, 118.

[74] R. to K., Apr. 4, 1884, RVP, I.S., 290/5, No. 18.

[75] K. to R., Apr. 4, 1884 (priv.), RVP, I.S. 290/5, No. 19.

opinion, unwise after the emotional eruption among Europeans over the Ilbert Bill. He was painfully aware of the fact that Ripon's pro-Indian measures, quite apart from the bill, had provoked the Europeans in Bengal and Bihar to engage in social strife. Strife, however limited, was what Kimberly was determined to avoid. In Calcutta it had brought policy-making and administration at Government House to a virtual standstill during 1883, and had prevented the Viceroy and the Secretary of State's Council from dealing effectively with such affairs as the renewed Russian advance on Merv and French diplomatic and commercial moves in Upper Burma. These were matters imperatively needing decision, upon which Kimberley had wished Ripon to concentrate and formulate a firm and clear policy. But this became impossible, given the rapidly mounting disagreements between the two men regarding both domestic and, later, foreign policy. Such disagreements were not to Kimberley's liking; and, if concessions to "educated India" were going to bring more of the same, he preferred not to take them.[76] His negative decisions on the Bengal Local Self-Government Bill and the Roorkee Resolution,[77] his negative answer to the British Indian Reform Association about raising the age limit for the Covenanted Service examination,[78] and his negative attitude toward the Bengal Tenancy Bill, to which he feared hostility from zemindars and European planters,[79] clearly indicated his trend of thought. Kimberley, in short, wished to walk between Lytton's and Ripon's solutions. He wished the Indian government to return to an impartial course with no favors for any nonofficial group, and to restore peace and harmony to the Indian social scene, thereby leaving the government free to concentrate upon the more important matters of Afghanistan and Upper Burma.

When Ripon, tiring of his labors and disappointments and sensitive to his deepening differences with Kimberley and the Home Government, advised Kimberley that once the Bengal Tenancy Bill had been completed in March 1885, he wished to resign,[80] Kimberley saw an opportunity to replace him with a new personality more closely in tune with his own views. On the pretext that a possible General Election in the autumn might lead to a Conservative victory and a Tory viceroy, Kimberley encouraged Ripon to think of returning that autumn.[81] To Gladstone, Kimberley was

[76] K. to R., May 2, 1884 (priv.), RVP, I.S. 290/5, No. 23.
[77] K. to R., Nov. 15 and Dec. 20, 1883 (priv.), RVP, I.S. 290/5, nos. 71, 77a.
[78] K. to R., Apr. 4, 1884 (priv.), RVP, I.S. 290/5, No. 19; *Times,* Apr. 4, 1884.
[79] K. to R., July 4, 1884 (priv.), RVP, I.S. 290/5, No. 36.
[80] R. to K., June 24, 1884 (priv.), RVP, I.S. 290/5, No. 35.
[81] K. to R., July 30, 1884 (priv.), RVP, I.S. 290/5, No. 42.

more candid: he did not wish Ripon to proceed with the Bengal Tenancy Bill, and a new viceroy would be "better able" to settle it and avoid another outburst.[82] As for Ripon's successor, Kimberley had no hesitation in recommending his friend and colleague, Frederick Temple Hamilton-Temple Blackwood, Earl of Dufferin and Baron of Clandeboye in County Down, Ireland.[83] Gladstone was not so enthusiastic. After all, Dufferin had differed sharply with him on Irish land legislation during the seventies, had accepted Disraeli's appointment to St. Petersburg in 1879, and had reorganized the Egyptian administration after Arabi Pasha's rising with more flurry than Gladstone had liked. Then, too, Dufferin's name had come before him in 1872 as a possible replacement for Mayo but had been set aside. Nonetheless, under Kimberley's polite yet persistent pressure,[84] the Prime Minister yielded. The Queen approved enthusiastically. She had known Dufferin ever since he had been one of her Lords-in-Waiting. Dufferin, then in residence at Clandeboye following his exertions in Egypt, hesitated at first because of age and family, but finally, inasmuch as he had always been ambitious for the appointment, accepted gratefully.[85] Ripon, duly notified,[86] was pleased to learn of his Liberal successor.[87] Arrangements were made posthaste for Dufferin to reach India by early December. Kimberley had secured the services of the man he wanted for the job.

Dufferin possessed singular qualities for the viceroyalty.[88] Of middling stature, nearly 60 years old, with aristocratic features accentuated by his flowing hair and full moustache, he outwardly portrayed the ideal proconsul. Upon first acquaintance, he seemed superficial and affected, with his eyeglass, elegantly tailored clothes, studied courtesy, and air of aloofness. This appearance was deceptive, arising largely from self-consciousness over a speech impediment and from his preference for aloofness in his initial relations

[82] K. to G., July 23, 1884, Gladstone Papers, BM Add. MSS 44228, pp. 144-147.

[83] B. 1826; Eton and Christ Church, Oxford; Lord-in-Waiting, 1849-1852, 1854-1858; Peer, 1850; special foreign mission to Vienna, 1855; British Commissioner in Syria to investigate Levant Massacre, 1860; K.C.B.; Under-Secretary of State for India, 1864-1866; for War, 1866; Earl, 1871; Governor-General of Canada, 1872-1878; G.C.M.G.; Ambassador to St. Petersburg, 1879-1880; Ambassador to Constantinople, 1881-1882; Special Commissioner to Egypt after Arabi's rebellion, 1882-1883; G.C.B., 1883.

[84] K. to G., Aug. 6, 1884, Gladstone Papers, BM Add. MSS 44228, pp. 150-151.

[85] K. to G., Aug. 12, 1884, Gladstone Papers, BM Add. MSS 44228, p. 154.

[86] Secretary of State to Viceroy, telegram, Aug. 12, 1884 (priv. and most confid.), RVP, I.S. 290/6, No. 82.

[87] Viceroy to Secretary of State, telegram, Aug. 13, 1884 (priv. and most confid.), RVP, I.S. 290/6, No. 83; R. to K., Aug. 22, 1884, I.S. 290/5, No. 44a.

[88] A. C. Lyall, *Life of the Marquis of Dufferin and Ava*, 2 vols. (London, 1905); H. Nicolson, *Helen's Tower* (London, 1937).

with others. In reality, he was a sensitive individual with a warm personality and charm, a keen wit and kindly sympathy toward those about him. His interests and tastes were cosmopolitan, his views tolerant, and his values set in the romantic idiom of Sir Walter Scott—"the soul of purity, chivalry, respect for women and healthy religious feeling." His intellect was quick and versatile rather than profound, enabling him to grasp with alacrity the key facet of any question. Generally cautious in all decisions of importance, he persevered in all tasks. Quick in temper, he was quick to forgive, being generous in condemnation of his own shortcomings and indulgent to those of others.

In addition, Dufferin possessed a broad and varied experience. At an early age he learned about agriculture and the administration of his own estate, and he became conversant with Parliamentary affairs by his intermittent attendance in the House of Lords during the 1850s and 1870s, where he concerned himself with Irish land legislation principally on Gladstone's behalf. Thereafter he undertook a succession of difficult imperial and diplomatic assignments: Governor-General of Canada (1872-1878), Ambassador to Russia (1879-1880), and Ambassador to Turkey (1881-1883) during which time he took charge of the British Commission in Egypt following Arabi Pasha's uprising. By 1884, Dufferin was not only popular and respected among his friends and colleagues, but was also recognized by both parties as a gifted imperial administrator and one of the most skilled diplomats of the Crown. It was the sum of his versatile personality and valuable experience that had led Kimberley to seek his services for the viceroyalty.

With Dufferin's strengths came some weaknesses which could not be overlooked in such a demanding post. He rarely tried to gain a thorough grasp himself of all aspects of a problem but instead sought the advice of those who were experienced and knowledgeable. This was sound administration insofar as he could select competent, frank, and unprejudiced advisers, but in the past he had not always been successful, and he would find it a precarious method in the Indian government of late 1884, torn as it was by strong official prejudices for and against Ripon and his policies. Dufferin was also most sensitive to criticism and dreaded public comment and ridicule as incidents in Canada and at the Porte had revealed.[89] He sought to please; he wanted to be accepted by those he served and popular with those he ruled. In the face of twisted personal relations with friends and foes alike, he readily betrayed his disap-

---

[89] Lyall, I, 224-227, II, 25-29.

pointment and his Irish temper. He disliked yet did not try to understand the petty self-seeking and the ungentlemanly behavior of the English official and mercantile middle class abroad, many of whom he encountered seeking title or wealth, or both, through influence and devious means that were odious to his aristocratic code of values. Moreover, given his training and experience in fulfilling imperial and diplomatic assignments, he had learned to conduct his mission in strict accordance with the instructions of the Home Government, and hence rarely, if ever, did he deviate from his allotted course. He willingly minimized his own judgment to avoid disagreement and disruption of policy. He was, in short, self-effacing, dedicated, and subservient to the wishes of his superiors; in this sense he was an ideal proconsul. But whether such traits were ideal for administering India by late 1884, given the impact of Ripon's administration and his vigorous attempt to implement the Act of 1858 with its definition of the viceroy as one who was to serve not only the interests of the Crown but also those of the Indian people, remained to be seen.

Dufferin was thoroughly briefed for the viceregal task. He met daily with Kimberley and "the Pandits of the India Office" to discuss all aspects of the policy to be followed by the Government of India.[90] He was given lengthy "coaching" sessions by Kimberley, who placed before his "pupil" his private correspondence with Ripon.[91] In this way, Kimberley disclosed most candidly his disagreements with Ripon and explained how such differences could best be avoided in the future by a proper understanding of the relationship between the Secretary of State and the Viceroy. Kimberley laid down very clearly the lines Dufferin was to follow: he was to restore domestic tranquility, thereby allowing the Government of India to give its undivided attention to the foreign dangers confronting the Empire,[92] and to postpone any further reforms which Ripon had proposed on behalf of Indian interests.[93] The emphasis, therefore, was to be external and imperial. That Dufferin fully understood Kimberley's instructions was revealed during his farewell address at Belfast when he gave notice that, with foreign problems on the horizon, he had no intention of engaging in any dramatic performances such as the annexation of new territory or "the revolutionizing of established systems."[94] He meted out praise

[90] D. to R., Sept. 26, 1884, RP, BM Add. MSS 43635, pp. 69-70.
[91] D. to R., Nov. 7, 1884, RP, BM Add. MSS 43635, pp. 88-89.
[92] K. to G., Oct. 5, 1884, Gladstone Papers, BM Add. MSS 44228, pp. 158-161.
[93] D. to C., Aug. 28, 1885, DVP, R. 517, No. 51.
[94] D. M. Wallace, ed., *Speeches Delivered in India, 1884-8, by the Marquis of Dufferin and Ava* (London, 1890), pp. 9-10.

to the Covenanted officials and had a pat on the back for the European community, but he was conspicuously silent about the educated Indian class. Thus prepared, Dufferin, acompanied by his attractive and capable wife, left for India at the end of October. The transition from one viceroyalty to another had begun, and the modification of Ripon's policy was already under way.

But neither the transition nor the modification were to be smooth or quiet. During November as Ripon made his final journey from summer quarters at Simla across northern India to Calcutta, and into the early weeks of December to the very day of his departure, Indian demonstrations in his honor, vast, impressive, and unprecedented in British-Indian history, took place in all the principal cities and towns. Hume and his friends, Lala Baijnath, M. M. Ghose, Sen, Malabari, and others, were instrumental in arranging some of the demonstrations,[95] but their efforts would never have been sufficient to produce what followed, had not a spontaneous sentiment among all groups of the Indian population, high and low, sparked the demonstrations and caused them to spread like fire. At railway stations in the Punjab, the Northwest Provinces, and Bihar, maharajahs, rajahs, Punjabi sirdars, Oudhi talukhdars, sayyids and khans, wealthy seths and merchants, learned pandits, barristers and *vakils,* journalists, university and college lecturers, school teachers and villagers gathered to honor the departing Viceroy with memorials and gifts in gratitude for his noble work.[96] The reaction in Madras was described as "very remarkable":[97] spontaneous meetings erupted throughout the Madras Presidency,[98] and leaders of the newly formed Madras Mahajana Sabha, the Triplicane Literary Society, and other Madras associations sent a major deputation to Bombay in Ripon's honor.[99] The public reception given to him upon his arrival at Calcutta was so extraordinary that even the usually hostile *Pioneer* described it as "unique in local history";[100] Justice Mitter presided over an impressive and moving meeting of some 2,000 influential members of Bengal and Bihar society.[101] The demonstrations upon his arrival in Bombay "surpassed beyond comparison" those in Calcutta: his train was virtually stopped just outside the city by thousands of cheering mill hands

[95] Baijnath to H., Nov. 28, 1884, RP, BM Add. MSS 43616, No. 30.
[96] Meetings, Nov. 13-25, *Pioneer Mail,* Nov. 19, 26, 1884.
[97] *Madras Mail,* Nov. 18, 1884.
[98] Nov. 16-30, *Madras Mail,* Nov. 17 to Dec. 1, 1884.
[99] *Madras Mail,* Nov. 18, 1884.
[100] Dec. 2, *Pioneer Mail,* Dec. 10, 1884.
[101] At "Balagatchia Villa," Dec. 12, *Bengalee,* Dec. 20, 1884.

from the cotton mills of Parel, while the following day the parade led by Indian gentlemen of all walks of life from Bombay, Madras, the Deccan, Khandesh, Gujerat, and Sind and bearing him to the Town Hall was described as "unparalleled" in Bombay's history.[102] And at the hour of his departure from the Apollo Bunder, the crowds and emotions were so overwhelming that they had to be seen and sensed to be believed.[103]

Such were the scale and pitch of Ripon's departure from India. His staunch critics among the editors of the English-controlled press of Bengal, Bihar, and the Northwest Provinces dismissed the meetings as having nothing to do with Ripon and his work and described them as "political demonstrations against England [and] the superiority of the English people" which had been planned and plotted by a mere handful of "wire-pullers and obscure agitators"[104] who were dissatisfied with British rule in India and who possessed "few or no followers."[105] Their colleagues in the Bombay and Madras presidencies refused to be tainted with such "ill-temper and passion."[106] They reached the markedly different conclusions that the meetings were "strange and significant" and were expressions of gratitude to Ripon, less for what he had acomplished and more for his efforts to serve all inhabitants of India no matter what their color, race, or creed. More important, the meetings showed that "for the first time in Indian history the people of India have learned how to demonstrate and agitate as a whole, irrespective of caste and race."[107] Few members of nonofficial circles in northern India, Bombay, and Madras were willing to reach such conclusions. Neither were members of official circles.

Sir Auckland Colvin,[108] the Finance Member, who had served in Egypt after Arabi Pasha's rising and who had been instrumental in producing the compromise to end the Ilbert Bill crisis, was an exception. He wrote an unsigned article, entitled "If It Be Real— What Does It Mean?," which the editors of *The Pioneer* publish-

[102] Dec. 18, 19, *B.G.O.S.*, Dec. 19, 26, 1884.
[103] Dec. 20, *Pioneer Mail*, Dec. 24, 1884. See also *Tribune*, Nov. 22, 29, *Indian Mirror*, Dec. 12, *Indian Spectator*, Dec. 14, 1884; *V. of I.*, III, Jan. 1885, on Farewell to Ripon.
[104] *Englishman's Overall Mail*, Nov. 18; *Indian Daily News*, Dec. 13, 1884.
[105] *Pioneer*, Dec. 10, 1884.
[106] *B.G.O.S.*, Dec. 26, 1884.
[107] *Madras Mail*, Nov. 18; *Times of India*, Dec. 19, 1884.
[108] B. 1838; Eton and Haileybury; Bengal Civil Service, 1858; Northwest Provinces, 1858-1879; Comptroller-General, Egypt, 1880-1882; K.C.M.G., 1881; Financial Adviser to Khedive, 1882-1883, assisted Dufferin on his mission; Financial Member, Viceroy's Executive Council, 1883-1887.

ed.[109] He not only agreed with those who found the demonstrations remarkable, but he added that the event was another profound indication that the Indian political mind was "at length awakening to the consciouness of its own powers and the assurance of its own success." Moreover, it placed before the European official and non-official class in no uncertain terms the question as to what was to be done with this awakening political consciousness. Was it to be officially nurtured to the benefit of all as Ripon had tried to do, or was it to be officially ostracized to the danger of all as Lytton had done? Colvin thought that there could be only one answer—an answer which the demonstrations themselves had given. Greeted silently by the English-controlled press while enthusiastically "printed and circulated in thousands by the native press," Colvin's article met with a "horrified" reaction in the Viceroy's Council, with Ilbert alone welcoming its liberal spirit.[110] Throughout the senior ranks of the Raj it caused a wave of amazement. Only Justice Raymond West, the thoughful, cultured member of the Bombay High Court and Vice-Chancellor of Bombay University, in his Convocation speech honoring Ripon the day before his departure, gave public expression to sentiments like Colvin's.[111] As for Ripon himself, he considered the meetings less a personal tribute and more an effective answer to those of his critics who had doubted the significance of the educated Indian class and had condemned his efforts to meet its grievances. In his final speeches he laid stress upon the importance of the new class and its press, its need to be recognized by the government, and its rightful claim to "a gradual but extending share of public duties and high places in the land."[112] His words deepened the significance of the demonstrations.

Whatever the interpretations of these extraordinary happenings, they had serious repercussions for the transition from Ripon to Dufferin and for the modification of Ripon's policy. They completely overshadowed Dufferin's arrival in India. Indeed, on December 9, it was reported from Bombay that its inhabitants were so engrossed in preparing Ripon's farewell that "a transparently apparent indifference existed on the subject of Lord Dufferin's arrival

[109] *Pioneer Mail*, Dec. 17, 1884, pp. 622-624. Colvin admitted his authorship to a family friend some months later. See J. Pullen, ed., *The Journal of Miss Adelaide M. Shuckburgh*, Apr. 30, 1885: selections were reprinted in *Missionary Times* (Mar.-Apr. 1948). Courtesy of Lady Ragnar Colvin.

[110] *Shuckburgh's Journal*, Apr. 30, 1885.

[111] Dec. 19, *B.G.O.S.*, Dec. 26, 1884.

[112] St. Xavier's College, Bombay, Dec. 19, *Pioneer Mail*, Dec. 24, 1884; Municipal Hall, Bombay, Dec. 19, *B.G.O.S.*, Dec. 26, 1884.

up to within twelve hours of the noble earl's coming ashore."[113] In Calcutta, the enthusiasm and display which greeted him were as much for Ripon who stood beside him as for himself, while the incessant Indian deputations in and out of Government House, the fireworks and the public dinners, and the final salutes fairly eclipsed Dufferin in the presence of his predecessor.

This disquieting experience left a deep impression upon Dufferin. "No Viceroy," he wrote Kimberley, "has ever left India amidst such general and genuine expression of good-will on the part of the Indian population."[114] Disturbing to him were the old wounds which the demonstrations had reopened. The English editors in the Bengal press took to the warpath again, deriding Ripon for playing up so unbashedly to Indian applause and condemning him for deepening the breach between European and Bengali by his "parting utterances of flimsy *ex parte* radical benevolence."[115] The party passions and racial discord of 1883 were rekindled. Nor did criticism stop with the English editors in Bengal. Senior officals wrote hastily to Dufferin deprecating Ripon's warm response to the demonstrations and venting their wrath on his policy of encouraging Indian political aspirations.[116] Last but not least, the Ripon farewell demonstrations made it evident to the new Viceroy and numerous officials that educated Indians could take effective political action. "India has proved herself capable of organization," wrote "S," a senior member of the Bombay Judicial Service.[117] With political ambitions fired and political capabilities realized, it would only be a matter of time before educated Indians took an independent line of action unless Dufferin pursued Ripon's policy of meeting their grievances and keeping their activities within bounds.

Ripon had repeatedly stated that there were only two solutions to the problem of the educated Indian: his own or Lytton's. Kimberley, however, had chosen to strike for a compromise between these alternatives, and to this end had so instructed Dufferin. He had forgotten what Ripon had predicted: that by restoring the confidence of the educated Indian leaders and strengthening their vital role in

[113] *Pioneer Mail,* Dec. 10, 1884.

[114] D. to K., Dec. 5, 1884, DVP, R. 517, No. 1.

[115] *Englishman's Overland Mail,* Nov. 18, *Pioneer Mail,* Dec. 10, *Indian Daily News,* Dec. 13, 1884.

[116] A. E. Hardinge (Commander-in-Chief, Bombay Army) to D., Dec. 21, Sir James Fergusson (Governor of Bombay) to D., Dec. 22, 1884, M. E. Grant-Duff (Governor of Madras) to D., Jan. 3, 1885, DVP, R. 528, nos. 6a, 9, 30.

[117] Letter to the editor, "'The True Meaning of the Ripon Ovation," *Times of India,* Dec. 26, 1884.

forming public opinion, Ripon's solution could never be undone.[118]
The Indian farewell demonstrations in his honor with their obvious
political implications indicated that his prediction had not been idly
made. Such was Ripon's legacy to his successor. Indeed, the political
climate within India had altered radically between the time of Kimberley's briefing of Dufferin and the new Viceroy's acceptance of
the seals from Ripon. Dufferin, although sensitive to this change,
nevertheless proceeded to execute Kimberley's instructions. He
sought to appease all parties with sympathetic nods and generous
statements: there would be strict impartiality to all, yet a pat on the
back for the Covenanted officials so vital to British rule;[119] there
would be continuity of policy,[120] yet no radical reforms or "Mid-
lothianizing" of India;[121] there would be concern for Indian interests, yet an emphasis only upon fostering local self-government.[122]
Such was Dufferin's interpretation of Kimberley's policy. It brought
a prophetic warning: "He who tries to please all pleases none, and
must perforce swerve from the path of duty and justice."[123] The
question was: Within such a changed setting could Dufferin succeed
in carrying out Kimberley's solution to the problem of the educated
Indian; or would he have to swerve from the middle of the road to
either Lytton's path or Ripon's, with fateful consequences for the
character of Indian political expression? Though he little realized
it at the time, he would be compelled by the events of the ensuing
year to answer this question in a manner which would lead him and
the British administration one way and the educated Indian leaders
with their political ambitions another. 1885 was to be a decisive
year.

[118] R. to K., July 10, 1883, RVP, I.S. 290/5, No. 53; R. to H., Jan. 21, 1883 (priv.),
I.S. 290/8-I, No. 3.

[119] Speech, Bombay, Dec. 9, *Times of India,* Dec. 10, 1884.

[120] Address to Calcutta Corporation, Dec. 13, *Bengalee,* Dec. 20, 1884.

[121] D. to Grant-Duff, Dec. 15, D. to Fergusson, Dec. 19, D. to Hardinge, Dec. 29, 1884,
DVP, R. 528, nos. 5, 6, 20.

[122] Speech to British Indian Association and Indian Association, *Bengalee,* Dec. 27,
1885.

[123] *Sadharani,* translated and reprinted in *Englishman's Overland Mail,* Dec. 23,
1884.

I

Kimberley's Policy and Ripon's Legacy

As the year 1884 quietly receded, Dufferin looked ahead hopefully to the success of Kimberley's policy. "There is a fair prospect of my getting our party-coloured team to jog along together in peace and good fellowship," he wrote.[1] His hopes were not unfounded. The Indian politicians remained quiescent; their journals, although still ringing with tributes to Ripon, were filled with expressions of loyalty. The Anglo-Indian community throughout northern India, especially in Bengal, relaxed. Everyone eagerly looked forward to Christmas as an occasion on which to erase the unpleasantness of the past two years and to greet the New Year "with a hearty faith in future peace and good will to all men."[2] Minds turned with excitement and expectancy to the brilliant Calcutta social season about to unfold: the horse racing at Burdwan, the Assembly dances and Saturday Club balls, the polo tournament, the cricket matches with Ceylon, the theater, and the dazzling spectacle of the Soldiers' Exhibition. Everyone hoped that 1885 would bring a return to the pattern of life before 1883 with its cordial understanding between the Englishman and his viceroy and its proper relationship between European and Indian. Even the meddlesome *Pioneer* voiced the wish: "Let the ledger of 1883 and 1884 be closed and carefully put away until the historian of the future needs to open it to instruct generations yet untold."[3] Early in the new year Dufferin confidently concluded that "the storm in a tea-cup created by the Ilbert Bill has passed out of sight, and my party-coloured

[1] D. to K., Dec. 15, 1884, DVP, R. 517, No. 1.
[2] *Pioneer Mail,* Dec. 10, 1884.
[3] *Ibid.*

team is jogging along in more or less amity."[4] He had spoken too soon, however. The Lieutenant-Governor of Bengal, Augustus Rivers Thompson, had no intention of forgetting the Ilbert Bill and the farewell demonstrations for Ripon.

Rivers Thompson[5] had certain qualities which made him a popular and respected member of the Anglo-Indian community and the Indian Civil Service. A product of Haileybury and of solid years spent in the Revenue and Judicial Service, Thompson had advanced slowly but steadily to the senior level of the Bengal Civil Service and to the Viceroy's Council. He blended the Haileybury tradition of responsibility and dedication with the Dalhousian values of imperialism and superiority. Unlike the leading men of his day, he lacked distinction—the perceptiveness of Aitchison, the brilliance of Lyall, the energy of Elliott, or the ability of Eden. But his demonstrated capacity for work and administrative ability made him the logical successor to Sir Ashley Eden as Lieutenant-Governor of Bengal. Ripon had appointed him partly because he was a gentleman and also familiar with Bengal administration, but mainly because he wished to get Thompson out of the Viceroy's Council and into a subordinate position where Thompson would feel less compulsion "to express his opinion freely" about the government's policy.[6] Lord Hartington, then Secretary of State for War, although he disliked Thompson's "intemperate disposition," mediocrity, and jingoistic ideas, reluctantly agreed.[7] In managing Bengal, Thompson's traditionalism and prejudice ultimately clashed with Ripon's liberal views on the repeal of the Vernacular Press Act, the Bengal Local Self-Government Bill, and the Ilbert Bill. His failure to support Ripon during the Ilbert Bill controversy won the applause of the Anglo-Indian community of Bengal, but it cost him the support of Kimberley and the India Council,[8] and any rapport with the Bengali politicians and editors, whose scathing indictment Thompson neither forgave nor forgot. As his anxieties rose and his health deteriorated, he became ill-tempered and impetuous. By 1884, he had entirely lost Ripon's confidence and so alienated the Bengali political leaders that Ripon advised Duf-

    [4] D. to J. K. Cross, Jan. 28, 1885, DVP, R. 525, No. 7.
    [5] B. 1829; Eton and Haileybury; I.C.S.; served in Revenue and Judicial Departments, 1850-1869; Secretary to Bengal Government, 1869-1875; Chief Commissioner, British Burma, 1875-1878; member of Viceroy's Council under Lord Lytton, 1878-1882; Lieutenant-Governor, Bengal, 1882-1887; K.C.S.I., 1885.
    [6] R. to Hartington, Jan. 7, 1882 (priv.), RVP, I.S. 290/5, No. 2.
    [7] Hartington to R., Feb. 3, R. to Hartington, Mar. 31, 1882, RVP, I.S. 290/5, nos. 8, 20.
    [8] K. to R., Apr. 13, 1883 (priv.), RVP, I.S., 290/5, No. 21.

ferin that Thompson was "very unpopular with the natives" and "unfortunately so committed to the Anglo-Indian party as to make it unsafe to rely upon his opinion on questions in which their interests are concerned."[9] This was soon demonstrated to Dufferin.

The annual Calcutta Trades Association Dinner, held in 1885 on January 30, had always been considered an important event of the New Year, at which leading Anglo-Indians and Indians of the Calcutta business community, the press, and the government gathered, and to which important guest speakers were usually invited. The Ilbert Bill controversy had interfered with the custom of recent years of inviting the viceroy to give the key address,[10] to say nothing of the intercommunal nature of the dinner. But this year the invitations—to Lord Dufferin and Rivers Thompson, who were asked to speak, and to various persons, both British and Indian, immediately involved in the Ilbert Bill controversy[11]— gave evidence of the desire to return to normality, to heal the wounds of the past, and to join hands for the future.

Dufferin chose this occasion to reiterate more fully Kimberley's policy. He wished to meet "the just and legitimate aspirations" of both communities and to be guided by "a justice which neither prejudice nor self-interest can pervert and an impartiality between all religions and races, which refuses to be irritated by criticism or cajoled by flattery."[12] No words could have been more appropriate, tactful, and sensitive, and had Rivers Thompson not spoken that evening, Dufferin might have found his gracious words accomplishing the task for which he had intended them.

But Rivers Thompson did speak—frankly and bluntly in words which beckoned to the past and catered to Anglo-Indian prejudices.[13] He reminded everyone that the British mission in India was "to restore the light" which had faded in Indian civilization "by the spread of Western knowledge and Western culture." British rule now stood upon the threshold of fulfillment, but this

[9] Ripon's Notes on Personalities, Dec. 1884, RP, BM Add. MSS 43616, p. 90.

[10] At this dinner in 1883, Ilbert announced his Criminal Procedure Amendment Bill, which provoked the Ilbert Bill controversy.

[11] C. P. Ilbert of the Viceroy's Council, the drafter but not really the originator of the bill; Griffith Evans of the Calcutta High Court, representative of Anglo-Indians in reaching a compromise with Ripon; A. MacDonald, editor of *The Englishmen*, and S. E. J. Clarke, editor of *The Indian Daily News*, both bitterly opposed; R. Knight, proprietor and editor of *The Statesman and Friend of India*, R. Sarvadhikari and Raja R. L. Mitra, editors of *The Hindoo Patriot*, organ of the Bengal zemindars and businessmen, and N. N. Sen, proprietor and editor of *The Indian Mirror*, all supporters of the bill.

[12] Viceroy's speech, *Statesman and Friend of India*, Jan. 31, 1885.

[13] Thompson's speech, *ibid*.

progress was threatened with disruption by "the misdirected aspirations or the exaggerated pretensions of a small section of the country" which claimed national rights, and with which Thompson defiantly owned, "I confess I have no sympathy." Since India was a vast area of many peoples, tribes, tongues, and creeds, he considered it "ethnologically impossible and historically improbable that any human effort or will could ever weld these into one nation." He dismissed such aspirations as mere theory "which might be called dangerous if we ever thought of carrying them out." He preferred to ignore them and to proceed with the important task at hand—the glorious mission of the British Empire in India. This was "Lyttonism" at its most extreme. As he sat down amid waves of applause and volleys of cheers, it was obvious that the brief interlude of harmony and goodwill following Ripon's departure was at an end.

The following day, editors of the Anglo-Indian press applauded Thompson for his "courage and precision"[14] in speaking for all Anglo-Indians against "the Bengali Babus and schoolboys, whose aspirations have, for the last year or two, been running riot amid dreams of an approaching epoch of emancipation" and against the Bengali press, especially *The Indian Mirror,* which had "insulted, traduced, misrepresented and denounced" him.[15] They felt that Thompson had a right to "sneer" and to call a halt to the government's drift toward a liberal policy, and they found Dufferin's speech too moderate, vague, and conciliatory—"a laboured complication of resonant platitudes"[16]—and warned him to cease the diplomatic two-step and to mold a policy in terms of Thompson's forceful attitude.

A few of the more liberal Anglo-Indian editors of Bengal and Madras and practically all Indian editors rose in a chorus to attack Thompson's "ill-conceived speech,"[17] condemning it as "deplorable,"[18] "unwise and impolitic,"[19] and as "a declaration of undying hostility,"[20] the petty comments of an "old Haileybury man" and a "disappointed official" with "narrow and illiberal views" who had been "nurtured in the tradition of a bygone generation of paternal officialism."[21] His words served no constructive purpose, but only

[14] *Englishman's Overland Mail,* Feb. 4, 1885.
[15] *Pioneer Mail,* Feb. 4, 1885.
[16] *Civil and Military Gazette,* Feb. 6, 1885.
[17] *Indian Mirror,* Feb. 1, 1885.
[18] *Statesman and Friend of India,* Feb. 6, 1885.
[19] *Behar Herald* (quoted in *Indian Mirror,* Feb. 13, 1885).
[20] *Reis and Raiyyet* (quoted in *Indian Mirror,* Feb. 11, 1885).

reawakened old animosities "just at a time when the Natives and Europeans were both trying their utmost to heal up old differences."[22] For those educated Indian leaders who had held out hopes for a sound rapprochement, Thompson's utterances produced "a sense of despair and bitter ill-will";[23] Lord Dufferin might as well cease his appeals to the good sense of the Indian and Anglo-Indian communities—"they can work to no purpose."[24] How could the Indian community come forward in goodwill when Thompson, other senior officials, and the Anglo-Indian press would not support Dufferin?[25] Under such changed circumstances, educated India should still rely on Dufferin, but, at the same time, renew its political activities to shape its own destiny.[26]

For Dufferin, Thompson's speech was like a bolt of lightning from a clear sky. Listening to it, he was visibly embarrassed.[27] Though he said nothing to Thompson,[28] he was concerned with its effect on his policy of rapprochement. He could not ignore the renewal of polemics in the Indian and Anglo-Indian journals or the political rumblings ringing with the words, "race" and "rights," or the bitterness engendered in the revival of the theme of English superiority and Indian inferiority. It was precisely this group consciousness and divisive particularism which Dufferin had come to India to check by making Europeans and Indians of all creeds and stations in life less self-conscious and more aware of their common identity under the Crown. Thompson's speech had rendered such efforts nugatory. The educated Indian leaders adopted increasingly divergent attitudes toward Dufferin, some optimistic, some sceptical. Both communities, Indian and European, now called upon him to strip away the facade of impartiality and to declare himself.

As a result of his Trades Dinner speech, one group of Indian leaders began optimistically to look upon Dufferin as the newly emerg-

[21] *Indian Mirror*, Feb. 1, *Bombay Native Opinion* (quoted in *Indian Mirror*, Feb. 13), *Behar Herald*, Feb. 13, *Indian Spectator*, Feb. 15, 1885.

[22] *Indian Mirror*, Feb. 1, *Statesman and Friend of India*, Feb. 6, *Behar Herald* (quoted in *Indian Mirror*, Feb. 13), *Indian Spectator*, Feb. 15, 1885.

[23] *Indian Spectator*, Feb. 15, 1885.

[24] *Amrita Bazar Patrika*, Feb. 5 (*V. of I.*, III, Feb. 1885).

[25] *Bombay Samachar*, Feb. 3, *Subodh Patrika*, Feb. 15 (*V. of I.*, III, Feb. 1885); *Indian Mirror*, Feb. 7, "Gup and Gossip," *Indian Mirror*, Feb. 11, *Indian Spectator*, Feb. 15, 1885.

[26] *Hindu*, Feb. 6, *Mahratta*, Feb. 8 (*V. of I.*, III, Feb. 1885); *Bengalee*, Feb. 7, *Indian Spectator*, Feb. 15, 1885.

[27] *Statesman and Friend of India*, Feb. 6, 1885. The editor, R. Knight, was at the dinner.

[28] At least there is no evidence in the DVP.

ent savior of Indian political development.[29] "We have in the speech
. . . a clear and emphatic announcement that the legitimate aspirations of the people will be gratified," wrote Banerjea,[30] and he in-
duced the committee of the Indian Association of Bengal to pass
resolutions acknowledging how "deeply grateful" the association
was to the Viceroy for his encouraging words.[31] Such sentiments fostered the hope that Dufferin had the makings of another Ripon;
this, in turn, generated unrealistic expectations about Dufferin's
future relationship with the Indian community which made his
position increasingly awkward.

The difficulties of this undue optimism became apparent when
the question of the reform of the provincial legislative councils
arose. Indian political circles began a moderate agitation for this
reform—by no means recently conceived or with high priority on
the list of Indian grievances[32]—during late 1884 and early 1885,
since it seemed the logical next step after Ripon's successful implementation of the elective franchise at the municipal level. Moreover,
Dufferin, with his councils reform in Egypt[33] and avowed interest in
Indian political aspirations, seemed the logical person to initiate
it.[34] Thompson's speech provided the Indian politicians with added
reason to press for the reform. As long as Indians were nominated,
not elected, to the legislative councils, Thompson and other officials
could decry the ability of Indians to undertake political responsibility and claim incorrectly that Indian political ambition involved
only a disgruntled few in Bengal.[35] Indian representation in the
councils was deemed essential to disprove these prejudices, and Dufferin was urged to move such a reform. "Will Lord Dufferin deny to

[29] *Indian Mirror*, Feb. 1, *Indian Spectator*, Feb. 15, *Bombay Samachar*, Feb. 3, *Mahratta*, Feb. 8, *Bangabasi*, Feb. 14, *Subodh Patrika*, Feb. 15 (*V. of I.*, III, Feb. 1885).

[30] *Bengalee*, Feb. 7, 1885.

[31] Report of committee meeting, Feb. 9, in *Bengalee*, Feb. 14, 1885.

[32] See above, pp. 14-15. Resolutions favoring such reform were proposed by the East India Association (London) in 1867, the Bombay Association from 1868 through 1871, the Indian Association (Bengal) in 1883, and the Madras Mahajana Sabha in 1884.

[33] Dufferin's reforms consisted of an appointed, solely advisory Legislative Council for the Khedive and an Assembly with a majority of elected members and with powers of interpellation, budget debate, and veto over new taxes. See *P.P.*, 1883, Vol. 83, Com. 3529, pp. 95-96; Earl of Cromer, *Modern Egypt* (London, 1908), I, 331-375. Historians have failed to note that Dufferin based his reforms in Egypt on Ripon's suggestions and scheme for Indian local self-government. See their corres-pondence, Nov.-Dec. 1882, RVP, I.S. 290/7, nos. 148, 155, 134, 135 with enclosures.

[34] *Native Opinion*, Jan. 25, *Indian Nation*, Jan. 26, *Bengal Public Opinion*, Jan. 29, *Indian Mirror*, Feb. 6, *Indian Spectator*, Feb. 8, *Indian Union*, Feb. 9 (*V. of I.*, III, Feb. 1885).

[35] *Statesman and Friend of India*, Feb. 6, *Bengalee*, Feb. 7, *Indian Spectator*, Feb. 15, 1885; *Amrita Bazar Patrika*, Feb. 5, *Sind Times*, Feb. 7 (*V. of I.*, III, Feb. 1885).

us what he has given to Egypt?"[36] Various schemes, all including the elective franchise, the right of interpellation, and budget debate, were put forward,[37] but Dufferin gave no sign. His inaction disconcerted the editors, who had relied upon his interest and support, but they made excuses for him and assured him that Indian political leaders would continue to look to him "with confidence," trusting that he would move the councils reforms soon.[38]

In contrast, the other group of educated Indian leaders, frankly sceptical, assumed that Dufferin's impartiality would not last long and considered reliance on him and expectation of his continuing sympathy unrealistic, and also unfair to him. Thompson's speech seemed to bear this out, and, when Dufferin failed to rebuke Thompson publicly, as some Indian politicians had hoped he would,[39] their doubts increased. "We will wait and hope," wrote one editor, "that Lord Dufferin will not become an Anglo-Indian and learn to despise our best hopes and aspirations."[40] They felt it now unwise to place full confidence in the Viceroy until he translated words into action.[41] His silence on the proposed councils reform showed he had no intention of rushing to promote Indian aspirations. Indians in the near future would have to organize to secure their own interests.[42]

While in Bombay, Madras, and the Punjab, where no issues arose to involve Dufferin immediately with Indian politicians, an attitude of cautious optimism continued to prevail, in Bengal both optimists and sceptics looked upon the next six months as a time of testing. In this period, Dufferin, who, as Governor-General in Council directly responsible for Bengal legislation, had to approve or disapprove all proposed legislative measures, was compelled to pass judgment on the recommendations of Rivers Thompson. In so doing, Dufferin ran afoul of the political situation in Bengal and Bihar, and in the ensuing entanglement the original support of the optimist group steadily weakened.

The Bengal Tenancy Bill, part of his inheritance from the Ripon administration, proved the most detrimental to Dufferin's reputation. The bill proposed by Ripon, based on the recommendations

[36] *Bengalee*, Feb. 7, 1885.
[37] *Hindoo Patriot*, Feb. 9, 1885. See also *Punjab Courier*, Feb. 11, *Mahomedan Observer*, Feb. 14, *Sind Times*, Feb. 25, *Bengal Public Opinion*, Feb. 26, *Subodh Patrika*, Mar. 4, *Charuvarta*, Feb. 9, *Swadesa Mitran*, Feb. 26 (*V. of I.*, III, Mar. 1885).
[38] *Bengalee*, Feb. 21, 1885.
[39] *Indian Mirror*, Feb. 7, *Hindu* (quoted in *Indian Mirror*, Feb. 19, 1885).
[40] *Bengal Public Opinion*, Feb. 5 (*V. of I.*, III, Feb. 1885).
[41] *Hindu*, Feb. 6, *Tribune*, Feb. 7 (*V. of I.*, III, Feb. 1885).
[42] *Mahratta*, Mar. 1 (*V. of I.*, III, Mar. 1885).

of Eden, Thompson, and other officials, aimed to amend the definition of the occupancy right to land of the ryot, or tenant cultivator, which, by Act X of 1859,[43] was determined by twelve continuous years of cultivation of the same soil. Encouraged by this static provision, the zemindars, or landlords, and Anglo-Indian indigo farmers shifted the ryots directly or forced them to move by rent enhancement, in order to prevent their gaining occupancy tenure. These practices inevitably led to agrarian disturbances, such as the ryot outbursts in eastern Bengal in the years 1873 to 1875, which upset the security of the region and seriously disrupted the flow of land revenue to the Indian government. Ripon's bill, designed to prevent similar costly outbreaks by providing the ryots with occupancy tenure and protection under law, was criticized— particularly the clauses on rights of tenure and limitation of rent enhancement—as racial and injurious by the zemindars and also by the upper-middle classes of Bengal and Bihar with their absentee interest in land.[44] When this opposition threatened to extend to Parliament and to join the Anglo-Indian opposition against the Ilbert Bill, Ripon was instructed to have the bill redrafted.[45]

With Ripon's departure the task fell to Dufferin, who immediately instructed Thompson and his staff to pluck from the bill a large number of the clauses weighted in favor of the ryot against the zemindar.[46] But Thompson refused to yield on certain clauses concerning the rent enhancement which he felt the cultivator interests deserved, and Dufferin was forced to support him to get the bill through his Council.[47] By early March, although the two zemindari representatives in the Viceroy's Council cast adverse votes and the Bengal government still had misgivings regarding some of the discarded clauses, the Bengal Tenancy Bill, to supersede Act X of 1859, was passed.[48]

Dufferin's decisiveness and skillful compromise in carrying the act won him instant praise from Indian editors in Bombay, Madras,

[43] R. to Hartington, Mar. 17 (priv.), Mar. 24, 1882, RVP, I.S. 290/5, nos. 18, 19.
[44] The land of Bengal was divided into 110,456 estates, owned by some 130,000 proprietors with about one million middlemen and some ten million ryots, or cultivators, of whom 60 to 90 per cent were occupancy ryots. See CRO, Abstract, Governor-General, Feb. 27, 1885, pp. 84-85.
[45] K. to R., Feb. 15, July 4, 1884 (priv.), RVP, I.S. 290/5, nos. 12, 36.
[46] D. to K., Dec. 30, 1884, Feb. 13, 1885, DVP, R. 517, nos. 3, 11; D. to Queen, Feb. 16, 1885, DVP, R. 516, No. 5a.
[47] D. to K., Mar. 10, 1885, DVP, R. 517, No. 14. See also council sessions, Mar. 4, 5 on enhancement, and Dufferin's summary remarks, Mar. 11, CRO, Abstract, Governor-General, 1885, pp. 209-212, 278-290, 449.
[48] Mar. 11, 1885, CRO, Abstract, Governor-General, 1885, p. 450.

and the Punjab.[49] In Bengal the verdict was different. Just four newspapers[50] congratulated him for his efforts; one, *The Bengalee,* edited by S. Banerjea, declared that the act was a decided improvement over the act of 1859.[51] But these praises were lost in a sea of negative criticism. The Bengal zemindars, although not overly dismayed with the act,[52] were displeased by the clause limiting rent enhancement which Thompson, with Dufferin's support, had successfully maintained.[53] Their colleagues in Bihar held stronger views: Dufferin's conduct and the resulting act were inimical to their interests.[54] The landlords in the Northwest Provinces and Oudh regarded the act as the government's first step in undoing the Permanent Settlement.[55] The liberals' indictment was equally severe: Dufferin was surrendering the property not only of the zemindars but also of "the State" to "middlemen usurers" merely to pass the bill and accommodate his Council.[56] The argument was pursued in more acrid tones by those Indian editors, such as Sambhu Chandra Mukerji and the Ghose brothers, Shishir and Motilal, who represented the entrepreneurial interests and absentee landlords of the Bengali upper-middle class. They claimed that Dufferin and his Council had proceeded hastily with the bill[57]—a charge which reached Parliament and required an explanation from Dufferin;[58] that they had purposely avoided any public discussion of the measure;[59] and that they had shown no consideration to the interests of middlemen.[60] Yet certain Bengali vernacular editors condemned the act as disastrous to ryoti interests because of Dufferin's surrender to the zemindars.[61] Finally N. N. Sen, viewing the act less in terms of the effects on interested parties and more from the standpoint of the crucial constitutional issue involved, claimed that Dufferin had "defied" public opinion and

---

[49] *Indian Spectator* and *Rast Goftar,* Mar. 8, *Bombay Chronicle,* Mar. 8, 15, *Jam-e-Jamshed* and *Bombay Samachar,* Mar. 13, *Kesari,* Mar. 14, *Mahratta,* Mar. 15, *Prabhakar,* Mar. 17, *People's Friend,* Mar. 21, *Gujerati Mitra,* Mar. 22 (*V. of I.,* III, Mar. 1885); *Tribune,* Mar. 21, 1885.

[50] *Liberal,* Mar. 8, 15, *Bangabasi,* Mar. 14, *Indian Nation,* Mar. 16 (*V. of I.,* III, Mar. 1885); *Bengalee,* Mar. 14, 1885.

[51] Mar. 14, 1885.

[52] See D. to K., Mar. 17, 1885, DVP, R. 517, No. 15.

[53] *Hindoo Patriot,* Mar. 9, 1885.

[54] *Nababibhakar,* Mar. 16 (*V. of I.,* III, Mar. 1885).

[55] *Indian Union,* Mar. 23 (*V. of I.,* III, Mar. 1885).

[56] R. Knight to D., Mar. 7, 1885, DVP, R. 528, No. 135a.

[57] *Reis and Raiyyet,* Mar. 9 (*V. of I.,* III, Mar. 1885).

[58] See n. 52 above.

[59] *Indian Chronicle,* Mar. 9 (*V. of I.,* III, Mar. 1885).

[60] *Amrita Bazar Patrika,* Mar. 19 (*V. of I.,* III., Mar. 1885).

[61] *Sanjibani,* Mar. 14, *Shamaya,* Mar. 15, *Sadharani,* Mar. 16 (*V. of I.,* III, Mar. 1885).

advanced the bill with "the iron hand of despotism."[62] Zemindari, entrepreneurial, ryoti, or constitutional—these views, while they represented half-truths and prejudices, also represented the opinion of important political groups in Bengal and Bihar. Dufferin's handling of the bill and his apparent support of Thompson made these groups apprehensive of the Viceroy's domestic policy.

The passage of the Bengal Local Boards Bill did little to offset these apprehensions. This bill formed part of the proposals of the Bengal Government to implement Ripon's resolution of May 18, 1882, calling for increased nonofficial, and particularly Indian, representation, with elective franchise, on municipal and local boards.[63] Kimberley had postponed action on the bill until Dufferin was in the saddle.[64] The bill, placed by Dufferin before a Select Committee of the Bengal Government, emerged in March 1885 with a number of changes which provided for increased centralization and official control of the Boards,[65] arousing the opposition of two important Bengali associations. In its memorial to Rivers Thompson, the Indian Association of Bengal stated that the bill was "less liberal" than similar acts approved for the Central and Northwest Provinces, both of which were considered less civilized and politically less developed than Bengal.[66] The Association advocated that the Bengal Government be allowed at least the reforms adopted in the other provinces, namely, that there be nonofficial majorities, of at least two-thirds, elected to the local and district boards and that these boards elect their own chairmen. Furthermore, the reforms should encompass all forty-five districts of Bengal instead of the sixteen listed by the Bengal Government, and the power vested in the lieutenant-governor should be restricted. The Indian Union, a small association formed after the passage of the Bengal Tenancy Act by "representatives of the landed, commercial and professional sections of the community," and led by the eminent barrister Man Mohan Ghose, officers of the British Indian Association, the wealthy landholder, the Maharaja of Durbhanga, and others, also opposed the bill in a memorial, drafted by the formidable pens of Rajkumar Sarvadhikari and N. N. Sen, who supported amendments similar to those of the Indian Association.[67] But, for administrative reasons, Thompson did not accept

[62] *Indian Mirror,* Mar. 12, 1885.
[63] *P.P.,* 1883, Vol. 51, Ret. 931, p. 25.
[64] See above, p. 16.
[65] Report of Select Committee, 1884, 1885, *Calcutta Gazette,* Pt. IV, 1884, p. 61, and 1885, p. 13.
[66] *Bengalee,* Mar. 28, 1885.
[67] *Indian Mirror,* Apr. 5, 1885.

these amendments, and the bill was duly passed in the Bengal Council with few changes.[68] Only the clause inserted in the original bill to deal with nonofficial, elected majorities met the wishes of the associations.

Thompson's Local Boards Bill was just and sound. True, it was not as liberal as his Municipal Act of 1884, but he, his advisers, and his district officers, when applying such reforms to rural Bengal, had to take into account administrative considerations, as well as the express wishes of the Secretary of State for India and of the India Council that a greater degree of centralization be written into the bill.[69] But these ingredients made little sense to the Bengali associations, and thus they dismissed the bill as "a satire on self-government"[70] and as another example of Thompson's determination "to thwart and frustrate the aspirations and pretensions of the educated classes of Natives in Bengal"; an appeal was made to Dufferin to veto the bill on behalf of Bengali interests.[71] Dufferin, however, made no move, private or public, and once again it appeared to the Bengali leaders that he had yielded to Thompson. Some months later, he gave his assent to the bill,[72] which thereupon became the Bengal Local Self-Government Act (III) of 1885.[73]

By late March, few Bengali politicians remained unshaken in their belief in Dufferin's sympathy with Indian political aspirations, and many owned pessimistically that he was rapidly replacing his impartiality with Anglo-Indian prejudice. They were puzzled and dismayed, and could only conclude that Dufferin had been more in step with Thompson at the Trades Dinner than he had led them to believe. Yet Dufferin's conduct was in keeping with Kimberley's policy. He did not deal forcefully and publicly with Thompson because such action would have produced the very result Kimberley wished to avoid, namely, a recurrence of the impasse between the Government of India and the provincial government of Bengal which had existed during the latter half

[68] *Calcutta Gazette*, Supp. 1885, pp. 549, 658, 683. For completion of bill, see CRO, Abstract, Lieutenant-Governor, Apr. 6, 1885.

[69] Dispatch of Secretary of State, No. 68, Pub., July 5, 1883, CRO, Jud. and Pub. Disp., 1883.

[70] *Hindoo Patriot*, Apr. 14, 1885.

[71] *Indian Mirror*, Apr. 1, 1885.

[72] Secretary, Government of India, Legislative Department, to Secretary, Government of Bengal, Legislative Department, July 11, 1885, CRO, Govt. of India, Legis. Dept. Procs., Vol. 2572, 1885, Pt. I; *Report of the Administration of Bengal 1885-86* (Calcutta, 1887), pp. 80-81.

[73] CRO, Govt. of India, Legis. Dept. Procs., Vol. 2572, 1885, Pt. I.

of Ripon's viceroyalty. Both the Bengal Tenancy Bill and the Local Boards Bill could have sparked agitation and public controversy if not dealt with circumspectly. Dufferin therefore maintained a discreet silence on Thompson's Trades Dinner speech and other public utterances, struck a compromise with Thompson over those clauses in the Tenancy Bill about which Thompson felt strongly, and gave his assent to Thompson's Local Boards Bill. By so doing, Dufferin reestablished the sound working relationship between the Supreme Government and the Government of Bengal which Kimberley wished.

In further regard for Kimberley's express instructions, Dufferin chose the Bengal Tenancy Bill as the first matter to be passed by his Council.[74] After studying the bill more closely and becoming aware of its weaknesses, he wrote Kimberley that he would prefer to postpone consideration for a year while a commission gathered the necessary supporting opinions and data that were lacking in the proposed bill[75]—the very course the Bengali politicians had advised—but he did not do so because Kimberley expressed his "desire to get the matter settled this year."[76] Kimberley, pleased to learn that Dufferin had overcome his reluctance to press ahead, wrote in reply that "the Ilbert Bill was a serious warning against the consequences of hanging up a measure which excites acrimonious feelings."[77] So in moving the Tenancy Bill, Dufferin never allowed his Council to become diverted from the central issues. Patiently listening to the claims of both Thompson's advisers and the zemindars, he relentlessly pressed the bill forward while he consulted Kimberley upon all its major clauses[78]—to such an extent that Kimberley advised him to use his own judgment.[79] The result was precisely what Kimberley had wished: the bill was completed with all parties reasonably amenable to the compromise and with agitation avoided. Kimberley "greatly rejoiced" and congratulated Dufferin for his "firmness and decision," emphasizing that "it was peculiarly important to get this question settled, with foreign troubles of such magnitude impeding."[80]

Dufferin also followed Kimberley's wishes on the demand of the educated Indians for changing the age limit for the Covenanted

[74] D. to K., Dec. 15, 1884, K. to D., Jan. 8, 1885, DVP, R. 517, nos. 1, 11.
[75] D. to K., Dec. 30, 1884, DVP, R. 517, No. 3.
[76] *Ibid.*
[77] K. to D., Jan. 22, 1885, DVP, R. 517, No. 14.
[78] Viceroy to Secretary of State, telegrams, Jan. 3 (priv.), Jan. 10, 16, 1885, DVP, R. 519, nos. 38, 57, 77.
[79] Secretary of State to Viceroy, telegram, Jan. 21, 1885, DVP, R. 519, No. 86.
[80] K. to D., Mar. 13, 1885, DVP, R. 517, No. 22.

Civil Service examinations in England. By 1884 Kimberley and Ripon no longer saw eye-to-eye on this issue.[81] Kimberley advised Ripon that any reappraisal of the age limit, let alone of Lytton's Rules, was out of the question.[82] Unless Ripon could provide valid evidence that Lytton's scheme had failed or that the age limit was deterring Indians from standing for the Covenanted examination in England, Kimberley was not going to rekindle the "bitter feeling" which had occurred within the India Council over the Ilbert and Local Self-Government bills by complying with such a demand.[83] Just prior to his departure from India, Ripon did forward to Kimberley a weighty official dispatch which had been given the "unanimous" approval of the Viceroy's Council.[84] Leading officials —Fergusson, Thompson, Aitchison, and Crosthwaite[85]—and sundry Indian associations in the Madras and Bombay presidencies[86] supported Ripon's scheme, which recommended that examination, instead of official nomination, be reestablished as the primary avenue for Indian entrance into the Covenanted Service and that the age limit be raised to 21 to facilitate Indian participation in the examination.[87]

Kimberley's official decision, in the negative[88] and forwarded to Dufferin, would undoubtedly have caused Ripon to resign instantaneously had he received it. Kimberley pointed out privately to Dufferin that, after exhaustive study of Ripon's dispatch, neither he nor his Council could find reason to reverse their former decisions and approve Ripon's recommendations. Kimberley's reasons (and his very expressions) were precisely those of Argyll and Salisbury. He had no intention of "modelling our rules for the examination with the special purpose of facilitating the admission

[81] See above, p. 16.

[82] K. to R., May 2, 1884 (priv.), RVP, I.S. 290/5, No. 23.

[83] K. to R., May 22, 1884 (priv.), RVP, I.S. 290/5, No. 29.

[84] R. to K., Sept. 11, 1884, RVP, I.S. 290/5, No. 48.

[85] Dispatch of Govenor-General-in-Council, No. 51, Pub. (Home), Sept. 12, 1884, CRO, Pub. Let., 1884, pp. 793-1270, enclosing confidential comments by J. Fergusson, Governor, Bombay, June 12, pp. 815-817, by A. R. Thompson, Lieutenant-Governor, Bengal, June 12, pp. 825-828, by C. U. Aitchison, Lieutenant-Governor, Punjab, July 11, pp. 877-882, by C. H. Crosthwaite, Chief Commissioner, Central Provinces, June 11, 1884, pp. 908-910.

[86] *Ibid.*, enclosing memorials from associations in the Punjab, pp. 937-952, in Northwest Provinces and Oudh. pp. 953-1040, 1215-1218, In Madras, pp. 1093-1096, in Bombay, pp. 1097-1215, 1219-1270. But no memorials from associations in Bengal were enclosed.

[87] *Ibid.*: recommendations of Governor-General-in-Council, pp. 793-800, minute by Viceroy on raising the age qualification for the Covenanted examination, Sept. 10, 1884, pp. 911-936.

[88] Dispatch of Secretary of State in Council, No. 1, Pub., Jan. 8, 1885, CRO, Selections from Disp., Ser. 28, Vol. 27, Pt. I.

of natives."[89] The annual number of Indian appointments to the Covenanted Service was increasing, and he feared that any changes in the Covenanted examination or its age limit would only accelerate this increase; such changes would produce no reasonable cross section of Indian candidates but only more Bengalis. Thus the existing Covenanted examination must remain unchanged, and the Statutory Service must continue to serve as the primary means of Indian entry into the Covenanted Service.[90] Kimberley instructed Dufferin "to use every effort to improve" the Statutory scheme and to make it more acceptable to Indian aspirants, and he encouraged him "to face the educated Baboo and not from fear of him impair the efficiency of our European bureaucracy on which we must after all mainly depend."[91]

Without hesitation, Dufferin accepted Kimberley's decision and at once put the latter's instructions into effect. He raised no questions with Kimberley, nor did he make any public comments, but, as in the case of the Bengal Tenancy Bill, he merely followed Kimberley's lead and turned his attention to the improvement of the rules by which Indians could enter the Statutory Service.[92] Upon receipt of the official dispatch from the India Office, he informed Kimberley that the India government was preparing an official statement on the age limit, based upon Kimberley's decision, to be forwarded to one of the Indian associations that had memorialized the India Office.[93] In addition, he would investigate the ways in which the local governments had implemented the Act of 1870 and the results achieved. Kimberley could have asked for nothing more. Dufferin had quietly relegated the inflammable Civil Service question to the background of Indian domestic affairs.

Dufferin had begun to forge his domestic policy with the necessary caution which Kimberley and the India Council wished and with the firmness and official self-interest which members of the Viceroy's Council and local governments favored. He had placated Thompson, restored official confidence in Government House, and done nothing to disturb the Anglo-Indian community. But he had done so by shelving and ignoring the demands of the educated Indians. By February the declaration he had made at the outset of his administration regarding a fair and impartial hearing for all groups could no longer apply. As a result of following instruc-

[89] K. to D., Jan. 8, 1885, DVP, R. 517, No. 12.
[90] See n. 88 above.
[91] See n. 89 above.
[92] D. to K., Feb. 3, 1885, DVP, R. 517, No. 9.
[93] D. to K., Mar. 2, 1885, DVP, R. 517, No. 13.

tions, he had reintroduced strong official prejudice into domestic policy at the expense of the claims of the educated Indian. This prejudice, moreover, contained an anti-Bengali tinge. In words reminiscent of Salisbury, Lytton, Eden, and Kimberley himself, Dufferin admitted that even from his brief acquaintance he found "the Bengali Baboo a most irritating and troublesome gentleman with a great deal of Celtic perverseness, vivacity and cunning." He agreed completely with Kimberley that the Viceroy and his Council must stand firm against the "Baboo," and not fear him. This was his point of view on the Civil Service question; it was the same concerning the councils reform. Official support and Anglo-Indian rapport with Government House were not to be set aside for Bengali interests. Even though the Bengali politicians seemed to Dufferin to be employed in "devising the machinery for a repeal agitation on the lines of O'Connell's Patriotic Association" in order to press their claims,[94] he did not intend to change Kimberley's policy one iota unless Kimberley so instructed him.

[94] See n. 92 above. Daniel O'Connell (1775-1847), who attempted to organize a mass Irish movement for repeal of the Union in 1843 by means of his Repeal Association (1831-1843), failed because he was too moderate for the revolutionary "Young Ireland" party. See W. E. H. Lecky, *Leaders of Public Opinion in Ireland*, new ed. (London, 1903), II, 233-255.

II

Plans for National Organization

Although Dufferin gave no reasons, his conclusion that the educated Bengalis were engaged in mounting a repeal agitation was undoubtedly based upon two developments reflected at the time in the Bengali press: the moderate agitation for councils reform[1] and, more novel and more arresting, the editorials of N. N. Sen[2] in mid- and late January in *The Indian Mirror* of Calcutta. These were concerned less with immediate issues such as councils reform than with the political organization of the educated Indian in the year ahead. What Sen proposed was a well-considered plan[3] for a national movement with "the regeneration of India" as its goal. This ambitious task was to be accomplished by building an organization upon the political base which Lord Ripon in particular and English rule in general had bequeathed to India and from which "the first germs of union and co-operation" had begun to sprout among the English-educated Indians. For this legacy, Sen was most grateful. While always unpleasantly outspoken in instances of obvious British miscarriages of justice, he was always the first to declare that India was fortunate to be under British rule, which was preparing India for its entry into the modern world of nations. "Till we learn all that we have to learn from them [The British] to our advantage, it is not likely that their rule will pass away." The English people had learned the lessons of the value of national union and cooperation, and of improving

[1] See above, p. 30.

[2] B. 1843; Hindu College; trained in law; cousin of Keshub Chandra Sen; proprietor and editor of *The Indian Mirror* (1879), which, founded by him in 1861, became the only Bengali daily printed in English; founder also of Brahmo Samaj (1866); attorney in the 1870s; Municipal Commissioner of Calcutta, 1880; Theosophist; supporter, then critic, of Ripon; member of Indian Association.

[3] "The Present Revival of National Life in India and Our Immediate Duty," *Indian Mirror,* Jan. 13, and editorials, Jan. 18, 20, 28, Feb. 3, 7, 13, 1885.

the condition of their masses by reliance on themselves and not on their government, and these lessons, especially the latter, Sen wished educated Indians to learn by heart. He was convinced that Indians must act "independently" of the government in seeking to better themselves and secure their rights. For this end, he published his plan.

Sen advocated the establishment of "associations" in all the principal district towns of India "to improve the condition of the people of India, political, material, moral, social and intellectual." These general goals were "the same as those of existing Political Associations" in Bombay, Poona, Madras, and Calcutta, but, in addition, and more particularly, the new district associations were to better the material condition of the Indian peasants, raise the status of women, remove the "shortcomings" in "the national character, customs and institutions," and devise the best ways to improve Indian primary and higher education. "Central Associations," located in the capital cities of the presidencies and the provinces, and consisting of representatives drawn from the municipalities and each district association, were to supervise the latter. Working together, yet independently, at these two levels, the associations would initiate the programs necessary to achieve the goals; they would, likewise, along the lines of the agitation of S. Banerjea's Indian Association on the Civil Service issue in 1877 and 1878, "adopt measures for constitutional agitation" in concert for redress of grievances, which the government alone could, but had failed to, correct. Beyond the provincial limits, the central associations would cooperate with each other "on all subjects of national interest," in order to avoid ineffective isolated action by any central association on a major critical issue. To ensure this cooperation, "delegates" from the central associations would meet "annually at all the Presidency and Provincial capitals by turns, discuss all matters of general interest, and come to some definite conclusions as to them for the guidance of the Associations collectively." This meeting "might be called the National Assembly for all India." Finally, funds, raised within the district associations by having "every Native of India with an income of Rs. 20 and above set apart one pice out of every rupee spent," and managed at the district level, would constitute a national fund, modelled on the proposal of S. Banerjea and his friends, to pay for "the Association programme," as well as for "new industries," the education of poor young men and women, and other aspects of Indian welfare requiring serious attention and reform.

Neither new nor original, Sen's plan was essentially a synthesis of three strands of political thought evolved within educated Indian circles in 1883 and 1884. First was the increasing tendency among the majority of the educated Indian leaders to favor some form of independent political action in order to secure their rights and redress their grievances. Ripon's acceptance of a compromise with the Anglo-Indian community on the Ilbert Bill demonstrated conclusively to many educated Indians that Government House was incapable of acting in their behalf,[4] and they asked, "If, with such a Viceroy, things are to be thus, what hope is there for the future?"[5] The answer was simple—there was little hope; obviously, they would have to look to themselves, not to the viceroy, and take independent political action if they wished to realize their aims and ambitions.[6]

Second, the idea of an organization, liberal in spirit, political in bent, and national in scope, originated after the Delhi Durbar in 1876 when N. N. Sen, S. Banerjea, B. Malabari, S. K. Chatterjee, S. H. Chiplonkar, and other Indian editors tried unsuccessfully to establish a press federation to meet annually to discuss political questions of national importance.[7] Unsuccessfully canvassed again in 1882 by Sen, the idea of national federation was projected into the political arena by the momentous events of 1883, when the Anglo-Indians and Eurasians, rallying behind the European and Anglo-Indian Defence Association, brought to the attention of Parliament and the London press their opposition to Ripon's policy and the interests of educated Indians by their manipulation of the English-controlled press in India and the Calcutta correspondent to *The Times.* The threat posed by the Defence Association, the pernicious misrepresentations spread by the English-controlled press, and the brief imprisonment of S. Banerjea for contempt of court in the Saligram Idol case,[8] which A. Bose, Sen, Banerjea, and other members of the Indian Association considered unjust, led them to formulate a scheme for national political action.[9] A national fund was to be raised from the existing associations in Calcutta, Madras, Bombay, Poona,

[4] See *V. of I.,* I, Dec. 1883, II, Jan. 1884.

[5] H. to R., Mar. 4, 1884, RVP, I.S. 290/8-I, No. 87a.

[6] "The Outlook," *Liberal and New Dispensation,* Dec. 23, 1883; "The Ilbert Bill and Our Future Course of Action," *Indian Mirror,* Jan. 19, 1884. For more on Ilbert Bill, see *V. of I.,* II, Jan. and Feb. 1884.

[7] "The Federation of the Native Press," *Indian Mirror,* Nov. 28, 1882.

[8] See D. Argov, *Moderates and Extremists in the Indian Nationalist Movement, 1883-1920* (Bombay, 1967), p. 6.

[9] Editorials, *Indian Mirror,* July 14, 16, *Bengalee,* July 14, 1883.

and Lahore, to be used by a national committee or council to promote "constitutional agitation for political advancement" and defend Ripon's policy in India and England,[10] but the scheme never materialized. Interest but no tangible support came from Bombay and Madras,[11] while the influential and wealthy British Indian Association of Calcutta refused to participate.[12] At the end of 1883, Banerjea shifted his emphasis and called a National Conference in Calcutta to discuss Indian grievances and plan all-India agitation,[13] but again, lacking broad and influential support, the conference turned out to be little more than a political rally of Bengalis representing the Indian Association.[14]

Ripon's compromise with the Defence Association on the Ilbert Bill[15] and the founding of the Indian Constitutional Association early in 1884 by leaders of the British Indian Association and the Defense Association to oppose any liberal measures—rural, legal, or political—inimical to their interests,[16] caused a revulsion of feeling. The more advanced educated leaders in Bengal were stirred to renewed efforts for a national association.[17] A notable series of letters, signed "A Hindu," appeared in the spring of 1884 in Sen's paper,[18] outlining a plan for "an organization of a really national character" to mobilize public opinion and forward petitions to John Slagg, M.P. for Manchester, and other M.P.s who were advocating the extension of Ripon's policy and the dismissal of the obstructive India Council, and who were willing to press for redress of Indian grievances in the Commons. But Banerjea, disregarding "A Hindu" and proceeding along the lines already laid down by himself and his colleagues, carried the scheme for a national fund into the Northwest Provinces and the Punjab by organizing concerted protests,[19] in the press and by petition, on the part of editors and associations throughout India against the age limit of 19 for the Covenanted Service examinations and

[10] Meeting of July 17, *Indian Mirror*, July 18, *Bengalee*, July 21, Aug. 4, 1883.
[11] Interest expressed by *Indu Prakash, Hindu, Behar Herald, Native Opinion, Indian Spectator, Tribune*. See *Bengalee*, Aug. 4, 11, 18, 1883; also *V. of I.*, I, Aug. and Sept. 1883.
[12] *Bengalee*, Aug. 18, 1883.
[13] *Bengalee*, Dec. 22, 1883.
[14] Conference, Dec. 28-30, 1883. See *Bengalee*, Dec. 29, 1883, Jan. 5, 1884; *Indian Mirror*, Dec. 29, 30, 1883, Jan. 1, 1884; Blunt, *India under Ripon*, pp. 114, 166, esp. 118.
[15] Editorials, *Indian Mirror*, Jan. 19, Mar. 26, Apr. 3, 1884.
[16] Circular, listing members, *Indian Mirror*, Mar. 12; meeting, Mar. 15, *ibid.*, Mar. 18, 1884.
[17] Editorials, *Indian Mirror*, Mar. 18, 19, 25, *Bengalee*, Mar. 15, 22, 1884.
[18] *Indian Mirror*, Mar. 25, 29, Apr. 1, 6, 7, 17, 24, 25, May 1, 8, 20, 1884.
[19] *Bengalee*, May 17, *Tribune*, May 17, 31, June 7, 14, 21, 1884.

against Lytton's discriminatory Statutory Service rules of 1879.[20]
The farewell demonstrations for Ripon showed the educated Indian leaders that their capacity for united action to influence those
below them was greater than they had realized.[21] At the end of
1884, Sen published a series of letters by "A.B.," urging the educated Indian leaders to focus all attention on the extension of
Ripon's proposal for self-government by pressing for a "National
Assembly," modelled after the English Parliament, with an Upper
House of nobles and titled zemindars, and a Lower House of
members elected from the provincial councils, which in turn would
be elected by the municipalities and district boards.[22] Thus by
the outset of 1885, the demand was swelling for a national fund
committee, a national conference, or a national association to
sponsor constitutional agitation in India and in England.

Third was the discussion concerning the form the national organization should take—should it be exclusively national or should
it allow for provincial variations? Here sharp differences of opinion appeared. N. N. Sen and other leaders of the Indian Association, as well as other vernacular editors in Bombay and Calcutta, favored national direction by one association with the others
subordinate to it.[23] But the Ghose brothers of *Amrita Bazar Patrika*
and other editors in the Bengal-Bihar area, and the members of
the British Indian Association, including Kristo Das Pal, editor of
The Hindoo Patriot, thought that national political agitation controlled by one association would be premature and impossible,
given the strong provincial character of India; consequently, they
advocated agitation on local, or "federal," lines with questions
of mutual concern settled bilaterally and not through a national
committee or council.[24] B. Malabari of *The Indian Spectator,*
G. S. Iyer of *The Hindu,* and certain Punjabi and Marathi editors
formulated a compromise: instead of a national fund, the presidency or provincial associations would hold funds in common to
pursue federal aims; and instead of a national committee or council, members of the various associations would meet annually to
discuss matters from an all-Indian perspective.[25]

[20] See *V. of I.,* II, May-Sept. 1884; for memorials from associations, see above, Ch.
I, n. 86.

[21] See above, pp. 20-21.

[22] Letters on "A National Assembly for India," *Indian Mirror,* Dec. 20, 30, 1884,
Jan. 20, 1885.

[23] *Bengalee,* July 21, 1883.

[24] *Hindoo Patriot,* Aug. 13, 1883.

[25] *Indian Spectator,* Sept. 9, 1883; see also *V. of I.,* I, Aug.-Sept. 1883, on National
Fund.

The collapse of the scheme for a national fund committee at the end of 1883 was a victory for the "Federalists," and thereafter political activity among educated Indians had a strong provincial bent. For example, the Madras Mahajana Sabha was formed in late 1884 on the ruins of the Madras Native Association by G. S. Iyer, R. Naidu, V. Chariar, A. Charlu, S. R. Mudaliar, Peter Pillai, and others of the younger men, and by Sir Madhava Rao and the wealthy former Diwan, Raghunath Rao, among the more elderly leaders of the earlier association. The Sabha was to be an association, as well as a conference, for exchanging ideas on political and social reform between members in Madras city and in the mofussil, and for developing and concentrating Madras public opinion on provincial matters. At the four-day session of the first Sabha, lengthy discussion on the reconstitution of the Madras Provincial Council, the separation of the collector and magistrate functions in the districts, the extension of local self-government, and the material condition of the agrarian classes,[26] as well as on the merits of the Ceylon Legislative Council and "native" magistracy, led to the conclusion that the key issues of councils and legal reform and agrarian improvement should be pressed upon the Madras Government and other Indian associations.[27] The influence of the Madras Mahajana Sabha and its program spread to Bombay where the younger leaders began preparations to rejuvenate the flagging Bombay Association. By 1885, any form of national organization would have to incorporate provincial aims and interests.

These three strands of thought—the need for political action independent of government, for national organization, and for inclusion of provincial aspirations—were naturally reflected in N. N. Sen's plan of January 1885, since he himself had actively participated in Bengali politics, had published and commented on the letters of "A Hindu" and "A.B.," and, while attending the Theosophical meeting at Adyar in Madras in December 1884,[28] had witnessed the emergence of the Madras Sabha and grasped the significance of its provincial character. There is reason to believe that, before leaving Madras, he conceived his own plan and discussed it with R. Rao, A. Charlu, and others connected with the Theosophical Society and the Madras Sabha.[29] Certainly, all

[26] Circular, *Madras Mail*, Dec. 19, 1884.

[27] Meetings of Dec. 29, 30, 1884, Jan. 1, 2, 1885, *Madras Mail*, Dec. 30, 31, 1884, Jan. 3, 5, 1885.

[28] Meetings of Dec. 27, 28, *Madras Mail*, Dec. 28, 29, 1884, listing members who attended and speakers; *Indian Mirror*, Jan. 4, 1885.

[29] See "Data for History," *Theosophist*, 10, Supplement (Sept. 1889), 169-170, an

these strands of thought and diverse influences were apparent in his plan, but, in addition, it represented a timely endeavor to promote national action among the educated Indian leaders on issues where Government had failed and, in Sen's opinion, would continue to fail to support Indian interests. It was a call for action independent of official influence or guidance, the very thing Ripon had sought to prevent by increasing the participation of educated Indians in the Government.

At no point, however, was it the aim of Sen or his colleagues to work for the repeal of British-Indian union as O'Connell had sought unsuccessfully to do in the Irish repeal agitation of the thirties and forties. Had Dufferin studied these stirrings in Bengali circles more closely and objectively, he would have realized that his analogy to Irish politics was as misconceived as his reference to O'Connell was misleading. Being new to the scene, and confined to Calcutta while the Supreme Legislative Council was in session, he was completely exposed to the anti-Bengali sentiments then rife in the Anglo-Indian official and nonofficial community of Bengal. Like numerous of his predecessors, Dufferin fell readily a victim to the anti-Bengali prejudice, and, preoccupied with more pressing matters, reached the convenient yet erroneous conclusion that Indian politics began and ended with the ambitious Bengali. Under these circumstances, not only did he entirely misjudge what Sen and his colleagues were saying and trying to do, but also he remained completely unaware of what was happening in educated Indian circles elsewhere, particularly in Bombay.

In mid-January, a meeting was held at the bungalow of Professor W. Wordsworth, Principal of Elphinstone College, Bombay University, which was attended by many leading personalities— Parsi, Gujerati, and Maratha—of the Bombay British East India

---

article which quotes verbatim an editorial by N. N. Sen in *The Indian Mirror,* Sept. 1889, in which Sen claimed that the idea of the Indian National Congress was based on discussions he held with other Theosophists at Adyar in 1884. I question this because Sen in his editorial refers to persons at the Theosophical meeting who were not listed in December 1884 as attending (see n. 28 above) and because of statements by Sen and others between January and December 1885. It seems probable that what Sen discussed at Adyar was his plan of January 1885, which differed in one fundamental from the scheme leading to the Congress, and that Sen made his claim because he was piqued by the adulation of Hume as "the originator of the Congress," and sought in his editorial to give other "workers" and himself credit by deflating Hume's image. The article in *The Theosophist* was probably the source of Annie Besant's interpretations of the founding of the Congress (*How India Wrought for Freedom* [Madras, 1915], pp. 1-6, and *India: A Nation* [London, 1915], pp. 66-67), which established and perpetuated the Sen version.

Association and the Poona Sarvajanik Sabha.[30] They had come together to consider two matters which had arisen toward the end of Ripon's viceroyalty. First, they were concerned to find an antidote to the activities of J. C. Macgregor, the Calcutta barrister who acted as the correspondent for *The Times* of London,[31] and who, they felt, had caused incalculable damage to Ripon's reputation and the cause of Indian political reform by his purposely distorted telegrams to *The Times* throughout 1883 and 1884, culminating in his pernicious misrepresentation of the farewell demonstrations.[32] Should his reports continue unchallenged, the British public would become wholly prejudiced against the Indian point of view and insensitive to Indian grievances. They therefore decided unanimously that arrangements should be made to send to a leading London daily, such as *The Pall Mall Gazette,* then edited by the radical Liberal, W. T. Stead, a weekly telegram dealing with "the important political questions" confronting the Indian people and the Government, so that objective news on India would reach the British public and its representatives in Parliament, especially those favorable to Indian interests, who would then have the facts of the Indian case which Macgregor always saw fit to exclude from his telegrams. Second, they were concerned about national reform. The younger men, particularly Mehta, Telang, Yajnik, Wacha, and Chiplonkar, wished to revive reformist activity in the Bombay Presidency. The pledges of the Queen Empress in the Proclamation of 1858 for Indian participation in the higher administration of the government remained unfulfilled and had now become "grievances that required systematic action on the part of natives for their removal." Ripon's departure made such action all the more necessary, and the farewell demonstrations in his honor showed that it could be undertaken. So they agreed that a "National Indian Association" should be formed in place of the all but defunct Bombay British East India Association, to parallel the action taken in Madras, with the difference that the new association would be more national

[30] Meeting of Jan. 18, *B.G.O.S.,* Jan. 23, 1885. Those present included: K. T. Telang, P. M. Mehta, D. Naoroji, N. Furdunji, M. G. Ranade, R. M. Sayani, F. R. Vicaji, J. U. Yajnik, S. P. Pandit, W. A. Modak, J. K. Dalal, D. E. Wacha, B. M. Malabari, K. N. Kabraji, D. Thackersey, V. Purshotumdas, S. H. Chiplonkar, W. Wedderburn, Dr. Peterson, W. Wordsworth, A. O. Hume; also, in all probability, B. Tyabji and G. Geary. There is no mention of this meeting in the biographies of Malabari, Naoroji, Tyabji, Mehta, Wedderburn, and Hume listed in the Bibliography (see below, pp. 347 ff.).

[31] The report of the meeting does not mention Macgregor by name, but refers to his activities as *The Times* correspondent.

[32] "A Most Mischievous Act," *B.G.O.S.,* Jan. 2, 1885.

than the Madras Sabha. To implement both objectives, a committee, composed of Naoroji, Tyabji, Mehta, and Telang, was appointed to work out arrangements with newspapers in London and the provinces, and a meeting was scheduled for early February to inaugurate the new association.

The inaugural session of the new association took place early in February at the Framji Cowasji Hall.[33] Convened by the principal organizers, Tyabji, Mehta, and Telang, who formed a triumvirate of the younger leaders in Bombay politics, the session was chaired by Sir Jamsetjee Jeejeebhoy, the aging doyen of the Parsi community of Bombay, whose efforts and wealth had contributed to the founding of the Bombay Association in 1852 and the subsequent formation of the British East India Association. In opening the proceedings, Jeejeebhoy stressed the need for forming a new association "because the regime of Lord Ripon has given a weight and power to native opinion which it had rarely had before." He continued: "Our present Viceroy has declared that this administration will proceed on the lines of the policy chalked out by Lord Ripon, and so it is plainly desirable that the opinion of all sections of our community should be organized and concentrated so as to be systematically available for the information of Government." His words were echoed by Tyabji who moved the resolution officially forming the association. Striking a stridently provincial note, he contended that a city like Bombay, "the best centre of political thought in India, . . . cannot afford to be satisfied with [being] the branch of any association, however powerful, eminent, or useful that association may be," but must produce "a well-organized, strong, and truly national association for the purpose of watching over the interests of this country" while showing "unimpeachable loyalty to the Throne." With the elderly Naoroji Furdunji, former leader of the "Young Bombay" party and founder of the Bombay Association, giving Tyabji's words his blessing, the Bombay Presidency Association was voted into existence with unanimous approval and much enthusiasm.

The meeting proceeded to choose officers, on the motion of Telang. Sir Jamsetjee Jeejeebhoy was elected President; the vice-presidents[34] were virtually the men of the older generation who had led the earlier associations; and the secretaries were Telang, Mehta, and Tyabji. Both officers and the members were drawn

[33] On Feb. 5. See "Native Political Association in Bombay," *B.G.O.S.*, Feb. 6, 1885.
[34] H. H. Aga Ali Shah, D. M. Petit, Sir Manguldas Nathubhoy, B. Jeejeebhoy, V. Madavadas, F. N. Patel, Nathabhoy Haridas, V. N. Mandlik, Sorabji Bengali, D. Naoroji, D. Framji, N. Furdunji, Ragunath Khote, and J. Peerbhoy.

from the Gujerati, Parsi, Borah, Osval, and Maratha communities of Bombay city. Mehta concluded the session by quoting Dufferin's remarks in a speech in Canada on the impoverishment of national life when the people of a country failed to contribute to its history and progress and "do not throb in unison with the vital pulse of national existence." The new association would strive toward these goals, and both the older and younger leaders would work together for "the cause of the country." On this optimistic note, the inaugural session ended. Yet it was apparent that the older leaders, with the exception of D. Naoroji and V. Mandlik, preferred to concentrate on Bombay affairs and grievances, while the younger leaders looked to the new national horizon as their goal. Tyabji and Mehta gave ambitious, nationalistically inspired speeches, but the name of the association and its senior officers bore the indelible imprint of Bombay City. This was a realistic compromise; the wealth remained with the elders, while the energy rested with the young. But those present in the inaugural session could have had few doubts as to the direction in which Tyabji, Mehta, and Telang were heading. They had called for an organization which would move outward from Bombay to give expression to Indian national, political development and to press the Government of India to extend Ripon's reform program, and they intended to lead, not to follow, the national reform movement.

Though the Bombay editors, B. Malabari and others, greeted the new association as a landmark in Indian political development and as an organization which would fully express Indian public opinion to the government,[35] the activities of the Bombay politicians were received with less enthusiasm elsewhere. N. N. Sen, possibly out of jealousy, with his national association in mind, never forthrightly acknowledged the national aims of the younger men in Bombay. Although he considered the telegraphic news service a reasonable proposal, he was at pains to point out that it was neither original nor restricted to Bombay: it had been recommended before the Ilbert Bill controversy and was being considered at that very moment in both Madras and Calcutta. He thought it self-evident that agitation in India on any major issue was practically of no use without complementary agitation in England and that a telegraphic service could make this possible. But he could not envisage a Bombay committee conducting an all-India telegraphic service. "It should be remembered that each

[35] "The New Political Association," *Indian Spectator*, Feb. 8, 1885; also *Subodh Patrika, Indu Prakash, Bombay Chronicle, Deen Bhandu, Bombay Samachar, Sumsher Bahadur, Kaiser-i-Hind* (*V. of I.*, III, Feb. 1885).

Presidency or Province has its own particular grievances to be redressed ... Bombay cannot represent them for the other Presidencies and Provinces." This conclusion could lead to only one solution, his national association plan onto which he was quick to tack the idea of the telegraphic service. Each provincial association should meet and agree on the service, then formulate their grievances, and forward them to the national association, which would be linked by cable either to the Central News Agency of London or to "a strong representative Committee or Association in England" with contacts in English press circles.[36]

The new association in Bombay Sen treated as only "a Native Political Association on the lines of the defunct Bombay Association," and slightingly compared it to associations started in lesser places at earlier dates. In his ardent advocacy of his own plan, he was obviously concerned lest the Bombay leaders steal a march on him. He called upon S. Banerjea and A. Bose to transform the Indian Association into a National Indian Association and to undertake a rapid expansion of its branches throughout India.[37] Reprinting editorials from other newspapers which advocated support for his plan, he used them skillfully as springboards from which to plunge into further details about his own plan.[38]

The same coolness toward the Bombay Presidency Association could be detected in Madras. G. S. Iyer and V. Chariar ignored the national aims of the Bombay association and declared themselves in support of Sen's scheme.[39] They thought that it was all very well to counter the biased reporting of *The Times* correspondent by developing telegraphic links with London, but this step was peripheral to the main task of creating "a *healthy* public opinion" in India which would refute *in toto* "the ill-merited reproach that a few of the educated Natives of the Presidency are, with the selfish view of getting the administration of the country in their hands, raising an unnecessary clamour against the bureaucratic Government of India, and are setting themselves up as the nation's champions." This task could not be carried out by a provincial association in Bombay; only the national association proposed by Sen could fulfil it. "The plan is simple and can be worked successfully in the present state of the country," given such "central associations" as the Madras Sabha, the newly formed

[36] Editorials, *Indian Mirror,* Jan. 20, 21, 1885.
[37] Editorial, *Indian Mirror,* Jan. 28, 1885.
[38] Editorials, *Indian Mirror,* quoting *Hindu* and *Liberal,* Feb. 7, 10, 1885.
[39] Editorial, *Hindu,* reprinted in *Indian Mirror,* Feb. 7, 1885.

Bombay Presidency Association, and others. The next step was to bind these associations with "all Mofussil stations"—a process which, they happily noted, was well under way in the Madras Presidency. Clearly, they preferred Sen's plan, which allowed for the strong provincial bias of the Madras Sabha.

N. N. Gupta, the editor of *The Sind Times,* which represented the interests of the Sind Sabha and the Karachi politicians, was even more outspoken against the Bombay Presidency Association. "Bombay is but one part of India."[40] If the new association was to be truly national in aim, then "the other Provinces have an equal right to be represented and to mingle their voice with that of Bombay. . . . Let a prospectus of the Association, detailing its objects and its aims, be scattered broadcast all over the country" to win "the countenance and co-operation of the many centres of education, and of all classes and creeds" throughout the subcontinent. Only if the Bombay leaders really intended to make the Association national would he be willing to follow them.

Further comments came from influential Bengali editors. The Ghose brothers regarded the new Bombay Presidency Association as simply another provincial association.[41] They maintained a discreet silence on the subject of national organization, since they firmly believed that all-India political cooperation lay far in the future. Kristo Das Pal's successors at *The Hindoo Patriot,* R. Sarvadhikari and Raja Rajendra Lal Mitra, both members of the British Indian Association, took the same attitude.[42] Subtly inferring that the British Indian Association had been, and was still, the true leader of political associations in India, both men defended provincialism as a political strength, not a weakness as the "nationalists" contended. In Bengal alone, they noted eight associations,[43] and this proliferation led them to conclude: "Each shade of opinion on public questions has thus the opportunity of being laid before the Government, and the chances of their being more impartially dealt with become all the greater." They welcomed the new Bombay association as "the key-stone of the system of national political associations in Western India"—their emphasis clearly on the word "Western"—and they ignored the national aims of Tyabji and Mehta, even when quoting from

---

[40] *Sind Times,* Feb. 14 (*V. of I.,* III, Feb. 1885).
[41] *Amrita Bazar Patrika,* Feb. 12 (*V. of I.,* III, Feb. 1885).
[42] "Representative Political Association," *Hindoo Patriot,* Feb. 23, 1885.
[43] British Indian Association, Indian Association, Indian Union, Indian Constitutional Association, Landholders and People's Association, Calcutta Mahomedan Literary Society, Central Mahomedan Association, and Indian League.

Tyabji's speech. Bombay had spoken for Bombay, not for Bengal. "Every organization is a part and parcel of, and intimately connected with a grand, and hitherto unperceived national movement." They preferred a natural growth, slow but sure. This was laissez-faire federalism pure and simple.

Whatever the course of national organization was to be, it was apparent that the desire for action was strong within the educated Indian community throughout the provinces and the presidencies. This development neither Dufferin nor his advisers could ignore. To make certain that they would not, Mehta, in his speech before the Presidency Association, pointedly referred to the Viceroy's active interest in similar developments in Canada and Egypt. Sarvadhikari and Mitra, however, preferred viceregal understanding, not meddling, either positively or negatively. "It is sheer folly to try to nip such a national movement in the bud by throwing cold water on it," they warned, adding that "a wise administrator should try to enlist the loyal sympathies of the people by fostering this phase of our national character."[44]

Both points of view seemed to make sense to Allan Octavian Hume, who had participated in the meetings leading to the formation of the Bombay Presidency Association, and he intended to do something about them.

[44] *Hindoo Patriot*, Feb. 23, 1885.

III

Allan Octavian Hume and the Indian National Union

By 1885, Allan Octavian Hume[1] held an anomalous position in India. In his late fifties, tall and erect, with a round, rather commonplace face, and beady, squinting eyes which seemed ever suspiciously on the alert, and with a protruding walrus moustache which engulfed his mouth and gave him an authoritative, pontifical air, he had retired from the Indian Civil Service three years earlier and taken up residence at Simla. Here he came to straddle the two worlds—of the official and the educated Indian. Treated as a confidant by Ripon and as a colleague by prominent figures on the educated Indian side, such as Malabari, Sen, Shishir Ghose, Subba Row Pantalu, Grattan Geary, Alfred Percy Sinnett, and Sir William Wedderburn, he had access to the inner circles of both worlds but was never fully accepted by either. Partially rejected by officialdom because of his controversial reputation and by the Indian camp because of his late arrival on the Indian political scene, he owed his influence and status to the fact that he had an entrée into both worlds. He himself admitted, "I borrow no plumes, but others choose to invest me with an appearance of what I do not possess—personally I have no power."[2] Thus he moved at the centers but lived on the fringes in the role of a go-

---

[1] B. 1829, son of Joseph Hume, M. P.; Haileybury; medicine and surgery at University College Hospital, London; Bengal Civil Service, 1849; District Officer, Etawah District, Northwest Provinces; excellent service in Mutiny; C.B., 1860; Commissioner of Inland Customs, 1867-1870; negotiated salt treaties with Rajputana Feudatories, 1870-1877; Secretary, Revenue, Agriculture, and Commerce Department, 1870-1879; Northwest Provinces, Revenue Board, 1879-1882; retired, 1882; ornithology and theosophy.

[2] H. to R., Dec. 25, 1883, RVP, I.S. 290/8-II, No. 215a.

To his colleagues a reformer and a prophet from beyond, to his official contemporaries and Anglo-Indian critics an eccentric and a renegade, he was, indeed, a controversial, yet seemingly influential, person, to be treated with both caution and respect. This curious position many persons questioned but failed to explain. Had they possessed more knowledge of Hume as an individual, his complex personality and disappointing past, they would have understood.[3]

Basic to any understanding of Hume's personality was his dedication to radical liberalism. From his Scots-family background and the teachings of his father, Joseph Hume, radical M.P. for Dulwich, from Chartism and Corn Law reform, from the writings of Bentham and J. S. Mill, and from Free Masonry and the Secret Societies of Paris in 1848,[4] Hume in his youth inhaled a heady dose of radical liberalism that lasted him a lifetime. Intelligent, sensitive, with the burning conscience of an Evangelical, he early became ill at ease with the world around him—with privilege and with existing institutions which perpetuated political injustices and social and economic ills. Thus the radical aims and progressive methods of the utilitarians and radical reformers shaped Hume's outlook and aspirations, and permeated his career in India.

As District Officer of Etawah District in the Northwest Provinces (1849-1865), he became conspicuous for his unprecedented innovations: creation of a model school system, encouragement of local newspapers to develop public opinion, reform of the legal administration, a program of land redistribution and agrarian education.[5] Later, as Chief Commissioner for Inland Customs (1867-1869) and Government representative in the salt negotiations with the princes of Rajputana (1868-1869 and 1876-1878), Hume recommended that any surplus from the tax settlements, resulting from these negotiations, should be placed at the dis-

[3] W. Wedderburn, *Allan Octavian Hume* (London, 1913). Except for a brief but helpful obituary in *The Times*, Aug. 1, 1912, this book is the only study of Hume's life and work; it is not an objective biography, but rather a eulogy by a very close friend and colleague. Wedderburn refers to his use of Hume's "documents" (p. 19) and "private papers" (p. 35), which must have been largely minutes and memoranda written while in official service. My fruitless search in libraries and my correspondence with descendants of Hume lead me to conclude that no other "papers," or substantial manuscripts, are now extant. By using the Wood-Canning, Mayo, Lytton, Ripon, Dufferin, and Mahatma Papers, and various Indian newspapers for the 1880s, I have attempted to add depth to Wedderburn's study and give some perspective to Hume's character, political thought, and work.
[4] H. to R., Jan. 11, 1884, RVP, I.S. 290/8-I, No. 136.
[5] Wedderburn, pp. 15-25.

posal of the princes for the sole benefit and welfare of their people,[6] but this radical proposal was unacceptable to the Government.

Again, as Secretary to the Revenue and Commerce Department (1869–1871) during Mayo's viceroyalty, he showed his radical bent in a number of ways. Concerned with the rising cost of British administration to the Indian peasants and their lack of political education, Hume spoke out strongly for the devolution of certain financial and administrative responsibilities of the Supreme Government to the provincial and district levels,[7] and contributed, along with his seniors, John Strachey and Richard Temple, to Mayo's decisions of 1871, which "decentralized" British Indian administration. A persistent critic of the Bengal Permanent Land Revenue Settlement (1793), which, in his opinion, favored a small group of zemindars at great cost to the Government, and which put the entire tax burden on the ryots, and dismayed by official apathy, he sought unsucessfully to persuade the Bengal Government to introduce a land cess drawn principally from the net profit of the zemindars after the revenue had been paid to the Government.[8] He had more success in influencing Strachey and Mayo to consider revising the Bengal Settlement so as to make permanent the share that the zemindar derived from any increase in quantity or quality of produce but variable the share derived from any rise in price.[9] Furthermore, Mayo enthusiastically adopted Hume's plan for an Agricultural Bureau along the lines of the German *Landwirtschaftenbureau* to collect statistics and set up model farms and agricultural training for the ryots.[10] But the plan was altered beyond all recognition because of the bureaucratic rivalry between Strachey and Temple,[11] and the emphatic disapproval of Argyll;[12] consequently, the proposed bureau became part of a hodge-podge Revenue, Agriculture, and Commerce Department, with Hume as Secretary.[13] With such wide responsibilities, in addition to his continuing role in the salt negotiations, Hume was unable to carry

[6] J. Strachey to Mayo, July 26, 1869, Mayo Papers, University Library, Cambridge, Add. MSS 7490, XLIV, Bundle 60, Corr. 10; Strachey to L., June 27, 1877, LVP, Eur. E. 218/519/5, No. 166.

[7] Note by H., No. 9, Jan. 19, 1871, enclosed in No. 847, Local Cesses for Local Purposes, Mayo Papers, Add. MSS 7490, Bundle 14, Finance III, No. 2.

[8] Notes by H., nos. 8, 10, (Draft Bill), *ibid.*

[9] Note by H. (printed), Feb. 25, minute by Mayo, Feb. 7, enclosed in Revenue Dispatch, May 24, 1871, Mayo Papers, Add. MSS 7490, IV, Bundle 18, nos. 2, 8.

[10] A. O. Hume, *Agricultural Reform in India* (London, 1879) pp. 24-30.

[11] Strachey to Mayo, Oct. 18, 1871, Mayo Papers, Add. MSS 7490, XLIV, Bundle 60, Corr. 10.

[12] Hume, *Agricultural Reform*, pp. 21-22, 30.

[13] *Ibid.*, pp. 13-20.

out his plans for the resurvey and resettlement of land tenures, and for model farms and agricultural training to improve crop yields. In the years following Mayo's murder, from 1872 until 1879, personal misunderstandings and budget retrenchment brought Hume's efforts to naught.

After he left the Government in 1882, Hume continued to pursue a radical reformist line on Indian problems, giving full support to Ripon's scheme for local self-government,[14] advising the Viceroy on agrarian and revenue matters,[15] encouraging the principle of equality between Englishman and Indian that underlay the Ilbert Bill,[16] and drawing attention to the manifest injustices in the Salem Riots Case.[17] Indeed, instead of diminishing, his radicalism increased with each passing year in India.

As a radical, Hume was an individualist with the advantages and disadvantages inherent in such a character. On the credit side, he was energetic and self-reliant, with a keen, analytical mind;[18] he was original and far-sighted,[19] and expressed his ideas bluntly and candidly with a sharp, witty turn of phrase. He disliked any form of pretense and sought diligently to deal straightforwardly with others. He was responsible in his duties, and devoted in a paternalistic fashion to Indians, whether as subordinates or as colleagues.[20] Above all, he was courageous, as his service during the Mutiny testified,[21] and he was dedicated to his convictions. Canning described him as "rather strange and flighty in his manner and not always quite subordinate, but a most valuable man."[22] John Strachey, who was Hume's colleague in the Northwest Provinces and who rose rapidly under Lawrence's aegis, recognized Hume's assets—his originality, energy and experience—and carried Hume with him to the top.[23]

[14] H. to R., Nov. 6, 1882 (priv.), RVP, I.S., 290/8-II, No. 342; letter to the editor, *Pioneer,* Nov. 4, 1882.

[15] H. to R., Apr. 2, 1883, RP, BM Add. MSS 43616, pp. 22-23.

[16] H. to R., Dec. 18, 1883, RP, BM Add. MSS 43616, pp. 54-65.

[17] H. to R., Mar. 4, 1884, RVP, I.S., 290/8-I, No. 87a.

[18] As shown by his reports from the 1850s to the early 1870s on education, land revenue and cess, and sale negotiations.

[19] His singular ideas in the early 1870s on self-government and agriculture were adopted by Ripon and, later, by Curzon.

[20] He referred to his Indian colleagues as his "children" and "flock."

[21] Awarded C.B. in 1860 for bravery at Etawah (Wedderburn, pp. 9-15).

[22] Canning to Wood with letter of introduction for Hume, Apr. 22, 1861, Wood Papers, CRO, Eur. F. 78, Box 2(B).

[23] The Mayo Papers, especially the sections on revenue and salt, reveal Strachey's high opinion. Even during Lytton's administration, when the tide had swung against Hume, Strachey wrote: "I have always personally liked Hume, and have believed the opinion of the world regarding him, notwithstanding his obvious faults, to be

On the debit side, Hume was eccentric, or "flighty," by the norm of mid-Victorian official decorum; he was offhand in manner, something of a mystic, and had an absorbing scientific interest in birds and animals.[24] He succumbed to the adulation showered upon him early in his career, and became conceited, overly ambitious, and self-seeking. Fear of a recurrence of the Mutiny became an obsession which prejudiced his assessment of Indian problems to such an extent that he pressed obstinately for radical reforms even when these were neither advisable nor possible.[25] Having little patience in working with others, he never hesitated to go over their heads to get his way, even though he himself hated to be overruled.[26] Lacking tact and a sense of timing, he was a bitter critic of those who were second rate and gained advancement by favoritism.[27] He misjudged the limits of his own endurance and, by the 1870s, had drained himself of his energy and vitality.

Yet Hume remained on a fairly even keel, so long as he had Strachey for his mentor and Mayo as Viceroy. Both men looked for originality, clear heads, and energy in their subordinates; they appreciated these qualities in Hume and were willing to overlook his eccentricities, high-handed manner, and extremist ideas. They tamed his radical schemes, protected him from undue criticism, and made allowances for his personal, informal approach. In fact, they pampered him, and he came to enjoy their pampering and their confidence. But with Mayo's assassination in 1872, Northbrook's assumption of the viceroyalty, and Strachey's promotion to Lieutenant-Governor of the Northwest Provinces and Oudh, the scene shifted and Hume's weaknesses became more sharply exposed, with unfortunate results. He reacted against the excessive departmentalization and bureaucratic regimentation introduced by Northbrook, and disliked the new Viceroy, because, unlike Mayo, Northbrook failed to treat him informally and displayed no per-

---

unjust . . . he possesses much greater ability than any other candidate [for the Council seat]." Strachey to L., Oct. 13, 1877 (priv.), LVP, Eur. E. 218/519/6, No. 54.

[24] Known in India as "the Pope of Ornithology," Hume formed an excellent ornithological collection, which he presented to the British Museum in 1885, and published ornithological studies (Wedderburn, pp. 40-46).

[25] Evident in his years under Lytton and in his advice to Ripon.

[26] See Hume's treatment of A. Arbuthnot (ranking Member for Revenue, Agriculture, and Commerce Department under Northbrook and Lytton) and R. Thompson, Arbuthnot's successor. Arbuthnot to L., July 26, 1876, LVP, Eur. E. 218/519/1, No. 109, with enclosure by H., July 14, 1876; Strachey to L., Apr. 21, 1879, 218/519/10, No. 125.

[27] Hume claimed that A. Eden, Arbuthnot, and Thompson had been appointed over his head by favoritism.

sonal interest or confidence in him.[28] He bitterly resented the appointment of Ashley Eden, a man whom he considered his junior and his inferior, with only family ties to assure his career, to a senior post in the Revenue, Agriculture, and Commerce Department which Hume had coveted, and the clashes arising from their relationship led to an incident in which Hume was charged with lying. Northbrook threatened to dismiss Hume from the service and turned the matter over to a secret investigating committee, which found that Hume was overworked and recommended that he take a long leave.[29]

But leave and change of scenery could not conceal the fact that Hume was rapidly falling out of step with the system. Soon after Lytton's arrival in India, Hume bluntly asked the Viceroy for support in securing an appointment to the Executive Council and in implementing his proposals for agricultural and land revenue reforms.[30] Strachey, who had returned to the Viceroy's Council as Lytton's right-hand adviser on finance and revenue, blocked the proposed reforms as too advanced, but tried to help Hume win Lytton's recommendation for the Council by warmly promoting Hume's appointment to conclude the salt negotiations in Rajputana.[31] Lytton, who attached great political and financial importance to the mission,[32] heartily concurred in Strachey's opinion that "Hume possesses so much knowledge of the whole subject that there can be no one better capable of making the necessary inquiries."[33] But Hume bungled the mission by misinterpreting his instructions, clashing with the political agents, crossing departmental lines, and advocating radical ideas which even Strachey termed "absolutely crazy."[34] With the greatest reluctance, Strachey finally withdrew the confidence he had invested in Hume over the years.[35]

In spite of what Hume insinuated later, Lytton did, in fact, support his candidacy for the Council and stood by him as long as he could. When Lytton initially submitted Hume's name, Salisbury, then Secretary of State, wrote back discouragingly: "I am

[28] See H. to D., May 15, 1885, DVP, R. 528, No. 314a.

[29] See Arbuthnot to L., May 21, 1879 (priv.), LVP, Eur. E. 218/519/11, No. 27.

[30] See Strachey to L., Oct. 13, 1877 (priv.), LVP, Eur. E. 218/519/6, No. 54.

[31] H. to L., Aug. 18, 1876, LVP, Eur. E. 218/519/2, No. 14.

[32] L. to S., Aug. 27, 1876, LVP, Eur. E. 218/518/1.

[33] Strachey to L., Aug. 5, 1876, LVP, Eur. E. 218/519/2, No. 4.

[34] H. to L., Feb. 27 (priv.), Strachey to O. Burne (Secretary to Viceroy), Mar. 7, Strachey to L., Apr. 25, 1877, LVP, Eur. E. 218/519/4, nos. 55, 60, 121; L. to H., Feb. 24 (priv.), Mar. 2, 1877, 218/518/2; H. to L., June 5 (priv.), Strachey to L., June 27, 1877, 218/519/5, nos. 39, 166.

[35] Stracney to L., Jan. 25, 1878, LVP, Eur. E. 218/519/7, No. 46.

most doubtful [about] the elevation of Hume to the Council. I do not know him, but his papers give me the impression of a man more effusive than solid, and the stories I hear of him represent him as little better than a charlatan."[36] Salisbury's views were principally those of his Permanent Under-Secretary, Louis Mallet, and of Sir Henry Maine and other potentates on the India Council with whom Hume had crossed swords during the administrations of Mayo and Northbrook.[37] Lytton, however, was not persuaded. Only when Hume had clearly made a mess of the salt negotiations, and Strachey had given the final verdict,[38] did Lytton withdraw Hume's name.[39] Even while agreeing with Salisbury that Hume was "viewy and cantankerous [with] many enemies,"[40] Lytton still maintained that Hume "is unquestionably clever, to myself very loyally devoted, . . . but he is full of crotchets and, with great intellectual arrogance, he has no knowledge of human nature and tact in his dealings with others."[41] Hume sensed what Lytton's decision would be and, writing to thank the Viceroy for his efforts, acknowledged that he was ill-adapted to the "official struggle for existence" and possessed "more ill-wishers than any man in India." Honestly yet sadly he concluded that "this, of course, can only be due to something in myself, but it has culminated now in this final and irretrievable failure, which closes my public career."[42] Rivers Thompson, Salisbury's choice but not Lytton's,[43] received, and accepted, the appointment,[44] much to Hume's discomfiture.[45]

Virtually superseded by A. C. Lyall, his subordinate, as head negotiator of the salt mission,[46] Hume returned to the Revenue, Agriculture, and Commerce Department a crushed and most unhappy man. A sense of inferiority, frustration, and embitterment welled up within him, all of which he expressed with a more obnoxious egotism and extreme radicalism, making mountains out of molehills. He was angered when his name was not listed for the

---

[36] S. to L., Oct. 27, 1876, LVP, Eur. E. 218/516/1, No. 58.

[37] Strachey to L., Oct. 13, 1877 (priv.), LVP, Eur. E. 218/519/6, No. 54.

[38] *Ibid.;* L. to Strachey, Nov. 3, 1877 (priv.), LVP, Eur. E. 218/518/2, p. 989.

[39] L. to S., Nov. 30, 1877, LVP, Eur. E. 218/518/2, p. 1041.

[40] S. to L., Nov. 2, 1877, LVP, Eur. E. 218/516/2, No. 44.

[41] L. to S., Jan. 4, 1878 (priv.), LVP, Eur. E. 218/518/3, pp. 22-23.

[42] H. to L., Feb. 8, 1878, LVP, Eur. E. 218/519/7, No. 59.

[43] L. to S., Feb. 8 and 22, 1878 (priv.), LVP, Eur. E. 218/518/3, pp. 102-103, 121.

[44] Thompson to L., Feb. 23, 1878, LVP, Eur. E. 218/519/7, No. 75.

[45] H. to L., Apr. 3, 1878, LVP, Eur. E. 218/519/7, No. 123.

[46] L. to Lyall, Feb. 12, 1878 (priv.), LVP, Eur. E. 218/518/3, pp. 105-106. A. Aitchison wrote later to Ripon on Hume's supersession by Lyall: "I believe, if Mr. Hume had been allowed to go on as he began, we should have had the whole of Rajpootana in a blaze" (Nov. 17, 1880, RVP, I.S., 290/8-II, No. 91).

Committee of Secretaries on Retrenchment;[47] he ran down the reputation of Rivers Thompson;[48] distrustful of Lytton's instructions and confidence, he balked at the Siam mission tentatively offered him; and he reproached Lytton for a draft report on the salt negotiations, which he thought failed to give him proper credit.[49] The final blow fell when Lytton, on the advice of Eden, then Lieutenant-Governor of Bengal, set aside Hume's scheme of a model farm for Lower Bengal as a dangerous experiment, impractical and expensive.[50] Disagreeable, petty, and obstructive, Hume had become a problem to the administration, and Strachey, then in charge of plans for retrenchment to pay for the mounting charges of the Second Afghan War, decided to merge the Revenue, Agriculture, and Commerce Department with the Home Department, thereby cutting staffs and "getting rid of Hume." "His insolence and his improprieties are really becoming insufferable . . . poor Thompson finds it impossible," Strachey wrote the Viceroy,[51] who supported Strachey's plan and duly advised Lord Cranbrook, then Secretary of State.[52] To Eden, Lytton confided: "This will get rid of a very troublesome Secretary."[53] When the Viceroy personally informed Hume of the decision, Hume, sensing Lytton's coolness, pleaded that they might at least remain friends,[54] and, at his request, Lytton, with great difficulty, arranged for him to be sent back to the Board of Revenue in the Northwest Provinces.[55] In this ignominious manner, Hume was dropped in 1879 from the senior level of the Government and concluded his official career. To justify himself, Hume published *Agricultural Reform in India,* which reviewed the establishment of the Agricultural Bureau under Mayo, its immediate restriction by Strachey, and its decline under Northbrook and Lytton, and blamed the Government for the downfall of the bureau and the resulting failure to alleviate the tax burden of the people, to improve land revenue and agricultural produc-

[47] H. to Colley, Aug. 8, 1878 (priv.), LVP, Eur. E. 218/519/8, No. 69.

[48] H. to L., Sept. 4, 1878 (priv.), LVP, Eur. E. 218/519/9, No. 3.

[49] L. to H., Sept. 27, 1878 (priv.), LVP, Eur. E. 218/518/3, pp. 692-693; H. to L., Sept. 27, 1878 (priv.), 218/519/9, No. 45.

[50] L. to Thompson, Mar. 26 and Apr. 13, 1879 (priv.), LVP, Eur. E. 218/518/4, pp. 214-216, 266-267.

[51] Strachey to L., Apr. 18, 21, 1879, LVP, Eur. E. 218/519/10, nos. 118, 125.

[52] L. to Cranbrook, Apr. 21 and May 1, 1879 (priv.), LVP, Eur. E. 218/518/4, pp. 300-301, 312-314.

[53] L. to Eden, May 10, 1879 (priv.), LVP, Eur. E. 218/518/4, pp. 337-342.

[54] H. to L., June 10, 1879 (priv.), LVP, Eur. E. 218/519/11, No. 27; L. to H., June 11, 1879 (priv.), 218/518/4, p. 457.

[55] L. to G. Couper (Lieutenant-Governor, Northwest Provinces), June 5, 1879 (priv.), LVP, Eur. E. 218/518/4, pp. 412-413; Couper to L., June 18, 1879, 218/519/11, No. 78.

tivity, and to raise the Indian standard of living.[56] What he did not publicly admit was that his own personal ambition had ruined the plan; in seeking his own ends, he had lost sight of the true goal. It was the realization of this shortcoming more than any other which haunted him until the end of his days and which he attempted to redeem by personal services to the Indian people.

A sense of failure and personal inadequacy, a bitterness against the bureaucracy, and a retreat into mysticism, esoteric philosophy, and things Indian characterized the years immediately following 1879. With time for reflection and introspection, Hume deplored his own selfishness, shed all personal ambitions, and sought to contribute to a cause above and beyond mere personal concerns yet in keeping with his original radical aspirations, his love for India, and his faith in the basic goodness and wisdom of British rule. Few people understood. Those associated with him in the higher posts of Government or during the years of failure remembered only the unpleasant facets of his personality and damned him. "Hume was said in my time to be the greatest liar who ever came to India," candidly declared Sir Henry Maine.[57] This and other unpleasant images of the man remained in people's minds, and Hume became *persona non grata* in senior official circles in India and at the India Office. By late 1879, he was living in Allahabad with summer quarters at Simla. His lesser duties at the Revenue Board brought him in touch largely with the lesser run of civil servants. He turned away from Anglo-Indian society, with a few interesting exceptions, such as A. P. Sinnett, the editor of *The Pioneer,* and became increasingly absorbed in Indian philosophy and the ferment then taking place in Indian cultural circles.

Four years earlier, Dayanand Sarasvati, "the Luther of Hinduism," had founded the Arya Samaj in northern India. Its aims were to attract young Hindus to Hindu theism based solely upon the Vedas, and to the task of restoring the Hindu way of life and freeing it from corrupt Puranic accretions, such as idolatry, caste intolerance, and the Brahmanic marriage code, and from the influences of Christian missions and the Brahmo Samaj.[58] With branches in Bombay and the Northwest Provinces and the Punjab, the Arya Samaj grew rapidly during the late seventies, as did Sarasvati's reputation. By 1877, his teachings had become known to Madame Helena Petrovna Blavatsky, the rotund, wild-eyed, spurious Russian noblewoman who, claiming mystical experiences in Tibet,

[56] Hume, *Agricultural Reform*, p. 32.
[57] Maine to D., June 2, 1886 (priv.), DVP, R. 525, No. 114.
[58] O'Malley, *Modern India*, pp. 315, 347, 462, 495.

had written *Isis Unveiled,* and to her bizarre, Santa Claus-like companion, the American Colonel Henry Steel Olcott. In 1875, they had founded the Theosophical Society in New York City,[59] and then, through friends in the Bombay Arya Samaj, Olcott arranged with Swami Dayanand for the Theosophical Society to become part of his movement. In 1879, the year after this development, Madame Blavatsky and Olcott arrived in India to sit at the feet of Swami Dayanand and begin propagating the "Theosophist Samaj" cult to the "lost souls" of India.[60] By the end of the year, their names were well known throughout India. In official circles, Madame Blavatsky was regarded as a Russian spy. Olcott's speeches at the Bombay Arya Samaj on the revival of Hindu culture won a wide hearing,[61] and he was befriended by a large group of Indians, chiefly from educated circles, including Furdunji and Telang of the Bombay Association, M. B. Namjoshi of the Poona Sarvajanik Sabha, B. Malabari of *The Indian Spectator,* and S. K. Ghose of *Amrita Bazar Patrika* of Calcutta. With the advice of Ghose, Telang, and others, Olcott brought out the first number of *The Theosophist* with articles mostly devoted to the Vedas and Swami Dayanand. A. P. Sinnett also became a good friend and devotee, and placed his influential newspaper, *The Pioneer,* behind the Theosophist Samaj.[62] When, in December 1879, Olcott and Madame Blavatsky visited Sinnett at Allahabad, he introduced them to Hume,[63] and, at a meeting of local pandits where Olcott spoke on the new cult, Hume chaired the meeting and, in Olcott's own words, gave "an eloquent and altogether excellent address, far better than my own."[64]

Thereafter Hume took a deep interest in theosophy, although he did not join the Society until 1881.[65] When, in 1880, Madame Blavatsky visited Simla to demonstrate to selected groups her "magnificent powers of psychological telegraphy with her occult friends" or *mahatmas,* living in a secret brotherhood in Tibet,[66] Hume became completely absorbed in her occult performances.[67] He began "corresponding" with one of her *mahatmas* named "Koot Hoomi

[59] H. P. Blavatsky, *From the Caves and Jungles of Hindostan* (London, 1892); H. S. Olcott, *Old Dairy Leaves: The True Story of the Theosophical Society,* I (New York, 1895), II, III (London, 1900, 1904); J. Symonds, *Madame Blavatsky* (London, 1959).

[60] Blavatsky, pp. 3-23; Symonds, pp. 100-102.

[61] Mar. 23, 1879, Olcott, II, 40.

[62] Olcott, II, 21-114.

[63] Olcott, II, 115.

[64] Dec. 7, 1879, Olcott, II, 118-119.

[65] Letter by D. K. Malavarkar of the Theosophical Society to *Madras Mail,* reprinted in *Indian Mirror,* Mar. 13, 1884.

[66] A. P. Sinnett, *The Occult World,* 2nd ed. (London, 1881), pp. 14-29.

[67] Madame Blavatsky called upon her *mahatma* to return Mrs. Hume's brooch

Lal Sing," but only through Madame Blavatsky or her Indian assistant, for reasons of "transmission and translation."[68] He learned that Koot Hoomi wished him to join the theosophist movement; he also learned that the invisible brotherhood gathered and sent intelligence on Indian affairs via select initiates, known as *chelas*, in the bazaars, before such intelligence reached British headquarters, and that the *mahatmas* had used this means in 1857 to control the Indian masses in the belief that British rule was best for India.[69] When, in furtherance of this belief, Koot Hoomi advised Hume that the Indian government should "countenance and support" the theosophical movement, Hume in the summer of 1881 helped found a branch, the Simla Eclectic Society, which began receiving letters from Koot's brother, "Morya Hoomi."[70] Hume became a generous financial supporter and ardent defender of the new faith. After Swami Dayanand broke off relations with the theosophists, ostensibly because of Olcott's curious entanglements with the Buddhists of Ceylon,[71] but more probably because the overpowering Madame Blavatsky was talking less about the Swami and the Vedas, and more about herself and the *mahatmas,* Hume took issue with the Swami on the Vedic approach to Indian philosophy, which brought a sharp retort from the Swami.[72] Likewise, to counter allegations of newspapers in India and in London that theosophy was a fraud, a cloak to hide Madame Blavatsky's spying activities, Hume wrote to *The Saturday Evening Review* in an attempt to clear both her and the Colonel's names.[73]

Undoubtedly, Hume genuinely believed in the new cult. He was interested in the occult powers by which the *chelas* could learn the truth and righteousness of life, in time present and future. He became convinced of "Hoomi's" claim that the *mahatmas* had saved British rule in 1857 and that they would prevent a similar holocaust in the future.[74] Moreover, the cultural and social ideas behind

---

which had been lost for years. She then led the guests into the garden and dug up the brooch. Olcott, II, 237-242.

[68] Symonds, pp. 147-148.

[69] Sinnett, p. 103, n., quoting from third Koot Hoomi letter. This letter appeared in the first edition (late 1880) of Sinnett's book, so it was probably written in mid-1880 when Madame Blavatsky visited Simla. See also Symonds, p. 148.

[70] Sinnett, pp. 151-152.

[71] Blavatsky, p. 24.

[72] In reply, the Swami wrote in the introduction of his *Satyanthaprakash*: "If Mr. Hume has any objection against the Vedas, he should publish it in a newspaper"; quoted in Symonds, p. 127.

[73] Symonds, p, 152.

[74] Even after Hume in late 1881 had learned that Madame Blavatsky was probably

Olcott's theosophy appealed to him, for he saw in them what many
educated Indian leaders had begun to see, namely, a means of re-
generating all phases of Indian life, long neglected under British
rule. Theosophy to Hume was a vehicle for social interaction with
Indian leaders. As the Society expanded,[75] Hume became acquainted with many of its members, particularly Shishir Ghose and N. N.
Sen, and learned of their aspirations and interests.[76]

It was inevitable that Hume, with his individualism and scientific
curiosity, in his zealous quest after occult powers, should clash with
the self-willed, high-handed Madame Blavatsky. Toward the end of
1881, he and Sinnett inadvertently discovered, when trying to contact a *mahatma,* that "the Old Lady" was probably one and the same
person as the astral communicants with whom they were "communi-
cating," but, when questioned, she flew into a rage.[77] By mid-1882,
as Madame Blavatsky herself realized, other developments increased
Hume's doubts, and his attempts to get at the facts rekindled her
anger.[78] She affirmed that all was well with the Society which was
"good enough for the masses" until Hume assumed "the role of its
benefactor, father and patron," when it began to fall apart. In blistering tones, she asked: "Why then, should he come in like an *African Simmoon* blasting and destroying all on his passage, impeding
my work, showing my *mediocrity* in a blaze of light, criticizing all
and everything, finding fault with everybody and forcing the whole
of India to point a finger of scorn at me—call me a *liar* and that's
him, who is never himself spoken of but as the biggest liar in creation. . . . " She became still more enraged when letters to the astral
brotherhood concerning herself and the Colonel, written by Hume
in his impatience to acquire occult powers, passed through her
hands for "transmission." But Hume controlled the purse strings
of *The Theosophist* and called upon her to publish his article criticizing her "sham occult phenomenon" and warning the people
against "selfish ascetics."[79]

By 1883, this clash of personalities had about run its course, and
Hume began to pursue his own form of theosophy. Madame Bla-

"Koot Hoomi," he continued to believe the story about 1857. See H. to R., Jan. 11,
1884, RVP, I.S. 290/8-I, No. 13c.

[75] Olcott, II, 341-348.

[76] Ghose to H., May 24, enclosed in H. to R., May 28, 1882, RVP, I.S. 290/8-I, No.
349; on Sen, see H. to R., Jan. 11, 1884, 290/8-I, No. 13c.

[77] Symonds, pp, 152-153.

[78] Blavatsky to Sinnett, July 21, 1882, Mahatma Papers, BM Add. MSS 45287, IV,
47-48.

[79] Blavatsky to Sinnett, Aug. 26, 1882, Mahatma Papers, BM Add. MSS 45287, IV,
55-59. A simoom or simoon is a hot, dry, suffocating sand wind of the Afro-Asian
deserts which blows in spring and summer.

vatsky charged that he deluded himself into believing that he was rapidly becoming an adept who saw mystical visions and had astral revelations through his new occult powers. "He is off his head and will yet become a spiritualist," she commented mockingly, for "he wanted *to force the hand, to out-Brother the Brothers.*" To achieve his goal, Hume formed a new group, which she disparaged as *"the new one that he has taken it into his head to found in India,* with the help of a few insane mystics—Spirits—, whom he will go on bossing."[80] She regarded this as a serious threat to the Society and her leadership, and charged Hume with being an arch-conspirator: "He wants to sink the old society and inaugurate a new movement *against* the Brothers." Sinnett, who had also withdrawn his support and was then in England, appears to have defended Hume by suggesting political reasons for Hume's actions. To this Madame Blavatsky responded tartly, "Such a stunt as his was more political than you aver."[81] In this, she was undoubtedly correct, for by late 1883 Hume was acting as an unofficial adviser to Ripon on Indian public opinion and politics. "I am associated with men, who, tho' never seen by the masses, I mean to recognize them, . . . are yet reverenced by them as Gods, . . . and who feel every pulse of public feeling."[82] On the split with Madame Blavatsky, he wrote:

Colonel O. and Madame B. are not quite honest; they have been to a certain extent aided by our people, and they began work unquestionably in the purest spirit of self-devotion to the cause of India, but . . . have drifted away into a maze of falsehoods, or at any rate exaggerations and deceptions, and have been gradually left almost wholly to their own devices . . . They are angry with me because I have similarly, while fully acknowledging and appreciating the great amount of good that they have done and are doing, moved apart from them, because they persist in mingling falsehood with truth.[83]

Within another year, the fraudulent activities of Madame Blavatsky, and, to a lesser extent, of the Colonel, were publicly disclosed, and "the Old Lady" was compelled to beat a hasty retreat to Europe. Although Hume broke with them, he never abandoned theosophy, which he continued to practice for most of the rest of his life.

While theosophy touched a mystical strain in Hume's personal-

[80] Blavatsky to Sinnett (priv. and not for Hume), undated (early 1883?, from context), Mahatma Papers, BM Add. MSS 45287, IV, 60-62.

[81] Blavatsky to Sinnett, Aug. 23 (1883?), Mahatma Papers, BM Add. MSS 45287, IV, 80.

[82] H. to R., Dec. 18, 1883, RP, BM Add. MSS 43616, pp. 62-63.

[83] H. to R., Jan. 11, 1884, RVP, I.S. 290/8-I, No. 13c.

ity and brought him into association with the cultural renaissance
in India, Ripon gave him a liberal political cause to work for and
restored his self-esteem. Their friendship, begun after Hume's
retirement from the government in 1882 when Ripon first announced his proposals for reform of local self-government, lasted
well beyond Ripon's departure from India in 1884 and was based
on mutual respect and confidence, derived from an honest exchange
of views. Hume regarded Ripon as another Mayo: he enjoyed
having Ripon's confidence, admired Ripon's liberal ideals, then
being put into practice, and respected Ripon's principles, his
tolerance, and his self-sacrificing devotion to a higher cause. "There
are probably not fifty men in the Empire," he wrote Ripon, "who
understand how marvelously rightly timed and rightly directed,
as though by the hand of God, has been your Policy. . . . I looked
upon you as I do upon myself and all other workers as an instrument in higher hands."[84]

Moreover, Hume was attracted by Ripon's sensitivity to the
changing nature of the Indian political structure and to the need
for training Indians at the local and provincial levels and developing Indian public opinion. In Ripon's plan for local self-government, Hume saw the fulfillment of reforms which he himself had
conceived at Etawah twenty years earlier and which were still
urgently needed.[85] Although for the moment he found no "germ
of any conspiracy in India," he wrote Ripon: "For years past,
India has been becoming more or less saturated with discontent,
with dissatisfaction if not positive disloyalty [which] was and is
increasing; partly owing to the gradual change in the character of
our Government, partly to the gradual change in the relations between district officers and their people, partly to the growth of
education and partly to other causes, [and] sooner or later a catastrophe was inevitable." Ripon's scheme for self-government was
the requisite "safe valve"; if implemented, "the tension will be
gradually lessened, and the coming danger averted." The success
or failure of Ripon's scheme would mean "the lives of hundreds of
thousands, . . . order, grace, happiness versus anarchy, bloodshed,
ravaged cities and burning villages."[86] So in December 1882, he
offered his services to Ripon. Thereafter, while giving freely of
his thought and energy to support the Viceroy's entire policy, he
became an important link between the Viceroy's inner circle and
the leaders of the educated Indian community. In his new role,

[84] H. to R., Dec. 30, 1882 (priv.), RVP, I.S. 290/8-II, No. 403.
[85] H. to R., May 28, 1882 (priv.), RVP, I.S. 290/8-I, No. 349.
[86] See n. 84 above.

which grew as his own form of theosophy took shape, he began to pursue an ancillary aim, namely, "to develop the national sentiment [of India] in the right direction."[87]

Ripon, on his side, valued Hume for his knowledge of Indian administration and revenue, his unique and progressive ideas, and his frank criticism of the static governing machine. Above all, Ripon prized Hume's interest in and devotion to the Indian people and his contacts with them, for Ripon's great hope was, by securing the loyalty of the educated Indian leaders, the key makers of public opinion, to restore the confidence of the Indian people in British rule, a confidence which, he thought, had been alienated by Lytton.[88] He confided to Hume: "It has been my aim to strenghten the influence of public opinion in this country ... in the extension of the power of public opinion lies the true safeguard of our work."[89] To achieve this, Ripon used Hume as "confidant" and emissary.

It is significant that Hume never fully enlightened Ripon on the extent of his contacts for measuring Indian public opinion. His correspondence with the Viceroy showed that he worked closely with certain Indian editors and lawyers, and liberal Anglo-Indians, basing his own views on their opinions and actions.[90] When, in 1883, George Allen, proprietor of *The Pioneer,* removed Hume's theosophist colleague of the Simla Eclectic Society, A. P. Sinnett, from the editorship, Hume bemoaned the loss of Sinnett's valuable assistance in advancing Ripon's policy. "I much fear," he warned Ripon just before the Ilbert Bill crisis broke, "that we shall have *The Pioneer* against us ... Allen is of the worst type of educated Englishmen, sneering at all things native and natives generally, ... always much guided by the opinions of a clique of civilians (of which Strachey was the head) who were uncompromising despots, who wanted and want to keep the people for ever in the cradle. ..."[91] He felt the same toward Kristo Das Pal and broke relations with him when Pal, following the lead of the British Indian Association over the Bengal Tenancy Bill, espoused anti-Riponism. Hume counted heavily upon B. M. Malabari and N. N. Sen, and was extremely worried lest his split with Madame Blavatsky and Olcott should damage his relations with Sen and alienate

[87] H. to R., May 23, 1883, RP, BM Add. MSS 43616, p. 33.

[88] See above, p. 11.

[89] R. to H., Jan. 4, 1883 (priv.), RVP, I.S. 290/8-I, No. 3.

[90] Persons mentioned as colleagues or friends were S. K. Ghose, S. K. Chatterjee, A. P. Sinnett, G. S. Iyer, K. D. Pal, B. M. Malabari, N. N. Sen, Lala Baijnath (subordinate judge, Meerut), and G. Geary.

[91] H. to R., undated (priv.) [except for date of receipt by Ripon, Jan. 23, 1883], RP, Add. MSS 43616, pp. 20-21.

an important leader of educated Indian opinion. "I cannot now trust him [Sen] as entirely as B.M.M.," Hume wrote Ripon. "He is entirely in the hands of Colonel Olcott and Madame Blavatsky . . . his mind is not his own, and he is, I fear, prejudiced against me . . . he is one of the very men mentioned to me from the first as likely to give us trouble in a quiet way (he will never be extreme). . . ."[92]

But for the most part, Hume did not refer to specific individuals or associations when advising Ripon. He preferred to deal in vague generalities couched in mystical language.

What you say . . . about my knowledge of the natives shows me that you altogether overrate me. In one sense as compared with many, perhaps the great bulk of Europeans, I do know the Natives, but when that is said, it comes to very little. . . . There are turns and twists in the Native Mind, that no European can ever fathom. There are whole groups of deeply rooted sentiments, that we not only do not know, but that when explained to us are practically unintelligible. . . . I generally can learn what will be the outcome of cogitations of the native mind, but not from any superior acumen or knowledge of my own, but simply because a body of men, mostly of Asiatic origin, who for a variety of causes are deeply and especially interested in the welfare and progress of India and who possess facilities which no other man or body of men living do, for gauging the feelings of the natives, have seen fit, knowing how thoroughly I also have the good of Aryavartha at heart, to give me their confidence to a *certain limited extent*. I feel all this is or may seem egotistical, but, you might at any time come to know of this, and I . . . feel anxious that none of the few men I love and respect should ever have their faith in me shaken, or have cause to think me an impostor sailing under false colours and taking credit due really to others."[93]

Again, in discussing his differences with Madame Blavatsky and Olcott, Hume told Ripon that his mystical advisers formed "the Association, to which I was first introduced in Paris in 1848 and which I broke off from within a year," and with which he had effected a "rapprochement" in 1880 through Madame Blavatsky and the Colonel, until they decided to work, not with "the Association" but with "a lower association of kindred origin." The mystical Brothers neither acknowledged nor approved the lower association because its principles were "not rigidly pure" nor its objects sufficiently "elevated." "Peace, order, brotherly love, freedom and progress are the keynotes of our people"; and these principles had led the Association to act swiftly against the revolutions

[92] See n. 83 above.
[93] H. to R., Dec. 25, 1883 (priv.), RP, BM Add. MSS 43616, pp. 72-73.

of 1848 in Europe, against nihilism recently, and especially against the mutineers in India in 1857. To prevent "the possibility of such a cataclysm recurring," the Association had organized the country since that time and was now working through Hume and others to carry out Ripon's policy of reform.[94] All this smacked of Free Masonry, spiritualism, Arya Samajist doctrines, theosophy with occult telegraphy, faithful *chelas,* and invisible omniscient *mahatmas* directing clandestine organizations from their astral community beyond the Himalayas. Thus Hume's estimates of Indian public opinion, while based partly on contacts with educated Indian friends, were largely his own personal estimates, disguised as intelligence imparted to him by his guardian *mahatmas.*

Nevertheless, Hume rendered valuable services to Ripon, while always maintaining that any success, "whether petitioning the Queen for your reappointment, tranquilizing the native press, . . . or preparing counter demonstrations of good will to rebut those . . . of the Europeans," was due to "the Association."[95] To further Ripon's scheme for local self-government, he circulated the Viceroy's personal views, with his own covering letters, among Indian editors, and paraphrased a confidential letter of Ripon's which was subsequently translated into the vernaculars and widely distributed to editors of the vernacular press.[96] When educated Indians became impatient with the Viceroy at the slow implementation of local self-government, Hume reminded them that Ripon could not afford to jeopardize the reform by hasty action which would only deepen official opposition. Bidding his friends to prove themselves worthy of the Viceroy's efforts, Hume wrote in a letter to *The Pioneer:*

If throughout the country during this coming year, any considerable fraction even of the educated and wealthy classes will show in practice a sincere interest in local self-government, . . . if they will put before them day and night the fact that their country will be on its trial, and that their success or failure will be *pro tanto* the honour or disgrace of India, then another year will not elapse without further important developments in the direction of self-government, nor another decade without a bloodless social revolution for which many true hearts have long yearned but never dared to look for as a practical possibility.[97]

[94] See n. 83 above.
[95] See n. 93 above, pp. 73-74.
[96] H. to R., Nov. 6 (priv.), Nov. 10, Dec. 18, 1882, RVP, I.S. 290/8-II, nos. 342,365, 374; Secretary of Viceroy to H., telegram, Dec. 14, R. to H., Dec. 14, 1882 (priv.), 290/8-II, nos. 244, 246.
[97] Nov. 4, 1882.

Ripon considered this an "excellent letter" which "already had a very useful effect."[98] Early in 1883 Hume wrote a circular letter of similar purport.[99]

In the Ilbert Bill crisis, Hume gave considerable services to Ripon. When the Viceroy asked Hume to use his influence to induce his Indian colleagues to remain aloof from the radical politicians, Wilfrid Blunt and Seymour Keay, then visting India, and to refrain from counteragitation against the European and Anglo-Indian Defence Association,[100] Hume approached Malabari, who, acting with friends in Bombay and Madras, prevented any demonstrations in honor of the visitors or against the association.[101] Later, Hume joined with some of his friends to defend Ripon's compromise with the Defence Association, pointing out that the compromise on minor details had saved the principle of the bill over which the battle had been fought.[102]

Again, when Kimberley rejected the Viceroy's recommendation to raise the age limit for the Indian Civil Service examination to 21, Ripon confidentially asked Hume to get the Indian editors to circulate for signatures memorials in favor of the reform, to be forwarded to Kimberley through official channels.[103] Hume, although ill, ably fulfilled his part,[104] but the memorials reached the India Office only after Ripon had left India.[105] Finally Hume, with Lala Baijnath and others, organized the initial farewell demonstration for Ripon,[106] which sparked the demonstrations elsewhere in India.

Though undoubtedly the working relationship between Hume and Ripon was valuable to the Viceroy, it had one grave weakness.

[98] R. to H., Dec. 6, 1882, RVP, I.S. 290/8-II, No. 236.

[99] Circular letter to the graduates of the Calcutta University, Mar. 1, 1883, of which I could find no copy in journals of the period, is published in part in Wedderburn, pp. 50-53. The parts given in Wedderburn closely resemble the letter in *The Pioneer,* Nov. 4, 1882 (see n. 97 above). Wedderburn cites the letter as evidence that Hume was calling for a national political organization, but this is not borne out by the portion he prints. In the light of Hume's deep interest in Ripon's scheme for local self-government, with its aim of Indian participation within, and not without, the Government, and in the light of the Ripon-Hume correspondence of 1883 (which contains no mention of any circular letter), I believe the circular letter was concerned with local self-government, *not* political organization.

[100] R. to H., Oct. 9, 1883, RP, BM Add. MSS 43616, pp. 47-48.

[101] H. to R., Nov. 22, 1883, RVP, I.S. 290/8-II, No. 164a.

[102] H. to R., Jan. 11, Jan. 14 (priv.), Jan. 23, 1884, RVP, I.S. 290/8-I, nos. 13c, 16a, 27b.

[103] R. to H., Apr. 4, 1884 (priv.), RVP, I.S. 290/8-I, No. 120.

[104] H. to Primrose, undated (early Aug., 1884 from context), RP, BM Add. MSS 43616, pp. 117-118.

[105] See above, p. 37.

[106] See Baijnath to H., Nov. 28, 1884, RP, BM Add. MSS 43616, pp. 134-138.

The closer Hume worked with Ripon, the more radical became his advice, which was based less on intelligence from his Indian informants than on mystical guesswork. Hume seemed to forget what Ripon could never afford to forget (and unfortunately did up to a point), namely, that a Viceroy was accountable to all his subjects—officials, Anglo-Indians, Eurasians, and Indians—and that his administration had to be conducted impartially. The dangers inherent in his relationship with Hume were revealed at a most critical stage of the Ilbert Bill controversy when Ripon, by telegraph, asked Hume's advice on a proposed compromise:[107] "If you think that the leaders of native opinion would acquiesce in such a settlement, telegraph 'yes'."[108] Hume, admitting that he had had no time to consult "any of the outside leaders," telegraphed "no" and wrote Ripon "to hold on course steadily, undismayed by the Envenomed local clamour," because his mystical advisers had told him that "never in any past time has the country as a whole been so moved, never has there been a crisis so important, and their distinct belief is that if any further concessions such that the people will look on them as a 'retreat' are made the result will be fatal to the future peace and progress of the country."[109] A closer reading of Hume's letter reveals that it was chiefly motivated by revenge against the Anglo-Indian community, the Bengal Civil Service, and Rivers Thompson, all of whom Hume could claim had ruined him; he even advocated that Ripon remove Rivers Thompson from the lieutenant-governorship and punish the Anglo-Indian community by moving the seat of government from Calcutta. Moreover, he was afraid that any surrender on Ripon's part would endanger the Viceroy's program of Indian political reforms. Ripon, recognizing Hume's bias and so not greatly surprised by his negative reaction, took instead the advice of his Council and of nonofficial advisers, Professor Wordsworth and Syed Ameer Ali, who both had wide contacts with educated Indians, and accepted the compromise.[110] Sifting fact from fancy, Ripon chided Hume for failing to realize that, without a compromise which would put an end to the agitation, the principle of the Ilbert Bill could not have been saved.[111] Hume, quick to perceive his mistake, and sensing Ripon's displeasure, reversed himself, and explained: "I led my

---

[107] A European being tried by an Indian judge in a criminal case could request either a mixed jury or a European judge to be associated with the Indian one.
[108] R. to H., Dec. 14, 1883, RP, BM Add. MSS 43616, pp. 51-53.
[109] H. to R., Dec. 18, 1883, RP, BM Add. MSS 43616, pp. 54-65.
[110] R. to H., Dec. 22, 1883 (priv.), RVP, I.S. 290/8-II, No. 146.
[111] R. to H., Dec. 22, 1883, RP, BM Add. MSS 43616, pp. 66-69.

advisers astray to a certain extent and partially vitiated the conclusions they desired to have pressed upon your notice."[112] He
sought to atone for his astral error by acting rapidly on Ripon's
request that he rally his educated Indian friends to support the
compromise.[113] Thereafter, although they continued to be friends,
and Ripon continued to use Hume as his chief link with educated
Indian circles, the Viceroy showed more caution in accepting his
advice.[114] "I do not say that I agree with all his views, but his experience gives him claim to be heard," Ripon later wrote to
Ilbert.[115].

Though Hume eventually came round to Ripon's view of the
compromise, one reason for originally opposing it was his fear that
the Indian leaders would interpret it as a retreat from the cause
of Indian reform, and, consequently, would feel forsaken and become distrustful of the Government as they had before Ripon
inaugurated his program of political reforms.[116] Should this happen,
Hume forecast that "the whole country would be honeycombed
with invisible cells of explosive hatred . . . that might deteriorate
in a frightful cataclysm." Momentarily after accepting the compromise, his apprehension was dispelled,[117] but it returned with
greater intensity following Ripon's visit to Madras. When Ripon
asked him for an assessment of popular feeling, he wrote: "I am
sorry to say that the prevailing feeling throughout the country is
one of sadness and dissatisfaction . . . no shade of unkindly feeling
towards yourself, no tinge yet of disloyalty; but there is a deep-
seated growing belief that the existing form of Government has
been weighed in the balance and found wanting." This feeling,
he then realized, stemmed partly from the "failure on the Ilbert
Bill matter," and partly from Ripon's failure to investigate alleged
injustices of the Salem Riots Case and the Chingleput Case, in
response to "numberless addresses" presented to him when visiting
Madras. Hume believed that these developments were causing the
Indian leaders to ask: "If, with such a Viceroy, things are to be
thus, what hope is there for the future? . . . Who are we to look

[112] H. to R., Dec. 25, 1883 (priv.), RVP, I.S. 290/8-II, No. 215a.
[113] See n. 102 above.
[114] See Ripon's reinvestigation of the Salem Riots case on Hume's urging, or Ripon's
consultation with Indian leaders on reform of the age requirement for the Covenanted Service examination, RVP, I.S. 290/8, vols. I and II, Lets. to and from Persons in
India, Jan.-Dec. 1884.
[115] R. to Ilbert (commenting on Hume's views on the Punjab Municipality Bill),
May 12, 1884, RVP, I.S. 290/8-I, No. 149.
[116] H. to R., Dec. 18, 1883, RP, BM Add. MSS 43616, pp. 54-65.
[117] H. to Primrose, Jan. 23, 1884, RVP, I.S. 290/8-I, No. 27b.

to?" Certainly not to the existing regime, which they viewed as "a great cruel, blundering machine running on its own weight," too powerful, too impersonal, too unsympathetic, and too incompetent "to meet and to satisfy the developing national mind."[118]

This feeling, according to "thinkers of our party," Hume continued, was "almost universal," "nascent," "not active or vivid" but "like a damp fog lying on the national mind, absolutely quiescent at the moment but carrying in its murky folds the germs of a dangerous political epidemic"; it could be "a very serious thing" in the immediate future, and he and his colleagues agreed that the only solution was the transformation of Ripon's scheme for local self-government into "some form of representative institutions." What form, neither Hume, after twenty years of studying this question, nor his friends could say, but they firmly believed that "the time has come to give the people hopes of something of the kind—to shadow forth representative institutions as a future probability more distinctly than ever . . . [and] the idea germinating in the mind of the country will by degrees evolve a demand for a form of representation that will be suited to India, tho' it will doubtless in some essential respects transgress western axioms on this subject."[119] Clearly Hume, like Ripon, wished to direct the rising discontent and aspirations of the educated Indians into constitutional channels, so that, given a responsible role in the existing system, they might be used for the betterment of India and the consolidation of British rule.

Ripon, uncomfortably aware that Hume's assessment might be nearer the truth than that of various Indian informants, was willing to discuss with Hume the subject of representative institutions, but frankly declared that to speak out publicly, as Hume suggested, was out of the question. "If I had committed myself on this point," he commented ruefully on his Madras visit, "I should probably have been recalled by telegraph."[120] Indeed, for the remainder of his viceroyalty, he adhered to a policy of official silence. Even in his farewell speeches, he ignored Hume's specific advice and talked in general terms of the advantages of giving educated Indians a greater share of the more responsible posts.[121] The question of representative institutions remained an open one. That Hume was still in search of an answer when Dufferin arrived seems clear

[118] H. to R., Mar. 4, 1884, RVP, I.S. 290/8-I, No. 87a.
[119] *Ibid.*
[120] R. to H., Mar. 13, 1884 (priv.), RVP, I.S. 290/8-I, No. 85.
[121] Bombay Town Hall, Dec. 18, *B.G.O.S.*, Dec. 26; St. Xavier's College, Dec. 19, *Pioneer Mail*, Dec, 24, 1884.

from the letters discussing a national assembly which appeared in *The Indian Mirror* in late December 1884 and early January 1885, and which, under the signature "A.B.," bore all the hallmarks of Hume's pen, symptoms of his fear of a cataclysmic revolution, and traces of his deep respect for and gratitude to Ripon.[122]

By 1885 Hume had come to occupy a unique position in the inner circles of the Viceroy and of the educated Indian leaders, both of whom tended to overrate his influence. Ripon had accorded him tolerance, respect, interest, and friendship; his Indian colleagues had come to regard him as their essential representative— their one ally—at Government House. Hume set himself the tasks in the months ahead of furthering Ripon's reformist ideals and removing the grievances of educated Indians by political reform. To achieve these tasks, he needed to establish close links with the new Viceroy, Lord Dufferin.

Upon Dufferin's arrival in Calcutta, Ripon advised his successor to talk with Hume "from time to time" on Indian questions because "he knew a good deal of the natives" and hence was in a good position to assess Indian public opinion.[123] Later, when Ripon bade farewell to Hume at Bombay, he informed him that he had spoken to Dufferin.[124] Meanwhile Primrose, Ripon's private secretary who had facilitated his contacts with Hume and other unofficial, "pro-native" personalities, warned Hume that Dufferin's private secretary, Mackenzie Wallace,[125] formerly one of *The Times* most talented foreign correspondents, would not only impede Hume's access to the new Viceroy but also be the "enemy" of educated Indian interests and liberal political reform in India.[126]

Hume lost little time in providing Dufferin with his thoughts on Indian reform. It so happened that during January Hume's close friend, B. Malabari, wrote a series of editorials for his Bombay newspaper, *The Indian Spectator,* in which he called on educated

[122] See Ch. II, n. 22. But there is no certainty that Hume wrote the letters. "A.B." could possibly be the initials of Hume's close friend, Captain A. Beynon, who did write under his own initials in support of Indian reform; see Wedderburn, p. 46.

[123] See D. to Reay, May 17, 1885, DVP, R. 528, No. 173.

[124] See H. to D., undated (placed among early Feb. 1885 letters), DVP, R. 528, No. 84.

[125] B. 1841, Edinburgh; educated in Edinburgh, Berlin, Heidelberg, and Paris; visited Russia 1874-1875; published *Russia,* 1877; foreign correspondent, *The Times,* Constantinople, 1878-1884, when Dufferin was H.M. Ambassador to the Porte; assisted Dufferin unofficially in Egypt in quelling Arabi Pasha's revolt, 1883-1884; published *Egypt and the Egyptian Question,* 1883; private secretary to Dufferin, 1884-1888.

[126] See H. to R., Jan. 13, 1889, RP, BM Add. MSS 43616, No. 33, p. 152.

Indians to inaugurate a movement for social reform to eradicate
the evils of child marriage and enforced widowhood. In reply,
Hume wrote a long letter to *The Spectator*,[127] condemning Malabari for various misstatements and for his misguided recommendations. Hume insisted that social reform should not be emphasized
at the expense of political reform, especially since an all-out as-
sault on Hindu customs was bound to cause dissension among
Indian leaders. Using theosophic concepts, Hume called for "national regeneration" to take place on many fronts simultaneously
and thus attract the largest number of "crusaders" as "interlinked
parts of one whole." In contrast to Malabari's narrow approach,
Hume declared: "It is only by starting on a platform co-extensive
with the aspirations of the country that we can hope . . . to labour
in any direction for the common weal." Sporadic, specialized efforts, such as Malabari advocated, were "an utter waste of power"
—a point which "A.B." had already made. It was imperative to
press for "the spread of liberal institutions," so that "the popular
voice becomes a more and more powerful factor in the direction
of public affairs" and thus able to formulate necessary, yet national,
social reforms. Hume's contention that political reforms leading to
representative government had to precede social and educational
reforms was pure "Riponism." He forwarded a copy of this letter
to Dufferin with a covering note deprecating Malabari's crusade
on the grounds that social reform of any kind was a touchy issue.[128]
Soon after, Dufferin replied, agreeing with Hume and asking to
talk with him at a later date.[129] In pursuit of the project foremost
in his mind, Hume still had access to the viceregal inner circle.

At the same time, Hume was beginning to work more directly
with colleagues in Bombay, Wedderburn and Wordsworth, and,
in particular, Malabari, despite the disagreement on the approach
to reform. Malabari moved at the hub of affairs and knew virtually
every leading Parsi, Borah, Gujerati, and Marathi editor and lawyer
in the Presidency, not the least of whom was his mentor of *The
Voice of India*, Dadabhai Naoroji. After Ripon's departure, Hume
had remained in Bombay to participate in the meeting at which
it was decided to start an Indian news service and to form a new
association.[130] In early February, Hume attended the inaugural
session of the new Bombay Presidency Association. He thus became

[127] "Prospects and Methods of National Reform," Feb. 1, 1885.
[128] See H. to D., undated, DVP, R. 528, No. 84.
[129] D. to H., Feb. 17, 1885, DVP, R. 528, No. 59.
[130] See above pp. 46 ff.

identified with the Bombay and Poona groups, with whose aims he seems to have had more sympathy than he did with those of their effervescent, highly individualistic colleagues in Calcutta. Had his confidence in N. N. Sen not been shaken by Sen's close ties with Madame Blavatsky and Olcott, Hume might at this stage have worked more closely with Sen and other theosophists in Calcutta. But his doubts of Sen and his friends led him to turn to Malabari, Naoroji, and other leaders in western India in order to further Ripon's policies and work for the political reforms necessary to offset distrust of the Government by educated Indians.

In the days following the inauguration of the Bombay Presidency Association, the comments of Indian editors in other parts of the country on the association's nonnational, strictly regional character appear to have struck Hume as they did other members of the new association. The question, whether or not a national organization was necessary, and possible, in India at the time, and, if so, what kind, had been forced sharply to the fore. The urge for action on a national scale was rising rapidly among educated Indian leaders; the method rested between the extremes of an independent national association as advocated by N. N. Sen, and the nonnational, provincial organization, advocated by R. Sarvadhikari and R. L. Mitra.[131] Neither extreme met the need to link Indian political development closely with the existing constitutional structure which Hume and others, following Ripon, had in mind. Should Hume and his friends fail in promoting their plan, very probably Sen, with the active interest and support already evidenced by groups in Madras, Karachi, Lahore, and Calcutta—and even by Malabari before the formation of the Bombay Presidency Association[132]—would succeed in carrying out his plan. So in early March Hume and his colleagues from Bombay and Poona met and drew up a plan for an Indian National Union.[133]

---

[131] See *V. of I.*, III, Feb. 1885; also letters to the editor: "National Assembly IV" by "A.B." and "A National Organization" by "A.K.B.," *Indian Mirror*, Feb. 13, 19, 1885; also editorials by Sen.

[132] See editorials in *Indian Spectator*, Jan. 1885.

[133] "Origin and Composition of the Congress," *Report of the First Indian National Congress . . . 1885* (Lucknow, 1886), p. 3, refers to a meeting in Mar. 1885. Since Hume was probably in Madras from mid- to late March (see n. 136 below), the meeting probably took place in early March. Although no reference can be found in the press at that time, in *The Quarterly Journal of the Poona Sarvajanik Sabha*, or in the studies written on Hume, Mehta, Tyabji, Naoroji, and Wedderburn, yet, from evidence in the DVP on the plan, it appears that such a meeting was held. See D. to Reay, May 17, Reay to D., May 24, June 4, 1885 (all priv.), DVP, R. 528 nos. 173, 331, 377.

The Union was to take the form of an annual conference, at which the leaders of the provincial associations could become personally acquainted and could decide what major reforms—political, social, educational, and economic—should be undertaken nationally and provincially during the ensuing year. Provincial, or special, committees would select delegates to represent provincial interests and opinion at the conference. The conference would be associated with the Government and be used as a sounding board for public opinion. Officials would be encouraged to participate, and the governor or lieutenant-governor of the presidency or province in which the conference was held would preside. The conference, to be held at a principal town or city in one of the presidencies or provinces, would, depending on the wishes of the delegates, rotate annually to a new site or remain at one central town for successive conferences. A reception committee, made up of members from the town at which the first conference was to be held, would prepare for the conference, and funds would be subscribed by the associations sending delegates.[134]

The Indian National Union was a compromise between Sen's national organization and provincial, or "federal," schemes. With distinct theosophical and utilitarian overtones, it followed the proposals Hume had advanced in his letter to Malabari to provide Indian reform on a national scale and absorb and integrate Indian political ambitions into the official governmental system as Ripon had aimed to do. It sought to provide a forum for Indian public opinion in order to make the Government more alert and responsive to the wishes and needs of its subjects. Such was the objective of Hume and his colleagues. Discussing some weeks later certain grievances in the Bombay Presidency, he emphasized that these could only arise and be left to fester in a system of "benevolent, bureaucratic despotism unchecked by public opinion" and that the educated Indian leaders contended that "some popular element must be infused into [the] Governments if these [were] to continue safe and the people to have fair play."[135] A system of representation to effect political reform had been Hume's aim in the spring of 1884; it was still his aim in the spring of 1885. It was the focus of the plan for the Indian National Union.

[134] No special circular or memo was written by Hume. This version is a reconstruction based on the sources cited in nn. 126 and 133 above; also H. to D., June 12, 1885, DVP, R. 528, No. 391.

[135] H. to D., Apr. 8, 1885, with enclosure: "Forest Conservancy in the Thana District of the Bombay Presidency" by "G.W.," whom Hume identified as himself (DVP, R. 528, No. 237a).

The key to the entire plan rested upon official sanction and participation. Having enlisted Indian supporters in Madras and in Allahabad,[136] Hume had now to place it before the new Viceroy for his support.

[136] Hume appears to have visited Adyar in mid- and late March to deal with the breakdown of the Theosophical Society; see Symonds, p. 210. In all probability, he spoke with R. Rao, G. S. Iyer, A. Charlu, and V. Chariar, all of the Madras Sabha, about the plan and enlisted their support. By early April, he was at Allahabad (H. to D., Apr. 8, DVP, R. 528, No. 237a) where he probably discussed the plan with members of the Prayag Hindu Sabha. These two sabhas, the Poona Sabha, and the Bombay Presidency Association were the only ones alerted to the plan for a conference at Poona later in the year. See editorial, *Indian Mirror*, Dec. 18, 1885.

IV

Imperial Themes and Indian Repercussions

While the Indian editors and politicians stood waiting in the wings—some optimistically, others sceptically—for signs that the new Viceroy intended to continue Ripon's political reforms, Dufferin entered fully into the spirit of Kimberley's instructions and, with the exception of the Bengal Tenancy and Local Self-Government bills, carefully set aside all questions of domestic policy. Isolating himself from the tugs and pulls of nonofficial opinion, Indian or non-Indian, he devoted himself to carrying out Kimberley's wishes on matters of broad imperial policy.

Two questions arising out of the Home Government's policy in Egypt and the Sudan—part of the aftermath of Gladstone's ill-advised intervention during 1882 and 1883—confronted Dufferin. First was the problem of the Somali ports of Zeila and Berbera on the Gulf of Aden, and second, the Suakin expedition. Berbera supplied fuel and food to the British base at Aden, which lay a short distance across the gulf, while Zeila, to the northwest of Berbera and strategically placed directly across from Aden, guarded the narrow neck of the gulf.[1] Both ports had been garrisoned by Egyptian troops and administered by the Khedive's agents, but, because of the bankrupt condition of the Egyptian Treasury, the troops had been withdrawn in 1884.[2] Gladstone's cabinet feared that this evacuation, just when the Italians were trying to squeeze into Abyssinia, when the French were tinkering with Madagascar, and when the Germans were stirring around Zanzibar and points northeast, would create a vacuum for European infiltration at or near Zeila and Berbera, which would menace the

---

[1] Earl of Cromer, *Modern Egypt* (London, 1908), II, 49-54.
[2] K. to R., Apr. 8, 1884 (priv.), RVP, I.S. 290/5, No. 20.

communications between England and India via the Cape and the Canal. The British cabinet, therefore, recommended that the Somali ports be made direct Indian protectorates administered from Aden and paid for by the Indian Exchequer.[3] When Ripon and his Council objected,[4] the cabinet directed Kimberley to bring the Viceroy and his Council into line.[5] Such was the situation, when Dufferin, upon taking over, broached the matter in the Executive Council. Colvin, Bayley, and Hope were still adamantly opposed, and saw no reason why the Indian Exchequer should "become saddled with expenses in relation to localities with which they have no concern, and at which British influence had been established in the political interests of England," and proposed that either the Colonial Office assume full responsibility for Aden and the Somali coast, at English expense, or that Indian troops be dispatched to Zeila and Berbera, with the English Treasury footing the bill.[6] Kimberley dismissed their suggestions as "useless" and "inconvenient," and threatened to overrule them if they failed to toe the line.[7] When Dufferin "insisted upon Colvin and the others agreeing to the arrangements," they gave in.[8] The Somali coast slipped silently under the protective wing of the British Indian Army, and a new annual charge of uncertain amount was thrown upon the Indian budget.[9]

At about the same time arose the controversy over the Suakin expedition. In May 1884, proposals were advanced in the cabinet and military circles to land a British-Indian force at Suakin on the Red Sea to establish a second front and to open up a supply line overland for Gordon and his small force confronting the Mahdi and his Dervishes at Khartoum.[10] On financial and military grounds, Ripon, Kimberley, and some other members of the cabinet resolutely opposed the idea as a wasteful and reckless "Mahdi manhunt."[11] But, as the cabinet received confidential intelligence, first of the investment of Khartoum, and then, in early February 1885, of the death of Gordon and his whole garrison,[12] Kimberley

[3] K. to R., May 9 (priv.), June 6, 1884, RVP, I.S. 290/5, nos. 24, 31.
[4] R. to K., May 27, 1884, RVP, I.S. 290/5, No. 14.
[5] Secretary of State to Viceroy, telegram, Dec. 25, 1884 (secret), DVP, R. 519, No. 13.
[6] D. to K., Dec. 30, 1884, DVP, R. 517, No. 3.
[7] Secretary of State to Viceroy, telegram, Jan. 21, 1885 (secret), DVP, R. 519, No. 85; K. to D., Jan. 22, 1885 (priv.), R. 517, No. 14.
[8] D. to K., Jan. 27, 1885, DVP, R. 517, No. 9.
[9] Viceroy to Secretary of State, telegram, Jan. 22, Secretary of State to Viceroy, telegrams, Jan. 25, Feb. 14, 1885, DVP, R. 519, nos. 91, 96, 164.
[10] K. to R., May 16, 1884 (priv. and confid.), RVP, I.S. 290/5, No. 28.
[11] R. to K., June 5, K. to R., June 6, Sept. 24, 1884, RVP, I.S. 290/5, nos. 32, 31, 52.
[12] Feb. 5, 1885; see J. Morley, *The Life of William Ewart Gladstone* (London, 1903), III, 166.

yielded to Hartington, the War Minister. Dufferin was alerted,
Sudanese policy was transformed, and the Suakin project became
a certainty.[13] The Home Government, taking a strong line to
offset the inevitable clamor once the public learned of Gordon's
disaster, and to extricate itself from its embarrassing position in
the Sudan, instructed General Wolseley, already at Cairo, to engage
the Mahdi, recapture Khartoum, and attack Berber, one of the key
Dervish centers.[14] Since no British troops were available in England to support Wolseley, and since Gladstone ran the risk of a
stinging defeat if he went before an unsympathetic Parliament with
a request for additional funds and troops (by 1885, the cost of the
Egyptian-Sudanese policy was running at £10 millions), the Indian
government had to bear the brunt. Kimberley instructed Dufferin
to dispatch to Suakin a brigade of 2,800 men and a regiment of
cavalry.[15]

His order meant that the Indian treasury would have to advance
a sum of about £1 million for the expedition, to be repaid by the
British Exchequer at some future date, which Kimberley did not
specify. Nor did he promise any assistance toward defraying the
cost of the troop replacements to be added to the British Indian
Army rosters, for security precautions devised after the Mutiny
made it axiomatic that the presidency armies be fully maintained
at a ratio of one British to two Indian soldiers.[16] To add British
soldiers from England would mean an increase in the Home Charges
on the Indian budget. Since Kimberley gave scant details, the members of Dufferin's Council concluded that the Home Government
was about to embark on another expensive imperial venture similar
to the Abyssinia, Perak, and Afghanistan ventures in the sixties and
seventies, and they vehemently expressed to Dufferin their opposition to placing this added burden on the shoulders of the Indian
taxpayer. Momentarily they cooperated in procuring men and ma-
tériel, but, once preparations were well advanced, they drafted an
official protest to Kimberley, stating that the Mahdi and the Sudan
had "no connection with any Indian interest, and lie altogether
outside the sphere of our [Indian] responsibilities."[17] Colvin, Ilbert,
Gibbs, and Bayley opposed the expedition for political and financial reasons, which would have appealed to Ripon, while the Mili-.

[13] K. to D., Jan. 8, 1885, DVP, R. 517, No. 11.
[14] Hartington to Wolseley, Feb. 6, 1885, see B. Holland, *The Life of Spencer Compton, Eighth Duke of Devonshire* (London, 1911), II, 11-13.
[15] Secretary of State to Viceroy, telegram, Feb. 9, 1885 (secret), DVP, R. 519, No. 129.
[16] Confidential Minute by Viceroy *re* Military Organization and Charges, May 1,
1879, LVP, Eur. E. 218/522/1, pp. 6-8.
[17] Dispatch to Secretary of State, No. 53, Fin., Feb. 17, 1885, CRO, Fin. Let., 1885,
Vol. 147.

tary Members, Generals Stewart and Johnson, were worried about weakening India's military position.

Initially, they received support from Dufferin. Having inhaled a heady whiff of Colvin's growing apprehensions about Indian finances, he reminded Kimberley of "the extreme poverty of the country and the instability of the financial system from the liability to famine, the outward tendencies of exchange and the fluctuation in the Opium trade." Was not this the wrong moment, Dufferin asked, to charge the Indian revenues for such expenditure? And was it not his duty as viceroy to play the role of "honest broker" in such conflicts between imperial and Indian interests?[18] Pressed by his Council, he answered in the affirmative. Though he had twice overruled them, he had finally come round to their opinion that "no part of the expenditure incurred . . . should be charged to Indian revenues." He drew Kimberley's attention to their warning that the use of Indian revenues beyond their "legitimate" application was watched "with increasing concern by all sections of the community" in India.[19] In fact, the leading newspapers were unanimous in insisting that the charges for the expedition be "paid to the last pie out of the treasury of the United Kingdom."[20]

Having written his dispatch and won the applause of his Council, Dufferin did not immediately advise Kimberley of the Council's opposition. Instead, he waited two weeks, and then, recognizing that Kimberley would never accept the Council's opposition, he reversed himself. In flat contradiction to his dispatch, he telegraphed: "All charges will be paid locally and extra costs debited [against] Imperial Government through [Indian] London Account current."[21] But this sleight-of-hand of Dufferin's did not fool Colvin, the Finance Member. The Indian budget had to allow £1,300,000 for the expedition, of which only £800,000 was eventually paid by the British Treasury.[22]

Colvin was disturbed that Dufferin had sided with the Home Government's decisions on both the Somali ports and the Suakin expedition. Colvin was then drafting the budget estimates for 1885, and the figures showed that Indian finances in the months

[18] D. to K., Feb. 13, 1885, DVP, R. 517, No. 11.

[19] See n. 17 above.

[20] *Bombay Chronicle*, Feb. 8, 1885; see also *Gujerati*, Feb. 8, *Indu Prakash* and *Indian Chronicle*, Feb. 9, *Subodh Patrika*, *Mahratta* and *Deen Bhandu*, Feb. 15, *Bengalee*, Feb. 21, *Native Opinion*, *Rast Goftar* and *Bombay Samachar*, Feb. 22 (*V. of I.*, III, Feb. and Mar. 1885).

[21] Viceroy to Secretary of State, telegram, Mar. 3, 1885, DVP, R. 519, No. 316.

[22] I.O./Treas. F. 643, F. 904, Feb. 17, Mar. 9, 1885, enclosed in nos. 2, 7 of Dispatches to Governor-General-Council, No. 76, Fin., Mar. 26, 1885 CRO, Selections from Disp., Ser. 28, Vol. 27, Pt. I.

ahead would be in no position to permit costly imperial ventures unless the Viceroy was prepared to resort to direct taxes. Colvin disapproved of taxation for imperial purposes; like Ripon, he was convinced that the Indian people should pay for only those charges of British rule which benefited them directly or indirectly. These charges, he thought, were already excessive. Those for official civilian and military personnel from England alone, which included salaries, pensions, furlough allowances, transport costs, and bonuses, and which had to be paid in sterling at a time when the value of the rupee was depreciating, were a great burden. Added to these were the charges for civil administration, military and public works, the famine protection fund, interest on loans placed in the London market for public works and the railways, and interest on the Indian debt, and the "loss by exchange" from payment in rupees of other Home Charges requiring payment in sterling. All these combined charges trod heavily upon the revenues available to the budget.[23] The principal sources of revenue were largely inelastic,[24] with land revenue virtually static, opium sales and *abkari* duties (excise on the sale and manufacture of spirits) fluctuating with the weather and humanitarian reform, import duties reduced to nil by the Free Traders, railway receipts just beginning to rise, and excises on tobacco, cloth, and liquor marginal. The only alternatives were direct taxation (income or license taxes), a measure politically sensitive as evidenced by public reaction during the viceroyalties of Lawrence, Mayo, and Lytton, or increased duties on the salt consumed by the ryots, a measure to be used only as a last resort. Of these realities of Indian finance, which Colvin, siding with Ripon, thought could not be juggled like so many balls in the air to provide for costly imperial schemes, Dufferin seemed completely unaware. So Colvin wrote hastily to the Viceroy, giving him the figures and urging him "to weigh most scrupulously the present state and the probabilities of our financial affairs."[25]

Colvin advised him that the surplus of £319,300, forecast for the

[23] E.g., total net expenditure 1879-80, excluding £5.9 millions in extraordinary military charges for Second Afghan War, amounted to £44,994,092, of which £15.8 millions were charges for the army, £12.2 millions for civil administration, £9.4 millions for interest, £3.8 millions for allowances, and £2.9 millions for "loss by exchange." See J. and R. Strachey, *The Finances and Public Works of India from 1869 to 1881* (London, 1882), Appendix Statement No. 3.

[24] E.g., total net revenue 1879-80 amounted to £49,801,664, of which net land revenue comprised £22.1 millions, net opium revenue £8.2 millions, net salt revenue £6.9 millions, or in total £37,271,328. The balance was distributed between customs duties, excise, license tax, and railway receipts. See J. and R. Strachey, Appendix Statement No. 2.

[25] Colvin to D., Feb. 23, 1885, DVP, R. 528, No. 96.

current fiscal year of 1884-85,[26] would probably be transformed into a deficit of £700,000 for various unforeseen reasons. The abnormal surplus of 1883-84 had inflated the surplus estimates for 1884-85; insufficient rains had necessitated the suspension of considerable land revenue in 1884 in Bombay and Madras presidencies; costs of harvesting and preparing the opium crops had been excessive; receipts from railway and customs duties had fallen sharply with the decline in exports of wheat and rice; and some £600,000 had been spent for military railways and roads on the frontier. Some of these deficiencies might be corrected during 1885, but the remainder would weaken the budget of 1885-86. "The fall in the exchange, co-incident with the immense increase in expenditure for railways of all kinds, and the state of the rice trade are matters for the gravest apprehension." For none of these possible deficiencies could Colvin frame a useful estimate. Should he peg the "loss by exchange" based on the rupee worth 1s. 7.3d. at £3,252,900 for the coming year, and then should the rupee decline to 1s. 7d., this would mean a further loss of £370,000. The value of the rupee depended on world supply and demand for silver, just as customs revenue from the rice trade depended on world conditions. The worst uncertainty, Colvin considered, arose from India's "political position," which, in his opinion, was "most serious" because of its vulnerability to imperial whims. As he had acted on the Suakin question,[27] he now again gave Dufferin a warning, all the more timely, since the Viceroy was on the verge of making decisions regarding Afghanistan which would most seriously affect the Indian budget.

The growing anxiety of the Home and Indian governments concerning Afghan affairs related directly to Russian expansion into Central Asia. The seizure of Merv, one of the principal Khanates of Turkestan, early in 1884, triggered off once again the question of Central Asian strategy, which had been intermittently a bone of contention within official and nonofficial circles in England and India since the late thirties. From the din and dither of debate had emerged two schools of thought: the Forwardists and the Anti-Forwardists. The former[28] contended that the Russians constituted a threat to Britain's prestige and her imperial mission in the Near East and Asia, that their southward expansion was aimed at the displacement of British political influence at the Amir's court in

[26] See Indian Financial Statement, Mar. 14, 1884, CRO, *Gazette of India Extraordinary*, pts. I and II, p. 59.

[27] See above, p. 81.

[28] H. C. Rawlinson, *England and Russia in the East* (London, 1875); S. J. Cotton,, *The Central Asian Question* (Manchester, 1873); C. Marvin, *The Russians at Merv and Herat, and Their Power of Invading India* (London, 1883).

Kabul and the deployment of Russian forces in northern Afghanistan in the key towns of Balkh, Kabul, Kandahar, and Herat, thus gaining strategic access to northern India. Having achieved these objectives, they could stir up disaffection with British rule, as a prelude to invasion, or put pressure on the British to respond to Russian interests elsewhere—in Turkey or the Balkans. To counter this threat, the Forwardists advocated a "forward policy" to ensure British influence at the Amir's court by treaty commitments and the establishment of a Political Resident, who would place British observers in the northern Afghan frontier towns and would give the Indian government a "scientific frontier" drawn beyond the Suleiman–Safed Koh ranges, and encompassing Quetta and Jellalabad as well as the Bolan, Kuram, Khost, and Khyber passes, through which British troops could be rapidly deployed to Kandahar, Kabul, Balkh, and Herat. The Anti-Forwardists[29] denied any Russian threat to British India. The Russian Foreign Office had repeatedly stated that the Russian aim was to carry civilization and trade into barbarous regions, and it had signed the Anglo-Russian Treaty of 1873, making the Oxus River the boundary. It would be years, they felt, before the Russians developed the requisite road, rail, and river communications between their Central Asian bases and northern Afghanistan to transport the men and the supplies needed to defend an Afghan position, let alone invade India. The Anti-Forwardists, therefore, advocated strict nonintervention in Afghan affairs, and a friendly understanding between Calcutta and Kabul on British interest in the maintenance of Afghanistan's sovereignty; they advocated, likewise, amicable boundary negotiations with the Russians, together with a firm and frank warning that any Russian interference within the British sphere of influence in Afghanistan and its outlying areas would be regarded by the British government as a *casus belli*. This policy, they believed, would achieve British aims at the least possible expense to India's economy and its people.

The views of both schools had been tested. The "forward policy" of the Whig, Lord Auckland, in the thirties and of the Tory, Lord Lytton, in the seventies had culminated in the First and Second Afghan wars with disastrous results for British prestige and the Indian debt. Later viceroys, both Liberal and Conservative—Lawrence, Mayo, Northbrook, and Ripon—who pursued the anti-forward policy of noninterference in Afghan affairs, accompanied by forceful diplomacy with the Russians, were able to achieve the

[29] E. Bell, *The Oxus and the Indus,* 1st and 2nd eds. (London, 1869, 1874); J. W. S. Wyllie, *Essays on the External Policy of India* (London, 1875); The Duke of Argyll, *The Eastern Question* (London, 1879), II.

desired effect. But the anti-forward policy was the more difficult
to pursue, and, with the Russian seizure of Merv,[30] Gladstone's
cabinet concluded that their confidence in Russian pledges had
been misplaced. A switch in policy was set in motion with "Forwardist" talk of an alliance with the Amir and other defensive measures.[31] In Calcutta, General Stewart and others in the Council
began to press for a military strategy to implement Lytton's "scientific frontier."[32] Ripon held firm against all proposals in London
or Calcutta, but when Dufferin assumed control at the end of 1884
it was evident that the days of the anti-forward policy were
numbered.

Dufferin had arrived in India with decided opinions on Afghan
policy, and his ideas accorded with those of his seniors at home and
many of his councillors in Calcutta. As Her Majesty's Ambassador
at St. Petersburg when the Russians first advanced toward Merv,
he had learned to be sceptical of the professed intentions of the
Russians.[33] From correspondence with Salisbury, he had gained
insight into the importance of Herat for the security of Afghanistan.[34] He was fully convinced that the Russians intended to subvert
northern Afghanistan, seize Herat, and establish a strategic line
linking Herat and Girishk to Kabul and Losh Jowain. As a result,
the Indian government would be confronted with the strategic and
psychological dangers which Lytton and others had dreaded, and
he, as Viceroy, would be left with the unpleasant alternatives of
either repeating Lytton's strategy of deploying British troops in
the triangle of Balkh, Maimena, and Kabul or of remaining behind
the Suleiman-Safed Koh ranges and the Indus River—a defensive
frontier which was "very bad indeed."[35] Nor did he put any hope
in diplomatic bargaining and boundary negotiations with St. Petersburg.[36] He condemned the initial Russian boundary proposals
as "impudent and outrageous," sound evidence that, until Russian

[30] Secretary of State to Viceroy, telegram, Feb. 15, 1884 (secret), RVP, I.S. 290/6-I,
No. 1990.

[31] K. to R., Feb. 22, Apr. 25 and June 2, 1884 (priv.), RVP, I.S. 290/5, nos. 11, 22,
31; Secretary of State to Viceroy, telegram, Mar. 2 (priv.), Apr. 22, 1884, I.S. 290/6-I,
nos. 2032, 2052.

[32] Memorandum by Stewart to R., June 5, 1884, RVP, I.S. 290/8-II, No. 238a; R.
to K., Jan. 24, July 24, 1884 (priv.), I.S. 290/5, nos. 35, 38a.

[33] See D.-S. correspondence, 1879-1880, *P.P.*, 1880, Vol. 78, Com. 2470, pp. 43-113,
P.P., 1881, Vol. 98, Com. 2844, pp. 1-2; D.-Granville correspondence, 1880-1881, *P.P.*,
1881, Vol. 98, Com. 2798, 2802, 2844, pp. 29-31, 1, 2-26.

[34] G. Cecil, *The Life of Robert, Marquis of Salisbury* I (London, 1921), 308-309.

[35] D. to K., Feb. 3 and 10, 1885 (priv.), DVP, R. 517, nos. 9, 10.

[36] Memorandum by Baron N. de Giers (Minister, Russian Foreign Office), Jan. 16,
forwarded to Granville, Feb. 7, 1885, *P.P.*, 1885, Vol. 87, Com. 4387; Secretary of State
to Viceroy, telegram, Feb. 7, 1885, DVP, R. 519, No. 122.

forces were well inside the Herat area and firmly entrenched to the south of the Hindu Kush and Paropamisus ranges, the Russians would be in no mood for demarcation.[37] The only way for the Indian government to keep Herat out of Russian hands was to pursue an active political policy and a bold military strategy.

Dufferin, therefore, lost no time in putting into effect Kimberley's original instructions to Ripon "to draw closer" to the Amir by sending him 5,000 rifles and asking him to come to Rawalpindi in April for a discussion of Afghan security and the commitments of both governments under the Agreement of 1880.[38] Dufferin proposed to Kimberley that the Amir be pressed to reinforce as quickly as possible the vast fortress of Herat.[39] But, when Russian boundary proposals and troop movements near Penjdeh led him to fear that the Russians would attempt a *coup de main* on Herat, these measures soon appeared inadequate, and he suggested the immediate dispatch of two corps of troops—15,000 European and 35,000 Indian—to Herat, if the Russians moved into position for attack.[40]

Dufferin's immediate advisers had no opportunity to criticize, because Dufferin held no extensive council sessions on the unfolding crisis. Instead, he discussed it with particular individuals such as H. M. Durand,[41] the persuasive Under-Secretary of the Foreign and Political Department, and General Stewart,[42] who were confirmed Forwardists, and who encouraged his Herat strategy. Kimberley, influenced by the intelligence sent to the Foreign and India Offices by the Military Attaché at St. Petersburg, F. C. Trench,[43] a devout Forwardist, concluded that the Russians fully intended to take advantage of England's difficulties in Egypt to break off negotiations and seize Herat at the opportune moment.[44] At no point did Kimberley or his council seek to dissuade Dufferin from the course he was pursuing.

At this juncture, Colvin, sensing the serious turn events were taking, advised the Viceroy of the grave uncertainties of the Indian budget for the coming year, and warned him against hasty imperial

[37] D. to K., Feb. 10, 1885 (priv.), DVP, R. 517, No. 10.

[38] D. to K., Dec. 23, 30, 1884 and Jan. 6, 1885 (priv.), R. 517, nos. 2, 3, 4.

[39] D. to K., Jan. 20, 1885 (priv.), DVP, R. 517, No. 7.

[40] D. to K., Feb. 3, 1885 (priv.), DVP, R. 517, No. 9.

[41] See D. to K., Feb. 24, 1885 (priv.), DVP, R. 517, No. 12.

[42] Stewart to D., Feb. 3, 4, 1885, DVP, R. 528, nos. 54, 55.

[43] F. C. Trench, *The Russo-Indian Question* (London, 1869); "The Late Russian Campaign Against Khiva," *Journal of Royal United Service Institution,* 17: 73 (1875), 212-226.

[44] Secretary of State to Viceroy, telegram, Feb. 20, 1885 (priv.), DVP, R. 519, No. 222.

[45] Colvin to D., Feb. 23, 1885, DVP, R. 528, No. 96.

decisions.[45] Dufferin, though he understood Colvin's "melancholy" and foreboding warning, chose to ignore it.[46] Indeed, he had no illusions about the costly nature of imperial obligations, but he justified them by their value to the Home Government.[47] Afghanistan was such an obligation; its cost, the Herat strategy; its justification, the security of the Indian Empire. The very day that Dufferin received and perused Colvin's note, he wrote Kimberley: "It is the loss of faith in our power and consequent hesitation and treachery in India, that we have to dread." Reports of Gordon's defeat by the Mahdi had caused "appreciable unrest" among the Indian population, especially within the Bengali commercial classes. The fall of Herat to the Russians would have threefold the effect. To offset this, he proposed the immediate demarcation of the northern Afghan frontier with or without Russian participation and simultaneously "to support the Amir in defending it against aggression."[48] Thus Dufferin listened to Durand and Stewart, not to Colvin. Moreover, by failing to give Colvin an accurate appraisal of his proposed policy, or to advise him to make provision for increased military costs in the estimates for the coming year, the Viceroy was working at cross-purposes with his Finance Member.

On March 2, Dufferin telegraphed Kimberley for instructions.[49] Kimberley, having consulted the cabinet, replied: "Every effort should be made to keep Herat out of [the] hands of Russia." Although he approved of Dufferin's steps to prod the Amir into action, he cautioned the Viceroy that "immediate defense must be by Afghans, aided, if the Amir desires it, by English officers"; the two corps which Dufferin had planned on for the dash to Herat should consist of 20,000 instead of 15,000 European and 30,000 instead of 35,000 Indian troops; reinforcements from England for the British garrison in India would be sent only upon a clear-cut Russian attack on Afghan territory, in order to avoid momentarily a heavy burden on Indian finances with its "consequent taxation and discontent," and to spare troop strength in England. Looking ahead, he asked Dufferin, "Is it not advisable to reinforce Quetta at once and make preparations for further advance of troops to support the Afghans?"[50] Dufferin had no doubt that it was advisable. He had received information about the growing uneasiness among

[46] D. to K., Feb. 24, 1885 (priv.), DVP, R. 517, No. 12.
[47] See D. to K., Jan. 20, 1885 (priv.), DVP, R. 517, No. 7.
[48] D. to K., Feb. 24, 1885 (priv.), and telegram of same date, DVP, R. 517, No. 12.
[49] Viceroy to Secretary of State, telegram, Mar. 2, 1885 (priv.), DVP, R. 519, No. 305.
[50] Secretary of State to Viceroy, telegram, Mar. 4, 1885 (priv.), DVP, R. 519, No. 320.
[51] Lyall to D., Feb. 25, 1885, R. 528, No. 105.

"natives of all classes" in the Northwest Provinces and Oudh[51] and Sind,[52] which was attributed to rumors of the Russian advance toward Herat, and this news convinced him that unless the Raj displayed a forceful policy over Herat, a mere ripple of rumors could "take hold of the popular imagination," shatter confidence in British arms, and breed discontent and agitation against British rule.[53] He at once instructed General Stewart to send three regiments to Quetta.[54] The stage was all but set for the Herat strategy.

Meanwhile, Colvin, only dimly aware of what Dufferin and Kimberley were planning, had taken limited steps to introduce a modicum of strength into the fiscal picture. With the approval of Dufferin and Kimberley, in order to forestall further decline of the rupee, he pegged its sterling value at the very low rate of 1s. 7d. for the coming year, and also arranged a considerable reduction in the Secretary of State's drafts on the Indian Treasury for the payment of rupee demands, thereby countering any loss by exchange on the Home Charges.[55] These measures, like those J. Strachey had used during Lytton's final year in order to give some strength to his budget, would permit the Indian Treasury to keep some £2.8 millions on hand, and so avoid "serious difficulty" in providing for the normal expenditure in the coming year. Colvin handled the estimates for "abnormal" expenditure with even more caution. His study, with his specialists, D. Barbour and J. Westland, of the Ways and Means Estimate for 1885-86 showed that the Indian Treasury could afford to borrow for railway development and harbor improvement not more than £2.3 millions.[56] This amount, Colvin and his colleagues were convinced, would have to be borrowed on the London market, despite the reluctance of the India Council to indulge in such dealings because of the strong Parliamentary injunction against increasing India's sterling debt by raising loans in England for public works. For the moment, they could not raise the sum in an Indian market already overloaded with issues; nor could they raise it in silver securities in Europe, where investors were alarmed by the precarious position of silver and would take silver securities only at an interest rate higher than that for gold securities. In short, it was slightly cheaper for India to borrow in gold, increase its interest on sterling debt, and add to its loss by exchange! When Kim-

[52] Fergusson to D., Feb. 27, 1885, DVP, R. 528, No. 110.
[53] D. to K., Mar. 2, 1885 (priv.), DVP, R. 517, No. 13.
[54] Viceroy to Secretary of State, telegram, Mar. 6, 1885 (secret), DVP, R. 519, No. 336.
[55] Viceroy to Secretary of State, telegram, Fin. Dept., Feb. 26 (confid.), Secretary of State to Viceroy, telegram, Feb. 27, 1885, DVP, R. 519, nos. 272, 278.
[56] Notes by Barbour and Westland, Mar. 4, 1885, DVP, R. 528, nos. 129, 130.

berley and the council gave their approval to Colvin's bid,[57] it
provided him with some degree of fiscal flexibility to meet the heavy
railway expenditure for 1885-86, even though it added some £60,-
000 to the annual interest charges paid in sterling on the Indian
debt and, in turn, inflated the loss by exchange.

But beyond these temporary palliatives, Colvin could not move,
and the fiscal picture remained far from bright. Barbour and Westland stressed the need for a specially close watch on finances during
the year. A serious failure of the revenue under any head or heavy
additional expenditure would necessitate a full review of the financial position, and might lead to the politically difficult and unpleasant alternatives either of increased taxation or administrative
retrenchment.

Early in March, just as Dufferin was about to present the Herat
strategy to the Council, Colvin forwarded to him a copy of the
Financial Statement and Estimates for 1885-86, which was to be
published on March 17. Since "it would be more than hazardous
to affirm that . . . there is at present no cause for anxiety," Colvin
insisted that the Indian revenues would have to be managed with
extreme parismony. He cultivated to the last pice every available
source of revenue, and gave a low estimate for military expenditure.
Although he looked forward to an improvement in the value of
silver, with President Cleveland's speech calling for a temporary
suspension of the coinage of silver, and with the forthcoming decisions of the Conference of the Latin Convention, he nevertheless
had to provide for any further decline in the value of silver, and for
the unsettling loss by exchange. He therefore retained the license
tax and the existing excise rate on salt, although he was aware that
Indian political circles had pressed for the elimination of the former
and the reduction of the latter. Then he gloomily predicted that if
"an abnormal expenditure" was forced upon the budget, within the
year the Indian government would be compelled "to choose between a deficit, or measures involving some degree of increase in
taxation."[58]

In the face of Colvin's tightly balanced and delicately interwoven
budget estimate, Dufferin brought before his Council for consideration the Herat strategy. The Council approved the "preparation"

[57] Viceroy to Secretary of State, telegram, Fin. Dept., Mar. 7, Secretary of State to
Viceroy, Mar. 10, 1885, DVP, R. 519, nos. 341, 353.

[58] See especially paragraphs 76, 80-82, 139 of Statement, CRO, *Gazette of India Extraordinary*, 1885, pts. I and II, forwarded to Secretary of State, Apr. 21, May 30, 1885.
CRO, Fin. Let. 1885, nos. 106, 143 in Vol. 147, and enclosures in Vol. 149.

of the Quetta–Herat corps, but nothing more.[59] Colvin, in particular, with his meagre budget in mind, wished no precipitate action which would hurl the country and its finances into troubled waters. The councillors refused to give the Viceroy carte blanche to move troops, and tore many holes in the logic of the Herat strategy. Their criticisms compelled Dufferin to make a painstaking review of policy, with Generals Stewart and Roberts, which resulted in the conclusion that the Indian government might not possess sufficient military strength for the Herat undertaking, and that it would be more sensible to limit any British forward deployment on Afghan soil to Kandahar, some 140 miles northwest of Quetta, and to undertake the Herat strategy only "in the last extremity" when it was apparent that the Afghans were willing to fight for their own soil, and that the Amir was truly a British ally.[60] Yet having made this compromise, Dufferin did not see fit to call another Council meeting. Instead he requested the cabinet's permission to begin transporting 25,000 troops (with two British combat soldiers for every Indian) to Quetta during the cold weather,[61] and to mobilize immediately another corps of the same size in India with a reserve of 25,800 to be held in readiness in England, irrespective of whether the Herat or Kandahar strategy was used.[62] The cabinet agreed to the dispatch of the troops to Quetta,[63] and Dufferin gave the order to Stewart and Wilson.[64] By March 21, the forward strategy was under way, and the whole of India was astir with the news.

At about the time Dufferin was ordering the mobilization of the first corps for Quetta, the Indian editors and politicians began publishing their reactions to the Financial Statement. Most sympathized with Colvin in his difficult task and complimented him for his "caution and candor," and "business-like" attitude.[65] They found "nothing new, nothing startling" in his Statement, which provided them with what they wished to know and what they thought the Indian taxpayer should know on how much the year

[59] Hope to D., Colvin to D., Mar. 15, 1885, DVP, R. 528, nos. 156, 157; D to Colvin, Mar. 25, 1885 (priv. and confid.), R. 528, No. 115.

[60] D. to K., Mar. 17, 1885 (priv.), DVP, R. 517, No. 15.

[61] Viceroy to Secretary of State, telegram, Mar. 19, 1885 (secret), DVP, R. 519, No. 2.

[62] Viceroy to Secretary of State, telegram, Mar. 20, 1885 (priv.), DVP, R. 519, No. 3.

[63] Secretary of State to Viceroy, telegram, Mar. 20, 1885 (secret), DVP, R. 519, No. 10.

[64] D. to Stewart, Mar. 21 (priv.), D. to Wilson, Mar. 21, 1885 (priv.), DVP, R. 528, nos. 103, 104.

[65] *Indian Mirror* and *Hindu*, Mar. 20, *Jam-e-Jamshed*, Mar. 19 *(V. of I.,* III, Mar.), *Indian Spectator*, Mar. 22, *Reis and Raiyyet*, Mar. 21, *Hindoo Patriot*, Mar. 23 *(V. of I.,* II, Apr. 1885).

ahead was probably going to cost him. Colvin's estimates were merely a review of the "status quo ante."[66]

Yet, had the Finance Member been looking ahead with any knowledge or imagination, he would not, they thought, have presented a budget with so slender a surplus. They wondered why Colvin had placed such emphasis on railway expenditures and their payment by a Public Works Loan approved by Parliament, when there were other, more pressing economic matters to which he had given scant attention.[67] On the devaluation of silver, some thought that Colvin should have proposed decisive action, such as levying a seigniorage charge of about 30 per cent upon all silver coinage as the English Exchequer was then doing, instead of merely waiting wishfully for international conditions to stabilize the value of silver. They considered the prospect of further decline in the value of the rupee sufficiently serious to have warranted an extensive comment by Colvin on taxation, and were perplexed by his vagueness on the subject.[68] Some editors maintained that since his budget had been framed on the basis of the status quo, he should have removed the unpopular license tax on trades and professions and reduced the incidence of the salt duty;[69] yet, "the Statement is worded with ample care to make it the basis for additional taxation in the future on a large scale."[70] This being the case, Colvin would have been wiser to expand existing tax revenues by extending the license tax to a broader range of incomes, including official incomes, and by reimposing the import duties on cotton, which had been so wantonly sacrificed by the Imperial Government to the demands of the English textile industry.[71] They regarded Colvin's failure to do this as the first real indication of Dufferin's policy toward Indian interests.

The editors were also distressed that Colvin had mentioned increased taxes as the sole means of meeting any unexpected rise in expenditure, but had said nothing about retrenchment in govern-

[66] *Bengalee* and *Reis and Raiyyet,* Mar. 21, *Mahratta,* Mar. 22, *Hindoo Patriot,* and *Indu Prakash,* Mar. 23 *(V. of I.,* III, Apr. 1885).

[67] *Hindu,* Mar. 20 *(V. of I.,* III, Mar.), *Liberal, Indian Spectator,* and *Bombay Chronicle,* Mar. 22, *Behar Herald,* Mar. 24, *Sind Times,* Mar. 28, *Punjab Courier,* Apr. 8 *(V. of I.,* III, Apr. 1885).

[68] *Bombay Samachar,* Mar. 19 *(V. of I.,* III, Mar.), *Native Opinion,* Mar. 22 *(V. of I.,* III, Apr. 1885).

[69] *Hindu,* Mar. 20 *(V. of I.,* III, Mar.), *Subodh Patrika,* Mar. 22, *Indu Prakash,* Mar. 23, *Indian Chronicle,* Mar. 30, *Advocate of the Agriculturists,* Apr. 10, *Yezdan Parast,* Mar. 22, *Rast Goftar,* Mar. 29 *(V. of I.,* III, Apr. 1885).

[70] *Indian Mirror,* Mar. 20 *(V. of I.,* III, Mar. 1885).

[71] *Indian Mirror* and *Hindu,* Mar. 20, *Jam-e-Jamshed,* Mar. 19 *(V. of I.,* III, Mar.), *Subodh Patrika,* Mar. 22 *(V. of I.,* III, Apr. 1885).

mental expenditure. Here G. S. Iyer and V. Chariar declared themselves emphatically: "The administration is extravagant, the expenditure has a constant tendency to increase, India is forced to
pay for purposes with which she has no concern whatever, and
the revenues are inelastic . . . The whole system needs overhauling
and readjustment."[72] Others added the important note—a domi-
nant theme thereafter in Indian political discussion—that the
time had come to allow increasing numbers of Indians, well
trained and competent, to enter the civil and military services and
replace the costly British personnel.[73]

The Indian editors considered Colvin's Statement weak, taken
as a whole, and they recommended that it be treated not as an
Executive Minute, but as a regular account to be placed before
the Viceroy's Legislative Council for discussion and debate, by
official and nonofficial members, pending approval for publication.[74] With such a routine, they hoped to obtain some semblance
of taxpayer opinion, albeit preponderantly Anglo-Indian by nature
of the existing nonofficial representation in the Legislative Council; even so, any reflection of nonofficial opinion, when Anglo-
Russian relations were rapidly deteriorating, would be valuable.
Although they were surprised that Colvin had not mentioned the
Afghan crisis, they were under no delusions about its impact on
the Indian revenue.[75] "We are likely to be called upon to pay
additional taxes, [so that] Amir Abdur Rahman may remain in
power, and the integrity of his territory may be maintained," N. N.
Sen brusquely pointed out.[76] Yet they knew that, until basic changes
were made and their opposition heard in the Legislative Council,
the Home Government would continue to draw upon Indian revenues to meet imperial ends. Dufferin disregarded their recommendation and approved the Statement.

Unbeknownst to the Indian editors, Colvin was challenging Duf-
ferin on his forward strategy.[77] Already troubled to learn that
Dufferin had ordered troops to Quetta without reference to his
Council, he became genuinely alarmed when, while travelling to
Bombay via the Northwest Provinces, he detected rising anxiety
throughout the Indian community about this military move and

[72] *Hindu*, Mar. 20 *(V. of I.,* III, Mar. 1885).
[73] *Indu Prakash*, Mar. 23, *Subodh Prakash*, Mar. 25 *(V. of I.,* III, Apr. 1885).
[74] *Bombay Samachar*, Mar. 19 *(V. of I.,* III, Mar.), *Hindoo Patriot*, Mar. 23, *Gujerati*, Mar. 22 *(V. of I.,* III, Apr. 1885).
[75] *Hindu*, Mar. 20 *(V. of I.,* III, Mar.), *Reis and Raiyyet*, Mar. 21, *Indian Spectator*
and *Subodh Patrika*, Mar. 22, *Indu Prakash*, Mar. 23 *(V. of I.,* III, Apr. 1885).
[76] *Indian Mirror*, Mar. 20 *(V. of I.,* III, Mar. 1885).
[77] Colvin to D., Mar. 22, 1885 (priv. and confid.), DVP, R. 528, No. 183b.

its probable costs. This discovery made him realize that Dufferin's policy was dangerously out of step with Indian opinion and rapidly "passing into the centre of warlike ambitions," and he bluntly warned Dufferin that "a false step in the direction of a forward movement at this moment may entail consequences other than those which are aimed at by a demonstration." It could be unduly provocative to both Russians and Afghans; it could easily force the hand of Gladstone's cabinet for war and saddle the Indian taxpayer with additional taxation. "Has the time come," he asked, "to further burden the country with the actual levy of 25,000 men?" He thought the Quetta advance was "premature," and the need for British reinforcements "not justified financially."

Dufferin replied immediately,[78] denying that he had acted prematurely, or had forced the hand of the cabinet. He had moulded his strategy in response to the Home Government's anxiety over the Russian advance, and had secured cabinet approval for the troop movement to Quetta. Similarly, he had requested cabinet instructions for the Herat strategy and approval for reinforcements from England. "The ultimate decision," therefore, rested entirely with the Home Government. "From the foregoing," he wrote, "you will see that I have no desire to precipitate matters, or to commit ourselves to a warlike expenditure which may prove unnecessary."

His comments to Colvin avoided all mention of the costs of his strategy or of Indian reaction to it. Yet just a few days before, he had admitted to Kimberley that his policy would be expensive. And, since the Nizam of Hyderabad and other princes had telegraphed support,[79] he concluded that Indian people were "fully aware of the critical nature of the situation," that the Herat strategy was acceptable to them, and that they would pay for it with little grumbling.[80]

Despite Dufferin's convictions, the final decision to pursue the Herat strategy rested with the cabinet, which initially opted for diplomacy rather than force. While the British ambassador in St. Petersburg warned Baron de Giers against any Russian advance on Penjdeh, just north of Herat,[81] Gladstone cleverly put the

[78] D. to Colvin, Mar. 25, 1885 (priv. and confid.), DVP, R. 528, No. 115.
[79] See D. to K., Mar. 17 (priv.), (for support from Nizam of Hyderabad), Mar. 23, 1885 (priv.), (for support from Maharajah of Durbhanga), DVP, R. 517, nos. 15, 16; also Maharajah Holkar of Indore to Viceroy, telegram, Mar. 18, Maharajah Sindhia of Gwalior to Viceroy, telegram, Mar. 21, 1885, R. 528, nos. 167, 183.
[80] D. to K., Mar. 23, 1885 (priv.), DVP, R. 517, No. 16.
[81] Granville to Thornton, Mar. 13, 14, 1885, *P.P.*, 1885, Vol. 87, Com. 4387, p. 167, No. 225, p. 171, No. 230.

Russian Foreign Office on the spot by stating before the Commons that the Russians had agreed to make no advance into the disputed territory while boundary negotiations were in progress,[82] and Granville politely but definitely rejected the initial Russian boundary proposal,[83] whereupon the Russians sent pledges to London not to occupy Penjdeh and to bring the boundary negotiations to a rapid conclusion.[84] As long as there was hope for an amicable Anglo-Russian settlement, Gladstone refused to go along with Hartington and Kimberley, and brought his influence to bear in the cabinet to check Dufferin's Herat strategy, not because of any concern for the Indian taxpayer, but because of the growing loss of confidence in his government as a result of British reverses in Egypt and his fear of similar misfortunes in Afghanistan.[85] The cabinet therefore advised Dufferin that it was "not in favour of an expedition at the present time to Herat," even though it would not recall the Quetta corps, just in case the Russians should seize Herat and the Amir should require military assistance.[86] Dufferin at his forthcoming talks with the Amir at Rawalpindi was to impress upon him that the Indian government was not obligated by the Agreement of 1880 to defend Herat with British troops, but that it would provide whatever money, arms, and ammunition the Amir thought necessary for its defense.[87] At the same time, the British government warned the Russian government that any further advance toward Herat would be construed as a *casus belli* not only in Asia but also in Europe.[88] To make good this threat, the Reserves and the Militia were called out in London.[89] By the end of March, Gladstone's cabinet had adopted an anti-Forwardist policy.[90]

When at the end of March the Viceroy received word of the cabinet's decision against the Herat strategy, the first army corps

[82] Parliamentary Debates, 3 *Hansard,* 295 (Mar. 13, 1885), 1084-1087.

[83] Granville to M. de Staal (Russian Ambassador), with memorandum, Mar. 13, Granville to Lumsden, telegram, Mar. 16, 1885, *P.P.,* 1885, Vol. 87, Com. 4387, pp. 167-170, No. 226 with enclosure, p. 174, No. 234.

[84] Thornton to Granville, telegram, Mar. 16, Mar. 17, 19, 30, 1885, *P.P.,* 1885, Vol. 87, Com. 4387, p. 174, nos. 234, 235, pp. 177-178, No. 244, p. 178, No. 245, p. 194, No. 269.

[85] Morley, III, 176-178.

[86] Secretary of State to Viceroy, telegram, Mar. 25, 1885 (priv.), DVP, R. 519, No. 15a.

[87] Instructions for the Viceroy, Mar. 20, 1885, Gladstone Papers, BM Add. MSS 44228, pp. 181-183; Secretary of State to Viceroy, telegram, Mar. 25, 1885 (secret), DVP, R. 519, No. 15b.

[88] Granville to Thornton, Mar. 27, 1885, *P.P.,* 1885, Vol. 87, Com. 4387, p. 183, No. 256.

[89] Royal Proclamation, *London Gazette,* Mar. 27, 1885.

[90] See speeches of Gladstone, Granville, and Kimberley, Parliamentary Debates, 3 *Hansard,* 297 (May 4, 12, 1885), 1559-1579.

for Afghan operations was moving into position at Quetta and Pishin.[91] Since Dufferin had advised Kimberley some days earlier that he was limiting his forward strategy to Kandahar,[92] it was in this context that he interpreted the cabinet's instructions. So, in early April at the meeting at Rawalpindi, although the Amir stated frankly that he was most willing to defend Herat with his own forces (if properly armed and paid) and requested that British–Indian troops be kept off Afghan soil even in a crisis because of Afghan tribal politics, Dufferin pointed out that a corps was in position at Quetta and Pishin, and that, should the Russians move upon Herat, these troops would "take up a position before Candahar."[93] Cordially acknowledged by the Amir in a public announcement,[94] Dufferin's statement virtually committed Gladstone's cabinet to his Kandahar strategy and obligated the Indian government to keep its troops at Quetta and Pishin. With Parliamentary support waning even within Liberal ranks, the cabinet was in no position to overrule the Viceroy, who was now enthusiastically espousing the Kandahar strategy with the same arguments he had used for the Herat strategy.[95] In May, Kimberley in an awkward statement in the House of Lords confirmed the cabinet's acquiescence to Dufferin's policy.[96] By this ironic twist of circumstances, Dufferin had successfully staged his forward strategy.

Immediately, the Indian government was confronted with extensive military problems—of manpower, transport, and supply. Troop requirements were complicated, for Dufferin's strategy involved not only the Quetta corps of 27,980 men, but a second corps of 25,000, and a reserve corps of 13,000 troops,[97] all of which sharply reduced the British–Indian garrison to an estimated 100,000-odd[98] troops. To strengthen this garrison, Dufferin recommended to Kimberley and the India Council increases in both the Indian

[91] Lyall to his sister, Mrs. B. Webb (from Rawalpindi), Mar. 31, 1885, Lyall Papers, Let. Bk. 1885-88. Courtesy of Mrs. R. C. Lyall.

[92] See above, p 91.

[93] See D. to K., Apr. 5 and 11, 1885 (priv.), DVP, R. 517, nos. 18, 22; Viceroy to Secretary of State, telegrams, Apr. 10, 1885 (priv.), R. 519, nos. 30, 31.

[94] Telegram, Rawalpindi, Apr. 8, *Times*, Apr. 10, 1885. The press in Europe and Russia erroneously printed the Amir's speech as Dufferin's own words.

[95] D. to K., Apr. 5 and 13, 1885 (priv.), DVP, R. 517, nos. 19, 25.

[96] Parliamentary Debates, 3 *Hansard*, 298 (May 12, 1885), 321-322.

[97] Final figures, all at ratio of one British to two Indian. See Viceroy to Secretary of State, telegrams, Mar. 30, Apr. 8, 1885, DVP, R. 519, nos. 10a, 20; Dispatches of Governor-General-in-Council, nos. 44, 69, Milit., Mar. 17, May 4, 1885, CRO, Bengal Milit. Let., 1885, vols. 482, 483.

[98] These troops consisted of 26,450 British and 76,532 Indian. See D. to K., Mar. 17, 1885 (priv.), DVP, R. 517, No. 15.

and British military establishments.[99] Adoption of the Kandahar
strategy meant a more difficult transport and supply problem,
necessitating the construction of new transport facilities. Railway
construction between Sibi and Quetta via the Bolan Pass, begun
under Lytton and suspended by Ripon, was now pushed with new
urgency; and a new rail line from Sibi to Pishin via the Harnai
Pass was undertaken. In anticipation of any move of the first corps
to Kandahar, 29,000 animals were sent to Pishin, and 220 miles
of rail and the necessary tools and supplies for a temporary railway via Chaman were stored at Quetta. Also, in addition to ordering 39,000 rifles and carbines and some four million rounds of
ammunition, Dufferin was committed to supplying the Amir with
some artillery, 20,000-odd rifles, ammunition, and money to pay
conscripts for the Afghan army.[100] Finally, in accordance with the
cabinet's wishes, the Indian government began construction of
fortifications, depots, and entrenched defences at Quetta, Pishin,
Peshawar, Multan, and other points on the Indian frontier.[101]

Upon his return from Rawalpindi, Dufferin finally took up the
question of the "enormous" expenditure his strategy might entail.[102] This, he estimated at only a million pounds sterling, but,
in the light of Colvin's Statement, this was an uncomfortably large
sum, which would eat away the meagre surplus and land the budget
with a severe deficit. The real problem, he realized, was the inability of the Indian government to meet such heavy expenditure
without increasing taxes. But a Viceroy, still facing his first budget

[99] For the Indian establishment, cavalry to be permanently increased from 17,384
to 21,956, with 56 new British officers, and infantry temporarily increased from 96,288
to 113,896; for the British establishment, 15,000 troops to be retained as a reserve in
England, 2,150 English drafts and 40 officers to be brought at once to India, and a
total increase of 10,980 men for 1885-86. See Viceroy to Secretary of State, telegrams,
Mar. 30, 31, Apr. 7, May 6, 1885, DVP, R. 519, nos. 10b, 11, 19, 100; Dispatches of
Governor-General-in-Council, nos. 63, 79, Milit., May 4, May 22, 1885, CRO, Bengal
Milit. Let., 1885, Vol. 483, paras. 8-9, 11, 13-16 (No. 63), 1, 5, 6 (No. 79). There was
confusion in the final figures, with telegram of Apr. 9 totalling 10,980 men and telegram of Apr. 21 totalling 13,600; see Viceroy to Secretary of State, telegrams, Apr. 9
(cancelled), Apr. 21, 1885, DVP, R. 519, nos. 26a, 48. Kimberley called this to Dufferin's attention in Secretary of State to Viceroy, telegram, Apr. 22, 1885 (priv.), R. 519,
No. 87.
[100] Viceroy to Secretary of State, two telegrams, Apr. 10 (priv.) and telegram, Apr.
23, 1885, DVP, R. 519, nos. 30, 31, 55.
[101] Military Department telegrams, nos. 535-D, 537-D, 540-D, Mar. 18, Commissary
General telegrams, nos. 5-T-A, Apr. 3, 245-A, Apr. 4, Military Secretary to Secretary,
Public Works, telegram, No. 3-M, Mar. 23, 1885, quoted in Dispatch of Governor-
General-in-Council, No. 69, Milit., May 4, 1885, CRO, Bengal Milit. Let., 1885, Vol.
483, paras. 8-10, 19; Viceroy to Secretary of State, telegrams, Apr. 24, 26, May 11,
1885, DVP, R. 519, nos. 61-62, 64, 79.
[102] D. to K., Apr. 6, 1885 (priv.), DVP, R. 517, No. 21.

after only five months in office and with a weak ministry to support him at home, who took this extreme step, ran the risk of being charged, like Lytton before him, with financial imprudence and recklessness by radicals in Parliament and by Indian editors and politicians. This charge both Dufferin and members of the cabinet all sought to avoid, even though disagreeing widely on how to meet the new expenditure.

Northbrook, First Lord of the Admiralty and the ranking expert in the cabinet on Indian finance, had, from the very start, been uneasy about Dufferin's Afghan strategy and its impact on the Indian budget. Colvin, in his Statement, seemed to favor direct taxation to cover increased military expenditure, and Northbrook warned Kimberley and Dufferin against the Indian political dangers of such a step and intimated that he would oppose it. As an alternative, he recommended floating a war loan in either the London or Calcutta market.[103] Dufferin, without consulting Colvin, proposed reducing current Indian capital expenditure and limiting to £4 millions the drawings of the Secretary of State against Indian revenues during the next six months for payment of the Home Charges.[104] Kimberley and the India Council favored neither Northbrook's nor Dufferin's recommendations. Limitation on the Secretary of State's drawings would deter rupee note sales, thereby interfering with the flow of English trade to and from India; on the other hand, a loan in England meant interest charges in sterling and hence "loss by exchange" to the Indian budget, whereas the interest rates in the Calcutta market were too high. On taxation, all agreed with Northbrook, and Kimberley advised Dufferin: "Pray avoid taxation"; instead, they recommended retrenchment in all nonmilitary or capital expenditure, especially in the Public Works Department.[105]

Colvin disagreed with all these proposals.[106] A tentative appraisal of the requirements of Dufferin's strategy convinced him that troop increases alone would amount to £1 million and that other costs would amount to two-and-a-half times that figure! Retrenchment could not possibly produce enough revenue; further-

---

[103] Northbrook to D., Mar. 14, 1885 (priv.), received *ca.* Apr. 4-5, DVP, R. 525, No. 20.

[104] Viceroy to Secretary of State, telegram, Apr. 3, quoted in Dispatch No. 174, Fin., June 20, 1885, CRO, Fin. Let., 1885, Vol. 147.

[105] Secretary of State to Viceroy, telegram, Apr. 15, quoted in Dispatch No. 174, Fin., June 20, 1885, CRO, Fin. Let., 1885, Vol. 147; K. to D., Apr. 17, 1885 (priv.), DVP, R. 517, No. 30, postscript.

[106] Colvin to D., Apr. 1885 *(ca.* Apr. 15, from order and context), DVP, R. 528, No. 276.

more, retrenchment in railways and famine-relief works could damage Indian interests. A loan in England would only add to the sterling debt paid on interest for loans and to the "loss by exchange." The only realistic alternative was direct taxation in the form of an extended license tax upon the incomes of the wealthy and official classes and, if necessary, an increase in the duty on salt consumed by the masses. There was the remote possibility the Home Government might shoulder a portion of the new expenditure on the grounds that the Afghan crisis was as much an imperial as an Indian responsibility. But Gladstone's attitude had changed since the days when the British Exchequer paid a portion of the costs of Lytton's war; he now had to worry about the English budget, and his remarks in the April debates revealed that he was in no frame of mind to assist India with the Afghan charges.[107]

Among all these proposals, Dufferin had no choice but to follow the orders of the Secretary of State in Council and embark upon a program of retrenchment,[108] however questionable it might be. Significant retrenchment in capital expenditure not only would retard economic and administrative development in the presidency and provincial governments, but also would curtail the Public Works Department's construction of railways, roads, and canals so vital to the expansion of trade and the welfare of the agrarian population, and would hamper government measures to deal with famine. Although no famine had occurred during Ripon's term, such a catastrophe might recur at any time, and the Government was responsible to itself and to its subjects to be always prepared. Though retrenchment was a step in the wrong direction, Dufferin pressed ahead, only to find that it raised more problems than it solved, and did not produce much revenue.

From the start, Dufferin maintained that Indian public opinion was behind his strategy and willing to accept whatever burdens it might entail.[109] To him, with his aristocratic outlook, "native public opinion" meant the Indian princes and the zemindars of Bengal and Bihar. Had he known anything of the structure of Indian opinion at the time, or attached any value to the opinions of educated Indians, and had he shown any interest in what this important segment of native opinion was saying about his Afghan policy, he would have learned that, by April, it was wholly out of sympathy with the course he was pursuing.

Not that these men welcomed a Russian victory! Far from it!

---

[107] Parliamentary Debates, 3 *Hansard*, 297 (Apr. 2, 27, 1885), 317-321, 848-865.
[108] D. to K., Apr. 19, 1885 (priv.), DVP, R. 517, No. 26.
[109] See above, p. 94

Loyal to British rule, the editors and politicians had no desire to see it replaced by a Czarist regime.[110] To a man, they would stand in support of the Indian government, should so much as one Russian soldier set foot on Indian soil. Early in the crisis a small group,[111] mostly editors of Gujerati and Urdu newspapers published in the Bombay Presidency, the Punjab, and the northern region of the Northwest Provinces and Oudh, accepted the Herat strategy in the belief that British prestige had to be upheld and that Indian Muslims and the Princely States would be called upon. By April, when no call came, and the financial implications of the strategy became clearer, their enthusiasm waned perceptibly.

But the larger, more influential group[112] never subscribed to Dufferin's policy. Less troubled by the Russian threat or a possible loss of prestige in Afghanistan, they placed full confidence in the Indian sepoy to defend the Indian frontier. By calling upon the princely armies and Indian volunteers, the Government could raise some 300,000 men in a week. The editors could find no justification whatsoever for the Viceroy's unfolding strategy of sending a predominantly British force into Afghanistan and reinforcing manpower in India in the event of war by bringing British troops from England at much expense to the Indian taxpayer. Consequently, S. Banerjea came to the conclusion that "our rulers have a sort of suspicion that the too near presence of Russia might produce a disturbing effect upon India and might unsettle the popular mind"[113]—an explanation rapidly and widely accepted. Various Anglo-Indian journals, known to have access to official thinking, corroborated it: *The Pioneer,* for instance, recommended a 3,000- to 6,000-man increase in the British garrison made up of "European and Eurasian" volunteers, with no reference to drawing upon the princely armies or Indian volunteers,[114] while *The Englishman,* in a similar vein, favored an increase in order "to guard against the error of pre-Mutiny days."[115] These comments, the Indian

[110] See *V. of I.,* III, Jan.-Apr. 1885, on Dufferin's Afghan policy and forward strategy.

[111] See *V. of I.* for twenty-seven editors, and the more important newspapers; *Bombay Chronicle, Bombay Samachar, Jam-e-Jamshed, Mahratta, Kesari, Akhbar-e-Am, Muslim Herald, Bengal Public Opinion,* and *Bangabasi.*

[112] See *V. of I.* for forty editors, and the more important newspapers: *Indian Spectator, Indu Prakash, Akhbar-e-Soudagar, Rast Goftar, Dnyan Prakash, Shivaji, Sind Times, Tribune, Punjab Chronicle, Oudh Akhbar, Indian Mirror, Hindoo Patriot, Mahomedan Obeserver, Reis and Raiyyet, Pravati, Amrita Bazar Patrika, Som Prakash, Sanjibani, Hindu, Dravidhavarthamani,* and *Swadesa Mitran.*

[113] *Bengalee,* Mar. 7 (*V. of I.* III, Mar. 1885).

[114] *Pioneer,* Feb. 10, 19, 27, 1885.

[115] *Englishman,* Jan. 13, 27, Mar. 10, 1885.

editors believed, represented official thinking. "The people," wrote
Sitala Chatterjee, "are allowed no share in trying to protect their
own country."[116] N. N. Gupta concluded that "we repose the full-
est confidence in our rulers, but are denied the privilege of cooperating with them."[117] "Distrust of the people" therefore became
the label which these editors affixed to the forward strategy. "Impoverishment of the people" was soon to follow.

By April, the optimism—or scepticism—of the Indian editors
concerning their new Viceroy was giving way to pessimism. His
decisions on imperial problems, culminating in his Afghan policy,
filled them with foreboding. It was not only educated Indian leaders in Bengal who were so affected, but many in other parts of
India also began to question his intentions. They had looked with
hope to him to continue Ripon's policy of reform; instead they saw
emerging the lineaments of Lytton's policy of imperialism. Dufferin's action in the Afghan crisis made them conscious of this fact;
his handling of the Indian Volunteer question bluntly brought it
home to them.

[116] *Tribune,* Jan. 31 (*V. of I.,* III, Feb. 1885).
[117] *Sind Times,* Feb. 4 (*V. of I.,* III, Feb. 1885).

V

Lord Dufferin's Lost Opportunity: The Indian Volunteer Question and the Indian National Union

The question of volunteering arose in 1885 when the Anglo-Indian and Indian communities became concerned that, in the event of a third Afghan war, the Government might be confronted with a shortage of troops, pending reinforcements from England.[1] Upon news of Government plans to expand the Volunteer Corps, both communities responded patriotically by offering to volunteer for garrison service. The Anglo-Indians urged the Government to reorganize the corps so that the majority of the 71,000 European and Eurasian males available for service might pass through volunteer training, thereby increasing the existing corps of 12,400 men to some 60,000;[2] the Indians—educated leaders, wealthy landowners, and the mercantile communities—suggested that, if it included "able Natives of birth and education who are physically qualified" and who wished to serve their country, the corps might well exceed 60,000 men.[3] The most effective solution would have been to combine the two proposals, but this was virtually impossible, given the prevailing interpretation of the Volunteer Act and official policy of recent years, both of which had transformed volunteering into an Anglo-Indian right and privilege.

[1] See above, pp. 99-101.

[2] Editorials, "Volunteering in India," *Englishman's Overland Mail*, Jan. 27, "The Volunteer Reserve," *Pioneer*, Feb. 10, 27, 1885.

[3] *Punjab Courier*, Jan. 7 (*V. of I.*, III, Jan.), *Tribune*, Jan. 24, 31, *Indian Nation* and *Indu Prakash*, Feb. 2, *Hindu*, Feb. 4, *Behar Herald*, Feb. 10, (*V. of I.*, III, Feb.), *Swadesa Nesan*, Feb. 18, *Indian Chronicle*, Feb. 23, *Dravidhavarthamani* and *Akhbar-e-Am*, Feb. 25 (*V. of I.*, III, Mar. 1885).

Originally, volunteering was an Anglo-Indian response to the Mutiny.[4] Confronted by a serious shortage of European troops, Lord Canning, the Governor-General, accepted the offers of Englishmen, Europeans, and Eurasians to serve as volunteers, and passed an act authorizing the formation of volunteer corps through out British India. The purpose of the corps was, first, to protect the life and property of the European communities, and second, to keep the peace in these communities during an emergency, thus releasing British troops for more urgent duties.[5] Canning and other officials considered it unlikely that Indians would risk life and limb as volunteers to protect Europeans and their property, and so the Volunteer Act of 1857 contained no clauses which specifically permitted or prohibited Indians from joining the corps or from forming corps of their own. Therefore, the regulations governing the conduct of volunteers were based on the Articles of War for European troops in India. Thus, the act was framed to assist the Anglo-Indian community during the Mutiny, with no intention to include Indians.

Yet underlying intent is different from intent precisely stated in law. On the face of the act, there was no reason why Indians should not volunteer, although from 1857 to 1860 only Europeans and Eurasians did so.[6] But in 1861, Parsi and Bengali gentlemen in Bombay and Calcutta respectively requested Canning's permission to form two corps. Canning, using the authority given the Governor-General under section five of the act, politely declined their request on the grounds that European corps were designed to act as short-term reinforcements for British troops in the event of an internal crisis, and, as it was quite unlikely that there would ever be a shortage of Indian recruits for the Indian part of the army, no need existed for a separate Indian volunteer corps. "Nevertheless," Canning added, "if any Natives, whether Parsees or others, should desire to take their place amongst the European members of the Volunteer corps, understanding sufficiently the English language, adopting the uniform of the corps, and being willing and able to share in its duties, the Governor-General in Council would be glad

[4] Act I of 1820 (1 Geo. IV, c. 99) permitted the Company to raise volunteers. See C. Ilbert, *The Government of India*, 2nd ed. (Oxford, 1907), p. 80. In 1854, Dalhousie sanctioned a Volunteer Corps for the Straits Settlements, then governed from Calcutta, see H. H. Collen, "The Volunteer Force of India," *Journal of the United Service Institution of India*, 12:58 (1883), 193.

[5] Act XXIII of 1857.

[6] Collen, p. 195.

to see them enrolled in it."[7] But he must have known that it would be virtually impossible for the Indians to be accepted within the European corps, for the racial prejudice, distrust, and bitterness toward Indians which the Mutiny had engendered within the Anglo-Indian community, and which were reinforced by the discretionary power vested by law in the commandants of the corps to pass upon prospective candidates, would have precluded any such arrangement. In fact, when the Parsis and Bengalis submitted their applications, they were rejected, and Canning did nothing to overrule the local decisions.[8] Thus precedents for exclusion of Indians from the Volunteer Corps were established under the existing law, and the official policy on Indian volunteering became stamped with exclusion. The Volunteer Amendment Act of 1869,[9] known misleadingly as the Indians' Volunteer Act, did little to clear up the imprecision of the act of 1857. Addressed to "all the loyal subjects of Her Majesty the Queen" serving as volunteers, it again contained no specific clauses on Indians, and in the regulations the Volunteer Corps was referred to as a "European force."[10] Thus, with intent still legally undefined, Anglo-Indian prejudice continued to determine the application of the law.

From 1870 to 1883 the Volunteer Corps expanded rapidly throughout India,[11] but Indians were not accepted into the new companies. This policy was challenged in June 1877 at a public meeting in Bombay, called by the Governor, Sir Richard Temple, to approve the resolution for European volunteers in response to the Afghan crisis. Mehta, Telang, and other young leaders moved an amendment to include Indians. Temple replied that the law recognized only European volunteers and recommended that the Indians forward memorials to the Bombay Government requesting permission to form an Indian volunteer corps, but, for some reason, Mehta withdrew his amendment, and the matter was dropped.[12] The Arms Act of 1878, with its discriminatory clauses on possession

---

[7] Minute, Aug. 1861, enclosed in Dispatch of Governor-General-in-Council, No. 166, Milit., Sept. 21, 1885, CRO, Bengal Milit. Let., 1885, Vol. 486, paras. 4, 6.

[8] See *Bengalee*, Apr. 18, *Tribune*, Apr. 25, 1885.

[9] CRO, Abtsract, Governor-General, 1869, Vol. VIII, pp. 237, 277-278.

[10] Act of 1869, para. 35.

[11] From 1861 to 1869 the Volunteer Corps had a total of 3,208 members, of whom 1,108 were serving in the East India Railway Volunteer Corps; from 1870 to 1883 10,933 members were added, 2,100 of them to the Railway Corps (serving principally on the Bombay and Central India lines), see Collen, Appendix.

[12] Mody, I, 90-92. There is no reference to this incident in the Temple Papers, see CRO, Eur. F. 86, Vol. 5, Lets. to Lytton 1877-80, vols. 193-194, Mins. of Gov., Bombay, 1877-80; or in the Lytton Papers, see Eur. E. 218/518/2, 218/519/5, 218/520/1.

of weapons by Indians,[13] confirmed the exclusion of Indian volunteers. The Ilbert Bill controversy, involving Indian rights versus Anglo-Indian status and privilege, brought the European Volunteers of Bengal and Bihar to near mutiny against Ripon, and further hardened the official policy of exclusiveness.

When Afghan developments in late 1884 made obvious the need for more volunteers, Sir Alfred Lyall, Lieutenant-Governor of the Northwest Provinces and Oudh, recommended to the Military Department of the Government a plan of Colonel Rivett-Carnac "for increasing the force of armed Europeans and Eurasians in the several provinces of India" by enlisting either the full-time or part-time service of 60,000 men to release sufficient British troops from garrison for combat duty and thus temporarily cover the deficiency of 5,000 British troops caused by rotation or by duty in Egypt. Although Rivett-Carnac included "Native Christians," for "in a time of trouble it would reflect on our rule were this class left to its fate," he omitted all reference to Indian volunteers.[14] The plan was given immediate support by Colonel George Chesney and the other ranking officers of the Military Department, who placed it before Dufferin and the council as the basis for expansion and reorganization of the Volunteer Corps.

By February 1885, Dufferin, intent upon his Herat strategy, realized the need for extra volunteers, and, apparently unaware of the suggestion then being made by the Indian editors to permit Indian volunteering, accepted Rivett-Carnac's plan. Early in March, after inspecting the Calcutta Volunteers, he called upon all existing units throughout India to bolster their strength and prepare to assist the regular army in defense of the Empire,[15] and, a few days later, he ordered Chesney to notify the provincial governments to expand the existing corps and recruit a Volunteer Reserve, following Rivett-Carnac's suggestions.[16] Apparently, in his pronouncements and orders, he purposely omitted all reference to Indian volunteers. In reply to a query by Charles Bernard, Chief Commissioner of

[13] Act XI of 1878, section 1(b).

[14] J. R. Reid, Chief Secretary, Northwest Provinces Government, to Chesney, Secretary, Government of India, Military Department, No. 862/III-454-2, Nov. 27, 1884, with memorandum by Lieutenant-Colonel J. H. Rivett-Carnac (Ghazipur Volunteer rifle Battalion), Aug. 12, 1884, CRO, Milit. Procs., Pt. A. 1885, Vol. 2553, No. 1935A.

[15] Telegram, Calcutta, Mar. 8, *B.G.O.S.*, week ending Mar. 13, 1885; *Englishman*, Mar. 9, 1885.

[16] Chesney to Secretary, Northwest Provinces Government, No. 586-E, Mar. 13, to Secretaries, Madras, Bombay, Bengal, Assam Governments, No. 578-E, Mar. 13, 1885, with memorandum, by Rivett-Carnac, CRO, Milit. Procs., Pt. A, 1885, Vol. 2553, nos. 1936A, 1937.

British Burma, on adding "native" volunteers to the Rangoon Volunteer Rifle Corps, he wrote: "it was not thought advisable to sanction the enrolment of Burmans, Karens, Chinese, and natives of
India in volunteer corps."[17] For Dufferin, "native" volunteering
was a dead letter, and so it would have remained had not the am-
biguities of the law given rise to an "incident" in Madras, which
provided the Indian editors and politicians with the opportunity
to challenge Dufferin and his Council on the Volunteer question.

Soon after the Viceroy's speech before the Calcutta Volunteers,
volunteering commenced in earnest in various parts of India. In
Madras City, on March 16, J. H. Garstin, Chief Secretary to the
Madras Government, acting on the instructions from Chesney,
publicly announced that a new Volunteer Corps would be organized to supplement the existing Madras Volunteer Guards and
Artillery, and that all "gentlemen" were eligible for recruitment.[18]
This was vague, or so it seemed to Major Spring Branson, a ranking
officer in the Madras Volunteer Artillery whose brother had led
the Calcutta Bar in opposition to the Ilbert Bill, and he called for
"gentlemanly" volunteers of a certain height to volunteer for artillery training.[19] Upon reading these notifications, officials in the
Madras Secretariat realized that Branson had gone too far, and
Garstin not far enough. The following day Garstin issued a supple-
mentary notification to the press stating specifically that "all the
European and Eurasian civilians of Madras, between the ages of
20 and 55, [were] to enrol themselves as volunteers," as long as they
were "of good education" and under no pressing obligations to their
employers;[20] and, to strengthen this, he added the public orders of
the Governor-General in Council to the Governor of Madras concerning volunteering.[21] But no official statement directly rescinded
Branson's notification, and this left the door ajar. On March 25, four
"native gentlemen" of the proper height and educational background volunteered for the Madras Volunteer Artillery and were
cordially accepted by Branson.[22] The deed was done; Indians had
been accepted for the Volunteer Corps.

Madras officials, stunned by this unforeseen turn of events, saw

[17] Bernard to Chesney, No. 299-4-V, Jan. 14, Chesney to Bernard, Feb. 14, and also
telegram, No. 349-E, Feb. 13, Bernard to Chesney, Feb. 25, Chesney to Bernard, Mar.
16, 1885, see CRO, Milit. Procs., Pt. B, 1885, Vol. 2553, nos. 101-107, 1625-1626, 1513-
1514. See also Memorandum on Native Volunteering, Mar. 14, 1887, DP, D. 1071H/
M10/6.
[18] *Madras Times*, Mar. 17, 1885.
[19] Branson's letter of Mar. 17, *Madras Times*, Mar. 18, 1885.
[20] Garstin's letter of Mar. 19, *Madras Times*, Mar. 20, 1885.
[21] Chesney to Secretary, Madras Government, Mar. 13, *Madras Times*, Mar. 24, 1885.
[22] Three pleaders in the High Court—Ramaswami Mudaliar, Sankara Nair, and

trouble ahead; Anglo-Indians, equally stunned, soon began to rally in defense of their privilege; educated Madrassis, elated by what had happened, spread the news throughout India. "The Native community are indebted for their honourable privilege to Mr. Spring Branson," wrote S. Iyer. "We cannot too highly applaud the wisdom and confidence that the Government have shown by having readily given their sanction to a step, which, if followed up by the native community and Government here and in other parts will lead to results of utmost importance."[23] Iyer's words, immediately telegraphed all over India, created a sensation. In Calcutta, N. N. Sen called upon the Viceroy and Commander-in-Chief to permit educated Bengalis to enroll in the Calcutta Corps, just as their Madrassi brethren were being permitted to do in Madras.[24] But he did not wish to see the privilege confined to Madras or Bengal alone. He advised Lord Dufferin to "give practical proof of his genuine appreciation of the loyalty and devotion of the Indian people by admitting Native Gentlemen to the Volunteer Corps throughout India." Failure to do so would result in "heart burning and discontent."[25] Sen's words found a ready response among the editors of the Bengal and Bihar press, who began to write enthusiastically about volunteering. Unfortunately, both Iyer and Sen had jumped to the unwarranted conclusion that the Madras Government had sanctioned Branson's action. Actually, official and Anglo-Indian groups, once they recovered from the shock of what had happened, fully intended to see Garstin's notification implemented.

When the news reached Simla, Chesney, acting for the Viceroy, then at Rawalpindi, advised the Military Department at Calcutta to instruct the Madras Government immediately to prohibit volunteering by the "native" classes.[26] Dufferin, immersed in talks with the Amir, wrote Chesney to treat the whole Madras affair as a minor incident,[27] but this was impossible. Branson had received anonymous threats that the admission of the four Madrassis into the corps would lead to wholesale resignations by Europeans and personal trouble for himself. The gathering storm broke in full force when Colonel Ross Church, Commandant of the Madras Volunteer

---

Gopal Nair—and one assistant professor at Presidency College, L. A. Williams (listed as Indian, though probably Eurasian), *Madras Times*, Mar. 26, 1885.

[23] *Hindu*, Mar. 25 (quoted in *Madras Times*, Mar. 26, 1885).

[24] *Indian Mirror*, Mar. 27, 1885.

[25] *Indian Mirror*, Mar. 28, 1885.

[26] Chesney to Military Department, telegram, No. 2-S-E, Mar. 28, and to Secretary, Madras Government, telegram, No. 71S-E, Mar. 28, and letter, Mar. 31, 1885, CRO, Milit. Procs., Pt. B, 1885, Vol. 2553, nos. 1515-1517.

[27] Private Secretary of Viceroy to Chesney, Apr. 2, 1885, CRO, Milit. Procs., Pt. B, 1885, Vol. 2554, nos. 727-728.

Corps, publicly denounced Branson for ignoring the published orders of the Supreme and Madras Governments, which specifically
disallowed the enrollment of "native" volunteers, adding that, even
if "native" volunteers were permitted to enroll, they would only
promote tension and complications, which should be avoided in
time of crisis.[28] But Branson, instead of backing down, gave a statement to the press in which he dismissed the anonymous threats and
declared that Europeans, far from withdrawing, were continuing to
enroll in his corps; in flat contradiction to Church, he maintained
that nothing in Government regulations prohibited Indian volunteering, and announced that the four Madrassis would not leave
the corps, but that, once their uniforms had been fitted, they would
report for duty.[29]

   This was a gallant, even heroic, position to take—Branson against
the Establishment—but it was a losing one. Church's words had
more weight than Branson's in the Madrassi and Anglo-Indian
communities, even though *The Hindu* was trumpeting loudly for
Indian support of Branson.[30] Some one hundred Indian graduates
of Madras University, who had intended to enroll in the Madras
Volunteer Infantry, were cowed by Church's statement, and, instead of filing their applications, they issued a disgruntled call to
their colleagues throughout the province to agitate for their right
to volunteer. A group at Bellary, led by S. Mudaliar, a group of
Mahajana Sabha members in Madras, led by Pulney Andy, and a
group formed by the leaders of the Triplicane Literary Society
submitted petitions to the Madras Government for presentation to
the Viceroy, requesting the right to volunteer.[31] The Anglo-Indians,
meanwhile, fully endorsed Church's words. *The Bangalore Spectator,* setting the tone for the Anglo-Indian press in Madras, warned
the Madras Government under no circumstances to entertain the
idea of "native" volunteering.[32] Only the liberal *Madras Times*
took issue with Church and attributed the loyal gesture of the
Madrassis "to that recognition of the right to equal citizenship and
privilege in all Her Majesty's subjects in India which Lord Ripon
nobly endeavoured to make a reality."[33]

   But *The Madras Times* was a voice crying in the wilderness.

   [28] Report of Mar. 30, Triplicane, *Englishman's Overland Mail,* week ending Apr.
7, 1885.
   [29] Interview, Mar. 31, *Madras Times,* Apr. 1, 1885.
   [30] Report of Mar. 31, Madras City, *Englishman's Overland Mail,* week ending Apr.
7, 1885.
   [31] *Indian Mirror,* Apr. 4, 7, 10, 1885.
   [32] *Bangalore Spectator,* Mar. 30, as quoted in report of Mar. 31, Madras City, *Englishman's Overland Mail,* week ending Apr. 7, 1885.
   [33] Apr. 9, 1885.

Church, sensing the alarm of the Anglo-Indians, announced that henceforth only European and Eurasian applicants would be accepted as volunteers and that the case of Branson and the four Madrassis would be submitted to the Madras Government for final decision.[34] Meanwhile, the orders of the Government of India on volunteers were republished by the Madras Government, with the added stipulation that "local committees, comprised of the chief civil officials and the principal members, European and Eurasian, of the unofficial community" would meet to recruit additional Volunteer Corps and a Reserve Corps.[35] Branson was conspicuously passed over in appointments to the committee for Madras province, which included Church and Garstin. The latter, as Chairman, officially announced that the kind offer of the four Madrassi gentlemen to volunteer had been declined by the committee, since "the Volunteer Corps, at present constituted, are regarded as an auxiliary force in India, and are, therefore, only open to Europeans and Eurasians."[36] Subsequently, the Government of Madras thanked the four volunteers but declined their services.[37] So ended the Madras incident, with volunteering still the preserve of the Anglo-Indians.

The storm in Madras was watched with mounting interest and anxiety by officials, Anglo-Indians, and educated Indians throughout India. Other local governments were careful to define precisely which groups were eligible for volunteering. The officials in Bombay, the Northwest Provinces, and the Punjab faithfully quoted Rivett-Carnac, stating that only "Europeans, Native Christians, and Eurasians" were eligible;[38] Bengal officials asked for only ablebodied Europeans, residents of Calcutta and the suburbs.[39] By mid-April, all local governments had so phrased their announcements as to make Indian volunteering impossible.

Anglo-Indian editors were divided on the question, with the more influential papers—*The Times of India* (Bombay), *The Civil and Military Gazette* (Lahore), and *The Englishman* (Calcutta)—opposing Indian volunteering. The artful H. Hensman and the unscrupulous G. Allen, editor and proprietor respectively of *The*

[34] *Madras Times,* Apr. 9, 1885.

[35] *Madras Times,* Apr. 6, 1885.

[36] Secretary, Madras Government, to Chesney, No. 1871, Apr. 8, 1885, CRO, Milit. Procs., Pt. B, 1885, Vol. 2554, nos. 728-729; *Madras Times,* Apr. 10, *Indian Mirror,* Apr. 11, 1885.

[37] Report of Apr. 15, Madras City, *B.G.O.S.,* week ending Apr. 7, 1885; Secretary, Madras Government, to Chesney, telegram, Apr. 17, 1885, CRO, Milit. Procs., Pt. B, 1885, Vol. 2554, nos. 1730-1731.

[38] *Times of India* and *Bombay Gazette,* Mar. 24, 1885.

[39] *Englishman* and *Indian Daily News,* Apr. 7, 1885.

Pioneer, struck the keynote for this group, reminding everyone that "the English in India are still a garrison in what was once a conquered country," warning that "any premature relaxation of all our safeguards might only encourage a revival of sedition among the evil-disposed," and concluding that Indians were therefore *"ipso facto* unsuitable material for the Indian Volunteer force."[40] The liberal voices in favor of Indian volunteering comprised *The Statesman* (Calcutta), *The Bombay Gazette,* and *The Madras Times,* while *The Madras Mail* favored separate units.[41]

The reactions of Indian editors and politicians to the stand taken by the provincial governments and the Anglo-Indian press were practically unanimous. Finding no legal basis for official policy, and puzzled by the inclusion of Indian Christians, Eurasians, and selected Parsis, and the exclusion of Hindus, Muslims, and Sikhs,[42] some ascribed it to distrust of Indians since the Mutiny,[43] some to protection of Anglo-Indian privilege,[44] and some to racial and religious prejudice,[45] but all agreed the policy was emotional and irrational. "The same sinister influence which stirred up the opposition to the Ilbert Bill is at work in Madras to prevent the admission of Natives into the Volunteer Corps," declared N. N. Sen,[46] while another editor added sourly, "The *amour propre* of the majority of the present Volunteers would be hurt if Natives were put on the same level as themselves."[47] The Indians recognized that as long as Anglo-Indian pride and prejudice remained, Indians would never be granted the right to enlist in the existing corps, and they had no option but to appeal by petition for separate corps to the only higher court available to them, namely, the Viceroy. At Poona, Lokamanya Tilak called upon educated Marathis to sign a petition;[48] at Patna, fifty leading Bihari gentlemen submitted a similar petition;[49] at Calcutta, Raja R. L. Mitra and some zemindari colleagues, incensed

[40] Editorials, *Pioneer,* Mar. 28, Apr. 16, 1885.

[41] Editorials, *Statesman,* Apr. 11, *Bombay Gazette,* Apr. 13, *Madras Times,* Mar. 26, *Madras Mail,* Apr. 13, 1885.

[42] *Bengalee,* Mar. 28, *Lahore Tribune,* Apr. 4, *Hindoo Patriot,* Apr. 6, 1885; also *Bangabasi,* Apr. 4, *Dravidhavarthamani,* Apr. 5, *Indian Chronicle, Sanjibani,* and *Shafeek-e-Hind,* Apr. 11, *Native Opinion,* Apr. 12, (*V. of I.,* III, Apr. 1885).

[43] *Indian Mirror,* Mar. 28, *Bengalee,* Apr. 4, 1885; also *People's Friend* and *Sind Times,* Apr. 11 (*V. of I.,* III, Apr. 1885); *Indian Chronicle,* Apr. 11 (quoted in Indian *Mirror,* Apr. 16, 1885); *Suravi* (quoted in *Englishman's Overland Mail,* week ending Apr. 14, 1885).

[44] *Hindoo Patriot,* Apr. 6, *Indian Spectator,* Apr. 12, 1885.

[45] *Subodh Patrika,* Apr 12 (*V. of I.,* III Apr. 1885).

[46] *Indian Mirror,* Apr. 2, 1885.

[47] *Vaidarbha, Apr. 11* (*V. of I.,* III, Apr. 1885).

[48] *Mahratta, Apr. 5* (*V. of I.,* III, Apr. 1885).

[49] Meeting, Apr. 5-6, *Indian Mirror,* Apr. 7, 1885.

by Dufferin's passage of the Bengal Tenancy Bill, urged in *The Hindoo Patriot* the formation of independent Indian volunteer corps;[50] J. C. Bose, editor of *Suravi,* a leading Bengali vernacular paper, supported Mitra's idea and called upon other vernacular editors to do the same.[51] Finally, with Bengali political circles primed for action, S. Banerjea issued a summons to interested Bengalis to sign a memorial to the Viceroy.[52]

The memorial, drawn up by Banerjca, declared that Indians wished to volunteer in order "to testify their sense of duty to their country and their devout loyalty to their Queen Empress" during the Central Asian crisis; "as citizens," they should "help in the defence of the Empire," and the Government should accept their services just as readily as it accepted those of Anglo-Indian, Eurasian, and "native" Christian volunteers. Failure to do so "would cast an unmerited slur" upon Indian loyalty and provoke a troublesome issue at a troubled time. This memorial, warning the Viceroy, was accompanied by an appeal in *The Bengalee* to Banerjca's Bengali and Indian friends: "The educated community owe their very existence to English education and English culture that have moulded their thought and aspirations"; their obligation to the Government at that critical moment was therefore greater than that of any other community in India; hence all educated Indians should come forward to support the memorial and secure the right to serve the Government. Whether they would be granted this right rested ultimately with the Viceroy and his councillors. "Upon that decision will depend very much the impression we shall form as to whether we are trusted or regarded as aliens, unworthy of the confidence of our rulers."

The response to the memorial was overwhelming. Four hundred Bengalis, chiefly *vakils,* undergraduates at Calcutta University, merchants, teachers, and zemindars, signed.[53] Intimate friends of Banerjca—N. N. Sen, A. M. Bose, N. N. Ghose (Principal of the Metropolitan College), and K. M. Chatterji, the latter three prominent in the Indian Association—as well as Raja R. L. Mitra, the Tagores, and other influential zemindars of the British Indian Association,

[50] Apr. 6, 1885.

[51] *Suravi,* Apr. 7 *(V. of I.,* III, Apr. 1885).

[52] Memorial circulated, Apr. 8, see *B.G.O.S.,* week ending Apr. 10; meeting held, Apr. 10, see *Indian Mirror* and *Bengalee,* Apr. 11 (with text of memorial), and *Times,* Apr. 13, 1885.

[53] Banerjea reported 30 zemindars, 7 talukhdars, 14 barristers-at-law, 107 *vakils,* 8 attorneys-at-law, 26 government officers, 50 professors and teachers, 4 editors, 15 graduates (3 M.A., 1 B.L.), 14 medical practitioners, 2 municipal commissioners, 7 mukteers, 64 merchants and clerks, and 66 undergraduates *(Bengalee,* Apr. 11, 1885, p. 176).

and Krishna Kumar Mitter of *Sanjibani* and S. P. Sarvadhikari of *Bharatbasi* among the vernacular editors, were among the signers. R. L. Mitra expressed the hope of all when he wrote: "We have too much faith in Lord Dufferin's statesmanship and large-heartedness to bring ourselves to believe that he will commit the fatal blunder of rejecting so loyal a prayer."[54] Thereafter, the agitation for petitions grew apace in Calcutta, Bombay, Allahabad, Benares, and Madras where all the leading Indian editors and politicians eagerly took up the issue.[55] Within a week, the plea in the memorial was being voiced far beyond Calcutta, and Dufferin's name had become inextricably linked with the Volunteer question.

Just as the agitation began in the Punjab, Dufferin, on his way from Rawalpindi to Simla, reached Lahore, and, on the assumption that Indians wished to hear about the Penjdeh incident and his talks with the Amir, he granted an audience to various local groups. He thus found himself confronted by representatives of the Singh Sabha and the influential Lahore branch of the Indian Association.[56] Founded in 1877 by Sirdar Dayal Majeetia, a wealthy Punjabi, and by S. Banerjea, then agitating on the Civil Service question, this branch was directed by talented lieutenants, Sitala Kanta Chatterjee, editor of *The Tribune* of Lahore, and Kali Prosanna Roy and Pandit Ramnarain, well-known barristers.[57] On this occasion, Pandit Ramnarain stepped forward, presented a memorial declaring their devotion to the Crown and their readiness to serve their country at such a critical juncture, and then read aloud the sections which asked the Viceroy to sanction "the formation of Volunteer Corps composed of respectable and educated Native gentlemen" and urged him to move "a revision of the Arms Act, and a partial relaxation of its stringent provisions as regards natives of India."[58]

Although he later denied it, Dufferin was apparently taken by surprise.[59] Speaking cautiously, with his soft intermittent lisp, he expressed appreciation for the interest shown by the associations, and then added, "Without pronouncing upon the merits of the representations you have made, either in regard to the revision of the Arms Act or the formation of Native Volunteer Corps, I

[54] *Hindoo Patriot*, Apr. 13, 1885.

[55] See *Indian Spectator*, Apr. 12, *News of the Day, Indian Union*, and *Hindu*, Apr. 13, *Indian Mirror*, Apr. 14, *Swadesa Mitran*, Apr. 15, *Amrita Bazar Patrika*, Apr. 16, *Mahomedan Observer* and *Indian Courier*, Apr. 18, *Rast Goftar*, Apr. 19 (*V. of I.*, III, Apr. 1885).

[56] Apr. 17, see *B.G.O.S.*, week ending Apr. 24, 1885.

[57] Banerjea, pp. 46-47.

[58] *Tribune*, Apr. 18, *Indian Mirror*, Apr. 19, 1885.

[59] D. to Reay, May 17, 1885 (priv.), DVP, R. 528, No. 173.

must frankly tell you that both are matters which must be discussed and adjudicated upon their own merits apart from the
circumstances of the hour." "The Government," he pointed out,
"could not commit a greater mistake than to allow itself to be
hurried incidentally into a decision in respect of two such grave
and important questions." Conscious of the effect that this non-
committal statement might have upon his audience and also on
the Indian press, Dufferin took occasion to pay tribute to "the
very noble and generous loyalty" shown by princes and people
toward the Crown at "the first alarm" of the Central Asian crisis.
But now that the alarm had passed, he assured them that there
was no cause for public concern; hence, though he did not say so
openly, there was no need for Indian volunteers and princely
armies. "The normal forces of the Empire," he emphasized, "are
more than sufficient to maintain the inviolability of our territory."[60]

Dufferin's statement was a keen disappointment to most Indian
editors. Only a few were optimistic as to the Viceroy's ultimate
response, and urged moderation and patience.[61] Some Bombay
editors, dejected because Dufferin had not at once replied favorably to the request of the Lahore memorial, hoped he would reconsider;[62] others felt that more than hope was needed to secure
their demand. "Though the Viceroy is not inclined to support the
movement, we believe that a persistent agitation will at last compel
our rulers to yield to Native demands."[63] Sharing this view, Iyer,
Charlu, and Chariar in Madras considered that Dufferin's hesitancy was part and parcel of the Government's policy as reflected
in the handling of the Madrassi volunteers.[64] N. N. Sen in Calcutta declared that Dufferin's "unfavourable, if not an ungracious
response" was unwise,[65] for the Volunteer question had wider implications than either the Viceroy or his advisers realized. Indian
reaction to the question had conclusively demonstrated that "different races of the Indian population, widely separated from each
other heretofore, have now cordially joined in working together
to the same ends."[66] "We are living in different times," Sen wrote
with a nod toward history. "The Government should know it and

[60] Reply by Dufferin, enclosed in D. to K., Apr. 19, 1885, DVP, R. 517, No. 26; telegram, Lahore, Apr. 17, *B.G.O.S.*, week ending Apr. 24, 1885.

[61] *Tribune*, Apr. 25, *Gujerati Mitra*, Apr. 26 (*V. of I.*, III, May 1885).

[62] *Rast Goftar*, Apr. 19, *Bombay Samachar*, Apr. 20 (*V. of I.*, III, Apr.), *Sind Times*,
Apr. 25, *Nyaya Darshak*, Apr. 27, *Hitechhu*, Apr. 30 (*V. or I.*, III, May 1885).

[63] *Yezdan Parast*, Apr. 19 (*V. of I.*, III, Apr. 1885).

[64] *Swadesa Mitran*, Apr. 23, *People's Friend*, Apr. 25, *Hindu*, Apr. 29 (*V. of I.*, III,
May 1885).

[65] *Indian Mirror*, Apr. 22, 1885.

[66] Editorial, "Germs of a New National Life in India," *Indian Mirror*, Apr. 25, 1885.

mark it, so that they may deal with old India. Our ancient civilization by coming in contact with the modern civilization of the West has been impregnated with a new vitality . . . the Indian people are being fast saturated with a new set of ideas; their feelings and aspirations are undergoing a thorough change; they are becoming a new nation altogether." Should the Government fail to respond to this change, such as in the case of volunteering, Sen. predicted "serious political disaster,"[67] and urged Dufferin to move with the tide of history and decide in favor of Indian volunteers, while still there was time.[68] Likewise, S. Banerjea cautioned: "Let not the words 'too late' be marked upon every privilege and upon every concession"; otherwise "the most splendid rights will fail to conciliate or to awaken gratitude."[69] Should this happen, India would be transformed into another Ireland, on a larger and more destructive scale, and he called on all Indian groups to draft new memorials, assuring the Viceroy of the sincerity of their plea and impressing him with their intention to act. By the end of April, Volunteer agitation was in full swing,[70] and telegrams and memorials were reaching the Viceroy's desk.[71]

Dadabhai Naoroji tried a more immediate approach. In a private letter to Ilbert, he expressed his hope that Indian volunteering would receive from the Viceroy and his councillors that "correct consideration" which had been conspicuously lacking in the past owing to official "prejudice and pusillanimity."[72] He had no doubt that the volunteer movement was an expression of a genuine loyalty, because "Lord Ripon left the Indians a nation" with hopes "of partnership with the English." Nor did Naoroji think it impossible for the Government to devise a scheme to select Indians by "the property and education test"; indeed "Mr. Hume had a scheme in his pocket" which was worthy of the Viceroy's attention. "We have not been going forward since the Viceroy came," or at least this was "the feeling of the most enlightened" of his friends,

[67] *Indian Mirror*, Apr. 23, 1885.
[68] *Indian Mirror*, Apr. 28, 1885.
[69] *Bengalee*, Apr. 25, 1885.
[70] Meetings at Barisal, Jamalpur, and Hugli, *Bengalee*, week ending Apr. 25; at Santipur, Meherpur, Khulna, Mozzaffupur, and also Shibpur (Lower Bengal and Bihar), *Bengalee*, week ending May 2; at Meerut (Northwest Provinces), Apr. 27, *Indian Mirror*, May 3, 5, 1885.
[71] Wallace to Chesney. Apr. 22, forwarding memorial from Indian Association (Lahore), Apr. 27, and telegrams from meetings at Meerut, Meherpur, and Santipur; Secretary, Punjab Government, to Chesney, No. 140-853, Apr. 30, forwarding petition from Bhagwan Singh Thapar and others; Secretary, Bengal Government, to Chesney, No. 142-T-G, Apr. 28, 1885, forwarding petitions from Patna and Calcutta, CRO, Milit. Procs., Pt. B, 1885, Vol. 2559, nos. 667-671.
[72] Naoroji to Ilbert, May 4, 1885, Ilbert Papers, CRO, Eur. D. 594, Packet 18.

Naoroji confided to Ilbert, noting that the Viceroy had concentrated upon Indian external affairs to the neglect of internal progress. A decision by the Viceroy in favor of Indian volunteering would help allay this feeling. Ilbert saw to it that Naoroji's hint was given to the Viceroy.

Dufferin had come away troubled from the audience at Lahore. A potentially dangerous issue had arisen at a moment when the foreign and financial crises demanded all his attention. To Kimberley he expressed his doubts: "The excitable Native Press has started a new question which will require some delicate handling." A group in Calcutta, he wrote, was forwarding to Simla a memorial similar to the one presented to him at Lahore. He enclosed a copy of his reply to the Lahore association and commented dubiously: "If the military enthusiasm of the authors of the agitation were genuine, it would be easy enough to manage, but the thoughts of some of them are of a different complexion."[73] Apparently the Viceroy had in mind S. Banerjea and his colleagues with their strong ties to the Lahore association.

Completely unconversant with the subject of Indian volunteering, though aware that it was a most awkward issue as it impinged directly on the privileges of the Anglo-Indian community, Dufferin hoped to delay reaching a decision. Awaiting him at Simla was a memorandum by James Gibbs,[74] a former member of the Executive Council, on the point of retiring to England. Gibbs had been one of the few councillors who had advised the Viceroy soon after his arrival in India on the political aspirations of the educated Indian community and who, conscious that these aspirations would eventually collide with the prejudices of the Anglo-Indians, had recommended to the Viceroy a cautious policy of gradual change.[75] Such a policy on the Volunteer question, he now maintained, would do more good than harm, for "the volunteer movement among the Natives is a real one and Government will have to take it up soon." A favorable response, he thought, would involve no insuperable difficulties. He supported the pleas from Bombay and Poona for separate corps with European and Indian officers, and, in regard to qualifications, he suggested drawing candidates of "respectability and education" from "the Native Gentry" or "graduates of the university, Justices of the Peace, Municipal Commissioners, Members of the Local Boards, and their relatives."

[73] D. to K., Apr. 19, 1885 (priv.), DVP, R. 517, No. 26.
[74] Gibbs to D., Apr. 26, 1885 (priv.), received *ca.* Apr. 29-30, DVP, R. 528, No. 266.
[75] Gibbs to D., Feb. 4, 1885, DVP, R. 528, No. 57.

As Gibbs had predicted, Dufferin was "soon" compelled to deal with the question when Hume, fresh from consultations in Bombay, Madras, and Allahabad on the plan for the Indian National Union,[76] and bringing also "a scheme in his pocket"[77] for Indian volunteering, returned to Simla. Acting on Dufferin's previous invitation, Hume requested an interview, and early in May the two men met for the first time.[78] Dufferin remained on his guard. All that he knew of the man made him suspect that Hume would prove unpredictable. Ripon, and Hume in his own letters, had told the Viceroy much. Dufferin also remembered well Hume's father, the radical "fiery Joe"; he knew that Hume had been "got rid of" by the government "on account of his impracticability," and that he was "a disciple of Madame Blavatsky." Now, Dufferin found Hume an arresting person: "clever and gentleman-like, but [with] a bee in his bonnet."[79] After a brief and pleasant chat, Hume broached the question of Indian volunteering, and Dufferin, assuming that this was what Hume had come to discuss, politely refused to be drawn. But immediately after their meeting, Dufferin, possibly on Ilbert's prompting, had second thoughts, and wrote Hume: "Far from being unwilling to discuss the question of volunteering with you, I shall be very glad to hear what you have to say on the subject." He even went so far as to say, "Personally I am rather favourable than the reverse to the idea—at all events I should be very unwilling to rebuff or treat otherwise than with sympathy and gratitude the loyal spirit which has been shown by the Native population at large."[80] And he arranged another meeting for that same week.

Having taken this step, which committed him to do something about the Volunteer question, Dufferin realized he was in no position, with only Gibbs' memorandum, and without other facts or figures, even to discuss the question intelligently with Hume or anyone else, much less to do anything about it. So he decided to seek expert advice and wrote hastily to Lyall, enclosing a copy of his "merely preliminary" reply to the Lahore Indian Association and asking Lyall to forward his ideas on the question as soon as possible.[81] But, much to the Viceroy's embarrassment, Lyall's reply failed to arrive before the second meeting with Hume.

[76] See above, pp. 75-77.
[77] See n. 72 above.
[78] In all probability, on May 4 or 5. See D. to H., May 5, D. to Reay, May 17 (priv.), H. to D., June 12, 1885, DVP, R. 528, nos. 148, 173, 391; D to R., July 8, 1886 (strictly personal), R. 525, No. 145.
[79] D. to Reay, May 17, 1885 (priv.), DVP, R. 528, No. 173.
[80] D. to H., May 5, 1885, DVP, R. 528, No. 148.
[81] D. to Lyall, May 6, 1885 (priv.), DVP. R. 528, No. 154.

On this occasion,[82] Hume went straight to the point. He recapitulated briefly the Indian editors' arguments for Indian volunteering either in separate or in integrated corps, and pointed out that their intentions were entirely genuine and loyal. They had suggested organizing a "five-thousand"-man force the first year, to be increased gradually each year until it represented an important element in the defense of the Empire. They were agreed that restriction and limitation of such a corps would be necessary and logical. They favored certain basic qualifications: every Indian candidate was to possess "a good education, adequate knowledge of English, an unblemished character and a respectable family." A recruiting committee, consisting partly of Europeans and partly of Indians in each major center of the presidencies and provinces, was to select candidates, who would enter mixed or unmixed companies of existing European and Eurasian corps, or, where necessary, "form new corps" if more than 400 Indian candidates were selected in a non-presidency town; all commissioned officers were to be European "at first," but the Government was "to hold the prospect of promotion to the commissioned ranks of Native volunteers." With such a plan, Hume believed the Government could safely satisfy the aspirations of educated Indians and, at the same time, cement this group's attachment to the Government and strengthen the Volunteer Corps.[83]

Dufferin listened attentively to Hume's statement, but then informed him that a subject of such importance would have to be discussed with his Council before he could even comment upon it. Moreover, he could not hold a Council until certain official papers on the question arrived from Calcutta, and, before he could give a final answer to either the Lahore or Calcutta memorial, he would have to obtain the approval of the Home Government. This would take time, and he asked Hume to relay this message to his Indian colleagues. Understanding the Viceroy's point of view, Hume agreed to do this.[84]

Their meeting appeared to be at an end when Hume brought

[82] The second meeting most probably took place between May 6 and 15; see n. 78 above. A brief résumé (but without details of Hume's plan for Indian volunteering) is contained in Hume's circular to Indian leaders, a copy of which he sent to Dufferin; see n. 90 below.

[83] See letter of H. to the editor, dated London, Sept. 3: "Native Indian Volunteers," *Evening Standard*, Sept. 4, 1885, in which Hume referred to his private interview with Dufferin and reviewed in detail the plan he put before Dufferin on behalf of Indian leaders.

[84] Enclosure *re* interview, H. to D., June 12, 1885, DVP, R. 528, No. 391.

up the subject of a national organization,[85] which he said was obviously needed to effectively represent and express to the Government Indian grievances and Indian opinion on matters of reform. The Indian press had hitherto shouldered this task but was no longer able to do the job in a manner beneficial to either the Indian community or to the Government. To correct this deficiency, he and his Indian colleagues proposed to form an Indian National Union. Hume went on to outline details of organization and program,[86] and then told Dufferin that plans were being made for the first meeting in Bombay at the end of the year with Lord Reay in the chair and other officials in attendance.

Dufferin showed considerable interest in Hume's plan, and, once he had a rough idea of what Hume was talking about, he "warmly approved the proposal, considering that it would at least furnish the Government with something like an authoritative statement of the views and wishes of the educated and intelligent classes throughout the country."[87] From what he had heard, he concluded that the Indian National Union was to be "a Political Convention of delegates on the lines adopted by O'Connell previous to the Catholic emancipation."[88] Though he had no thorough grasp of the plan or sound appreciation of its aims, the Viceroy objected immediately to any official link to the Union; had he taken time to think it over, he might have come to realize the possible advantage of an official connection. "The functions of such an assembly must of necessity consist in criticizing the acts or policy of the Government, in formulating demands which probably it would be impossible to grant, and in adopting generally the procedure of all reform associations." For this reason, official participation was "absurd." "Consider how awkward it will be for Lord Reay," he pointed out to Hume, "if Grant-Duff's administration comes to be severely criticized whilst he is in the chair." In effect, Dufferin was denying official recognition to the future Indian National Union and, in consequence, thwarting the hopes of Ripon and Hume for Indian political development in cooperation with the Government. Hume, seeing that Dufferin had made up his mind, did not press the point; rather, he deleted it, whereupon Dufferin accepted the revised plan and said to Hume: "I am perfectly satisfied and wish you every success." Indeed, as Hume

[85] Dufferin wrote to Reay (see n. 79 above) about his meeting with Hume and the proposed Indian National Union, but he did not advise Kimberley.

[86] See above, p. 77.

[87] H. to R., résumé of interview, Jan. 13, 1889, RP, BM Add. MSS 43616, No. 33.

[88] D. to Reay, see n. 79 above.

later declared, when the plan took shape in the form of the first National Congress in Bombay in December 1885, there was "not the smallest change in the programme." But when in Simla Hume received Dufferin's private blessing for the experiment, neither realized that they had laid the groundwork for India's national development.[89]

Following their meeting, Hume, as he had promised, wrote a private circular on the Volunteer question to the "special" committees of the National Union, urging patience. "Some considerable time must necessarily elapse before any *final* orders on this matter can possibly be issued." He assured his colleagues that the Viceroy appreciated the loyal spirit shown by those wishing to volunteer, and he concluded with a tribute to Dufferin: "The country cannot do better than trust in him and be patient—lay before him freely aspirations and grievances with a full confidence that these will receive his most earnest attention, but without expecting immediate practical results." In compliance with Dufferin's expressed wish, nothing was said in the circular about the Viceroy's approval of the Indian National Union.[90]

With Hume cooperating on the Volunteer question, Dufferin, at last, had time for reflection, though he realized that having asked Hume to relay a message to the Indian leaders, a decision had become imperative. He now instructed Ilbert to review the Lahore memorial,[91] and turned his attention to the opinions of government officials.

On May 13 he had heard from Lord Reay,[92] who on March 30 had succeeded Sir James Fergusson as Governor of Bombay, Though Dufferin did not know him personally, he had learned much about Reay's unusual background and liberal outlook from Fergusson, who knew him well,[93] and Dufferin looked forward to learning his views, coming as they did from one who was also

[89] From this reconstruction of the Dufferin–Hume interview based on their private papers, the reader will see that there is nothing to W. C. Bonnerjee's contention that Hume wished to use the plan for the Indian National Union for social reform, but that Dufferin persuaded him to make it political in aim. See W. C. Bonnerjee, ed., *Indian Politics* (Madras, 1898), pp. vii-viii.

[90] Circular, undated, enclosed in H. to D., June 12, 1885, DVP, R. 528, No. 391, but circulated before May 24 (see Reay to D., n. 110 below).

[91] Ilbert Diary, May 12, 1885, Ilbert Papers, CRO, Eur. D. 594/4.

[92] Mackay, Donald James, eleventh Baron Reay; b. 1839, the Hague; Leyden and Cambridge Universities; D.C.L., 1861; Dutch Foreign Office, Second Chamber, States General, Netherlands, 1871-1875; in England, 1875; inherited Scottish estates in 1876 on death of father; naturalized, 1887, by act of Parliament; befriended by Gladstone; Bimetallism Conference, 1881; Baron, U.K., 1881; educational and social reform, Scotland; Rector, St. Andrews, 1884; Governor of Bombay, Mar. 1885.

[93] Fergusson to D., Jan. 3, 1885, DVP, R. 528, No. 31.

fresh to India. These views were "tentative," but, Reay emphasized, Indian volunteering was a subject widely discussed in important circles of Bombay, and some solution must soon be found. Upon becoming Governor, he had taken counsel with one of his more liberal Bombay advisers, Maxwell Melvill, and had at first agreed with Melvill that the Government would have to meet this mani- festation of Indian loyalty by admitting Indians into the Volunteer Corps, the higher ranks of the army, and the civil administration. But Reay had tempered his opinion after discussing the question with General Hardinge, Commander-in-Chief of the Bombay Army, who was frank in his opposition to separate Indian volunteer regi- ments, preferring instead to draft native companies directly into the existing Bombay volunteer establishment and to place them under English officers, even though such an arrangement might create dissatisfaction among Europeans in the Volunteer Corps.[94]

On May 14, Dufferin held a Council meeting to discuss the Volunteer question.[95] Bayley and Colvin were chiefly concerned with the effect of Indian volunteers on the Europeans and the ad- ditional cost to the budget of this new personnel. Ilbert, upon Dufferin's instructions, had investigated the legal basis of the exist- ing Volunteer Corps and pointed out that, since the volunteers came under the Articles of War for European troops serving in India,[96] "the incorporation of Natives into independent Volunteer companies would be illegal," unless sanctioned by "the Secretary of State [and] in all probability, an Act of Parliament." Dufferin was much struck by this statement, and was further impressed when Hope, having listened to the others, warned Dufferin that the Volunteer question was "perhaps the most important question of internal administration which the Council has had before it since the Ilbert Bill was so light-heartedly accepted," and asked for a postponement of the decision pending further investigation.[97] Dufferin and the Council agreed. A day later, Lyall's letter ar- rived,[98] adding a further note of warning, and Dufferin began a cautious retreat from making a decision.

Lyall's attitude toward Indians was paternalistic. He held the nobles and the "martial races" in high esteem, but had little re- spect for the English-educated Indian class, most of whom he clas- sified loosely as "Bengalees." "The educated native is after all a

[94] Reay to D., May 10, 1885, received *ca.* May 13, DVP, R. 528, No. 299a.
[95] Ilbert Diary, May 14, 1885, Ilbert Papers, CRO, Eur. D. 594/4; D. to Reay, see n. 79 above.
[96] See above, p. 103.
[97] Hope to D., May 14, 1885, DVP, R. 528, No. 312.
[98] Lyall to D., May 13, 1885, received *ca.* May 15-16, DVP, R. 528, No. 308.

contemptible creature," who dabbles in "seditious agitations" against the Government, when they themselves are dependent upon the Government for their existence. "It is one thing to have won your liberties by the hard fighting of centuries; it is another thing to get them all freely given you, as a girl gets her trousseau." The bid to volunteer he attributed to "nervousness" on the part of this effeminate new class, but, with the aristocracy in mind, he admitted that "I am not sure I would not let some of the better sort of natives join us, if things looked bad."[99]

These prejudices Lyall amplified in his letter to Dufferin. Since the Volunteer Corps had evolved in India from "the feeling of insecurity left among the Europeans and Eurasians by the Mutiny of 1857," and not, as in England, from the threat of foreign invasion, the admission of Indians was, and would continue to be, out of the question. Western education and a more liberal spirit in the administration had caused "the more advanced section of the native community" to challenge from time to time the legality of this exclusion, and Lyall was apprehensive that the fact that "the Government of India has never ventured to lay down any distinct rule of exclusion" might soon be "pressed somewhere in India in a manner that will bring the question to an issue."[100] But, legality aside, Lyall questioned the sincerity of the Indian bid. In the Northwest Provinces, "insecurity" had sparked the volunteering enthusiasm. Fearing that the reduction of British garrisons for Afghan duty would lead to lawlessness, "the educated professional men" had sought to organize for defense. This was loyal and commendable. But Indian bids elsewhere bore all the traces of "a desire to make political capital out of an awkward demand,"[101] to grant which, under the circumstances, would be a "hazardous experiment." It would likewise be a gamble if selection was not "very closely" restricted so that the European element, especially in the mofussil stations, was not to be swamped by Indians who then "might become formidable politically." Moreover, always to be considered was the rift between the Hindu and Muslim communities which, in a crisis, would destroy the unity and purpose of the corps. Summing up, Lyall advised Dufferin "to stave off as long as possible any decision at all," with the hope that "interest in the question will probably subside with the disappearance of war preparations." If Dufferin were absolutely pressed to take

[99] Lyall to Mrs. B. Webb, Apr. 28, 1885, Lyall Papers, Let. Bk. 1885-88.

[100] Lyall seems to have been unaware of the Madras incident, see above, p. 106.

[101] Lyall was most probably referring to Calcutta and the educated Bengali, whose political influence extended to the Northwest Provinces and the Punjab, that is, the Indian Association of Lahore.

action, "the least objectionable alternative" would be to have "young native gentlemen" join the Volunteer Reserve, "the selection of which and the arms for which would remain under local administrative officers."

Lyall's advice reinforced the Executive Council's hesitancy, and determined Dufferin to retreat not only from the encouraging attitude he had initially shown Hume, but also from making any decision at all. "It will be better perhaps to refrain from showing any special sympathy with the idea," he wrote Reay; he did not wish "to encourage expectations which it is not certain we may be able to fulfill. . . ." The Indian bids, however "genuine and legitimate," were impossible to meet unless Indian volunteering was controlled by restriction "to particular classes," but such restriction meant selection by "arbitrary distinctions" which were "always obnoxious and difficult to maintain." For the moment, he thought it advisable to temporize, and to handle this "exceptional display of loyalty with the greatest deliberation and delicacy."[102]

Within the Executive Council, however, there was growing concern over the Volunteer question. All agreed that the Secretary of State and his Council would not favor introducing a bill to legalize Indian volunteering which might touch off a debate in the Commons far more explosive than the debate on the Ilbert Bill. At a special session of the Council, Ilbert therefore set forth alternatives to volunteering which would suit the "native" taste; he proposed either the formation of special regiments in the army to which Indians could apply for service, or an increase in the appointments of Indian officers at the senior levels.[103] Some days later the Council instructed the Military Department to draft a confidential memorandum on the Volunteer question and the Ilbert proposals to be sent to the senior officials of the provincial governments. By this step the Council planned to sound official opinions and also gain time, during which the agitation might subside.

At this juncture, a curious twist occurred which provided Dufferin and his Council with the solution they were seeking. In mid-March, Dufferin and the Council had forwarded to Kimberley proposals for putting the British Indian Army on a more effective combat footing to meet any major Russian threat to Afghanistan. One proposal, already suggested by senior officers and the Army

[102] D. to Reay, see n. 79 above.
[103] Ilbert Diary, May 16, 21, 1885, Ilbert Papers, CRO, Eur. D. 594/4.

Commission in 1879, called for the formation of a reserve for the Indian army, distributed on a territorial basis and with "Native officers and non-commissioned officers on the same scale as the regular army," to cover troop losses arising from combat and sickness.[104] The other proposal, echoing the aristocratic views of the late Sir Henry Lawrence and Lord Lytton, and based on memoranda prepared for Dufferin by Colonel George Chesney,[105] called for the appointment of "Native Gentlemen to the commissioned ranks of the army in the same grades as European officers."[106] Heretofore, only honorary commissions, limited to such persons as the maharajas of Gwalior, Kashmir, and Cooch Behar, had been given to Indians, but the time had come to make available an increased number of senior appointments in the infantry and calvary to "the higher classes of Native gentlemen" from "noble and respectable" families of Maharashtra, Oudh, Hyderabad, and the Punjab. "It is a class," the Council noted, "which perhaps above all others ought to be carried with us, and made to feel that their interest and fortune are bound with ours." The Mutiny had demonstrated the wisdom of this axiom. Now, with the Russian threat and the changing nature of the Indian political structure, it was important that this class should feel "that there is a place for them in the new state of things," not based wholly upon educational requirements, such as existed to their disadvantage in the Covenanted Civil Service. Appointments would be made not through open competition, but on the basis of "personal qualification, fitness, character and social position." To test the idea, it was proposed to form one infantry and one cavalry regiment, commanded by Indian officers transferred from regular regiments.

Not expecting an immediate reply, Dufferin was happily surprised to hear from Kimberley,[107] just at the moment when the Council was seeking some alternative to Indian volunteering. Kimberley was especially interested in the proposal for the appointment of Indian officers to higher grades in the army. Since Northbrook also favored it, Kimberley intended to give it "full and immediate consideration," although he predicted "serious opposition" from his council on the grounds that it would be "unsafe to

---

[104] Dispatch of Governor-General-in-Council, No. 44, Milit., Mar. 17, 1885, CRO, Bengal Milit. Let., 1885, Vol. 482.

[105] Memorandum, "Army Commissions to Native Gentlemen," Jan. 22, and note, "Advancement of Natives in the Army" with essay by H. Lawrence, Feb. 3, 1885, DP, D.1071H/M10/6.

[106] Dispatch of Governor-General-in-Council, No. 47, Milit., Mar. 21, 1885, Bengal Milit. Let., 1885, Vol. 482.

[107] K. to D., May 1, 1885 (priv.), received *ca.* May 21-22, DVP, R. 517, No. 33.

train up Native Officers, who might become leaders in another mutiny, [and] to place European officers under Native officers." It might be better to have separate Indian regiments and officers. With Turkomans at the senior level in the Russian Transcaspian Army, Kimberley wondered what effect the absence of senior Indian officers in the British Indian Army might have upon the "martial races." "The contrast between our system and the Russian is one which we cannot safely allow to continue," he confided to Dufferin.

Kimberley's letter caused Dufferin to reconsider Ilbert's proposal for Indian senior officers.[108] It would require no Parliamentary action; with Kimberley's support, it had a good chance of clearing the India Council; it would demonstrate the Government's confidence in the loyalty of Indians; and it would satisfy the group most genuine in its volunteering enthusiasm. Moreover, it would avoid the danger of separate Indian volunteer corps, loosely controlled and largely composed of "a parcel of hot-headed students or other citizen soldiers." The volunteering movement had been transformed into a "craze," Dufferin told Kimberley, "artificially stimulated by the press and the wire-pullers." By late May, the Viceroy had drifted poles apart from Hume.

To Dufferin, Hume had now become the wire-puller *par excellence.* In mid-May, the Viceroy, in a letter to Reay,[109] had described his meeting with Hume, and, while implying that he had given his approval to Hume's plan for the Indian National Union, he bound Reay to secrecy and warned him to be on his guard on this and the Volunteer question, for "it is our duty carefully to watch the signs of the times, and cautiously and conscientiously to liberalize the administration of India," but "I am sure it would be a mistake if we identified ourselves personally either with the reforming or the reactionary enthusiasts." Reay's long reply disturbed Dufferin.[110] Through a "most confidential" source,[111] Reay had discovered that Hume was "the head-centre of an organization" which had planned all the demonstrations in honor of Ripon, and which was "spreading" throughout India with the avowed "object to bring native opinion into a focus." Reay admitted that Hume's men in the Bombay Presidency were "very able co-adjutors," and

[108] D. to K., May 29, 1885 (priv.), received *ca.* June 15, DVP, R. 517, No. 36.

[109] D. to Reay, see n. 79 above.

[110] Reay to D., May 24, 1885 (priv.), received *ca.* May 28, DVP, R. 528, No. 331.

[111] Reay subsequently identified Sir William Wedderburn as "his personal friend" and contact within Hume's group who gave him "most valuable information about the advanced party." See Reay to K., Feb. 18, 1886, Kimberley Papers, D. 26b Box. Courtesy of Dr. S. Gopal.

some of the reforms they were pressing were justified, but he was worried by their use of the press and telegraph to develop their organization. He had heard nothing of Hume's "political convention," but, if approached, he would decline to preside. He had, however, seen Hume's circular on the Volunteer issue, which urged his cohorts "not to be hasty" inasmuch as his interviews with the Viceroy had been "very satisfactory."

Hume had kept his word, but Dufferin was troubled nonetheless by the link of Hume's "organization" to Ripon and his reforms, espcially since Hume had not disclosed that the Indian National Union was to be a monument to Ripon's memory. Furthermore, the Union was obviously a more mature political body than Hume had led Dufferin to believe. Voices round him were encouraging his initial doubts. Mackenzie Wallace, in particular, who had never liked Hume personally, and who had opposed the plan for the Union from the start, increased Dufferin's suspicions of Hume, and the Viceroy began to believe that the Union and the Volunteer issue amounted to the same thing—trouble to be kept at arm's length.[112]

Despite Hume's circular, throughout May Indian agitation continued in Lower Bengal, Bihar, Assam, Bombay, the Northwest Provinces, and the Punjab.[113] Banerjea, insisting that the Volunteer question was "a test" of the Viceroy's true intentions, set the pace.[114] Sen, Malabari, Grattan Geary, and some of the Bengali vernacular editors sought to allay the growing impatience with expressions of confidence in Dufferin's cautious handling of the question.[115] But this gave way to renewed activity when the Bengali press heard through an official leak to the Anglo-Indian journals that Dufferin and the Council were considering the appointment of Indian officers in the army.[116] Sen, Banerjea, and Motilal and Shishir Ghose welcomed the move;[117] the editor of *The Behar Herald*

[112] See H. to R., Jan. 13, 1889, RP, BM Add. MSS 43616, No. 33.
[113] Meetings at Berhampur, Jamalpur, and Murshidabad in Lower Bengal and Bihar, *Bengalee,* May 16, Bogra, *Indian Mirror,* May 15, Midnapore, *Indian Mirror,* May 19, Krishnagur, and Busishant, *Bengalee,* May 23, Ranaghat, Bali, and Cuttack, *Bengalee,* May 30, Ranaghat, Serajgunj, and Khulna, *Bengalee,* June, Darjeeling, and Sylhet in Assam, *Bengalee,* May 9, 16, Bombay City and Poona, *Bengalee,* May 2, Allahabad, Lucknow, and Aligarh in Northwest Provinces and Oudh, *Indian Mirror,* May 14, 27, June 2, 1885. In Madras, there was no new agitation.
[114] *Bengalee,* May 16, 30, also *Hindu,* and *Indu Prakash,* May 23, 1885.
[115] "New India and Old Policy," *Indian Mirror,* May 13, *Indian Spectator,* May 17, *Bombay Gazette,* May 22, *Charuvarta* and *Sangabad Pravakar* (quoted in *Englishman's Overland Mail,* week ending May 30, 1885).
[116] Telegram, May 19, Simla, *Englishman,* May 23, 1885.
[117] *Amrita Bazar Patrika,* May 21 (*V. of I.,* III, June 1885); *Indian Mirror,* May 22, *Bengalee,* May 30, 1885.

thought "this reform ought not to be delayed one moment longer";[118] editors in Karachi and Lucknow, Bombay, and Lahore
expressed the same opinion;[119] and the editor of the *Subodh
Patrika* characterized the rumored reform as the first official acknowledgment of Indian loyalty and declared, "after this, the
permission to form Native Volunteer Corps can be delayed no
longer."[120]

Public statements by government officials in favor of Indian
volunteering spurred on the agitation. A. H. Harrington, Collector
at Saharanpur, Northwest Provinces, in letters to *The Pioneer*,[121]
declared volunteering "the opportunity of associating the people
of India with the Government . . . more closely than hitherto in
the State duty of protecting property for external or local outbreaks"—a logical step in preparation for self-government and a
natural corollary to Ripon's reforms. Even stronger was the
pamphlet "Ought Natives to Be Welcomed as Volunteers?," signed
"Trust and Fear Not,"[122] whom S. Banerjea and other Bengali
editors identified as Mr. (later Sir) Henry Harrison, a member of
the Bengal Civil Service, Commissioner of Police, and Chairman
of the Corporation of Calcutta, a person possessed of a brilliant
mind, liberal outlook, and great faculty of expression, both oral
and written.[123]

The pamphlet warmly championed the idea of Indian volunteering, so fervently desired by the English-educted Indians—or
"Young India," as Harrison preferred to call them. And why was
it important to satisfy their desire when they represented a mere
200,000 souls among 200,000,000 with even more pressing grievances and aspirations? Because they were the political and social
future of India on whom depended the perpetuation of the British ideal in India. "Young India" was "clearly destined to be the
voice of India and the brain of India, [and] the masses will be
its hands and will reflect its teaching," since it possessed the educational training, the legal and scientific knowledge, and the tools
of journalism. Harrison warned officials against dismissing this
group as "politically insignificant," decrying its aims out of petty
jealousy and frustrated paternalism, or attempting to impede its

[118] *Behar Herald,* May 26 (*V. of I.,* III, June 1885).
[119] *Native Opinion,* May 24, *Hindustani,* May 29, *Sind Times,* May 30 (*V. of I.,*
III, June 1885); *Tribune,* May 30, 1885.
[120] *Subodh Patrika,* May 21 (*V. of I.,* III, June 1885).
[121] May 25, 26, 1885.
[122] Published, Calcutta, 1885, see also *Indian Mirror, Indian Spectator,* and *Bengalee,* May 31, 1885.
[123] Banerjea, pp. 90-91.

development by siding with reactionary Anglo-Indians. A major change was taking place in the social and political fabric of British India, whether the Government of India liked it or not, and "Young India" held the key to change. "The time has come, when we must re-cast our ideas of Indian administration . . . unflinching impartiality, equal justice to all parties, and sympathy with legitimate aspirations are what is needed to retain the increasing class of educated Natives as a party within the unity of the Empire [and] interested in its maintenance, instead of driving them to form a faction external to it, and seeking to overthrow it."

The Indian editors gave a warm reception to the pamphlet, which united them in renewed agitation with more cogent arguments. Hume read it, and while he wondered whether it might be official—written by Colvin or even Dufferin himself—wrote the Viceroy, urging him to read it. Hume considered it so effective that he withdrew a pamphlet he had just written on the subject. And he assured Dufferin that, whoever the author might be, it represented "the universal feeling in the inner circle of the National Party."[124]

In June, Dufferin's attitude toward Indian volunteering underwent further change. The sustained agitation of the Indian press, Harrington's letters, "Trust and Fear Not"'s pamphlet, and Hume's meddling had heightened Dufferin's suspicions. Now, to his relief, he heard from Kimberley.[125] "You gave a very judicious answer to the Lahore Association," he complimented the Viceroy. "Clearly we cannot have Native Volunteers." The near mutinous performance of the Bengal and Bihar volunteers during the Ilbert Bill crisis had alarmed him, as it had Ripon and Lyall, and Kimberley concluded that the Government would be throwing oil on the fire if it permitted Indian volunteers. He favored the proposal of two regiments officered entirely by Indians and was confident of approval by his Council. As far as Kimberley was concerned Indian volunteering was a dead issue. Dufferin's reluctance to enlist Indian volunteers began to harden into quiet opposition.

Letters from senior officials in the provinces did nothing to dissuade him from this attitude. Grant-Duff, scribbling in his gossipy manner from Madras, informed Dufferin that public opinion there on issues such as volunteering was "a commodity manufactured to order by small cliques"; the "intelligent part of the community"

---

[124] H. to D., May 31, 1885, DVP, R. 528, No. 363.
[125] K. to D., May 15, 1885 (priv.), received *ca.* June 5-6, DVP, R. 517, No. 42.

was too interested in its own "material prosperity" to participate.[126]
Lyall confirmed this for the Northwest Provinces and Oudh. The
agitation was confined principally "to the professional and English-
speaking classes" and limited to Allahabad and Meerut. Moreover,
Lyall now believed the essential reason for the movement was not
the Russian threat, but "the desire to make political capital and
to assert equality with the English." An Indian volunteer corps
would become "the nucleus, in times of excitement, of political
organization and demonstration," and would endanger "the stability of British rule and order."[127]

Another letter from Reay crystallized Dufferin's opposition.[128]
Again, the note pertained to Hume's political activities and his
ties with Ripon. Reay had got hold of some private circulars and
a memorandum which Hume had distributed to the "special"
committees of the Indian National Union.[129] One circular reported
that Lord Ripon hoped to accelerate Indian reform once he became
Secretary of State for India and had dismissed the India Council,
and that he had grave misgivings about Dufferin's Afghan policy
because it would retard Indian reform. Another circular concerned the radical Liberal, William Digby, who was willing to
stand for Parliament on the question of Indian reform, provided
he received the pertinent facts and sufficient monetary backing
from India. "It shows clearly," Reay concluded caustically, "that
as we have paid Irish delegates, we shall ere long have paid Indian
delegates of the least desirable description." But it was the memorandum, with Hume's "plan of agitation" for the Indian National
Union, which made Reay especially uneasy. "Only those matters
should be brought forward in which we are, as it were, at one
versus the administration." They should aim first at the reconstitution of the India Council—"the sworn defender of every abuse
against which the country desires to protest"—then at rectifying
abuses such as "the virtual exclusion of natives from the higher
posts in the judicial and other branches of the administration,"
"the entire absence of voice in the disposal of the proceeds of
taxation," and the lack of effective Indian representation in the
existing legislative councils. After discussion at the annual meet-

[126] Grant-Duff to D., June 3, 1885 (priv.), received *ca.* June 7-9, DVP, R. 528,
No. 373a.

[127] Lyall to D., June 4, 1885 (priv.), received *ca.* June 7-8, DVP, R. 528, No. 378.

[128] Reay to D., June 4, 1885 (priv.), received *ca.* June 8-9, DVP, R. 528, No. 377.

[129] Since these documents, despite diligent search, could not be found in any of the
Dufferin papers, it appears that Hume, because of Dufferin's wish not to have any
personal identification with or official participation in the Union, did not forward
them to Dufferin.

ing, " a formal monster memorial," setting forth these aims, should be drawn up to be submitted to Parliament eighteen to twenty-four months later. To achieve the necessary unanimity for this memorial, Hume had planned an English daily newspaper for Bombay to "advocate and defend native interests in the Presidency and Empire generally"; and he had arranged with particular "Native Princes," supposedly admirers of Lord Ripon's policy, to advance the necessary funds. "The country must henceforth keep steadily pushing on, and count nothing now till all is ours." Though Reay considered Hume's activities basically "disinterested," he was shaken by the scale and scope of Hume's plan.

In evaluating Hume's memorandum, Reay tended to exaggerate. The plan for the National Union, its principles and program, as outlined in the memorandum, were essentially the same as those he had discussed at his interview with the Viceroy,[130] and which the Viceroy, after deletion of the provision for any official link, had privately approved. The only new features in the memorandum were the provisions for a "party" journal and support from the wealthy princes. These were logical developments, since Dufferin had withheld official participation and patronage. But now, Reay's florid appraisal of the memorandum caused Dufferin to have misgivings. He had given his blessing to the Union and could not go back on his word, but he need not arm Hume's legions with weapons under the pretext of Indian volunteering.

Meanwhile Dufferin, not yet ready to risk an official announcement, acted upon his Council's decision to consult the provincial governments, and sent out the confidential memorandum drafted by the Military Department.[131] The memorandum briefly summarized, with quotations from Canning's Minute of 1861, the history of volunteering since the Mutiny and the government policy of discouraging "native volunteering."[132] It stated that there was still danger in arming a "large and influential portion of the native community," but that, by failing to meet the Indian aspirations for volunteering, the Government ran the risk, first, "of appearing to make a retrograde movement when it is said the

[130] See above, pp. 117-118.
[131] D. to Reay, Grant-Duff, Aitchison, Bernard, Crosthwaite, Griffin, Cordery, Girdlestone, Ward, June 8, 1885 (priv.), enclosing secret and confidential Memorandum on Native Volunteers with Minute by Lord Canning, Aug. 5, 1861, DVP, R. 528, No. 187; also D. to Thompson, Lyall, Bradford, June 8, 9, 1885, R. 528, nos. 188, 189, 190. Since this memorandum could not be located in any of the Dufferin papers, or in the Military or Home Department Records at the CRO, this résumé has been pieced together from extracts from the memorandum quoted in Griffin, Ward, and Thompson to D., June 21, 30, July 15, 1885, DVP, R. 528, nos. 421, 431, 42.
[132] See above, pp. 103 ff.

policy of Government is [moving] in the direction of more liberal treatment of the natives," and second, "of checking and chilling a feeling of loyalty which we ought to encourage and develop." The provincial governments were asked to analyze how widespread the demand was for Indian volunteering and the validity of the motivation behind it, to recommend how it could be successfully carried out and, if they deemed this impossible, to suggest an alternative.

That this was merely an official gesture is evidenced by the letter that Dufferin wrote Ripon, purposely to inform him of the complexities of the Volunteer question, in order to ward off any complaints Ripon might receive from Hume or other critics of the viceregal handling of the matter. In more moderate language than he had used in writing to Kimberley, Dufferin declared, "I am very doubtful about trying so novel an experiment. . . . However, I have written to some of the principal people of the country, asking their opinion, without giving the faintest intimation of the tendency of my own thought on the subject."[133]

When by mid-June, Hume had had no word from Dufferin since their interview in early May, he sent a copy of his circular on the Volunteer question to the Viceroy, and advised him that it was "very desirable" for him to speak out "soon," because impatience and dissatisfaction were rising among his "children."[134] He did not add that a prolonged silence could be as embarrassing to him as to the Viceroy. It would permit his Indian friends to conclude either that the Viceroy had misled Hume, or that Hume had misinterpreted the Viceroy's words and misled them. In either case, whatever confidence they had placed in the Viceroy would be sapped, and the value of Hume's liasion with the Viceroy would be seriously diminished. Dufferin ignored Hume's letter, seemingly for two reasons. First, he agreed with Lyall and Grant-Duff that the longer an official decision was delayed, the quicker the hue and cry for volunteering—in reality nothing more than a fit of midsummer madness by the disgruntled few—would pass. Second, he had come slowly to realize that the Anglo-Indian editors had managed to discover a great deal about supposedly confidential Council discussions[135] and about Hume's recent political activities in the Bombay Presidency; and that they were charging Hume with the ambition of getting Indians elected to Parliament in

[133] D. to R., June 11, 1885 (priv.), DVP, R. 525, No. 30.

[134] H. to D., June 12, 1885, DVP, R. 528, No. 391.

[135] Secretary, Home Department, to Chesney, No. 22-A (Special) June 3, Chesney to Secretaries, Provincial Governments, No. 336-B, June 19, 1885, CRO, Milit. Procs., Pt. B, 1885, Vol. 2555, nos. 1412-1413.

order to form "an Indian party on the lines of that which now represents the interests of Ireland."[136] Clearly, with leaks in his office, a snooping Anglo-Indian press, and sudden public interest in Hume, the less Dufferin had to do with Hume, the less risk he ran as Viceroy of being cast into the role of "the budding Parnell of India."

Dufferin's silence on both Indian volunteering and the appointment of Indian officers caused growing disillusionment among the Indian editors. They warned the Viceroy that he was ill-advised not to discuss these questions openly.[137] Again, it was Banerjea who spoke out. The memorials had been submitted to the Viceroy as early as April 10, but no reply had been given and no Indian volunteer units formed, even though new European and Eurasian volunteer regiments had been authorized. "The delay . . . in replying to the petitions . . . is as painful as it is unexpected." "We were given to understand" by Hume's circular "that the Viceroy was personally inclined to support the memorialists." In the light of the delay and the silence, Banerjea now questioned whether this was so. He hoped that the Viceroy had not decided upon a "quiet burking of the question," for this policy would not dissipate the agitation, which would be continued out of "national self-respect" —a point he feared the Viceroy and his advisers had not grasped. The official silence bore the hallmarks of the Irish policy with its "persistent disregard of popular opinion" which the Home Government had pursued in recent years, and which had compelled the Irish people to seek political action in "secret societies," costing both the people and the Government a high price in peace, property, and persons. "India has hitherto been free of them," Banerjea remarked, but if the Government continued to flout public aspirations and grievances, these societies would spring up overnight. He did not expect the Government to push matters to this extreme. "Least of all do we expect from Lord Dufferin a departure from the policy announced by the Queen's Proclamation and enforced in practice by his illustrious predecessor."[138] He called upon the Viceroy to make known the Government's decision. But Banerjea's plea had no effect.

By the end of June, most Indian editors and politicians held out little hope that Dufferin would permit educated Indians to

[136] *Pioneer Mail,* June 14, 1885.
[137] *Punjabi Akhbar,* May 30, *Indian,* June 1, *Sind Times* and *Hindu,* June 3, *Tanjore Varthamania,* June 4, *Deen Bhandu,* June 14, *People's Friend,* June 20 (*V. of I.,* III, June 1885).
[138] *Bengalee,* June 20, 1885.

volunteer. Although agitation sputtered out in Bengal and Bombay, the Volunteer question was by no means regarded as a dead issue. Irritated by the continued official silence, K. K. Mitter spoke out: "If there be no intention of admitting the natives as Volunteers, then it is better to tell them so plainly."[139] S. Iyer and N. N. Sen, convinced that the volunteer issue was hopeless, advocated compromising with the Government on its obvious preference for the appointment of a few Indian officers,[140] but Banerjea objected, for it was only "an effort to please old families" while neglecting "the claims" of the educated community.[141] He and Malabari obstinately pressed the Viceroy for a decision on Indian volunteering, and insisted on an answer to the memorials.[142]

The Afghan crisis brought Dufferin for the first time into contact with educated Indians other than Bengalis. While previously the Viceroy had had to deal primarily with Bengali political issues, such as the Tenancy Bill and the Local Self-Government Bill, and while criticism of his policy had been confined to Bengali editors and politicians, the events of February and March changed this pattern. With the Russian advance toward Afghanistan and its threat to Indian security and British rule, concentration upon provincial matters was eclipsed overnight by preoccupation with national defense, and it was this common denominator which brought out the divergent points of view of the Viceroy on the one hand and the educated Indian leaders of the whole subcontinent on the other. Dufferin, in choosing his costly forward strategy, with its reliance largely on European troops, had placed military requirements ahead of any consideration of the Indian budget or the welfare of the Indian people, whereas the Indian leaders, in proposing a less costly antiforward strategy, with reliance on princely armies and Indian volunteers, hoped to avoid increased taxation or retrenchment in public expenditure for the benefit of their countrymen. Moreover, the Indian leaders regarded volunteering as one of their inalienable rights, and the Viceroy had not granted it.

[139] *Sanjibani* (quoted in *Englishman's Overland Mail*, week ending June 27, 1885).
[140] *Hindu,* June 19, *Indian Mirror,* June 28, 1885.
[141] *Bengalee,* June 27, 1885.
[142] See "List of memorials and telegrams from Native Associations and Public Meetings in support of the Native Volunteer movement received by the Government of India," from Madras, Bombay, Bengal and Bihar, Assam, Northwest Provinces and Oudh, and the Punjab, enclosed in Dispatch of Governor-General-in-Council, No. 166, Milit., Sept. 21, 1885, CRO, Bengal Milit. Let., 1885, Vol. 486. For memorials and telegrams to and from Private Secretary of Viceroy and Secretary, Military Department, mid-Apr. to early July 1885, see CRO, Milit. Procs., Pt. B, 1885, Vol. 2559, nos. 1874-1900.

With these differences fully in evidence, the Indian leaders realized how distant and unresponsive the Viceroy was to their interests and aspirations. Whereas Ripon had regarded them as representatives of an emerging Indian public opinion and had encouraged them to act responsibly in their new role, Dufferin, disappointing all their hopes, had chosen to ignore them on the first major issue involving their interests. Their doubts of his professed liberalism began to rise, and their suspicions of his susceptibility to official and Anglo-Indian prejudice grew. By July, the warm rapport that had existed between Dufferin and "Young India" at the outset of the crisis had dwindled to a chilly formality marked by sullen criticism and apprehension of what lay ahead.

This sharp change coincided with Hume's efforts to bring the Indian National Union into existence. The Union, originally conceived as an organization in which officials and Indian leaders could meet to exchange ideas, now bid fair to become, thanks to the Viceroy's refusal to participate, a vehicle for criticism directed at him and his policy. Dufferin, less by his handling of the obviously awkward Volunteer question than by his failure to comprehend the novel character of Hume's plan for the National Union, had lost a unique opportunity to find some solution to the problem of the status of the educated Indians, and to give them a meaningful role in contemporary British–Indian society while winning their support at the same time. In his attempt to placate official and nonofficial Anglo-Indian opinion, he had strayed from the middle of the road in pursuit of a policy that was the very antithesis of Ripon's. The change of government at home and the advent of a new Secretary of State for India would carry him still further along the road away from any understanding with the educated Indian leaders and Mr. Hume.

VI

Lord Randolph Churchill: A Political Interlude

Throughout June, while Dufferin wrestled with Afghan strategy and Indian finance, and groped for a solution to the Volunteer question, the government at home faced a ministerial crisis, which resulted in the resignation of Gladstone.[1] Salisbury, after some reluctance, accepted the Queen's invitation to form an interim government, which Chamberlain dubbed "the Ministry of Caretakers," to carry on until the General Election could be held in November.[2] This new, Conservative government settled down to work on June 25, with Lord Randolph Churchill[3] as Secretary of State for India.

Then only in his thirty-sixth year, Churchill was wispy and slight, with a round, boyish face, protuberant, twinkling eyes, a disproportionately large moustache, and slicked-down hair. Add to this his liking for flamboyant, rakish clothes, and he was truly the caricaturist's delight. He was a complex individual, to his friends, engaging and imaginative, abrupt and assured, contemp-

---

[1] Morley, III, 200-202.

[2] Extract from Queen Victoria's Journal, June 10, Queen to S., June 23, 1885, G. E. Buckle, ed., *The Letters of Queen Victoria*, 2nd ser. III (London, 1928), 665, 678; Cecil, III, 134-135; A. L. Kennedy, *Salisbury 1830-1903; Portrait of a Statesman* (London, 1953), Ch. X; K. to D., June 19, 1885 (priv.), DVP, R. 517, No. 50.

[3] Churchill, Lord Randolph Henry Spencer, third son of the sixth Duke of Marlborough; b. 1849; Eton and Merton College, Oxford; B.A., 1870; Conservative M.P. for Woodstock, 1874, 1880; made reputation in 1878 for his attacks on subordinate members of Diseraeli's cabinet; formed the "Fourth Party" with D. Wolff, J. Gorst, and A. Balfour to expound aggressive, resolute Toryism; extended Conservatism to middle and working classes by clubs and the Primrose League; advocated concilia tion and extension of franchise to Ireland but not Home Rule; India, Jan.-Mar. 1885; Secretary of State for India, June 1885 to Feb. 1886.

tuous of the conventional, sympathetic and generous to the weak, disarmingly frank, witty and outrageous in speech, and with a talent for capitalizing on a changing situation, to his opponents, brash, ill-tempered, and wayward, ambitious and opportunistic, unscrupulous in tactics, extremely partisan, and devastatingly sarcastic and destructive in debate. To both friend and foe alike, he was a brilliant politician, actuated not necessarily by lofty principles but by a bluff honesty and sincerity of purpose.[4]

Political expediency alone dictated Churchill's inclusion in the cabinet. Salisbury, himself a man of fixed principles, greatly preferred guarded, reflective men who shunned the limelight, and he had never been attracted to Churchill. Salisbury disliked his impulsiveness, his volatile temper, and the strain of demagogy in his make-up.[5] However, it was not the established Tory Front Benchers, but Churchill and his young colleagues, who, in 1885, in revolt against the "old guard," were the prime movers behind the incessant, blistering opposition which tumbled Gladstone and his party from power.[6] Salisbury had no choice but to include Churchill in his government.

But Salisbury had his reasons for appointing Churchill to the India Office. It was a senior appointment, yet one where Churchill's lack of official and administrative experience and his unpredictable, impulsive character could do least harm.[7] Moreover, Salisbury, always in favor of an empirical approach, knew that Churchill was the one member entering the cabinet with firsthand knowledge of Indian affairs. Armed with letters of introduction from his friend, the radical politician W. Scawen Blunt, and from friends in Parliament, Churchill had visited India in the winter and spring of 1885[8] and had met a broad cross section of persons.[9] He talked, particularly about Afghan affairs, with Lord Dufferin, Sir James

[4] H. W. Lucy, *A Diary of Two Parliaments* (London, 1885-1886), II, 180; Blunt, *India under Ripon*, p. 12; E. Finch, *Wilfrid Scawen Blunt 1840-1922* (London, 1938), pp. 207-209, Blunt on Churchill in spring of 1885.

[5] Kennedy, pp. 55-59, 189, 198; Cecil, III, 26, 29, 88, 111.

[6] W. S. Churchill, *Lord Randolph Churchill* (London, 1906), I, 302-331; Lucy, pp. 453-454, 471; R. R. James, *Lord Randolph Churchill* (London, 1959), pp. 130-156, 175-176; editorial, *Times*, May 7, 1885; Northbrook to D., June 12 (priv.), June 19. 1885 (confid.), DVP, R. 525, nos. 41, 44.

[7] James, p. 189, quoting Northcote's diary: "Randolph was to have India, where, as Salisbury remarked, he would be prevented from doing much mischief by the Council at one end and Lord Dufferin at the other." See also extract from Queen Victoria's Journal, June 12, 1885, Buckle, III, 663; S. to D., Aug. 7, 1885 (priv. and personal), DVP, R. 525, No. 3.

[8] See Blunt, *India under Ripon*, pp. 9, 12, 230-231.

[9] See Churchill's letters of Jan.-Mar. 1885 to his wife and to his mother, in W. S. Churchill, I, Appendix IV.

Fergusson, A. C. Lyall, and General Roberts.[10] He met also the Maharaja of Indore, who left him with a lasting impression of the grievances of the Indian princes, and Raja Siva Prasad at Benares, James Wilson of *The Indian Daily News* and other members of the Anglo-Indian Defence Association, and Maharaja Jotindro Tagore and his colleagues of the British Indian Association, who were then opposing the Bengal Tenancy Bill.[11] In Bombay, he discussed Indian political reform with the younger Indian leaders, in particular Hume's friend, Lala Baijnath, and suggested the novel step of bringing Indian editors and politicians to England each summer to work with Parliamentary members in educating the British electorate on Indian affairs.[12] After these varied discussions, Churchill returned home with some idea of the difficult problems confronting the Indian government and of the issues exercising the minds of the landed aristocracy and the educated Indian leaders.

More important to Salisbury, Churchill returned with a deep sense of the British achievement in India and its significance for the far-flung Empire. His visit reinforced his belief that England derived her reputation and greatness in the eyes of the world from fulfilling her responsibilities to the Empire. The Empire was a traditional institution to be preserved at all costs; British rule in India was justified by this imperial mission and by the British investment in India that was so valuable to England. "Without India, England would cease to be a nation."[13] Thus Churchill was as much a dedicated "Disraelian Imperialist"[14] as Salisbury, who, as Foreign Secretary, wished to have someone at the India Office with identical interests when dealing with the Egyptian problem or the Russian threat, both of which were directly relevant to Indian policy.

But, unlike Salisbury, Churchill approached the problems of Empire from the standpoint of party politics. Convinced that the

[10] At the time, Dufferin wrote no one about Churchill's visit, although in mid-1885 and ten years later, after Churchill's death, Dufferin referred to their meeting; see D. to S., July 3, 1885 (priv. and personal), DVP, R. 525, No. 35, and James, p. 160.

[11] *Indian Mirror,* Feb. 12, *Hindoo Patriot,* Feb. 16, 1885.

[12] Meeting of Jan. 7, with B. M. Malabari, D. Naoroji, B. Tyabji, J. U. Yajnik, K. Telang, R. Sayani, D. E. Wacha, and N. Furdunji, see *Bombay Gazette,* Jan. 9, *Indian Spectator,* Jan. 11, *Bengalee,* Jan. 17, 1885; for Baijnath, see Churchill to his mother, Mar. 3, W. S. Churchill, I, 564, and Agra correspondent, *Indian Spectator,* Mar. 8, 1885.

[13] Speech at Paddington, May 6, *Times,* May 7, 1885; also at Aylesbury, June 18, 1884, and London, Apr. 18, 1885, L. J. Jennings, ed., *Speeches of the Right Honourable Lord Randolph Churchill, M.P., 1880-1888* (London, 1889), I, 152-158, 207-214.

[14] Blunt, *India under Ripon,* p. 9.

security of the Empire and India depended on a Conservative victory in the General Election, he "fought," as his close friend, Lord
Rosebery, remarked, "with any weapon that came to hand, intent
on the end rather than on the means. . . ."[15] In the years before
taking office, persistently and with withering effectiveness, he had
attacked Gladstone for enlarging the Empire in the wrong place,
Egypt, or for diminishing it, as in the Transvaal,[16] just when English industry needed markets to counter the effects of a world
depression.[17] Churchill felt strongly on this point. Since 1870,
American and German production had shaken the stability of
English production and distribution in home and foreign markets,
resulting in a depression which reached its lowest point in 1884
and 1885,[18] and adversely affected voters newly enfranchised in
1884, especially the wage-earners in the Midlands and northern
England, and also the small landholders and farmers.[19] Churchill
attacked the Liberals for failing to produce a remedy and called
for a greater imperial effort in Asia.[20] "India," he reminded the
Paddington voters just before his party took office, "is the only
free foreign market which we have at present." Gladstone's timid
and ineffective policy had shaken Indian loyalty and undermined
confidence in English investment in India and had added staggering
costs to the Indian and English budgets. To correct this rapidly
deteriorating situation, Churchill advocated a new—a Tory—
policy: externally, no further boundary concessions to the Russians
and immediate fulfillment of British pledges for the security of
India's frontier; internally, "a real and comprehensive Parliamentary inquiry into the whole operation of the Government of India"
with a view to possible areas of reform.[21]

Although Dufferin suspected that staying at his post under the
Tories would bring him "nothing but uneasiness and disquiet,"[22]
he chose to remain for financial reasons (the income from his estate
had fallen as a result of Irish land troubles and politics), and also

[15] Lord Rosebery, *Lord Randolph Churchill* (London, 1906), p. 27.

[16] Speech at Aylesbury; also at Edinburgh, Dec. 18, 1883, Blackpool, Jan. 24, 1884,
and Leeds, Oct. 3, 1884, Jennings, I, 70-85, 97-117, 164-183.

[17] Speeches at Blackpool and London; also at Birmingham, Apr. 15, 1884, Jennings,
I, 118-130.

[18] W. Ashworth, *An Economic History of England: 1870-1939* (London, 1960); also
E. Halévy, *Imperialism and the Rise of Labour*, 2nd ed., V (London, 1951), 292,
296-298.

[19] E. L. Woodward, *The Age of Reform, 1815-1870*, 7th ed., (London, 1958).

[20] Speech to Blackpool Conservative Association, Jan. 24, *Times*, Jan. 25, 1884.

[21] Speeches at Paddington, May 6, Tower Hamlets, June 3, Bow, June 4, *Times*,
May 7, June 4, 5, 1885; at London, Apr. 18, 1885, Jennings, I, 213-214; in House of
Commons, May 4, 1885, Parliamentary Debates, 3 *Hansard*, 297:1524-1541.

[22] D. to K., June 12, 1885 (priv.), DVP, R. 517, No. 39.

to keep the viceroyalty out of "the vortex of party politics."[23] He little realized that the Queen was determined that he should remain,[24] and that both Salisbury and Churchill had made his continuance at Calcutta a precondition for accepting office. In greetings to Dufferin on behalf of the cabinet, Churchill defined their working relations: "Our one desire . . . [is] to be mainly, and even entirely, guided by your advice, and to support, to the utmost of our power, the policy which you may recommend to us."[25] Yet Dufferin was uncertain. He was fully alive to Churchill's political foibles, his irritating espousal in Parliament of the zemindari opposition to the Bengal Tenancy Act,[26] and his disastrous wooing of the Parnellite vote.[27] So Dufferin wrote Salisbury, asking that he act as "an additional safeguard" against any indiscretion on Churchill's part.[28] Worried especially about Indian external affairs and Indian finances, Dufferin wanted a strong, intelligent lead from the Secretary of State for India. He soon learned that Churchill was thinking about the same problems—but with decidedly different ideas.

During his initial three months in office, Churchill concentrated exclusively and deliberately on Indian external and financial policy, since these would have a direct bearing on the General Election. Churchill and his colleagues were not pleased with the late government's Afghan policy. They wanted an immediate solution to the Russo-Afghan imbroglio so that they could cut the soaring military charges, which were embarrassing for any English peacetime budget, especially in an election year. Specifically, they wanted to be able to release the English Reservists called out in April and still awaiting orders for Kandahar, in the event of hostilities, and also the Militiamen, on orders to replace the Reservists whenever the latter left for India.[29] Furthermore, convinced that the Liberals' policy had been so favorable to Russian aims in Central Asia that the Russians would seek "to influence the November elections and impair the position of the Tory party," and recalling Gladstone's performance in 1879, when, to the detriment of the Tories, he persuaded the public that the Christian, civilizing mission of the

[23] D. to S., July 3, 1885 (priv. and personal), DVP, R. 525, No. 35.
[24] Extract from Queen Victoria's Journal, June 24, 1885, Buckle, III, 679-680.
[25] C. to D., June 26, 1885 (priv.), DVP, R. 517, No. 53; also S. to Queen, June 25, 1885, Buckle, III, 680.
[26] D. to K., Feb. 13, 1885 (priv.), DVP, R. 517, No. 11.
[27] D. to Reay, June 18, 1885 (priv.), DVP, R. 528, No. 195.
[28] D. to S., July 8, 1885 (priv. and personal), DVP, R. 525, No. 195.
[29] See Parliamentary Debates, 3 *Hansard*, 299 (July 9, 1885), 127-139; editorial, *Times*, July 10, 1885; C. to D., July 24, 1885, DVP, R. 517, No. 60, Secretary of State to Viceroy, telegram, July 30, 1885 (secret), R. 519, No. 231.

Russians made it wrong for England to support the "heathen" Turk, Churchill feared a repeat performance over Afghanistan.[30] He also feared that a successful Russian *coup de main* on Herat just before the election would have "disastrous effects" on English and Indian public opinion and expose the Tories to charges of having failed to defend the town and of having smeared a new blot upon the British imperial escutcheon.[31] Finally, he feared that the Russians might purposely protract the boundary negotiations in order to force the British government to maintain "a scale of military preparations unendurable to peace and . . . with no inconsiderable humiliation and discredit to the Imperial Government."[32]

To forestall these developments, Churchill set to work to scrap the existing policy of the Indian government and devise a more aggressive policy, which would compel the Russians to accept the English position in Afghanistan and Central Asia, and convince the British public that the Tory cabinet intended to settle the question in a manner consonant with British honor and imperial interests. Suspicious of the intentions of both the Russians and the Amir, Churchill maintained that both St. Petersburg and Kabul required what had been so conspicuously absent in the Afghan policy to date: firm handling and veiled threats. He urged wooing Bismarck away from the Russians by purchasing his support for British policy in Central Asia with a quid pro quo in Africa. He advocated warning the Russian Foreign Office that failure to accept the original British boundary proposals, which had held the Russians well to the north of the Afghan-Turcoman territory, and to dispatch a team to delimitate the area within a fixed time period would cause the British government to break off all negotiations and that any Russo-Afghan clash would be considered as a *casus belli*.[33] Furthermore, he wished to impress the Russians by holding extensive military manoeuvres with one of the *corps d'armée* and some of the princely armies at Delhi or Amballa at about the time of the election, with foreign, especially Russian, military attachés in attendance. Churchill also proposed that, under threat of tearing up the Agreement of 1880 and leaving the Amir to his fate,

[30] C. to D., July 10, 1885, DVP, R. 517, No. 56; also C. to Queen, July 11, 1885, W. S. Churchill, I, 485-486.

[31] C. to D., July 17, 1885, DVP, R. 517, No. 58; Secretary of State to Viceroy, two telegrams, July 21, 1885 (priv.), R. 519, nos. 215, 216.

[32] Secretary of State to Viceroy, telegram, July 30, 1885 (secret), DVP, R. 519, No. 231.

[33] Secretary of State to Viceroy, telegrams, June 27 and July 8 (priv.), June 27, 1885 (secret), DVP, R. 519, nos. 174, 191, 175; C. to D., June 26, July 2-3, 17, 24, R. 517, nos. 53, 54, 58, 60.

he be forced to fulfill the agreement, accept a British Resident or officers to supervise the defense of Herat as well as officers to be posted along any future Russo-Afghan boundary, and make proper use of British military aid then being supplied.[34]

By the end of June, when Churchill's communications on Afghan policy began arriving in Calcutta, Dufferin's conception of the forward strategy had changed from an active one aimed at Herat and Kandahar to a passive one with troops held in readiness for advance to Kandahar in an emergency.[35] So Dufferin found himself in the position of having to concentrate most of his thought and energy on opposing Churchill's many suggestions on external problems, at the expense of other phases of Indian administration. With the concurrence of his chief advisers on strategy—Durand and Lyall, and Generals Stewart, Johnson, and Roberts—Dufferin informed Churchill that the Executive Council believed that the Herat strategy was not only dangerous and unnecessary, but also impossible so long as the Amir refused to go along with it.[36] Moreover, at the outset of the crisis, he had mistaken for public support of the forward strategy what were really loyal manifestations for the defense of India and India alone.[37] But in June, when the offers of Indian money and volunteers had ceased, and the leading Indian journals were bitterly criticizing him for indulging in a recklessly expensive strategy, based upon distrust of Indians, he began to realize for the first time what Colvin had sensed much earlier, that educated Indian opinion was out of sympathy with the Afghan and financial policies of the Government. The recent "monster public meeting" in Bengal, at which "the preservation of peace was vehemently insisted on," had further enlightened him.[38]

He was referring to the meeting at Jhinkergatchi in Jessore, where certain zemindars, pleaders of the Jessore and Calcutta Bar associations, and members of the Indian Association had staged a rally of some 25,000 to 50,000 ryots.[39] Resolutions calling for peace,

[34] Secretary of State to Viceroy, telegrams, July 3, 4, 8, 9, 15, July 8 and Aug. 4 (priv.), two on July 3 (secret), July 30, 1885 (secret) , DVP, R. 519, nos. 185, 186, 190, 196, 204, 191, 239, 183, 184, 231; C. to D., July 2-3, 10, 1885, R. 517, nos. 54, 56.

[35] See above p. 91.

[36] Viceroy to Secretary of State, telegram, June 29, 1885 (priv.), DVP, R. 519, No. 124; D. to C., July 3, 1885 (priv.), R. 517, No. 41.

[37] D. to Northbrook, May 5, 1885 (priv.), DVP, R. 525, No. 23.

[38] Viceroy to Secretary of State, telegram, June 29, 1885 (priv.), DVP, R. 519, No. 124.

[39] See *Statesman*, June 21, *Indian Mirror*, June 21, 23, 24, 26, 27, *Bengalee*, June 27, 1885. The idea of the meeting was attributed to Shishir and Motilal Ghose. Leaders included Piari Mohan Guha, pleader and Chairman of Jessore Municipality; Prosunno Kumar Dass, pleader, Judge's Court, Jessore; Kali Nath Mookerjee, pleader

because the people, overburdened with taxes, were in no position to pay for extra military preparations, had been circulated previously for discussion among the important villages. One thousand *mundals,* or village head men, were on hand to support the resolutions, which were incorporated in a memorial. With the formation of a ryoti political organization, the Barwari Association, the meeting adjourned. The Anglo-Indian editor, Robert Knight, concluded that the meeting "inaugurated a new era in the history of political agitation in India," one in which ryots would organize en masse to seek political ends, and he warned the Government that it would be well to pay attention to its significance.[40]

For once, Dufferin did pay attention, and he telegraphed Churchill: "I do not think a war with Russia would be popular in India."[41] To reinforce this view, he wrote a few days later: "It is known that our preparations for sending an army corps to Quetta have cost more than two millions, and everybody understands that a declaration of hostilities would imply heavy additional taxation." The Indian government could not possibly pursue any other Afghan policy than that which he and Kimberley had developed.[42] In opposing Churchill, Dufferin won Salisbury's support for his "buffer" policy. The boundary negotiations were continued, with no time limit or threat of military action; neither British officers nor troops were pressed on the Amir.[43] Dufferin had prevailed.

Meanwhile, the problem of imperial markets for English industry was also occupying Churchill's attention. Soon after taking office, he was confronted with the pleas of British merchants for assistance from the Indian government in expanding British trade in the East. In dealing with these, he became directly involved with the "Burmese question."[44] Ever since Dalhousie's annexation

and landholder, member of Jessore Indian Association; Umesh Chandra Ghosh, pleader, member of District Board and Jessore Indian Association; and Tarapada Banerjee, pleader, member of Indian Association who conceived the scheme for the National Fund.

[40] *Statesman,* June 20, 1885.

[41] Viceroy to Secretary of State, telegram, June 29, 1885 (priv.), DVP, R. 519 No. 124.

[42] D. to C., July 3, 1885 (priv.), DVP, R. 517, No. 41.

[43] See C. to D., July 2-3 (priv.), D. to C., July 10, 30, July 3 and Aug. 7, 1885 (priv.), DVP, R. 517, nos. 54, 43, 47, 42, 48; Viceroy to Secretary of State telegrams, July 4, 8, two on July 4 (secret), July 10 and Aug. 2 (secret), July 5, 10 and Aug. 3, 1885 (priv.), R. 519, nos. 132, 139, 129, 131, 141, 186, 134, 142, 187.

[44] For the Burmese question, see J. Nisbet, *Burma under British Rule—and Before* (London, 1901), I; the chapters by G. E. Harvey in *The Cambridge History of India,* ed. H. H. Dodwell, V, VI; A. C. Banerjee, *Annexation of Burma* (Calcutta, 1944), based solely on *Parliamentary Papers;* J. F. Cady, *A History of Modern Burma* (New York, 1958), a broad survey with minimal reference to viceregal MSS; D. Woodman,

of the lower, or Pegu, portion of the Kingdom of Ava, both the Home and Indian governments had treated Upper Burma as a British sphere of influence, from which all foreign intervention, political and commercial, was to be excluded. They feared that Europeans, especially the French, might gain the upper hand at the Court of Ava and use Mandalay as a base for military or subversive operations against British Burma, or across the Assam hills into India. Such a development would adversely affect mercantile interests not only in Rangoon, Bombay, and Calcutta, but also in Manchester, Sheffield, Leeds, Liverpool, Glasgow, and London, to say nothing of the revenues of the Indian government. From 1880 to 1884 alone, the total value of British exports to British Burma was £6,875,000; this was owing to the high per-capita consumption of the Burmese, especially the prosperous small landholders who controlled the bulk of the rice-growing "industry" and whose principal market was Upper Burma, where from 1880 to 1884 the total value of British Burma's export trade (mostly rice) amounted to £3,224,814. Should British Burma lose this market, much of its prosperity and trade with England would also vanish. This lucrative export trade meant an average revenue surplus of £750,000 per year for British Burma from 1876 to 1883, and £885,663 in 1884, which directly and indirectly benefited the supreme government.[45] Thus, British officials and traders looked upon Upper Burma as personal property not to be trespassed upon by outsiders.

But King Mindon, his successor, King Thibaw, and their ministers looked at it from a very different angle. They steadfastly refused to conduct their relations with Her Majesty's Government through the Government of India, and pressed for full diplomatic status at the Court of St. James. The Hlutdaw (Council) regarded treaties made with the Indian Government as articles in no wise binding, since they were signed under duress and not by accredited representatives of the British Crown. This was particularly applicable to commercial and juridical clauses relating to British trade: in the face of the treaties of 1862 and 1867, the Hlutdaw continued the royal monopolies[46] and applied Burmese royal law

The Making of Burma (London, 1962), misleading as to available official and vice-regal MSS, especially the few references to the Dufferin MSS; A. Fytche, *Burma Past and Present*, 2 vols. (London, 1878); W. F. B. Laurie, *Our Burmese Wars and Relations with Burma*, 2nd ed. (London, 1885).

[45] Laurie, pp. 137, 163, 164, 166.

[46] Dispatches of Governor-General-in-Council, No. 59, For., Mar. 7, 1879, No. 6, For., Jan. 14, 1880, with memorandum by C. U. Aitchison (Chief Commissioner, British Burma), Dec. 6, 1879, *P.P.*, 1886, Vol. 50, Com. 4614, pp. 11-19, 66-69, 72-73; Anglo-Burmese negotiations of 1882-1883; *P.P.*, 1883, Vol. 50, Com. 3501.

to British merchants and sailors on the Upper Irrawaddy.[47] Since the Hlutdaw never officially acknowledged the British Resident or allowed him to deal with disputes between British traders and the Court of Ava, in 1879 the British withdrew the Resident and representation at the Court ceased. Acting with the same independence, the Hlutdaw sent two diplomatic missions to Europe, one in 1873 and another in 1883, which established relations with the French and the Italians. Premier Jules Ferry, whose imperialist ambitions had led to rapid French expansion in Tunisia, West Africa, and Tongking, in January 1885 signed a diplomatic and trade agreement with the Court of Ava,[48] and, in July, a Burmese plenipotentiary was assigned to Paris while a French Vice-Consul, M. Haas, arrived at Mandalay accredited to handle all commercial and political matters between the two governments. This Franco-Burmese rapprochement shook the confidence of the British trading community in Rangoon, and created an immediate stir in commercial circles in England.

Soon after taking office, Churchill was visited by representatives of A. Milne and Company of Glasgow, a Scots firm with extensive commercial interests in Rangoon, and by K. B. Murray, the Secretary of the London Chamber of Commerce.[49] Speaking on behalf of the Rangoon Chamber and all the London shippers and merchants with a stake in Burmese and Southeast Asian trade, they drew Churchill's attention to the deteriorating situation in Upper Burma and to the ominous predictions in the press of Rangoon, Calcutta, and London concerning the future of British trade at Mandalay, coupled with rumors of preferential privileges for the French. The representatives of A. Milne and Company charged that the late Government's policy toward Ava was "feeble and vacillating," and wished to know whether the new cabinet would reverse this policy "either by annexation or by the establishment of a protectorate . . ." Representatives from Wallace Brothers, managing agency for the Bombay Burma Trading Corporation, Ltd., urged Churchill to give the question his immediate attention.

This joint-stock company was the largest British timber concern in Burma, conducting extensive teak logging operations under

[47] See incidents *re* the river steamers "Shwe Myo" and "Yunnan," 1879-1881, *P.P.,* 1886, Vol. 50, Com. 4614, pp. 66-71, 88-91, 91-93, 100-102.

[48] Franco-Burmese Commercial Convention of Jan. 15, 1885. See Lord Lyons (British Ambassador in Paris) to Granville, Jan. 16, 1885, and copy of convention, *P.P.,* 1886, Vol. 50, Com. 4614, pp. 122, 240-246; Secretary of State to Viceroy, telegram, Jan. 31, 1885 (secret), DVP, R. 519, No. 103.

[49] Milne and Co. to C., July 6, Murray to C., July 16, 1885, *P.P.,* 1886, Vol. 50, Com. 4614, pp. 166-167.

contracts with the Court of Ava in the royal forests of Ningyan and Chindwin Moo.[50] In 1885, with teak exports and profits declining because of the industrial depression in England and Europe, the Court decided to raise the royalties for the logging leases, and, at the height of the brief logging season, to investigate charges brought against the corporation by Burmese foresters, who claimed that they had not been paid for all logs felled and that the corporation had attempted to conceal the fact by bribing Burmese officials. The Rangoon management, fearing a complete loss on the corporation's large capital outlay and, angered by the investigation, refusing to admit even the possibility of illegal activities, looked to London for help when the Chief Commissioner of British Burma, Charles E. Bernard,[51] declined to interfere. They telegraphed Wallace Brothers a report from their representative at Mandalay, the Italian Vice-Consul, Andreino, that there was reason to believe that the Hlutdaw planned to fine the corporation heavily or retract the leases *in toto* in order to acquire greater capital resources for entering into railway and banking contracts with the French. Milne and his colleagues had merely issued warnings; Wallace Brothers intended to enlist the services of the Secretary of State to solve the Burmese question and save the corporation.

Churchill responded with enthusiasm and lost no time in telegraphing the intelligence to Dufferin and asking for his "views as to the course which should be followed."[52] Dufferin was guarded in his response. The previous winter the Gladstone government had rejected forceful intervention when the Rangoon Chamber of Commerce had started agitating about disorder in Upper Burma and the alleged ill effects on British trade of the Franco-Burmese commercial treaty, and when Bernard had proposed sending a 3,000-man force to Mandalay. Dufferin concurred, but with one reservation: "If the French intrigues should eventuate in any serious attempt to forestall us in Upper Burma, I should not hesitate to annex the country."[53] When Churchill's telegram arrived, Duf-

[50] Nisbet, I, 76. For lease agreements between Court of Ava and Bombay Burma Corporation, charges against the corporation by Court of Ava, Bernard's action, and Andreino's letters, with enclosures, see *P.P.*, 1886, Vol. 50, Com. 4614, pp. 185-188, 179-180, 182, 172-175.

[51] B. 1837, nephew of John Lawrence; Rugby, Addiscombe, Haileybury; Bengal Civil Service, posted to the Punjab and Central Provinces, 1858-1871; Secretary, Bengal Government, member of Bengal Legislative Council, 1871-1875; Famine Secretary during Bihar famine of 1874; C.S.I., 1875; Secretary to Sir R. Temple's famine mission, 1877; Home Secretary, Government of India, 1878-1880; Chief Commissioner, British Burma, 1880-1888.

[52] Secretary of State to Viceroy, telegram, July 25, 1885, DVP, R. 519, No. 223.

ferin had already received the same intelligence from Bernard, who recommended that the Indian government should officially call upon the Court of Ava to break off negotiations with the French, and, if it failed to comply, the Government should intervene and annex the Kingdom.[54] But Dufferin, aware of Bernard's excitable temperament, preferred to see copies of the contracts and ascertain for himself how far negotiations had progressed before acting forcefully.[55] He accepted the advice of Ilbert that an ultimatum to the Court of Ava on such flimsy information was certain to be refused, thereby compelling the Indian government to make good its threat of force at a moment when the Indian army and budget were overstrained to meet the requirements of the Quetta-Kandahar strategy. Ilbert also warned of the uncertainties as to the reactions of the Indian Princes and the Imperial Government of China with its nebulous ties to Ava. On Ilbert's proposal for the announcement of a British "Monroe Doctrine" for Upper Burma, coupled with a diplomatic understanding with the French, Dufferin gained unanimous agreement from the Executive Council, although they added that, if the French did not desist from meddling, or if the contracts revealed that the negotiations were completed, Bernard's recommendation should be acted upon. Colvin, looking ahead, disliked Bernard's glib logic that interference meant annexation; knowing only too well what financial burdens annexation would entail, he persuaded the majority of the council to append a warning statement to the official telegram to Churchill: "We should consider it a misfortune on many accounts to be forced to adopt coercive measures. The time is most inopportune; we are opposed on principle to an annexationist policy, and the acquisition of Upper Burma would entail upon us considerable responsibilities."[56] Dufferin, in sharp contrast to his action earlier in the year on Afghanistan, now followed the advice of Ilbert and Colvin rather than

[53] D. to K., Jan. 12 and Feb. 10, 1885 (priv.), DVP, R. 517, nos. 6, 10; Viceroy to Secretary of State, telegram, Jan. 12 (priv.), Secretary of State to Viceroy, telegram, Jan. 14, 1885 (priv.), R. 519, nos. 62, 70; K. to D., Jan. 29 and Feb. 13, 1885 (priv.), R. 517, nos. 15, 18; D to Bernard, Feb 25, 1885 (priv.), R. 528, No. 71b. Also Bernard's Secretary to H. M. Durand, Secretary, Government of India, Foreign Department, Jan. 15, Durand to Bernard, Feb. 10, Dispatch of Secretary of State in Council No. 13, For., May 1, 1885, *P.P.*, 1886, Vol. 50, Com. 4614, pp. 145-146, 156, 160-161.

[54] Bernard's telegram quoted in full in Viceroy to Secretary of State, telegram, July 29, 1885 (secret), DVP, R. 519, No. 171.

[55] D. to Napier, July 30, 1885 (priv.), DVP, R. 525, No. 39.

[56] For council session and recommendations, see Viceroy to Secretary of State, telegram, Aug. 2, 1885 (secret), DVP, R. 519, No. 185; Colvin to Wallace, Aug. 2, 1885, R. 528, No. 109.

that of his generals and political officers, and he considered Indian finances first in making his decision.

With this decision the cabinet readily agreed.[57] Salisbury, then trying to settle the Afghan and Egyptian questions, did not wish to provoke the French by precipitous action in Upper Burma, and began making plans to take up matters with the French Foreign Office. Churchill, then preparing the Indian Budget Statement, momentarily agreed to hold in abeyance Bernard's plan of intervention, and Dufferin, having studied the documents, reassured Churchill that the Franco-Burmese negotiations were far from being concluded.[58]

The Indian Budget Statement, Churchill considered, would have wide political significance for the fortunes of the Tory Party in the November election. From the moment he stepped into office, he was aware of the unsatisfactory position of the Indian finances. While the Indian government needed funds for railway construction during 1885, it would have to expand its revenues by direct taxes during 1886-87 if certain military proposals materialized. Once Churchill began to seek a solution to these difficulties, it quickly dawned on him how serious the political implications of the Indian financial jumble could be for the Tory Party.

This lesson he learned from the debate on the East India Railway Loan Bill (No. 109), introduced by the late government, to allow the Indian government to borrow £10 millions sterling for its program of railway construction and other demands. Churchill proceeded with the bill once the cabinet had agreed to continue the Afghan "buffer" strategy, but charges levelled during the debate by Radicals, Independents, and liberal-minded Tories that the bill would increase the Indian debt, necessitate heavy Indian taxation, and have adverse effects upon commercial railway development and the investors' confidence,[59] made Churchill realize that Salisbury's cabinet was being held responsible for the bill and being severely criticized for proceeding with it. Although he advanced the bill to the Upper House, he came away irked that he and his colleagues had been criticized for an Indian financial policy that was not of their own making. He needed to put the record straight as soon as possible, and so he wrote Dufferin: "It is absolutely due to the present government that I should take the earliest opportunity to divest them of all responsibility for the

[57] Secretary of State to Viceroy, telegram, Aug. 3, 1885 (secret), DVP, R. 519, No. 234.
[58] Viceroy to Secretary of State, two telegrams, Aug. 4, 1885 (secret), DVP, R. 519, nos. 189, 190.
[59] Parliamentary Debates, 3 *Hansard*, 298 (July 6, 1885), 1777-1789.

events which have necessitated an increased expenditure. This I should not be doing if I failed to give the House of Commons some preliminary information as to what may be the state of Indian finances next year."[60] The best moment, Churchill decided, for releasing this information would be the evening in the first week of August when he presented the Indian Budget Statement before the Commons. On July 28 he telegraphed Dufferin to send along figures on "the amount of extra charge which Indian finance will have to bear in consequence of frontier defences and the increase of the army."[61] On July 30 Dufferin telegraphed that the estimates and final proposals would be examined in Council within a week or so.[62] Back came a telegram the same day from Churchill saying this would not do and that the Viceroy was to send the best information available "without waiting for Council."[63] Dufferin, somewhat shaken by this urgency and unclear why Churchill wanted the information, sat down with Colvin and hastily prepared a concise summary of the military proposals and financial recommendations for 1886-87.

The summary[64] included alternative proposals for troop increases. The Commander-in-Chief, General Stewart, proposed an increase of 16,000 British troops and 24,470 Indian, while the Military Department proposed an increase of 10,657 British troops and 17,840 Indian. Colvin and the Financial Department estimated that the former would cost annually £1,900,000, and the latter £1,500,000. For additional frontier railways and defensive works, the Military Department submitted new estimates for the five-to-six-year program, amounting to some £3 millions, instead of £1,600,000 as forecast earlier. As for Ways and Means to cover the increased troop expenditure, Colvin proposed expanding the existing revenue by £1,300,000 per year, of which £700,000 was to come from converting the license tax into an income-license tax of 2 per cent on all incomes of 500 rupees and above per annum, and of 2.5 per cent on incomes of 2,000 rupees and above. "The rest," Colvin advised, "could be furnished by raising 4 annas on the Salt Duty . . ." To pay for the frontier railways and fortifications, he recommended, first, decreasing the amounts drawn annually from revenue and from the Famine Insurance Fund for internal (commercial) railways, second, giving priority to frontier

[60] C. to D., July 17, 1885, DVP, R. 517, No. 58.
[61] Secretary of State to Viceroy, telegram, July 28, 1885, DVP, R. 519, No. 228.
[62] Viceroy to Secretary of State, telegram, July 30, 1885, DVP, R. 519, No. 175.
[63] Secretary of State to Viceroy, telegram, July 30, 1885, DVP, R. 519, No. 229.
[64] Viceroy to Secretary of State, telegram, Aug. 2, 1885 (priv.), DVP, R. 519, No. 183.

defense railways over commercial and famine railways, and third, capitalizing £200,000 of the famine grant to meet annual interest on the three railways assigned to guaranteed companies. Colvin omitted any mention of a further depreciation of the rupee and its probable charge against Indian revenues.

When on August 2 Dufferin telegraphed this summary to Churchill, he added a specific request: as the figures had not been examined in Council, they should "not be disclosed at present in Parliament, where discussion would be premature and prove very embarrassing to this Government."[65] But Churchill, with three days to go before the Budget Statement, discussed Dufferin's summary as well as the whole state of Indian finances with an array of wizards, including Sir John Strachey, whom Churchill was about to appoint to the India Council, Sir Evelyn Baring, then on home leave from Egypt, and Lord Lytton.[66] Of the three, Lytton gave Churchill the recommendations that best fitted his political designs.

Lytton pointed out to Churchill that an income tax would raise "a howl in India," as in Lawrence's time, and an increase in the salt duty would be "powerfully opposed in England," whereas the part of Colvin's proposal calling for an extension of the existing license tax to official and other incomes would have no adverse political effects. Lytton favored the income-license tax together with severe retrenchment of Hope's vast public works program, a step which, he charged, Ripon had failed to take and so left no surplus. Lytton also suggested that Churchill discontinue the construction out of revenue of "famine-protective" railways and other projects and employ the Famine Insurance Fund and the provincial governments' surpluses "for general imperial purposes *in case of necessity*" as originally specified by Strachey. Finally, Lytton recommended the construction of all frontier fortifications and railways—military, commercial, and famine—from loans. Churchill accepted all of Lytton's ideas.[67] Shortly thereafter he drafted the Indian Budget Statement for 1885-86, drawing upon the meaty ingredients of Dufferin's military facts and figures, Lytton's recommendations, and his own political genius.

On the evening of August 6, Churchill presented the Statement before the Commons.[68] It was an unusually crowded occasion for an Indian budget because of the keen interest in everything Churchill

[65] Viceroy to Secretary of State, telegram, Aug. 2, 1885 (priv.), DVP, R. 519, No. 184.
[66] See C. to D., July 2-3, 31, 1885, DVP, R. 517, nos. 54, 62; Secretary of State to Viceroy, telegram, Aug. 7, 1885 (priv.), R. 519, No. 243.
[67] See L. to D., Sept. 1, 1885, DVP, R. 525, No. 73.
[68] Parliamentary Debates, 3 *Hansard,* 300:1286-1315.

had to say. Speaking crisply and punctuating his remarks intermittently with gestures directed at the Opposition benches, he reviewed in a detailed yet lucid manner the trials and tribulations of the Indian government in meeting the financial ills of the year. The net result was "an unprovided charge of £1,500,000 and the celebrated Famine Insurance Fund practically eaten up." "Not a very exhilarating financial statement," he affirmed, lowering his voice, "and it is rather hard upon a Minister coming into office so recently." Continuing in a sombre tone, he pointed out that the picture for the coming years was even darker. Commencing in 1886, the Indian government would have to spend an extra £2 millions annually from Indian revenues for "an indefinite period of time" on new weapons and troop increases. This was the high price of Indian security, but he for one thought it could not be paid soon enough. Here he introduced *in extenso* Lytton's recommendations, which, he agreed, were drastic, but absolutely imperative under the circumstances.

At this point, he turned to the central issue of his Statement. He had given all these facts, figures, and prognostications not to alarm anyone about the condition of Indian finances, but "to fix the responsibility for the present state of things on the right shoulders, and to interest public opinion, and bring home to the electors, the real nature and character of the case." He believed that the Viceroy's most important duty was to look ahead and make provision for the future. Living in a despotic paradise without the trammels of influential political parties, powerful newspapers, and critical electors to worry about, the Viceroy could plan for the future as effectively and freely as he liked, and failure to do so was tantamount to irresponsibility and shortsightedness. Unfortunately, the depressing figures that he had laid before them showed that irresponsibility and shortsightedness had been present in Indian financial policy. Who was responsible for this appalling state of affairs? Lord Dufferin? Certainly not. "Neither the Government of Lord Dufferin in India nor the Government of Lord Salisbury at home can in any way be held responsible." He made no mention of Dufferin's costly Herat and Kandahar strategies. Raising his voice and casting a lowering glance at Hartington, J. K. Cross, and others lolling on the Opposition front bench, he answered, "Lord Ripon," and, to uneasy coughs and a sudden stirring in the House, he began a withering indictment of the late Viceroy's policy "of recklessness and carelessness." Kandahar and the Quetta railway had been abandoned, the British and Indian garrisons dangerously reduced in strength, customs duties all but abolished and excise on salt reduced, yet public works had been greatly increased; and all because "Lord Ripon slept lulled by the languor of the land of the lotus. . . . I disown and repudiate on behalf of the present Government," he growled, "all responsibility of any sort or kind for that policy, and I hold up that Viceroyalty and the Government responsible for it to the censure and the condemnation of the British and Indian peoples." Fortunately, he added, all was not lost, thanks to the foresight and genius of Lord Lytton and Sir John Strachey, who had decentralized Indian finance, stimulated construction of commercial railways, and equalized the excise on salt. Indian revenues possessed "vitality" and would recover, and the Indian government would be able to surmount Lord Ripon's legacy of irresponsible blunders.

Bursts of cheers and angry yells greeted his remarks about Ripon, and virtual pandemonium broke loose upon his vindication of Lytton. But he had not yet finished. He still had a word for each of the groups who might well prove troublesome for his Indian policy. After allotting tasty political plums to the Anti-Opium party, the old India hands, and the Liberal Imperialists, he turned toward John Slagg and the Manchester Radicals, and to the Irish group, and announced that "Her Majesty's Government have decided that, if they are in office next year, they will propose a Parliamentary inquiry into the system of government in India." This was long overdue; in the forty-seven years since the last inquiry, India had changed socially and politically. Like his friends Blunt and Baring, he admitted that this change had produced "a large body of intelligent native opinion, which, perhaps, has not been allowed to exercise that amount of influence on the Government of India which may now be regarded as reasonable, healthy and safe." This opinion as well as that of "experienced Anglo-Indian authorities" would now be sought to ascertain the defects of the governing machinery. Finally, looking ahead to the election, he appealed to the English electorate and the members of Parliament "to watch, develop and guard with undying resolution, the land and the people of Hindusthan, that most truly bright and precious gem in the crown of the Queen, the possession of which, more than that of all your colonial dominions, has raised in power, in resources, in wealth and in authority this small island home of ours far above the level of the majority of nations and of States." With this ruffle on the imperial drum, he took his seat amidst the cheers and demonstrations of the Tory benches, while the Liberals looked on, frozen with anger.

Churchill had scored all his points. He had set forth an Indian financial policy to appeal to Independents and radical Liberals; he had given notice that the Tory cabinet was providing for the defense of India at no cost to English taxpayers; and he had placed the responsibility for Indian financial ills upon Ripon's shoulders and avenged the reputation of Lytton and the Tory Party. How effectively Churchill had done his work was demonstrated by the disarray of the Opposition during rebuttal. He had won hands down. Even the adverse reactions in the days to follow did not trouble him. Of the editors, only his friend George Buckle of *The Times* "found much that was substantially just" in Churchill's criticism and supported his Statement.[69] Northbrook, though admitting it was "a very good speech," tossed it off as "an electioneering attack on Ripon."[70] Kimberley frowned upon it, but considered it "very important" as it came from "the chief Power on the Tory side."[71] Salisbury greeted it offhandedly as "an oratorical success, but it will produce rebutter and sur-rebutter."[72] Churchill apologized for having taken it upon himself to exceed Dufferin's instructions, but in reality he had no regrets. "It was absolutely incumbent on me," he explained to the Viceroy, "to divest the present Government of all responsibility from the heavy expenditure entailed upon India by the Russian advance, and this led me into a criticism of Lord Ripon's policy, which was no doubt of a very controversial character, and of which the other side strongly complained. But self-preservation is the first law of nature, and of Governments, and in view of the coming election and of a possible second Midlothian campaign, and of the extreme unscrupulousness of the Radical Party in attributing every kind of foreign difficulty and of large expenditure to Tory Jingoism and extravagance, I had no other course open to me." And he added, "It would have been a pity not to have prepared the House for a considerable increase of military expenditure, for which the Parliament and the public is at present in the most favourable mood."[73] By using the Indian Budget Statement in this way, he had executed a skillful opening gambit for the political contest which lay ahead.

The policy of maximum Indian military strength at minimal increase of Indian taxes which Churchill had set forth in his budget speech was very different from the recommendations that he

[69] *Times,* Aug. 7, 1885.

[70] Northbrook to D., Aug. 7, 1885 (priv.), DVP, R. 525, No. 61.

[71] K. to Godley, Aug. 20, 1885 (priv.), Kilbracken MSS, CRO, Eur. F. 102, Bundle 3.

[72] S. to D., Aug. 7, 1885 (priv.), DVP, R. 525, No. 63.

[73] C. to D., Aug. 7, 1885, DVP, R. 517, No. 63. See also the *Times* report of Budget Statement, as sent by Secretary of State to Viceroy, telegram, Aug. 7, 1885 (priv.), R. 519, No. 243.

received from Calcutta the following day.[74] Dufferin and his Council had agreed on the troop increase proposed by the Military
Department, costing some £1.5 millions, to be paid for by an income
tax on all official and nonofficial incomes, except those derived from
land, at a rate of 2 per cent on incomes of 500 rupees or above and
at 3 per cent on incomes of 2,000 rupees or above per annum. This
marked a sharp shift from the proposals for raising revenue in the
summary Dufferin had forwarded to Churchill before his Budget
Statement.

The genius behind this sudden change was Mr. Hope, the Public
Works Member, whom both Lytton and Ripon considered one of
the most clever, unscrupulous officials in the Indian government.
Recognizing that some increase of troops was a virtual certainty,
which would entail either taxation or retrenchment, Hope decided
beforehand to influence the Viceroy and the Council in favor of a
large income tax instead of broad retrenchment, which necessarily
would fall upon his vast empire of railway, dam, roads, and building
projects, and he set about striking down Colvin's proposals for light
direct taxation and a small increase in the salt duty, both of which
Hope thought would be insufficient to cover the additional military
expenditure. Keenly alive to the Viceroy's weaknesses, especially his
sensitivity to Ripon's extraordinary popularity, Hope wrote Dufferin two days before the council session. "A full direct tax" was not
to be dreaded, "while an increased Salt Tax, except in the greatest
emergency, is so. . . . The latter would probably be greatly directed
against your Lordship personally, in contrast to Lord Ripon, in a
way which, though quite unjust, would be none the less regretta-
ble."[75] As Hope subsequently noted, he was apprehensive lest the
government and particularly Dufferin himself would be "attacked
for reversing the beneficent policy of Lord Ripon."[76] Although
irritated by Hope for suggesting a course which would save his
personal reputation,[77] the Viceroy, when the Executive Council
met, nevertheless supported Hope against Colvin. Only Ilbert sided
with Colvin.

Echoing Hope's argument that the salt duty was "a reserve for an
emergency and a poor man's tax," Dufferin admitted privately to
Churchill[78] that he was averse to "meddling" with it so soon after

[74] Viceroy to Secretary of State, telegrams, Aug. 6, (priv.), Aug. 7, 1885, DVP, R. 519,
nos. 191, 192.
[75] Hope to D., Aug. 4, 1885, DVP, R. 528, No. 126.
[76] Hope to D., Aug. 7, 1885, DVP, R. 528, No. 139.
[77] The gist of Dufferin's reply to Hope, which appears to have been oral, can be
deduced from Hope to D., Aug. 7, 1885, DVP, R. 528, No. 139.
[78] D. to C., Aug. 7, 1885, (priv.), DVP, R. 517, No. 48.

Ripon had reduced it, fearing that any increase in the duty might expose the Indian government to attack by "the Radical Party" in England for paying military charges by taxing the impoverished masses. Even though the income tax would excite "the opposition of those classes who are best able to influence public opinion, and to give vent to their resentment through the newspapers and elsewhere," he averred that he would sooner strike these classes than any other section of the Indian community. They numbered only about 350,000; they had received the benefits of lowered import duties and no direct taxation for some years; and since Anglo-Indians would also be subject to the tax, they could not accuse the Government of discrimination. True, "3 per cent is a very heavy tax and is equal to about 8 pence in the English pound," and British taxpayers would be highly agitated if their income tax went above 4 pence! But as this would be the only tax for this Indian group, and as 3 per cent on Rs. 2,000 per annum was only 62 rupees, the tax would "not after all be so very great a hardship." Thus the Viceroy rationalized his surrender to Hope on the income tax.

But Churchill, unaware of Hope's role, overruled Dufferin and telegraphed back[79] Lytton's recommendations for "large economies in Civil Building expenditure and suspending, or almost suspending, all expenditure from Revenue on Railways and Irrigation until revenues by natural increase shall have again exceeded expenditure, which might well occur in three or four years' time"; and this, with retention of provincial government surpluses, would release "another million or thereabouts . . . to go to military expenditure." Since fortifications and heavy armament were to be met by loan, the outstanding deficit in any one year would be £500,000, which could be met by Colvin's original license tax. On an increase in the salt duty, he agreed with Dufferin that "Tories and Radicals" in Parliament would "strongly condemn it"; on the income tax, he said nothing, but later wrote Dufferin that for political reasons it would also be out of the question;[80] on the increase of troops, he left the decision entirely to Dufferin, so long as Indian revenues paid for the increase.

Dufferin forwarded Churchill's reply to Colvin, advising him that it "throws a good deal of light upon the wishes of the Government" and asking him what it meant for the future.[81] Colvin could see at once: it meant deluding themselves about the salt duty, which

[79] Secretary of State to Viceroy, telegram, Aug. 7, 1885 (priv.), DVP, R. 519, No. 243; C. to D., Aug. 7, 1885, R. 517, No. 63.
[80] C. to D., Sept. 8, 1885, DVP, R. 517, No. 70.
[81] D. to Colvin, Aug. 9, 1885 (priv. and confid.), DVP, R. 529, No. 36.

would have to be raised eventually to meet the new expenditure; it meant reliance upon the provincial governments and retrenchment in the Public Works Department; and it meant the destruction of the Famine Fund,[82] since revenue allotments to it would probably have to be suspended.[83] At the same time Colvin warned Dufferin that Churchill had made no allowance for further depreciation in the rupee's value.[84]

Dufferin, though confused about the complexities surrounding the depreciation of the rupee, did grasp the seriousness of touching the Famine Fund for military expenditure. Indian editors and politicians had come to treat the Fund as security paid by Indian taxpayers against the contingency of famine; any abuse of the Government's "pledge" on the Fund would certainly trigger a stormy agitation which could easily reach Radical ears in the Commons. Not believing that Churchill would take such a step, Dufferin challenged Colvin's interpretation and asked Churchill for clarification.[85] Back came Churchill's reply: "I think suspending for a time [the] contribution from the Famine Fund to Public Works a less evil than [that] of taxation."[86] That settled matters. The Secretary of State wished to hold taxation down yet maintain India's security for imperial and political reasons, and, if this entailed snuffing out the Famine Fund for a while, then it should be done. Colvin began drafting a new financial policy. And the Viceroy, by the sale of surplus transport animals and stores initially earmarked for the two army corps under the Quetta–Kandahar strategy, and by paring slightly the figure for troop increases, trimmed the annual increase in military expenditure by some £250,000, to £1,259,000, thereby permitting Colvin to redraft his financial scheme without touching the Famine Fund and with merely a moderate license-income tax.[87]

The undivided attention Churchill lavished upon Indian ex-

[82] Of £750,000 drawn annually from revenues for the Famine Insurance Fund, £500,000 was for famine railways and £250,000 for irrigation works constructed by the Public Works Department.

[83] Colvin to D. (with detailed comment on C.'s telegram No. 243), Aug. 9, 1885, DVP, R. 528, No. 138.

[84] Colvin to D., Aug. 9, 1885, DVP, R. 528, No. 142.

[85] Viceroy to Secretary of State, telegram, Aug. 10, 1885 (priv.), DVP, R. 519, No. 195.

[86] Secretary of State to Viceroy, telegram, Aug. 10, 1885 (priv.), DVP, R. 519, No. 244.

[87] D. to C., Aug. 21, 1885 (priv.), DVP, R. 517, No. 50; Dispatch of Governor-General-in-Council, No. 234, Fin., Aug. 22, 1885, CRO, Fin. Let., 1885, Vol. 148 and enclosures in Vol. 150. Troop increases pared to 10,600 British, 16,540 Indian, and 23,000 Indian reservists, see Dispatch of Governor-General-in-Council, No. 135, Milit., Aug. 14, 1885, Bengal Milit. Let., 1885, Vol. 485, paras. 23, 61, 64.

ternal and financial affairs throughout July and August left him little time for, and but passing interest in, Indian domestic policy. He believed that the external and financial aspects of Indian administration had political significance for the Tory Party because they concerned the threat of war and the existence of economic depression, both of which had become immediate issues for the majority of the British electorate. To Churchill, imperial issues were sound politics. But, with each passing day the Viceroy had to give ever increasing time and thought to assessing, countering, rejecting, or accepting the proposals which streamed from the pen of the young, energetic Secretary of State sitting on the *gadi* at the India Office. Domestic policy played second fiddle throughout this exercise.

VII

At Cross-Purposes Over Domestic Policy

In response to Dufferin's request for instructions on domestic policy, Churchill replied frankly that he would have neither time for nor interest in this aspect of Indian administration. "As long as you remain Viceroy," he wrote, "my intention and desire is to support to the utmost whatever you may recommend"; he urged Dufferin to settle the grievances of the Maharaja of Indore, and he approved the Viceroy's proposal to return Gwalior Fort to Maharaja Scindhia and to lay down "a more generous and pleasing policy" toward the princes while putting a tight rein on the petty interference of the Foreign Department, about which some of the princes had complained.[1] While Dufferin seemingly had been given *carte blanche,* it became apparent almost immediately that Churchill would support only those measures which did not weaken in the slightest degree his imperial policy. He took a personal interest in Lyall's request for a legislative council in the Northwest Provinces and Oudh, since he believed that this would bring more aristocratic leaders to the forefront in those provinces and "would be in accordance with the ideas of Parliament and thoroughly agreeable to the natives,"[2] but he treated quite differently Lyall's proposal to amend the Northwest Provinces Tenancy Act of 1868. The views of the Strachey brothers had dampened his initial enthusiasm for this proposal and made him apprehensive lest the Oudh talukhdars in angry opposition to the amendment join their disgruntled zemindari friends in Bengal, and so he washed his

[1] C. to D., Aug. 7, 1885, DVP, R. 517, No. 63.
[2] C. to D., Aug. 14, 1885, DVP, R. 517, No. 64.

hands of the matter and left the final decision to Dufferin with the warning that "a moment might come when there was a great strain on India, when the irritated Talookhdars might play an analogous part to that which they did in 1857."[3]

Obviously, Churchill had no intention of embarking on reforms which would jeopardize India's internal security. In speeches to the public and in the Commons, he had declared that the reckless Indian domestic policy of the Gladstone administration had seriously damaged Britain's imperial position in India. Like Salisbury and Lytton, Churchill subordinated Indian domestic policy to Indian external policy, and measured it by its appeal to the English electorate. Dufferin never fully understood this facet of Churchill's thinking, and so never gauged correctly the probable response of Churchill to domestic issues. From the beginning, they worked at cross-purposes and by September they had not worked out any Indian domestic program, much less come to an agreement on the most pressing domestic problem, the Indian Volunteer question and the proposal for Indian officers.

By mid-July, Dufferin had received from the senior officials of the provincial governments their reports on the Volunteer question in reply to his inquiry of early June.[4] Based on information supplied by town, city, and district officers, the reports provided Dufferin with an excellent introduction to the regional variations in the Indian political and social scene for policy-making, and gave him a valuable insight into the attitudes of senior officials toward English-educated Indians, their newspapers, and their emerging political role in British-Indian society. The reports confirmed his doubts about Indian volunteering, the new class, and Hume.

Although their opinions varied and their analyses were vague at times, all the officials agreed that, in their respective regions, some kind of a political movement, comprising a distinct minority of the population, had emerged to give expression to the demand for volunteering privileges. Neither Lyall nor Grant-Duff had anything new to add to their previous reports on the Northwest Provinces and Madras. In the Punjab, Sir Charles Aitchison wrote that the

[3] C. to D., Aug. 16, 1885, DVP, R. 517, No. 72.

[4] See DVP, R. 528: No. 406, Aitchison to D., June 17; No. 422, Reay to D., June 22, enclosing memoranda by Harding, Phayre, Peile, and Melvill; No. 421, Griffin to D., June 21; No. 426b, Grant-Duff to D., June 24; No. 3, Crosthwaite to D., July 2; No. 16, Bernard to D., July 7; No. 42, Thompson to D., July 15, enclosing memoranda by MacDonnell, Edgar; No. 431, Ward to D., June 30; No. 4, Cordery to D., July 3; No. 10, Bradford to D., July 4; No. 43, Reay to D., July 16, enclosing memoranda by Cunningham; No. 141a, Girdlestone to D., Aug. 8, 1885. See also Chap. V, p. 127. and nn. 126, 127 for earlier letters of Lyall and Grant-Duff.

movement had been initiated by "native gentlemen of mature years and tried loyalty," by some "young and advanced politicians," and by the English-educated members of the important "native" communities in Lahore, Amritsar, Gujranwalla, and Rawalpindi. In the Bombay Presidency, Lieutenant-General Phayre, a senior officer of the Bombay army, wrote that it was sponsored by "the educated Hindoo classes" and influenced by Brahmin leaders, and M. Melvill, a ranking member of the Bombay Council, emphasized the active participation of Parsis. In contrast, Sir Lepel Griffin, the Government Agent for Central India, having found no meaningful traces of the movement there, concluded that it was an urban phenomenon restricted to Bombay, Lahore, Calcutta, and Madras, and supported by "the two dissolvent forces of our Indian Empire, the extreme Radical party in England who wish to run all Indian measures into English moulds and the middle or lower class natives of India, who have received a more or less superficial English training and whose conceit is only surpassed by their ignorance." C. H. T. Crosthwaite, Chief Commissioner of the Central Provinces, found little interest in the movement there, except among "the more advanced class of clerks and others in the employment of the Government"; and C. E. Bernard, Chief Commissioner of British Burma, thought what little interest in volunteering existed in Lower Burma stemmed from the influence of the Bengali newspapers among the educated groups in Arakan and at Rangoon. In Bengal, Rivers Thompson insisted that the movement, centered in Calcutta, was not "a popular movement (for the masses know and care nothing about it) or a movement in which even all the socially higher and educated classes are interested (for there are very many who openly oppose it), but the outcome of an agitation of a very limited body," namely, the Indian Association led by S. Banerjea which, unlike the British Indian Association, was "landless, comparatively poor and socially inferior." A. P. MacDonnell, a rising young officer in the government of Bengal and one of Thompson's key advisers, agreed but argued that the significance of the movement rested less upon its numbers and more "on the enthusiastic, forward and undoubtedly growing class who support it; on the importance of the principle involved; and on the strength which their case acquires from previous declarations of Government." MacDonnell's opinion was unique.

As might have been expected, all the officials saw a clear link between the movement and the "native press." The reports cited, among others, the Marathi *Dnyan Prakash* at Poona,[5] *The Tribune*

---

[5] See Reay to D., May 31, 1885, DVP, R. 528, No. 360.

of Lahore, a "distinctly seditious" paper,[6] the *Amrita Bazar Patrika* in the Central Provinces, "a very widely circulated paper, [which] represents the views of a small section of really disaffected and malignant men,"[7] the influential papers, *The Bengalee* and *The Indian Mirror,* and various "minor Anglo-native papers and vernacular papers" in Bengal. J. W. Edgar, another political adviser of Rivers Thompson, analyzed the Bengali press in some detail, stressing the "absence of unanimity among the advocates of the measures as to what they really want." For example, *The Indian Mirror* of May 21 proposed separate corps for Europeans and Indians, and, under certain favorable conditions, mixed corps with mixed officers, but *The Bengalee* of May 30 wished "a volunteer corps recruited wholly from among natives," even though both papers favored selection from the educated class only. Edgar concluded that this lack of unanimity made it very difficult for the Government to judge intelligently the Volunteer grievance.

In assessing the genuineness of the demand for Indian volunteers, the loyalty of the agitators, the actual need and practicability of Indian volunteer corps and how to control them, if established, the officials were divided into two schools: the Imperialist and the Progressive. The majority, forming the Imperialist school, considered the Indian demand to volunteer "insincere and factitious,"[8] motivated by a "lying spirit,"[9] with the intent "to make political capital,"[10] and "used to conceal ulterior designs"; it would evaporate at any rumor of a British reverse in a brush with the Russians.[11] The function of a volunteer corps was to protect the home community in internal as well as external crises, and, for this, absolute trust must be reposed in the corps. This would be impossible with Indian volunteers. Rivers Thompson voiced the general view: "To those who passed through the great Mutiny of 1856-57, the facts must be familiar enough . . . regiment after regiment revolted and massacred their officers who declared that, though every regiment in the country failed, their own would remain firm, and who perished for their implicit confidence in their own men." J. B. Peile, one of Lord Reay's key advisers and a ranking member of the Bombay Council, after referring to "the Sikhs and Goorkhas, who saved us against the high-caste Hindu soldiery of 1857," maintained

[6] Griffin.
[7] Crosthwaite.
[8] Griffin.
[9] Thompson.
[10] Lyall.
[11] Grant-Duff.

that "we can trust these warlike tribes to be faithful to our standards" only because "their natural instincts are gratified by war, and [because] we can set off one race against another." Who would be available for "native" volunteering? Certainly not the Sikhs, Rajputs, and Jats, most of whom were already serving in the army or were preoccupied with agricultural responsibilities.[12] Nor could the other martial groups of North India, the Brahmins of Oudh and the Rajputs, the Wahabis of Patna and the Bengali Ferazis, who had given disloyal performances in the past, be included.[13] The Maratha Brahmins were not to be trusted, judging by their intrigues at the Satara and Poona courts and their anti-British influence upon other caste groups of the Deccan and the Konkan;[14] neither were the Kayastha clerks and writers of the Punjab, for they were "the most ambitious, discontented and unsettled of all classes in India and the very last to whom arms should be given."[15] Nor were the "weaker and more effeminate" Bengali Hindus any better, for with their "considerable aptitude for organizing political agitation . . . it would be very inconvenient that they should appear to enforce concessions with arms in their hands."[16] Undoubtedly a "Native Volunteer Corps would become the nucleus of political organization and demonstrations,"[17] like the Indian Association in Calcutta.[18]

Loyalty aside, the Imperialist school pointed at other obstacles to any scheme for Indian volunteering. "If the Government were to force natives into English Corps a violent European agitation against the Government would be the instant result."[19] Even with separate Indian corps, race consciousness would become intensified, and "the native attitude would become more hostile to those who in India represent authority." Furthermore, "Mahomedans, Hindus, and the multitude of other castes and races who live side by side peaceably under [British] paramount rule yet who hate each other with a deadly and undying hatred, would be extravagantly and dangerously conflicting in such a movement."[20] Even if it were possible to form Indian corps, these extra Indian troops would dangerously unbalance the established ratio of two Indians to one

[12] Griffin.
[13] Edgar.
[14] Phayre, Peile.
[15] Griffin.
[16] Edgar.
[17] Lyall to D., June 4, 1885, DVP, R. 528, No. 378.
[18] Thompson.
[19] Griffin.
[20] Cordery, Bradford.

British.[21] Finally, Indian volunteering might "promote a fusion of religious classes and forms a bond of union between different races," which would encourage "a transient and spurious union . . . for independence."

Since the Imperialists deemed Indian volunteering both impracticable and dangerous, they advised Dufferin to "act as if Great Britain were to govern India for all time," and eschew any "proposal so calculated to undermine our self-confidence in the stability of our position in a land won and hitherto held by the sword."[22] More than half advocated a "simple" and "firm" refusal of separate Indian volunteer corps,[23] based upon Canning's Minute of 1861,[24] which allowed for Indians joining European corps. Lieutenant-General Phayre spelled this out by suggesting that the Viceroy increase the existing European corps by admitting "natives of good character employed by Government or by Railway and other companies [which] are under tangible control." Edgar preferred to treat the Bengal and Calcutta volunteer movement independent from the rest of India, and he arrived at a tentative solution for Calcutta alone, whereby persons "having some recognized position" and with a knowledge of English or a university degree should be allowed to form a corps controlled and supervised by the Government. Cunningham thought Indian volunteering could be tried in certain areas, if it was entirely controlled by European officers and separated from European volunteers. Peile felt the answer to the agitation was "to admit native gentlemen" as officers into the British Indian Army. But Lyall and Grant-Duff, the chief protagonists of the Imperialist school, were adamant against Indian volunteering in any form and advised the Government to reject all demands to volunteer, and instead to consider other grievances of the educated Indian—the Arms Act or the age-limit requirement for the Covenanted Service.

The Progressives, in the minority, held views more in keeping with the paternalistic tradition of Munro, Elphinstone, and Metcalfe. They had little doubt that the Indians were genuine and loyal in their desire to volunteer. Their aspirations emanated from "the present days of enlightenment, of liberal education, and of material and social progress, when there has sprung up a strong feeling of loyalty and attachment to the person of our Queen, when the peace and blessings secured to the country by British rule are

[21] Phayre, Peile.
[22] Bradford.
[23] Griffin, Phayre, Ward, Cordery, Bradford, Thompson.
[24] See Chap. V, n. 7.

widely appreciated and when a feeling of community of interest
between Government and the people is slowly but surely taking
root in the native mind." The question therefore "must not be
considered exclusively . . . from the standpoint of 1857," especially
as "experience and events since 1857" had compelled officials to
abandon their attitude of suspicion.[25] To condemn the loyal enthusiasm expressed by this new Indian class, which had not been
involved in the Mutiny, was unfair. Even Crosthwaite, a cautious
Progressive, admitted that "there is no doubt a real feeling of
loyalty among the motives at work." Some pointed out that educated
Indians wished "to be treated as if they were on the same level with
Europeans."[26] Discrimination was involved in the Volunteer question, just as it had been in the dispute over the Ilbert Bill, and
constituted a bona fide grievance, crying out for solution.

They acknowledged that Indian volunteering would be "a new
departure in policy," which would produce "a state of relations
between the rulers and the ruled which does not at present exist"
and would entail some risk.[27] But, in their opinion, the prospective
benefits, contingent on the reform, far outweighed the risks. "Let
the natives learn that we do not wish to treat them as a conquered
race," they maintained, "but that we consider our relations with
them to be those of a partnership, in which they shall have a fair
share of the business, but in which England must always be the
senior partner." Rule and reform were the essentials of this partnership. "The educated natives will no doubt continually demand,
and we shall have to yield to them, a greater share in the administration of the country." They believed that educated Indians had
no desire for self-rule but preferred a colonial status "enjoying
representative institutions, and with all appointments except that
of Viceroy, and perhaps the Governors, in their own hands." This
would come gradually and over a long period of time, during which
British responsibility would be to foster "a spirit of self-reliance"
and a climate of mutual trust and confidence. One step in this
direction would be to grant the request of Young India to serve
as volunteers.[28]

Unlike the Imperialists, the Progressives foresaw no increase
in racial tension, as long as the separate Indian corps were carefully selected and grouped, in accordance with the requirements
of a particular locality. Aitchson, writing on the Punjab, and

[25] Aitchison.
[26] Melvill.
[27] Aitchison.
[28] Melvill.

MacDonnell, on Bengal, thought that mixed companies of Europeans and Indians would pose no problems, and the latter warned against drawing any misleading conclusions from the Ilbert Bill excitement, which was by no means "a fair index to the general temper of the non-official European in Bengal, especially if questions of equality between them and natives are cautiously approached and put forward with judgment, tact and moderation." In sum, the Progressives thought that the Indian government could meet the volunteering grievance safely and usefully.

Despite their insistence on the great benefits and practicability of Indian volunteering, the Progressives forwarded to Dufferin recommendations of an essentially cautious character, with emphasis on controls and safeguards. The majority favored separate corps for Indians, but differed on the question of Indian or European officers. MacDonnell advocated adding Indians to the existing European corps, and Crosthwaite, rejecting both separate and mixed corps, recommended a "yeoman cavalry," made up of ranking Indians. But whatever the final composition, separate, mixed, or yeoman cavalry, all agreed on strict qualifications and careful selection of candidates. Aitchison thought that "admission to the force should be a matter of distinction and not of course," and suggested basing the selection at Lahore on the Lieutenant-Governor's Durbar list, and elsewhere on education and responsibility. Melvill believed competent officers could be drawn from "the great families of the country—the Maratha chiefs, the Talukdars of Guzerat and Kathiawar, and the ex-Amirs of Sind." Crosthwaite, Reay, and Hardinge advised the selection of candidates from the ranks of the "elite of native aristocracy." All were convinced that proper training would be absolutely necessary and could only be conducted by seasoned officers. Aitchison and Melvill thought that the "native corps" could produce its own officers; others were for selecting staff officers, either European or Indian, from the British Indian Army.[29]

Taken as a whole, the recommendations of neither school conceded the volunteering privileges which Indian leaders were seeking and which Hume had discussed with Dufferin in May. Even the Progressives, who professed to understand the aspirations of the educated Indians, recommended solutions designed largely for the landed aristocracy. The case of the educated Indian volunteering had been weighed officially and found wanting. This conclusion was neither displeasing nor unsatisfactory to Dufferin. The reports

[29] Crosthwaite, MacDonnell.

not only confirmed but also strengthened the tentative opposition
to Indian volunteering that he had expressed to Kimberley in late
May.[30] Whatever doubt he might then have had was removed.
Like Lyall and Grant-Duff, he considered Indian volunteering
quite out of the question.

He gave Hume no indication of his decision or of the drift of
official thinking, even though he had ample opportunity to do so.
Alerted by Reay to the pamphlets on Indian grievances which
Hume's colleagues in Madras and Bombay were circulating, Dufferin had a private talk with Hume in July, prior to his departure
for England. Following their chat, Hume sent the Viceroy copies
of the pamphlets, which dealt largely with discrimination against
Indian appointments to the Uncovenanted Civil Service, and which
were written by his friends, Javerilal Umiashankar Yajnik, an
editor and member of the Bombay Presidency Association whom
Hume considered the best Indian authority on Bombay revenue
questions, and Crawley-Boevey of the Bombay Civil Service.[31]
Hume took the opportunity to comment to the Viceroy on the
general hardening of Anglo-Indian attitudes, official and unofficial,
especially in Lower Bengal, against educated Indians in appointments to the Civil Service and in jury trials. Hume went on to
remark that Dufferin during their talk had either forgotten to
speak of the Volunteer question or did not wish to do so, and added:
"If the former, and you can tell me anything that I can send round,
it would do no good, for our people are still childish and have yet to
realise the moral of the Psalm of Life and 'to learn to labour and
to wait.' "[32] A few days later, Hume sent Dufferin three printed
notes by his Bengali acquaintance, Man Mohan Ghose, the Calcutta barrister who was active in the politics of the Indian Union
and in dealing with cases of discrimination in the administration
of justice against Bengalis in the mofussil.[33] Before sailing from
Bombay, Hume forwarded to Dufferin a copy of a private letter
from an Indian, which he had received and had translated for Lord
Reay, on the antagonism between Hindus and Muslims in Sind
arising from the English educational system. For the last time, he
broached the subject of Indian volnuteering. "I should not do right,
if I did not tell you that the delay in any expression on your part of
sympathy for the Native Volunteer movement is genuinely disturb-

[30] See Chap. V, pp. 123-124 and n. 108.
[31] Another Bombay pamphlet was prepared by M. M. Ghose; one Madras pamphlet
was possibly prepared by V. Chariar, an editor of *Hindu*, who later did pamphlet
work for Hume.
[32] H. to D., July 4, 1885, DVP, R. 529, No. 9.
[33] H. to D., July 7, 1885, DVP, R. 528, No. 15.

ing the native community."[34] He added that this was unreasonable, but, obviously, Hume himself was disturbed. Hume had looked upon Dufferin as Ripon's liberal-minded successor; he now began to have second thoughts. Dufferin let matters drift until the end of the month, and then wrote Hume in London.[35] He was "very sorry" if Hume's "clients" were impatient for an official answer, but he had "not yet received the opinions of several authorities whom I have consulted." Once all the reports were in and the Council had reached a decision, the Secretary of State in Council would have to be consulted "before any reply can be given to the memorials." Months, not weeks, would pass before the Oracle would hand down its decision, and Dufferin advised Hume to inform his "clients" accordingly. Inconclusive and evasive, a mere repetition of what he had said to Hume in May, Dufferin's letter gave no hint of developments since then.[36]

Though reticent with Hume, Dufferin was by no means reticent with Churchill. With some reports still to come in and discussion in Council still to be held, Dufferin wrote Churchill in the midst of their preoccupations with the Afghan and Burmese questions early in July.[37] After reviewing the reports of both Imperialists and Progressives, he told Churchill that "the movement is partly stimulated by designing people with a view to the creation of a Citizen Army to be hereafter used for political purposes," and he declared, "I am opposed to the idea" of Indian volunteering. He preferred the alternative, already recommended by his council in March and "approved" by Kimberley, of selecting trained youths from the Indian aristocracy and admitting them to responsible commands in the British Indian Army.[38] "Should you be able to see your way to acquiescing in such an experiment on a small scale," Dufferin concluded, "it would put us in a better position to deal with the petitions of the would-be Volunteers." This view he reiterated later in the month when he wrote to Ilbert that he anticipated an unfavorable response from Churchill to the demand for volunteering, but a favorable response to the proposal for Indian officers.[39] Clearly, he was looking to Churchill's support to get himself "off the hook" with the educated Indian leaders and Hume.

What Dufferin did not know at the time was that, with Churchill's concurrence, the proposal for "Native Officers" had been shelved at

[34] H. to D., July 12, 1885, DVP, R. 528, No. 31.
[35] D. to H., July 28, 1885 (priv.), DVP, R. 529, No. 38.
[36] See Chap. V, pp. 117, 122-123 and n. 107.
[37] D. to C., July 10, 1885 (priv.), received *ca.* July 31-Aug. 2, DVP, R. 517, No. 43.
[38] See above, pp. 122-124.
[39] D. to Ilbert, July 30, 1885, DVP, R. 529, No. 25, postscript.

the India Office. Opposition to the idea had appeared as early as May and June when experts at the War Office and the India Office, whom Kimberley had consulted, submitted their conclusions.[40] The two ranking generals of the War Office would accept the proposal as an experiment, if sharply modified and tightly controlled. Of the military advisers at the India Office, seven agreed to try it, but most added qualifications in order to ensure discrimination between English and Indian Officers in the matter of privileges and ranks, thus knocking the essential principle of the proposed reform on the head. The remaining six, including three of the most important members of the India Office's Military Committee, Generals Sir F. Haines, Sir Edwin Johnson, and Sir C. H. Brownlow, were unalterably opposed to the whole idea. Haines feared that "the principle of supremacy of European authority" would be threatened; he could not conceive of a parity of commands between British and Indian officers in the light of the poor performance of the "Native Gentlemen" who had received commissions during the past twelve years. Johnson, surprised that the Viceroy had recommended an experiment so dangerous to British supremacy in India, quoted the Army Commission Reports of 1858 and 1879 to the effect that the Indian government's security against another mutiny rested on having only European officers lead Indian troops. Brownlow considered the proposal as part of "a policy of sentimental adventure in India," evoked among officials by the recent outburst of Indian loyalty during the Afghan crisis. In view of this opposition, Churchill decided to seek more advice from a specially selected group.[41]

Sir Ashley Eden, upon whose counsel Churchill greatly relied, tore the proposal to pieces with devastating effectiveness. He based his opposition upon one overriding consideration: "a jealous regard for the safety of British rule in India." He had no sympathy with any proposal which would weaken the British hold upon India, and render the British Indian Army incapable of repelling invasion and quelling internal commotion. The Indian government was defying the lesson of the Mutiny, and was also disregarding the fact that a similar scheme, without parity between English and Indian officers, had been instituted by 1880 on a limited scale. There was no need

[40] See Appendixes of Dispatch of Governor-General-in-Council, No. 47, Milit., Mar. 21, with memoranda by Haines, May 18, by Johnson, May 20, by Brownlow, May 24, 1885, CRO, Bengal Milit. Let., 1885, Vol. 482, nos. 15-51.

[41] See Enclosure II, Confidential Memoranda to Secretary of State by Members of the Council of India *re* Native Officer Proposal, Confidential Dispatch of Secretary of State in Council, No. 88, Milit., Apr. 15, 1886, CRO, Selections from Disp., 1886, Ser. 29, Vol. 29, Pt. I, with memoranda by Sir A. Eden, Sir R. Montgomery, Sir P. Lumsden, Colonel Yule, Sir W. Muir.

to do anything more. The scheme would necessitate more British troops, and hence increase military expenditure; equal rank and pay between English and Indians would produce a military version of the Ilbert Bill crisis. Churchill, impressed by Eden's exhortations and troubled by the imperial aspect of the proposal, sent Eden's memorandum to Dufferin, as representing the current view within his Council.[42] Churchill added that the Duke of Cambridge, the Queen's cousin and the ruling potentate at the War Office, and his aged "war horses" were preparing "great opposition" to the proposal, but that he himself had been too concerned with other aspects of Indian policy (which he certainly had been) to find time to assess the proposal.

A few days later, upon receiving the comments of Sir Robert Montgomery and General Sir Peter Lumsden, both of whom cautiously supported the proposal, but agreed with Eden on the impossibility of granting equality of rank between British and Indian officers without provoking another Ilbert Bill crisis, Churchill dropped the whole proposal without even consulting his council. He himself added the final touch to the War Office's opposition. In a bitter dispute[43] with the Duke of Cambridge, when Churchill succeeded in blocking, for personal reasons,[44] the appointment of the Queen's son, the Duke of Connaught, as Commander-in-Chief of the Bombay Army, Churchill's pungent comments so alienated the Duke of Cambridge as to bring a virtual breakdown in military planning between the War Office and the India Office. By the end of July, Churchill had not the remotest chance of carrying the proposal for Indian officers through his Council or of placing it before the War Office. Nor did he intend to. Dufferin had incorrectly anticipated Churchill's response.

By the end of July, Dufferin learned for the first time that the proposal for Indian officers was encountering heavy opposition at home. The memoranda by Haines, Johnson, and Brownlow dropped with a thud on his desk, and these were followed in rapid succession by Churchill's private note and Eden's memorandum. Dufferin was irate over Brownlow's charge that the proposal was of an "emotional origin,"[45] but he followed Churchill's gentle hint to pay close attention to Eden's argument, which, Dufferin admitted,

---

[42] C. to D., July 10, 1885, received *ca.* July 29, DVP, R. 517, No. 56.

[43] This extraordinary incident is well summarized and documented in W. S. Churchill, I, 503-517.

[44] C. to S., July 25, 1885, James, pp. 200-201.

[45] See D. to Northbrook, July 30, 1885 (priv.), DVP, R. 525, No. 40, which was never sent.

was "very cogent and forcible in some respects."[46] But this was beside the point. What really mattered, Dufferin now realized, was that Churchill would only create trouble for himself and doom the proposal if he pressed ahead with it under existing circumstances. Since Churchill was a mere novice in Indian affairs and therefore "not in a position to press the point à outrance," Dufferin telegraphed Churchill not to act if the proposal would disrupt the India Council or Churchill's relations with the War Office at a moment when more important political and financial matters were before him. It could "very well lie over until the arrival in London of Sir Donald Stewart," the Commander-in-Chief, sometime in November.[47] Churchill, absorbed in the intricacies of the Afghan policy and of his Indian Budget Statement, and at daggers drawn with the Duke of Cambridge, readily agreed.[48]

But lest Churchill had failed to grasp the significance of the proposal, Dufferin, still convinced that it was feasible, trotted out for Churchill the pro-aristocratic logic of the Imperialist school: "At present, the only persons who are acquiring official influence and position in India are the Bengalee Baboo and the Mahratta Brahmin, both classes [being] instinctively inspired by questionable notions, [while] in the meantime the landowners, the leading Mahomedan families, and the aristocracy of the country have been relegated to obscurity and are losing alike their influence and their energies."[49] This sounded very like Lytton in his time. Military service was the best opening for these important classes; not only would it give them employment, it would also ensure their loyalty "to a certain degree." As the proposal was to be based upon official selection, not competitive examination, the Indian government could choose candidates from the neglected classes and make people in England realize there were "other interests and communities in India than those represented by the nimble-witted students from Bengal." This had been Dufferin's original aim in substituting the proposal for Indian officers in place of the proposal for Indian volunteers, and he still wished to achieve it, even if the opposition of Eden and the others meant that he would have to wait for five to six months before Stewart could defend the proposal before the India Council.

Meanwhile, Dufferin still had to place before his own Council the

[46] D. to C., July 30, 1885 (priv.), DVP, R. 517, No. 47.
[47] Viceroy to Secretary of State, telegram, Aug. 1, 1885 (priv.), DVP, R. 519, No. 179.
[48] Secretary of State to Viceroy, telegram, Aug. 3, 1885 (priv.), DVP, R. 519, No. 236; also C. to D., Aug. 7, 1885, R. 517, No. 63.
[49] D. to C., Aug. 7, 1885 (priv.), received ca. Aug. 28, DVP, R. 517, No. 48.

issue of Indian volunteering. The day before the Council meeting Ilbert, after taking stock of the reports, advised Dufferin that, on the basis of majority opinion, he would not be justified in advancing any other policy than that already laid down by Lord Canning. Ilbert himself thought the experiment of separate Indian companies should be tried wherever a local government was willing to do so. "I feel so strongly the importance of adopting every means in our power whereby the interests and sympathies of those classes who are influential from education, birth, or property may be enlisted on the side of Government that I should be in favour of trying the experiment where the requisite conditions are shown to exist." But he knew that his recommendation was "destined, for some time to come, to remain a 'pious opinion.' " Was there any alternative issue upon which the Government could concentrate in order to mollify "educated" Indian opinion? Possibly a concession on the age limit for admission into the Civil Service, a more liberal version of the Arms Act, the formation of a yeoman cavalry of landowners, or the admittance of "native gentlemen" to the officer ranks of the British Indian Army. Ilbert thought that these suggestions deserved "very careful consideration," because "it would be impolitic to adopt an attitude of *non possumus* on every side" to educated Indian griev- ances. If the Council vetoed any experimentation with Indian volunteering, he advised Dufferin to "find an early opportunity . . . of stating, on some public occasion, the conclusion of the Gov- ernment and the reasons upon which it is based"; "the speech would cause disappointment, but less than would be caused by silence."[50]

Ilbert's report held no surprises for Dufferin, and the Executive Council session went exactly as he had expected and as Ilbert had forecast.[51] Ilbert, supported only by Colvin, opted for a slight modi- fication of Canning's ruling and then proposed the experiment of separate companes. Hope, Bayley, and Generals Stewart and John- son immediately "offered a strong and uncompromising opposition to the whole idea" of Indian volunteering, arguing that such a privilege would only provide the Indian "political leaders and wire-pullers" with a well-trained youth cadre for armed agitation more dangerous than that of 1857, and at the very moment when "the national attitude of the educated class is in some measure that of hostility to existing administrative arrangements." They ex- patiated on every point made by the Imperialists, ranging from the

[50] Ilbert to D., Aug. 25, 1885, DVP, R. 528, No. 199.

[51] See résumé of council session held on Aug. 26 in D. to C., Aug. 28, 1885 (priv.), DVP, R. 517, No. 51; also Dispatch of Governor-General-in-Council, No. 166, Milit., Sept. 21, 1885, Bengal Milit. Let., 1885, Vol. 486.

possibilities of another mutiny or Ilbert Bill crisis, and Hindu–Muslim feuds, to the need for more British troops and greater military expenditure. Their views prevailed and the Viceroy voted with the majority. Then the discussion turned briefly to alternatives to volunteering. Dufferin, instead of bringing up Ilbert's suggestions, put forward the one proposal—for Indian officers—which had the least chance of success at the India Office, and this received the unanimous support of his Council. The councillors also agreed with Ilbert that the Viceroy should "take an early opportunity" to decline publicly the offers of Indian volunteering on the grounds that such were not required by the Government. Thus Canning's decision of 1861 remained in force, and any Indian wishing to enroll as a volunteer would have to do the impossible and enter the existing Anglo-Indian corps. Ilbert noted tersely in his diary: "prayers of memorialists to be negatived."[52]

About two days after the Council meeting, the receipt of a letter from Churchill, written on August 7, made Dufferin realize once again how incorrectly he had estimated Churchill's views on Indian domestic policy. "I think you know," Churchill wrote, "that I am not ultra-Tory in my political opinions, and as far as I am concerned I would gladly co-operate in a generous and trusting policy towards the natives." He would be pleased "if the native volunteer movement was not too strongly snubbed and if possible that it might be tried cautiously on a small scale."[53] In effect, Churchill saw no threat to the British imperial mission from Indian volunteering on a limited, experimental scale, but he did see a danger in appointing Indian officers. The two men were looking at the problem from opposite points of view, and their respective decisions cancelled each other out. They were working at cross-purposes on Indian domestic policy, with no results to show for their efforts.

The same could be said with regard to the age limit for the Covenanted Service examination. Dufferin was startled to read in the same letter of August 7: "I am very anxious, but subject to your better knowledge, that the age of admission to the Civil Service should be raised." In effect, he wished to throw over Salisbury's decision of 1876,[54] for a number of plausible reasons. The existing age limit greatly handicapped Indians in the London competition, and likewise yielded a crop "of half-grown, undeveloped, worn-out youths" from England who detracted from British rule in India. By a return to the age limit of 1854, Indians would be given an

[52] Aug. 26, 1885, Ilbert Papers, CRO, Eur. D. 594/4.
[53] C. to D., Aug. 7, 1885, received *ca.* Aug. 27-28, DVP, R. 517, No. 63.
[54] See above, p. 4.

equal opportunity to compete and enter the Covenanted Service as, by pledges of Crown and Parliament, was their right. With the aim of strengthening the British imperial mission in India, but not necessarily on Salisbury's or Lytton's terms, and with his eye cocked for reforms with a liberal appeal to Parliament and to the public, Churchill had chosen the very reform which Dufferin, in seeking an alternative to Indian volnuteering, had preferred to overlook.

Dufferin had been confronted with the question of raising the age limit during the winter and spring of 1885. Acting on instructions in a dispatch of January 8 from Kimberley, stating that the Secretary of State in Council had rejected the proposal to raise the age limit, previously agreed upon by Ripon and most members of the Executive Council, Dufferin had announced the official decision.[55] Meanwhile Kimberley, when Ripon threatened to take the entire question to Parliament, withdrew his instructions in the January dispatch and wrote Dufferin in April to make no public announcement concerning the decision against raising the age limit.[56] But the announcement had been made, and Dufferin instructed MacKenzie Wallace to make some discreet inquiries as to the reactions to the decision.[57] These revealed that the Indian leaders were profoundly disturbed by the decision, and that senior ranking officers, such as Aitchison, Lieutenant-Governor of the Punjab, and J. Nugent, Secretary to the Bombay Government and President of the Central Civil Service Examination Committee, favored raising the age limit (for reasons very similar to Churchill's).[58] Moreover, at the end of August, when Churchill's letter arrived, Colvin, Ilbert, and Grant-Duff were thinking along the same lines.

In his reply to Churchill,[59] Dufferin made no mention of all these developments but merely told Churchill that he had neither said nor done anything because "the question had been decided by

[55] See Dispatch of Secretary of State in Council, No. 1, Pub., Jan. 8, 1885, CRO, Selections from Disp., 1885, Ser. 28, Vol. 27, p. 1, paras. 9-11; Secretary, Government of India, to Secretaries, Governments of Madras, Bombay, Northwest Provinces, Punjab, Bengal, Mar. 23, 1885, enclosed in D. to K., May 18, 1885 (priv.), DVP, R. 517, No. 35. Also see above pp. 36 ff.

[56] K. to D., Apr. 17, 1885 (priv.), received *ca.* May 8, DVP, R. 517, No. 30.

[57] Wallace to Secretaries, Governments of Punjab, Northwest Provinces, Madras, Bombay, and Mysore Residency, May 19, 1885 (priv.), DVP, R. 528, No. 175.

[58] Secretaries of Lieutenant-Governors of Punjab, Northwest Provinces to Wallace, May 22, 28, Grant-Duff to Wallace, June 3, Secretary, Government of Bombay, to Wallace, June 18, enclosing memorandum by Nugent, DVP, R. 528, nos. 324, 349, 373a, 411.

[59] D. to C., Aug. 28, 1885 (priv.), DVP, R. 517, No. 51.

the India Office in an opposite sense" before Dufferin's appointment. He had, indeed, acting on Kimberley's instructions, taken some steps to see how the Statutory Service might be improved,[60] and he added cautiously that he had always been partial to a higher age limit, but he was not willing to do anything about it immediately. Dufferin's real views on the question may well have been reflected in his earlier letter to Churchill with its remarks on "Bengalee Baboos" and "Mahratta Brahmins," and he probably had no intention of taking up the question of the age limit unless overruled by the Secretary of State. He was more interested in restoring the sense of participation and responsibility of aristocratic Muslims and Hindus than in improving the status and influence of the English-educated class. His response to Reay's plea on behalf of Muslims and the Executive Council's resolution giving official encouragement to Muslim education,[61] his proposal for Indian officers, and his support for Lyall's land reforms and the proposed legislative council were all steps in this direction. To reconsider the age limit at this point would be an abrupt and uncertain shift. Moreover, with only a month before Simla officially closed, the Council dispersed, and he went to the plains for his official tour prior to returning to Calcutta, Dufferin had no wish to open up such a controversial subject while financial and Burmese affairs were engrossing the attention of himself and his colleagues.

By doing nothing about Churchill's suggestion, Dufferin set aside a possible alternative to volunteering. But from July onwards, he had lost interest in the Indian reform movement. His education, begun with Lyall, was completed with the reports on Indian volunteering. He was willing to wait some months until Stewart was at the India Office to deal with the proposal for Indian officers, which, if carried, would succor the aristocratic class. Thus Dufferin's and Churchill's views on the grievances of educated Indians diverged. With no understanding between them, nothing happened. The hiatus in Indian reform, begun in the previous year under Kimber-

[60] See Circular, Pub., Government of India to various local governments, No. 25/1074-83, June 18, 1885, enclosed in Dispatch of Governor-General-in-Council, No. 11, Pub.-Home, Feb. 9, 1886, CRO, Pub. Let., 1886, Vol. 7.

[61] See Reay to D., May 3, 1885, DVP, R. 528, No. 360, and D. to C., July 17, 1885 (priv.), R. 517, No. 44, in which Dufferin wrote: "I have been long anxious to see whether we could not do something to give the Mahomedans a lift in the world, for undoubtedly, owing to the ecclesiastical character of their education, they are being crowded out by the nimble-minded Bengalees . . . although we agreed that they must place their main reliance upon their own exertion. . . . We have been able to frame a Resolution the terms of which will make them feel that the Government has their interests at heart." See also Resolution, July 19, 1885, CRO, *Gazette of India, Extraordinary,* 1885.

ley, became complete under Dufferin. That fleeting moment, when something novel and eventful might conceivably have been done to deal with Indian grievances, passed. It was not to return. From September onwards, Churchill concentrated upon the approaching Tory campaign in the General Election and upon his own contest with the illustrious radical Liberal incumbent, John Bright, for the Birmingham seat. He gave his entire attention to bringing together the bits and pieces of his Indian policy into the grand imperial design that he had enunciated in his Indian Budget Statement. And Dufferin, heartened upon learning of Churchill's brilliant handling of the budget in the Commons and of his praises for the name of Dufferin,[62] acted in greater sympathy and harmony and he responded more readily to Churchill's bold and assured lead.

Together Dufferin and Churchill brought the Afghan question to a conclusion just as the latter opened the Tory campaign in the Midlands and north of England. The Russian Foreign Office, aware of Salisbury's successful wooing of Bismarck, and the Russian War Office, anxious about rising nihilist tension within its army, decided to agree to British terms for the settlement of the boundary.[63] By late August, just after Parliament had adjourned and Salisbury had gone on holiday, the final proposals of the Russians arrived.[64] Churchill stepped into the breach and instructed Dufferin to get his Council's endorsement of the Russian proposals,[65] which Dufferin did.[66] Salisbury, having hurriedly returned to London, accepted them on September 3.[67] That evening, Churchill, opening the Tory campaign at Sheffield, announced the news, which made a great impression and sent the newspaper reporters scurrying. He reminded his audience that the settlement was the result of the Tories' firm military and external policy in India with its aim of upholding British imperial prestige and honor.[68] To make good his words, he pressed Dufferin not to slacken his military preparations for the Kandahar strategy.[69] Although Dufferin gained

[62] D. to C., Aug. 28, 1885 (priv.), DVP, R. 517, No. 51.

[63] Secretary of State to Viceroy, telegrams, Aug. 5 (secret), Aug. 11, 1885 (priv. and most secret), DVP, R. 519, nos. 240, 246, 247; C. to D., July 24, Aug. 14, 1885, R. 517, nos. 60, 64.

[64] Secretary of State to Viceroy, telegram, Aug. 20, 1885 (secret and immediate), DVP, R. 519, No. 261.

[65] Secretary of State to Viceroy, telegram, Sept. 2, 1885 (priv.), DVP, R. 519, No. 287.

[66] Viceroy to Secretary of State, telegram, Sept. 3, 1885 (priv.), DVP, R. 519, No. 224.

[67] S. to Thornton, Sept. 3, 1885, *P.P.*, 1884-85, Vol. 87, Com. 4389, p. 69.

[68] Speech in Sheffield, Sept. 3, *Times*, Sept. 4, 1885; C. to D., Sept. 2, 1885, DVP, R. 517, No. 68.

[69] Secretary of State to Viceroy, telegrams, Sept. 1 (priv.), Sept. 11 (priv. and most secret), Sept. 11, 1885 (secret), DVP, R. 519, nos. 285, 294, 296.

Churchill's approval for some reductions, he kept 10,000 men in readiness along the Bolan Pass and at Quetta,[70] and, yielding to Churchill's demands, he overrode the objections of his Council to large-scale winter military manoeuvres of the British Indian and princely armies to impress the Russians.[71] "Strength and stability" was Churchill's motto for Indian policy and for the British voter; he applied it vigorously and made Dufferin follow suit.

Adopting the same motto for Burma, Churchill now intervened directly in the Burmese question. Advised by Wallace Brothers that the Hlutdaw, allegedly encouraged by the French Vice-Consul, M. Haas, had decided the log dispute against the Bombay Burma Trading Corporation and had fined it some £85,000, Churchill telegraphed Dufferin to act.[72] Dufferin, having listened to Bernard's advice that the Indian government should act whenever the Hlutdaw handed down its fine, had already secured his Council's approval.[73] On August 28, a letter from the Indian government was dispatched to Mandalay, defending the corporation and requesting the Hlutdaw to suspend its decree and let the Indian government appoint arbitrators.[74] At about the same time, Churchill persuaded Salisbury to warn the new French Premier, M. de Freycinet, to cease commercial meddling at Mandalay or serious consequences might follow.[75] By early September, Churchill, disregarding Ilbert's earlier warnings and recommendations,[76] and faithfully supported by Dufferin, had seen to it that what were virtually ultmata were sent to the Court of Ava and to the French Government. Should the one or the other fail to yield, British intervention was certain.

To Churchill, India's financial policy seemed out of step with his new imperial aims. He considered Colvin's latest fiscal plan too conservative and wholly insufficient for the broad commercial expansion and bold external policy he had in mind. By extending the license tax, retrenching civil expenditure, and placing priorities

[70] Viceroy to Secretary of State, telegrams, Sept. 1 (priv.), Sept. 9, 1885, DVP, R. 519, nos. 220, 232; D. to C., Sept. 10, 1885 (priv.), R. 517, No. 53.

[71] D. to C., Aug. 28 and Sept. 21 (priv.); C. to D., Sept. 22, 29, 1885, DVP, R. 517, nos. 51, 54, 73, 74; Viceroy to Secretary of State, telegram, Sept. 27 (priv.), Secretary of State to Viceroy, telegram, Sept. 29, 1885 (priv.), R. 519, nos. 252, 327.

[72] See Jones to Burgess, and Bombay Burma Corporation to M. Haas, Aug. 20, 1885, *P.P.*, 1886, Vol. 50, Com. 4614, p. 199; Secretary of State to Viceroy, telegram, Aug. 25, 1885 (secret), DVP, R. 519, No. 272.

[73] Viceroy to Secretary of State, telegram, Aug. 24, 1885 (secret), DVP, R. 519, No. 208.

[74] Secretary, Chief Commissioner, British Burma to Foreign Minister, Mandalay, Aug. 28, 1885, *P.P.*, 1886, Vol. 50, Com. 4614, pp. 206-207.

[75] Enclosure, C. to D., Aug. 28, 1885, DVP, R. 517, No. 67; S. to Walsham, Sept. 9, 1885, *P.P.*, 1886, Vol. 50, Com. 4614, p. 177.

[76] See above, pp. 145-146.

upon railway construction, Colvin had planned to meet the annual costs of India's administrative machine, the famine railways and irrigation program, and the new annual expenditures for the Kandahar strategy out of revenue, without affecting the provincial balances and the Famine Insurance Fund.[77] None of this appealed to Churchill. The plan depended upon additional taxation, which he had announced in his Budget Statement would be resorted to only if retrenchment failed; it provided no scope for Indian industrial and commercial development; and it provided no elasticity in case of an unforeseen emergency, such as a further fall in the value of the rupee, famine, or troubles beyond India's borders. With the approval of the India Council, Churchill proposed a radically different solution, which he forwarded officially to Dufferin and his Council as preferred policy.[78]

He proposed to increase Indian revenues in four ways: by sustained retrenchment at the supreme and provincial levels of Government, especially in the Public Works Department; by restrictions on the balances of the provincial governments and by arrangements with them for contributions to the supreme revenues to offset imperial charges; by the "temporary" suspension of the annual allotment of £1,500,000 from the revenues to the Famine Fund; and by the sale of certain famine railway lines then being constructed from revenues by the Government to private companies—a step which would reimburse the Indian government for its investment to date and permit it to undertake new famine railway construction. These measures, yielding some £2,500,000 to £2,900,-000, would pay for the increased annual military charges commencing in 1886, and would avoid additional taxation. He recommended covering the cost of unremunerative works, such as frontier and famine railways and fortifications by a large loan of £20 millions to be placed in the London market early in 1886.[79] Thus, with military and unremunerative charges covered, the remaining surplus could be used for unforeseen emergencies and private railway development.

But Colvin refused to budge, and the Council supported him. Colvin charged that Churchill's policy was an attack on the financial policy laid down by Ripon and Baring.[80] Dufferin, lacking confidence in his own knowledge of Indian finances, unable to effect a

[77] See above, p. 154.
[78] Dispatch of Secretary of State in Council, No. 239, Fin., Aug. 27, 1885, CRO, Selections from Disp., 1885, Ser. 28, Vol. 28, Pt. II.
[79] C. to D., Sept. 22, 29, 1885, DVP, R. 517, nos. 73, 74.
[80] Colvin to Wallace, Sept. 30, 1885, DVP, R. 528, No. 327.

compromise, and unwilling to overrule his Council, asked Churchill not to press his scheme.[81] He trusted in retrenchment, railway priorities, and the Parliamentary inquiry proposed by Churchill to save the situation.[82] "Provided no unforeseen emergency occurs, such as a further fall of silver, war, a Burmah expedition," Colvin's fiscal policy would balance the budget.[83] Dufferin, seemingly, overlooked the fact that Churchill's Burmese policy had already carried the Government to the point of a Burmese expedition.

In this ebb and flow of debate, nothing more was heard of Indian grievances or reform. Churchill wrote no more on the proposal for Indian officers and, sensing the listlessness in Dufferin's response to the idea of raising the age limit for the Civil Service, agreed to drop it until after the election. What thoughts on reform he did have concerned the military organization of the princely and aristocratic class. The Indian Government should pursue toward the Princely States a military policy analogous to that of Prussia toward the German States after 1866 and 1870, and incorporate the feudatory armies "effectively in the military resources of India," with each State maintaining a stipulated military force which would be inspected "frequently" by British officers, brigaded with British troops when on manoeuvres, and armed with the latest weapons. This would reduce military costs while increasing internal security. "Here, you might find your outlet for native military aspirations which our policy since the Mutiny has unduly, I think, repressed."[84] Indian reform had come to mean for Churchill what it meant for Lytton: changes benefitting those classes which were integral to the British imperial mission.

From July to early October, Dufferin had played host to Churchill's imperial policy. Indian domestic policy had been lost sight of, and Indian reform interred. None of these developments went unnoticed by the educated Indian leaders, and each heightened their opposition to the Viceroy.

[81] D. to C., Sept. 10, 1885 (priv.), DVP, R. 517, No. 53.
[82] Dispatches of Governor-General-in-Council, nos. 264, 275, Fin., Sept. 22, Oct. 6, 1885, CRO, Fin. Let., 1886, Vol. 148.
[83] D. to C., Oct. 5, 1885 (priv.), DVP, R. 517. No. 56.
[84] C. to D., Sept. 22, Oct. 16, 1885, DVP, R. 517, nos. 73, 76.

VIII

A Summer of Dissatisfaction

As July slipped by and August vanished into September, Indian editors and politicians became increasingly dissatisfied with Dufferin and his handling of major issues such as the Indian Volunteer question and the proposal for Indian officers. Unfortunately, his action on other matters by no means mitigated their growing disillusionment. Revision of the Copyright Bill occasioned much dissension.[1] In 1884, Ilbert had decided to revise Act XX of 1847 relating to copyright in order to bring it in line with revision of the law in England and to update it to meet the needs of contemporary India. In June, *The Times of India,* the best edited and wealthiest journal in India, called Ilbert's attention to the fact that since it was the only newspaper in India paying for and publishing Reuters' telegrams, it should have priority rights to this news, and that the hitherto unrestrained "piracy" of its columns by other newspapers, both Anglo-Indian and Indian, should be stopped.[2] This seemed a reasonable request, which could well be applied to official, nonconfidential telegrams that were appearing with increasing regularity in the press. Ilbert therefore included press telegrams as a category for copyright in his draft bill,[3] specifying under Clause IV that neither a foreign nor a domestic news telegram could be reproduced by other newspapers "except after 24 hours from the time of publication" by the original owner.[4] His intent was not discriminatory—the clause was to apply to Anglo-Indian and Indian newspapers alike. In fact, the clause would affect only a handful of Indian newspapers,

---

[1] Neither the Copyright Bill nor the press agitation are mentioned in the DVP. The draft bill was introduced in 1885 into the Governor-General's Legislative Council, but was deferred early in 1886 (see *Times,* Jan. 5, 1886); the bill was eventually treated as an amendment and dealt with by the Executive Council.

[2] June 22, 1885.

[3] Introduced on June 9, see *Times,* June 11, 1885.

[4] See résumé of draft bill, *Times of India,* June 22, *Hindoo Patriot,* July 27, 1885.

one English daily,[5] some thirteen vernacular dailies,[6] and four tri-weeklies,[7] while the majority, weeklies and bi-weeklies, including, for the vernacular press alone, at least four Indian newspapers in Bombay City, twenty-three in Calcutta proper, and seventeen in Madras City, would remain unaffected.[8]

Though the clause seemed just, straightforward, and uncontroversial, many journalists thought otherwise when Ilbert circulated the draft bill for comment. Led by the editors of *The Bombay Gazette, The Madras Times, The Pioneer, The Englishman,* and *The Indian Daily News,* the entire Anglo-Indian press attacked the clause on press telegrams as unfair and conducive to monopoly.[9] They, in turn, were followed by editors of the Indian dailies who, seeing their interests threatened, distorted the facts and, playing skillfully upon the dissatisfaction already rife among Indian editors over the Volunteer and Civil Service questions, stimulated opposition to the clause. In their criticism, all, with the exception of the editors of *Indu Prakash, Rast Goftar, The Indian Spectator, The Sind Times,* and *The Tribune,* blamed Dufferin.

In Bombay, Maneckji Minocher-Homji, the Parsi editor of *Bombay Samachar,* the oldest and most influential Gujerati daily on the west coast, charged Dufferin with promoting another reactionary bill that would effectively gag the vernacular press, and requested the Viceroy to withdraw it.[10] His Parsi colleague, editing *Jam-e-Jamshed,* the other influential Gujerati daily in the city, and his Gujerati friends, who owned the Anglo-Gujerati *Kaiser-i-Hind,* cited the bill as evidence of the influence wealthy Anglo-Indian editors were able to exert upon Dufferin's Council.[11] The editor of *Pravati,* the Bengali daily most widely circulated in Calcutta and Lower Bengal,[12] charged that the clause was discriminatory because Indian editors had not been consulted and could not possibly pay copyright

[5] *Indian Mirror,* Calcutta.

[6] Bombay: *Bombay Samachar, Jam-e-Jamshed,* and *Akhbar-e-Soudagar* (all Gujerati), *Prabhakar* (Anglo-Marathi); Calcutta dailies: *Dainik Varta, Samvad Prabhakar, Samvad Purnachandrodaya, Samachar Chandrika, Banga Vidya Prakashika, Pravati* (all Bengali), and *Urdu Guide;* Lahore *Rahbar-i-Hind,* and Lucknow *Oudh Akhbar* (Urdu dailies).

[7] Madras: *Hindu* (English), *Dravidhavarthamani* (Tamil); Lahore *Akhbar-e-Am* and Lucknow *Hindustani* (Urdu).

[8] See confidential list of native newspapers, Bombay, Madras, and Bengal presidencies, Jan. 1885-July 1886, DP, D. 1071H/M12/1, 7, 8.

[9] Though the Calcutta correspondent of *The Times* telegraphed that the measure was "'generally approved" by the Anglo-Indian press (see *Times,* June 29, 1885), a survey of the press disproves his statement.

[10] *Bombay Samachar,* June 24 *(V. of I.,* III, July 1885) .

[11] *Kaiser-i-Hind,* June 28, *Jam-e-Jamshed,* June 29 *(V. of I.,* III, July 1885).

[12] Some 1,100 to 1,300 copies daily.

charges without pricing themselves out of business.[13] N. N. Sen, writing in *The Indian Mirror,* produced the most damaging indictment. The clause was another example of Dufferin's duplicity, and Sen quoted from an official letter, written by Mackenzie Wallace at the end of May with the Viceroy's full approval, though for some reason not published by Indian editors until the end of June, in reply to the Native Press Association of the Northwest Provinces and Oudh, thanking its members for the loyal resolution submitted at the height of the Afghan crisis:[14] "Lord Dufferin is a sincere friend of the Native Press in India [and] an attentive reader of the Native journals, regarding them as a legitimate channel through which an independent Native public opinion expresses the wants and wishes of the community [and] as one of the most powerful assistants the Government can possess to the proper conduct of public affairs."[15] Sen, in first publishing the letter on June 23, chose to compliment the Viceroy fulsomely, but, a few days later, with the copyright clause on press telegrams before him, he caustically commented that, with such legislation, the Viceroy was absolutely crippling the "native Press," and demanded that the Viceroy make good his words and revoke the clause.[16] Toward the end of August, the Indian editors met to draw up memorials to the Viceroy, and, when no response was forthcoming from the Viceregal Lodge at Simla, they added this copyright clause to their list of unanswered grievances.[17]

Adding fuel to the fire was the news of the official decision against raising the age limit for the Covenanted Civil Service examinations. This reached Calcutta via the columns of *The Pall Mall Gazette,* whose editor, W. T. Stead, managed to obtain and quote verbatim paragraph eleven of Kimberley's January dispatch instructing the Viceroy to decline the request of the memorialists for a higher age limit.[18] Stead commented that this was the final act in the "virtual exclusion of Indian youths from the chance of rising to executive power in the public service of their own country," and called for either an increase in the age limit to 21 years or simultaneous

[13] *Pravati,* June 26 (quoted in *Indian Mirror,* June 26, 1885).

[14] At a meeting in Lucknow, Apr. 3, see *Tribune,* Apr. 3, 10, 1885.

[15] Wallace to Ganga Prasad Varma (editor-proprietor, *Hindustani*), May 22 (*V. of I.,* III, July 1885, p. 348).

[16] *Indian Mirror,* June 23, 27, 1885.

[17] See selections in *V. of I.,* III, July, Aug. 1885; also translations from Bengal vernacular press in *Indian Mirror,* June 26, July 23, *Englishman's Overland Mail,* Aug. 1, 15, 22, 29, 1885. The clause was eventually rescinded. Published in June 1886 as the grams; see CRO, *A Collection of Statutes Relating to India,* Vol. I. International Copyright Act (of 1886), the act included no category for press tele-

[18] See Chap. I, n. 88, and above, pp. 170-171.

examinations in India and England.[19] Stead's editorial was published immediately by Sen in *The Indian Mirror* and by Banerjea
ment of the Statutory Service, Sen criticized Dufferin for having
in *The Bengalee*,[20] and then by the leading vernacular and Anglo-
Bengali journals. Using the editorial to launch a scathing indict-
approved the candidate selected by Grant-Duff, who had passed over
K. Subba Rau, the top man among all the Madrassi candidates and
a member of the Madras Sabha, even though the Viceroy admitted
in private that Rau should have been selected.[21] "This is not the
sort of justice we expected at the hands of Lord Dufferin [who] has
committed a very grave error merely to please Mr. Grant-Duff,"
Sen wrote, adding, "it is needless to disguise the fact that the Native
Community is far from satisfied. . . . The Statutory Civil Service is
a perfect farce."[22] S. Banerjea directed his fire less at Dufferin than
at Kimberley's decision: it flouted justice; it would keep Indians in
an inferior position by making them enter the Civil Service through
"back-door patronage" of the worst sort; and it emanated from a
Liberal cabinet, members of which had pressed for reform of this
very system on the floor of the Commons in 1878-79. But "expectations have now been blasted . . . the defeat . . . gives rise to melancholy reflections regarding the character of British rule."[23] The
editors of *The Hindoo Patriot*, in similar vein, claimed that the
Viceroy had failed to make good the official pledge to draw upon
Indians "of good family, of appropriate loyalty and of good education."[24] Dissatisfaction concerning the Civil Service quickly became
mingled with that already engendered by the Copyright Bill.

In Bengal, the feeling was intensified by Dufferin's role in the
controversy raging between the Lieutenant-Governor, Rivers
Thompson, and the Municipal Commissioners of the Calcutta
Corporation. Ostensibly, the controversy arose over the matter of
sanitation in Calcutta and its suburbs, but actually it concerned
personalities and politics, and stemmed from the mutual antipathy
that had arisen between Rivers Thompson and his commissioners,
especially N. N. Sen, S. N. Banerjea, and Raja R. L. Mitra, during
the Ilbert Bill dispute and subsequently over Rivers Thompson's
reluctance to frame a liberal Local Self-Government Bill. Throughout 1884, both parties, increasingly at odds, awaited the moment of

[19] "Occasional Notes," *Pall Mall Gazette*, May 30, received in India *ca.* June 26-27,
1885.
[20] *Indian Mirror*, June 27, *Bengalee*, July 4, 1885.
[21] D. to K., Mar. 2, 1885 (priv.), DVP, R. 517, No. 13.
[22] Editorial, *Indian Mirror*, July 3, 1885.
[23] Editorial, *Bengalee*, July 4, 1885.
[24] Editorial, July 27, 1885.

collision, which was ultimately precipitated by the question of measures to control cholera in Calcutta and its suburbs.

Cholera had always been prevalent in India, particularly along the Ganges and the Hugli rivers, and, during the century, epidemics reaching pandemic proportions had occurred in 1826, 1832, 1840, and 1879. In Calcutta, the growth of population since the sixties and the resulting expansion of the city along the Hugli made the disease a constant source of anxiety to the Bengal authorities.[25] It could arise overnight in the congested, diseased riverine sections and could spread rapidly with serious consequences for the health and livelihood of the inhabitants. By the seventies, health specialists who had studied the etiology of the disease agreed that public quarantine was no longer sufficient to check the disease and that sanitary controls and inspection, particularly of public water supplies and the disposal of night soil, were required if the disease was to be isolated and stamped out. In 1876, one of the tasks allotted to the newly formed Calcutta Municipal Corporation was to deal with controls for cholera; and though the corporation took some action, progress was impeded by lack of funds and preoccupation with other problems. In mid-1884, when Bengal officials, concerned over the corporation's slow progress, brought the matter to Rivers Thompson's attention with a request for more decisive action, the results were explosive.[26]

Rivers Thompson charged the corporation with having failed conspicuously to formulate and to implement a sanitation scheme, and appointed a Special Commission consisting of three non-Bengali members of the corporation to assess the work already completed and recommend to the Bengal Government a plan for the future. The majority of the corporation countercharged that Rivers Thompson and the Bengal Government had failed to provide the corporation with the necessary funds and refused to approve the Special Commission, as was their right under the Municipal Charter. Rivers Thompson, relying upon executive clauses in the charter, overruled the corporation and, to the indignation of Sen, Banerjea, Mitra, and the entire Bengali press, proceeded with the Special Commission.

The report of the Special Commission, submitted in April 1885, upheld Thompson's charge against the corporation and included a long list of measures calling for immediate action. The commis-

---

[25] See *P.P.*, 1884, Vol. 54, chs. III, VII, Com. 4116, and *P.P.*, 1887, Vol. 63, chs. III, VII, Com. 5209, for sanitary reports for 1882-83 and 1885-86.

[26] For a summary of the sanitation question 1884-1885, not mentioned in DVP, see Calcutta telegrams, *Times*, July 13, 27, and editorial, *Hindoo Patriot*, July 20, 1885.

sioners, with reason, stressed the urgency of the situation, for the Sanitary Conference had just concluded its session at Rome with a decision that any port which did not provide sanitary controls against cholera should be placed in quarantine to all shipping. Following the wishes of Rivers Thompson and of Henry Harrison, the Chairman of the corporation, the commissioners recommended the appointment of a Special Committee to study the amalgamation of the municipality and suburbs into one corporate body, in order to facilitate uniform and economical sanitary arrangements.

Rivers Thompson forwarded the report and recommendations to the Home Department for Dufferin's approval.[27] He also used the report as a platform from which to lecture the corporation on its waywardness. The Municipal Commissioners had expected this, but they were wholly unprepared for Rivers Thompson's sudden appointment of the Special Committee on amalgamation, without referring to them, without appointing any members from the Suburban Ratepayers Association to the committee, and without paying any attention to the representative group which came to his office to appeal against amalgamation. R. Sarvadhikari, the editor of *The Hindoo Patriot,* spoke for R. L. Mitra and the Political Committee of the British Indian Association when he charged Rivers Thompson with acting in a high-handed fashion with no regard for "the sacred principle of local self-government."[28] Sen called him "despotic" and "autocratic," charged him with playing cheap politics with Harrison, and berated him for using an undemocratic, "packed Committee." Since Rivers Thompson had acted over the heads of the Municipal Commission and Suburban Ratepayers, Sen called for protests to the Viceroy. "Lord Dufferin, if he is at all friendly to local self-government as Lord Ripon was, should interfere in the present case. Otherwise, the whole Native community . . . will be profoundly alarmed, and even seriously discontented."[29] Sen's call for agitation to impress the Viceroy received an immediate response. The Political Committee of the British Indian Association, then planning to petition Rivers Thompson to suspend the implementation of the new Bengal Tenancy Act for one year, promptly announced a large meeting for early August,[30] and all the Bengali

---

[27] Secretary, Government of Bengal, to Secretary, Government of India, No. 824, Home, July 1, with enclosures, as cited in letter of Governor-General-in-Council, Aug. 31, published, *Indian Mirror,* Sept. 15, 1885.

[28] "'The Reason Why," July 20, 1885.

[29] Editorials, *Indian Mirror,* "The Threatened Extinction of Local Self-Government in Calcutta and the Suburbs," July 22, "The Autocrat of Bengal, and a Packed Committee," July 31, 1885.

[30] *Hindoo Patriot,* July 31, 1885.

editors, already directing their invectives against the copyright clause on press telegrams, readily joined in the protest. As in the early stages of the Volunteer question, all turned to Dufferin as a higher court of appeal.

It was this kind of situation that made the Viceroy's position difficult and unenviable. For better or for worse, his relations with the different groups composing Indian society were largely determined by the day-to-day relationship between the governors and lieutenant-governors and these groups. Where a reasonable degree of consultation was maintained, appeals on legislative or other policy matters of an ill-considered, vexatious character were unlikely to be made to the Supreme Government and put the Viceroy at odds with the Indian groups whose interests were involved. Lord Reay's actions in Bombay during his initial six months in office are illustrative of this happy relationship. He added two more Indians to the Bombay Legislative Council—Mahadev Ranade and Dadabhai Naoroji, two of the most competent and representative members of the Bombay educated Indian community.[31] He approved a Poona Municipal Board, consisting of twenty elected and ten nominated members, with an elected president, and he appointed a representative commission to investigate Indian grievances concerning the forest regulations in the Thana district—a measure which both Telang and Hume had encouraged him to take.[32] He set up a Bombay City Commission, including in it representatives of the Bombay Indian community, to investigate Indian grievances concerning the *abkari* regulations, and he wrote the Viceroy after hearing the grievances of the Anjuman-i-Islam regarding education and the insufficient representation of Muslims in the Civil Service, thereby giving the impetus to the Supreme Government's resolution on Muslim education.[33] He listened to the grievances of the Poona Sarvajanik Sabha and advised its leaders in their preparation of a petition to the Viceroy.[34] He issued a resolution prohibiting discriminatory treatment of Indians by Englishmen on trains,[35] and he accepted the invitation of the Bombay Presidency Association to preside at the Fawcett Memorial Meeting on September 2.[36] The

[31] Reay's appointment of Ranade in May and Naoroji in the summer, in addition to Fergusson's previous appointments of Telang and Tyabji, made the Bombay Council the most representative, in India, of Indian interests.

[32] Reay to D., May 24, July 27, Aug. 15, 1885, DVP, R. 528, nos. 331, 81, 166.

[33] Reay to D., July 27, May 31, 1885, DVP, R. 528, nos. 81, 360.

[34] Reay to D., Aug. 5, 1885, DVP, R. 528, No. 129.

[35] Aug. 4, see Reay to D., Aug. 11, 1885, DVP, R. 528, No. 148; also *V. of I.*, III, Aug. 1885, pp. 417-418.

[36] *Times of India*, Sept. 4, 1885.

influential Bombay leaders agreed that Reay, in his response to the problems and grievances of the Bombay Indian community, was just, impartial, and energetic. He acted so as to preclude any measures being submitted to the Viceroy which might put Dufferin in the awkward position of opposing Bombay "native" interests.

The same could not be said for Rivers Thompson. Bengali editors commented continually on the contrast with Reay. Rivers Thompson had taken no steps toward effective representation of Indian interests. He had not consulted Bengalis on critical measures such as the Bengal Tenancy Act and the Bengal Local Self-Government Act,[37] and he had consistently refused to meet with the leaders of the Bengali associations to discuss proposals for reform. They sensed in him the narrow caste prejudice of the civil servant toward Indians in general, in contrast to the refreshing objectivity of the true aristocrat, as exemplified in Reay. Rivers Thompson's inflexibility and lack of understanding irritated and alienated the Bengalis with the result that legislative recommendations, forwarded by Rivers Thompson to the Supreme Government for final approval by the Governor-General in Council, were usually unacceptable to the Bengalis. This put Dufferin in the invidious position of either coming into conflict with Bengali interests or overruling his Lieutenant-Governor who, the Viceroy had come to realize, was "very unpopular with the native community."[38]

In mid-September, Dufferin's reply to Rivers Thompson on the report of the Special Commission on sanitation was published.[39] The Viceroy approved the recommendations of the commission, declared that the Lieutenant-Governor had in no way infringed the principles of local self-government by his actions, and rebuked the corporation for raising so many "irrelevant issues," for being hypersensitive to criticisms by its executive government, and for failing to increase municipal rates to pay for adequate sanitation. Dufferin expressed interest in the forthcoming proposal of the new committee on amalgamation, a task, he thought, which should have been undertaken by the corporation. Despite a mild rebuke to Rivers Thompson for some tactlessness and haste on amalgamation—a rebuke which all the Bengali editors attributed to A. Mackenzie, the Home Department Secretary—Dufferin's reply constituted an endorsement of Rivers Thompson and a censure of the corporation.

The Bengali politicians and editors were stunned. S. Banerjea's

[37] See above, pp. 31-35.
[38] D. to C., Aug. 28, 1885 (priv.), DVP, R. 517, No. 51.
[39] See n. 27 above.

"deep disappointment" was "all the more keen, considering that we had been promised a continuity of the late Viceroy's policy at any rate, as regards Municipal institutions."[40] Imitating Sen, Banerjea reprinted Dufferin's statement made upon arrival in Calcutta pledging his support to Ripon's principles. He asked why Dufferin should reply with alacrity to Rivers Thompson on sanitation yet make no response to the Indian associations on volunteering.[41] Raja Norendra Krishna Deb, Raja R. L. Mitra, K. Lall Dey, L. Mukherji, Raja Chandra Singh, and others, all leading zemindars of the British Indian Association, who had learned a few days earlier that Rivers Thompson had declined their petition on the Bengal Tenancy Act,[42] joined with Banerjea, his colleagues in the Indian Association, and with Sen, Syama Churn Laha, and some 200 members of the Suburban Ratepayers Association, at the Town Hall, to criticize the Viceroy's decision and protest against amalgamation without representation.[43] Sen announced that it was but another indication of what they could expect from Dufferin as Viceroy. "It is useless to appeal at all to the Government of India against any decision of any Local Government"; henceforth neither the Viceroy nor his senior advisers would be looked upon as a higher court of appeal for the redress of Indian grievances. What were things coming to in India? Where were he and his colleagues to turn for a fair hearing? Where, but to themselves?

This was the conclusion reached by other Indian editors and politicians once they had grasped the import of Churchill's Budget Statement, telegraphic reports of which arrived by mid-August. It confirmed their suspicions: Churchill had shown his true colors, and Dufferin was in league with him. They were surprised and exasperated by Churchill's attack upon Ripon and his policy, especially as Churchill, when in India, had led them to believe that he sympathized with Ripon's views.[44] To a man, they rushed into print to defend the reputation of their viceregal patron saint.[45] No issue since volunteering provoked a more unanimous, deeply felt response. Even R. L. Mitra and Sarvadhikari and their colleagues at *The Hindoo Patriot,* none of whom had been stalwart advocates of Ripon and his work, took up the cudgels.[46] But the Indian editors

---

[40] *Bengalee,* Sept. 12, 1885.
[41] *Bengalee,* Sept. 19, 1885.
[42] Petition presented Aug. 23, see *Times,* Aug. 24; petition declined Sept. 10, see *Evening Standard,* Sept. 11, 1885.
[43] On Sept. 12, see editorial, *Indian Mirror,* Sept. 15, 1885.
[44] *Indian Spectator,* Aug. 16, 1885.
[45] See selections, *V. of I.,* III, Aug., Sept. 1885.
[46] Editorial, "Lord Churchill on Lord Ripon," Sept. 7, 1885.

knew that their protests were ex post facto and that Churchill's attack had been devastatingly complete, marking as it did the virtual end of Ripon's policy of restricted military expenditure, light taxation, beneficial public works, and political and educational reforms. Now this reform policy was to be replaced by a permanent increase in the British Indian Army costing an additional £2,000,000 per year. This was "a shocking proposition."[47] so much so that some declared that it would have been cheaper in the long run to have gone to war with Russia and won an enduring peace.[48] In the opinion of Malabari and many others, "it has yet to be proved *that a permanent increase in the army is really needed,*" particularly when the Russians were on the verge of burying the hatchet with England, when the telegraph, the Suez Canal, steamships, railways in India, and improved weapons made the existing force with fewer men twice as effective as in former days, and when the armies of the Indian princes stood ready and scores of educated Indians were awaiting permission to enroll as volunteers.[49]

"It is utterly incomprehensible to us," wrote the Ghose brothers, "how the Secretary of State means to raise these two millions from a people so hopelessly steeped in debt and poverty."[50] J. U. Yajnik, speaking at the meeting of the Bombay Presidency Association in honor of their late Parliamentary advocate, Henry Fawcett, found it inconceivable that India should be made to pay for this lavish expenditure. Churchill had announced that retrenchment was to precede taxation, but retrenchment of what and for how much?[51] Other Indian editors asked even more penetrating questions. Was the presidency army system to be abolished and the large net saving to be applied to the new military expenditure?[52] Would the Indian Civil Service be trimmed and would more Indians with lower salaries be used in place of Europeans at great annual saving?[53] Or would the Public Works Department provide still further scope for retrenchment?[54] These measures seemed highly improbable. Dedicated as Indian editors were to retrenchment, they seriously doubted whether it was the cure for the Indian budget. Ever since Mayo's time, they had heard about retrenchment, but it inevitably had resulted in sacking Indians from minor offices or reducing

[47] *News of the Day,* Aug. 17 (*V. of I.,* III, Aug. 1885).
[48] *Hindoo Patriot,* Aug. 24, 1885.
[49] *Indian Spectator,* Sept. 20, 1885.
[50] *Amrita Bazar Patrika,* Aug. 13 (*V. of I.,* III, Aug. 1885).
[51] On Sept. 2, *Times of India,* Sept. 4, 1885.
[52] *Native Opinion,* Aug. 9 (*V. of I.,* III, Aug. 1885).
[53] *Bengalee,* Aug. 15, 1885.
[54] *Amrita Bazar Patrika,* Sept. 3 (*V. of I.,* III, Sept. 1885).

fringe staffs, and had never involved "a careful and thorough over-hauling of the various branches of the public service,"[55] or what Banerjea preferred to call "bloated establishments and inefficient systems."[56] Nor had it ever entailed cutting the expensive "Simla exodus" of the entire secretariat from Calcutta during the hot weather, estimated at £800,000 per year.[57] Worse still, retrenchment had always taken its toll of productive public works, such as commercial railways, so essential to India's trade, and the Famine Insurance Fund.[58] To touch the Famine Fund would be tantamount to "a gross breach of faith," since Lytton's administration, in devising the fund, had pledged that it would be used only for works to prevent famine or for relief. Should the prevailing official view of retrenchment be to use the Famine Fund in 1885 entirely for military expenditure, as had been done once in 1879, the Indian editors were convinced that this "misappropriation" would be no cure for India's financial ills.[59]

Failing retrenchment, there remained taxation—"the very means which they [the Indian editors] most dread."[60] Churchill in his Statement had spoken of a light increase in taxation as a last resort —and then only in the form of an extended license tax, not an income tax. But Churchill, the editors maintained, was playing with words again. The license tax could only be extended horizontally to official and nonofficial Anglo-Indian incomes, certainly not vertically to Indian incomes lower than 1,500 rupees per year. "Indians have been pumped to the pice" and can assume no increase in taxes.[61] Moreover, if the license tax were extended to European incomes, would not this really be an income tax? Would not this, in turn, permit the Indian government to increase the incidence of taxation on Indian incomes? "If additional taxation is resorted to . . . it would fall as a calamity on the people."[62] The "discontent" which Churchill said he had found upon his arrival in India "would be greatly intensified if additional burdens were imposed upon the people."[63] "The people," of course, included the Indian editors, who warned the Secretary of State and the Viceroy that their patience and support of official policy were sorely over-

[55] *Tribune*, Sept. 12, 1885.
[56] *Bengalee*, Aug. 15, 1885.
[57] *Amrita Bazar Patrika*, Sept. 10 (*V. of I.*, III, Sept. 1885).
[58] *Hindoo Patriot*, Aug. 24, *Prabhakar*, Sept. 5, *Armita Bazar Patrika*, Sept. 10, *Liberal*, Sept. 13 (*V. of I.*, III, Sept. 1885).
[59] *Hindoo Patriot*, Sept. 7, 1885.
[60] *Hindoo Patriot*, Aug. 24, 1885.
[61] *Amrita Bazar Patrika*, Aug. 13 (*V. of I.*, III, Aug. 1885).
[62] *Rast Goftar*, Aug. 16 (*V. of I.*, III, Aug. 1885).
[63] *Hindoo Patriot*, Sept. 7, 1885.

strained, and that they had no wish to scrape their pockets for a policy on which they had never been consulted and which they had never wanted in the first place.

Furthermore, in their view, alternatives to taxation did exist, even though Churchill had not seen fit to mention them in his Statement. By reimposing the import duties on English cotton cloth and other goods entering India, the Government could raise at least £1.5 millions, or almost the extra annual military charge.[64] This alternative was supported by the influential Madras Chamber of Commerce, composed principally of Anglo-Indian business and professional men who saw their incomes threatened by the extension of the license tax. Largely out of self-interest, the chamber addressed a strong remonstrance to the Viceroy on the dangerous financial policy his administration had begun to follow, and advocated borrowing to cover military expenditure and reimposing the import duties.[65] The Indian press in Bombay, where many of the proprietors and editors of the Parsi and Gujerati journals were directly connected with the textile industry, overwhelmingly favored this step. They had always regarded the lowering of duties as the intensification of imperial discrimination rather than as the application of free trade principles, and, since Churchill had been so bold as to accuse Ripon of being the culprit who had finally removed the duties, they urged Churchill to reimpose them and aid the Indian taxpayer.[66] Failing this, the editors reverted to the original alternatives of using the armies of the Princely States or Indian volunteers.[67] And Malabari wondered, "Is there any hope of England sharing this burden, if she does not bear it herself entirely? Why should India pay for England's imperial policy?"[68]

But the Indian editors knew that none of these alternatives would be considered as long as Churchill and Dufferin determined policy, with the influential India Council behind them. Official factions would nullify any vigorous retrenchment or the substitution of lower paid Indian officials for higher paid Europeans;[69] the "lurking fear" concerning Indian loyalty would prohibit any effective use of the princely armies and Indian volunteers;[70] "the powerful cotton lords of Manchester" would dissuade Churchill

[64] *Jam-e-Jamshed*, Aug. 11 (*V. of I.*, III, Aug. 1885).
[65] Letter, July 25, published in *Madras Times*, Aug. 7, 1885.
[66] *Indian Chronicle*, Aug. 17, *Amrita Bazar Patrika*, Sept. 10 (*V. of I.*, III, Aug., Sept. 1885).
[67] *Hindu*, Aug. 20, and others (*V. of I.*, III, Aug., Sept. 1885).
[68] *Indian Spectator*, Aug. 16, 1885.
[69] *Amrita Bazar Patrika*, Sept. 3, *Liberal*, Sept. 13 (*V. of I.*, III, Sept. 1885).
[70] *Subodh Prakash*, Aug. 26, and others (*V. of I.*, III, Aug., Sept. 1885).

from reimposing the import duties;[71] while the pecuniary self-interest of any English government, be it Tory, Liberal, or Radical, and the impotence of India made sharing the new expenditure as an imperial charge a dream.[72]

Finally, might not Churchill's proposal for a Parliamentary inquiry into Indian administration prove a timely alternative? All the editors welcomed it as a step in the right direction, which should be used to good advantage,[73] but it would not parry the immediate threat of increased taxation, nor would it necessarily be of much use in the future. The inquiry depended on a Tory victory in the coming election, and the odds, they felt, were against this.[74] Furthermore, they soon learned that the proposed inquiry would canvass the opinions only of Anglo-Indian officials and members of Parliament,[75] and would be limited strictly to the administration of the acts which regulated the governmental machinery of India.[76] Churchill's promise was therefore merely a "half promise," and of these Indians had received too many in recent years to place any further confidence in the words of English statesmen. "We have ceased to believe in the profession and promises even of English statesmen . . . how can we trust to the sincerity of convictions which do not stand the crucial test of action?" wrote Sen.[77]

Sen and most of his fellow editors had ceased to rely upon Churchill or Dufferin; slowly but surely, they had come to realize that they must rely on their own political action. "It is the duty of our political associations," wrote the editors of *Jam-e-Jamshed*, "to supply Manchester, the Home Government, the Parliament, and the Government of India with the figures of the last seven years' imports of English-made cloth in India and then to raise an agitation on a large scale, both here and in England, for reimposition of the import duties."[78] K. Kabraji and D. Naoroji called for action against imperial charges: "The whole of India should protest against this crushing burden [before] it will be too late to protest against the new financial policy."[79] Some called for action directed at influential groups in England. "This burden which English politicians are imposing on India in the imperial

[71] *Hindoo Patriot*, Sept. 7, 1885.
[72] *Indian Spectator*, Sept. 20, 1885.
[73] See selections, *V. of I.*, III, Aug., Sept. 1885.
[74] *Hindoo Patriot*, Aug. 24, 1885.
[75] *Amrita Bazar Patrika*, Aug. 13 (*V. of I.*, III, Aug. 1885).
[76] *Hindoo Patriot*, Sept. 21, 1885.
[77] On retrenchment, *Indian Mirror*, Aug. 15, 1885.
[78] Aug. 24 (*V. of I.*, III, Aug. 1885).
[79] *Rast Goftar*, Sept. 6 (*V. of I.*, III, Sept. 1885).

interest of England, ought to be borne by the latter, and the efforts of our friends in that country, and also of our political associations, should be directed to secure this redress."[80] The moment had arrived "for carrying on an agitation for demanding the removal of the obstacles imposed on India . . . Native political associations, native publicists, young students and experienced merchants should now band together for raising a just cry for the wants of the country."[81] Some wished to aim a broad attack at Parliament,[82] and some to relate all agitation on economic matters to Churchill's Parliamentary inquiry.[83] Dissatisfaction with Dufferin and his financial policy was strong, the urge to protest real, and the plans for agitation rife. The ideas set forth in January for a national reform movement to extend Ripon's work had by September been transformed into talk of national political agitation to oppose Dufferin's administration.

In mid-July, just as this dissatisfaction was beginning to ferment, an Anglo-Indian writer in Bombay forwarded an article to *The Times* of London[84] a day or so before Hume sailed for England to carry out plans for the proposed Indian National Union and the Telegraphic Union.[85] The timing of the article was not coincidental, for rumors had been circulating in Anglo-Indian circles of Allahabad and Bombay that Hume was going to England on behalf of "Young India." Nor was it just another random article in the discursive manner of a *Times* foreign correspondent. Written in a style that betrayed an official hand, it was a classic exposition of the prevailing official theory of Indian domestic policy, clearly for the benefit of Churchill and his politically minded colleagues who, with an election coming up, might be inclined to listen to "either ignorant philanthropists in England or ambitious agitators in India" on the subject of accelerating the pace of Indian political reform.

The writer, primarily concerned with "the cold reality" of the internal policy of the Indian government and India's political future, neither of which, he thought, were thoroughly understood in England, pointed to a significant change which had taken place in the Government's task. Since the British had failed to colonize India intensively, and did not possess the requisite manpower and resources to provide the administrative staff necessary to meet the

---

[80] *Subodh Patrika*, Sept. 6 (*V. of I.*, III, Sept. 1885).
[81] *Kaiser-i-Hind*, Aug. 30 (*V. of I.*, III, Aug. 1885).
[82] *News of the Day*, Aug. 25 (*V. of I.*, III, Aug. 1885).
[83] *Hindustani*, Sept. 9 (*V. of I.*, III, Sept. 1885).
[84] "The Government of India," July 15, Bombay, *Times*, Aug. 19, 1885.
[85] See above, p. 164.

demands of the Indian people, which had been stimulated by British enlightenment, permanent British ascendancy over India was out of the question. The Government's task was no longer merely to rule the races of India, but now it was "to weld them into one great nation . . . fit to perform all the civic duties of a self-governing people." This could not be done in a day. India was still plagued by "the conflict of races, the diversity of creeds, the isolating effect of caste, and all the separating influences and disintegrating forces" which, for centuries, had thrust men apart on the subcontinent. These divisive elements produced heterogeneity, and the Indian government had first to bring about the homogeneity required for any nation. Also, the political capacity of the people, irrespective of what might be said about the centuries old traditions of village headmen and panchayats, was "simply *nil*" beyond the towns and left much to be desired in the towns and cities; "the people of India are not in the least ready for the self-government that their zealous friends would thrust upon them."

This, the writer quickly added, did not mean that the Government was not striving to develop the political capacity of the people. On the contrary, ever since the Queen's Proclamation of 1858, every Viceroy had steadily promoted local self-government. Moreover, "natives" had been selected for the central and provincial legislative councils; they had been appointed to the High Court and to the Statutory Service, and could compete, if they wished, for the Covenanted Civil Service. They were being educated for self-government; "in the whole Imperial administration of the country they have now a footing," and will rise "in time" to more responsible capacities, even though "higher capacity can only be attained after years of patient exercise of the lower duties." This whole experiment was "in its infancy and ought to be given time to show its results before any further advance is made." But gradualism was threatened by "the educated class in the towns" who were far ahead of the ignorant millions in political awareness. "This section of the people have been taught, perhaps, beyond the needs of their station, and they fret at the want of an opening. They are clerks, writers, editors, pleaders, doctors, and through the native Press many of them maintain a constant agitation in favour of the Native right to further political power. This cry, taken up as it is by ignorant philanthropy at home, is one of the greatest obstacles to true progress that the Indian government has to encounter." The writer cited as an example the fate of the reforms in local self-government. After a year's experience on the local boards, educated Indians were now shunning them and shouting for representation in the councils, with the result that the entire experiment was in danger of not receiving a fair trial. This led the writer to question whether the experiment in political education was really worth trying. Superficial and hasty training meant irresponsibility and inefficiency later. Would it not be better to keep the Government of India autocratic in accordance with its culture and traditions? And should not educated Indians concentrate on social reform, for which there was a great demand for their energies, and leave politics to the Government? If "these agitators found no sympathy in England," such might indeed come to pass. Thus it was absolutely incumbent upon "the true friends of India" not to respond to or to encourage these "hasty aspirations."

In mid-August just a few days after Hume set foot in England, this article was published in *The Times*. Whether or not it was written with Hume in mind, its publication could not have been better timed to make his mission more difficult. The article made an instant impression and stimulated Anglo-Indian prejudices against any thought of Indian reform.

Two days later, an article entitled "The Black Radical" appeared in the *St. James's Gazette*.[86] Edited by Frederick Greenwood, Tory in politics and imperial in outlook, the *Gazette* had a large circulation in influential political circles and published some of the most clever and informative articles in the London press. In this article, attention was focused on Lal Mohan Ghose, the Bengali barrister from Dacca who had spent the past two years in London working with the Indian Reform Association and who in early 1885 had been chosen by the Liberal Party to contest the seat at Greenwich. The writer sought to prove that Ghose and "the more adventurous of the Indian politicians" came to England to dabble in alien politics because they had a far better chance of convincing the credulous British public that they represented a whole people struggling to be free than they had of attempting the same stunt with the Indian people at home. He considered the work of such men an excellent study in deception, since they fanned the air with three serious "misrepresentations": first, that India was a nation resembling modern European democracies; second, that English senior officials in India were rapacious, indolent despots; and third, that the aspirations of the "natives" of India were represented by English-educated Indians. Parroting the expressions and ideas set forth in the article in *The Times*, he asked: "Is it

[86] Aug. 17, pp. 5-6, "Radical Types—V"; also editorial, Aug. 28, 1885, "Real Indian Reforms," with a similar attack on English-educated Indians and political reform.

to be supposed that a century of English rule has transformed such a population into a great quasi-European nation, ready to govern and legislate for itself, and to behave in all respects as if it were descended from Saxon forefathers? . . ." The very idea was absurd. Equally absurd was the idea that Ghose and other agitators from across the seas, whom he did not name, represented the aspirations of the Indian peoples. Their heterogeneity and their lack of education made this claim laughable. What educated Indians did not admit was that for every one of them there were twenty others who were contented with and deeply grateful for British rule, and who, if they had the opportunity, would annihilate this "insignificant section of pestilent rhetoricians" from the scene of British–Indian relations and stop the flow of venom that was poisoning the minds of Indians against the English and sapping the foundations of the Empire.

These articles were well timed to hamper Hume. They forced him to spend the rest of August and all of September refuting their arguments before embarking upon his task of attempting to persuade British politicians and the public of the pressing need for Indian reform. In letters to the press and in personal contacts he sought to counteract the effect of the articles.

On September 3, for instance, he sent to *The Evening Standard*, which had the largest circulation in London,[87] a letter in reply to an editorial by J. Robinson, the editor, who, using the arguments of *The Times* article, advised refusal of the Indian demand to volunteer.[88] Hume's reply was a significant addendum to his discussion with Dufferin in May.

Referring to himself "as the representative and delegate *pro tem* of the Indian National Union, an Association that includes the great majority of the foremost members of the Native community of all parts of India (excluding Burma and Assam)," Hume summarized for the editor the arguments he had made to Dufferin, and emphasized the controls and qualifications proposed by the Indian leaders, which would effectively counter the dangers the editor of *The Evening Standard* foresaw, notably its novel, uncontrollable character in a society where "volcanic religious fanaticism and race animosity" prevailed. The concepts of religious and racial conflicts were applicable only to the uneducated, unwesternized Indian masses, not to educated Indians. Having disposed of the editorial, Hume took the opportunity to appeal to the cabinet and

[87] 246, 470 copies.
[88] Editorial, *Evening Standard*, Sept. 3; Hume's reply, "Native Indian Volunteers," and editorial rebuttal, Sept. 4, 1885.

to potentates of the India Office to permit Indian volunteering. "Otherwise, the disappointment will be deep, widespread and lasting, [because] now the uneducated millions look up everywhere for guidance to the educated hundreds, and wish what these wish in a way that no one even five years ago could have deemed possible." In words curiously similar to those Churchill had used in writing to Dufferin, Hume declared that "nothing but direct necessity should lead us to 'snub' and throw cold water on the loyal impulses that have led to these offers." Although Robinson, not convinced, wrote another brief editorial in rebuttal, Hume had ably argued the case for Indian volunteering in one of the leading London newspapers and had made a bid far beyond Dufferin's circle for a fair hearing on the issue.

But for the most part, Hume's efforts to inform the British public on Indian issues were of a less public and more personal character. Acting on the suggestions of D. Naoroji, N. N. Sen, A. M. Bose, Motilal Ghose, and others that Indian grievances be placed before the British public and Parliament by a competent group sympathetic to Indian interests, Hume, through the efforts of Wedderburn, Ilbert, and Ripon, gained the able assistance of an influential group of Liberals and radical Liberals. He met Sir James Caird, the expert on Indian agriculture and famine, and through him, John Bright, who with the late Henry Fawcett and members of the Indian Reform Association had always shown an interest in Indian grievances. Hume was also introduced to Lord Dalhousie, the wealthy Scots landowner whose family ties with India were well known, to William Baxter, radical Liberal M.P. for Dundee, to R. P. Reid [later Lord Loreburn], Liberal M.P. for Hereford, and to John Slagg, radical Liberal M.P. for Manchester.[89] Hume's principal counsellor was Lord Ripon, with whom he stayed in mid-September at Studley Royal.[90] He also met Joseph Chamberlain, the mastermind of the radical Liberal campaign for the forthcoming election.[91] Through these men, he established links with British newspapers for the Indian National Telegraphic Union, to which Lord Ripon and Lord Dalhousie made generous contributions. By the time Hume departed from England in November, he had arranged with a goodly number of English and Scots

[89] Wedderburn, pp. 55-56.
[90] See R. to Malabari, editor, *Indian Spectator*, Sept. 10, 1885, RP, BM Add. MSS 43616, pp. 176-178.
[91] "Notes by the Way," *Christian World*, Oct. 29, 1885, p. 814, announcing Hume's arrival in England to bring Indian grievances to the notice of Liberal leaders and his meetings with Bright, Chamberlain, and Ripon.

editors to publish the weekly Indian commentaries telegraphed by the Union.[92]

Hume also discussed with these men the aim of the Indian National Union to stir the British public's interest in Indian issues. Their advice was unanimous. Since they would be unable to give detailed attention to Indian grievances during the election campaign, Hume should concentrate upon obtaining from the various candidates with Indian sympathies a pledge to refer to Indian affairs during the campaign. "I would recommend you," R. P. Reid wrote Hume, "to secure two or three men, as influential as you can, in as many constituencies as you can, and get them to write to the candidate, exacting no pledge as to the course of policy but a simple pledge to give attention to Indian affairs, and publish the correspondence in the local papers. . . . One in ten would keep the pledge (which would be easy) and thus give a nucleus of listeners in an Indian debate. The publicity of the correspondence would make them afraid wholly to neglect business they had so publicly engaged to consider." Beyond this, Reid impressed upon Hume the need for "coadjutors" in and out of Parliament—men like Hume himself, "high-class men" to "coach and inform members"; an Indian member of Parliament would also be an invaluable asset. Like Reid, the others who advised Hume all believed that the English public desired a just and generous policy toward India. But this desire, they warned him, would not be transformed into tangible results unless vigorous propaganda was undertaken throughout the country with public meetings, lectures, pamphlets, articles and correspondence in the press, and unless Hume and his co-workers could win the sympathy and interest of local associations and influential politicians.[93] With such support and encouragement, Hume began to enlist persons in and out of Parliament who would be willing to serve the cause of Indian reform and the proposed Indian National Union. Although the Union, per Lord Dufferin's request, was not to be linked with the Indian government, Hume intended to link it with Parliament through willing friends, who would make the wishes and grievances of the Indian people known to the Home Government and the British people.

[92] In London: *Pall Mall Gazette, Daily News,* and *Christian World* (bi-weekly); outside: *Cambridge Independent Press, Bradford Observer, Western Times, Sheffield Independent, York Herald, Birmingham Daily Post, Leeds Mercury, Manchester Guardian, Manchester Examiner and Times, Liverpool Daily Post, Scotsman, Glasgow Daily Mail, Dundee Advertiser.* See Report of Telang, Secretary, Indian National Telegraphic Union, Jan. 30, in *Times of India,* Feb. 5, 1886; also Wedderburn, p. 55.

[93] Reid's letter was probably written on Sept. 5, 1885, see Wedderburn, pp. 56, 92.

Hume was proceeding on the assumption that political action conducted along strictly constitutional lines in India and England would be sufficient to meet the needs of the Indian political scene, given the embryonic state of Indian politics, the aims of the educated Indian leaders, and their goodwill toward Government House. He was unaware of the dissatisfaction with Dufferin and his administration that had grown apace among Indian editors and politicians, and he did not realize how rapidly the goodwill and trust the educated leaders had initially shown the Viceroy were being replaced by hostility and distrust. But he soon learned of it when certain of the younger Indian leaders took matters into their own hands and gave a revolutionary twist to Indian political development, one which ultimately left its mark upon the Indian National Union and the Indian political reform which Hume was then planning.

IX

India's Appeal to the British Voter

A few days after Churchill's Indian Budget Statement in August, a letter, under the pseudonym "English Elector," appeared in *The Bombay Gazette*.[1] The writer was much interested in the telegraphic extracts of Churchill's Statement the *Gazette* had published, and concluded from the animated nature of the debate, with its extreme proposals of "threatened fresh military expenditure" and a Parliamentary inquiry, that "India is now evidently to the front in English politics." He continued: "Will you allow me, Sir, through your columns, to urge upon the native community the extreme importance of seizing the occasion to place before the English public the Indian view of Indian questions, and to make their voice heard at the coming elections? The exact time of the general election being known beforehand, there is now an opportunity which may never occur again."

To the question of "how best to make an impression upon the English electors," he proposed the following answer. In order "to inform and influence the general public, and especially the more important constituencies in the manufacturing districts of the north," he advocated "great public meetings" and the distribution, after the example of the Cobden Club, of leaflets and pamphlets

[1] Letter to the editor, Aug. 9, *Bombay Gazette*, Aug. 10, 1885; identity of "English Elector' is unknown. The letter is mentioned in Mody's *Sir Pherozeshah Mehta*, but not in the studies on Hume, Wedderburn, Naoroji, and Tyabji nor in N. G. Chandavarkar's excellent résumé of the delegates' activities in England, *English Impressions* (Bombay, 1887, CRO Tract 652). Despite suggestions resembling those Hume was currently pushing in England, and despite certain ideas and phrases reminiscent of W. Digby's pamphlet, *Indian Problems for English Consideration* (Plymouth, 1881), the letter's date and contents show it was written in Bombay—probably by Wedderburn (see C. to D., Nov. 27, 1885, DVP, R. 517, No. 80) though possibly by Naoroji or Wordsworth.

"in large numbers," which would give "brief but clear answers" to topical Indian questions and grievances.[2] To settle these grievances, "English Elector" wished a new perspective for English imperial policy. India had been and still was "the pivot" of English foreign policy. Throughout the past few years, whenever trouble had arisen in Afghanistan, Egypt, the Sudan, and Central Asia, British and Indian troops had been sent to these places supposedly in defense of India. Lives and money had been squandered merely because the Home and Indian governments had "not yet abandoned the old and mischievous policy of suspicion, treating India as a sort of powder magazine which no stranger can safely be allowed to approach." It was time that these extravagant activities ended and that Indian manpower was looked upon as a "tower of strength" and not as a point of weakness. But this would be accomplished only "if the English people will listen to wiser counsels, if they will understand that the real defence of India consists in gaining the goodwill and approval of this vast but reasonable and docile population." This education could best be provided by Indian leaders in an "appeal to the general English public."

In addition, "English Elector" thought it equally important to tackle those constituencies where the candidates were men who in the past had shown themselves either "friends" or "unfriends" of India. This meant assuring the electors that men like John Slagg, William Digby, and Sir John Phear held views consonant with those of "the intelligent classes" of India, and which, if acted upon in Parliament, would bring India prosperity and contentment. The converse would apply to an "unfriend" like Sir Richard Temple, and action should be taken to inform the electors accordingly within his constituency. It must be made clear, however, that "the people of India do not wish to say anything with regard to these gentlemen personally, or as to their general politics," but merely wish to portray such candidates as "unfriends" of the Indian people and as exponents of unsound Indian policy. For the results of such an endeavor "English Elector" held out great hopes: one election or one defeat would mean that in the future Parliamentary candidates could not afford to neglect either Indian questions or grievances. The redress of such grievances would harden "the friendly feeling" now existing in India toward England into "a permanent national sentiment," linking the two countries

----

[2] "Why does India prefer English to Russian rule? What is our interest in Central Asia? Is the Indian Council a benefit to India or the Reverse? Can India be defended within her own frontier and by her own citizen soldiers? What are the aspirations of her educated classes? What are the causes which impede her material progress and the development of her trade with England?"

into "a partnership of common interest and mutual goodwill."

The most singular feature of "English Elector" 's scheme was his advocacy of Indian intervention in a British election to secure redress of Indian grievances. Efforts had been made in the past to bring pressure to bear upon certain members of Parliament, the Secretary of State for India, or the Viceroy to redress specific grievances, but no attempt had been made to step outside these official channels and place before the British public the major Indian grievances. This was a most novel innovation for Indian politics at that time. Yet for all its novelty, it had a true imperial goal—the maintenance of British rule in India—and was entirely constitutional in scope and method. But "English Elector" did not state precisely "who" would distribute the leaflets and pamphlets, address the public meetings, and act within the constituencies; nor did he comment on the significance of this aspect of his scheme. His inference was that these tasks would be carried out by groups in England, probably by organizations friendly to Indian interests such as the Indian Reform Association, the Cobden Club, or the pro-Indian nucleus of the East India Association. The alternative would have been to hire an independent body, which would have to be sponsored and paid for, and this would be out of the question. Herein lay the weakness of the scheme. If the members of these groups, largely Liberals and radical Liberals with a sprinkling of Independents, intervened in the election of Digby or Temple, then their action would be greeted by the British press and political parties as radical Liberal intervention for the former and against the latter, but not as disinterested action on behalf of Indian reform. In the smoke and flame of the political exchanges that were certain to follow, the electors would quickly lose sight of Indian grievances, while the impact of India's appeal would be rendered ineffectual. On these significant aspects of the scheme—its novel method and its grave risk for the Indian appeal to the British electorate—"English Elector" had nothing to say.

The scheme received an immediate and enthusiastic welcome from all Indian editors and politicians. G. S. Iyer, in his Tamil paper, spoke out for immediate support of those Parliamentary candidates who were friends of India, but said nothing as to how this support should be given.[3] N. N. Sen called for complete implementation of the scheme.[4] The editor of *The News of the Day*, the other major Bengali-owned, English daily of Calcutta, proposed that the plan should be supported *"first,* by sending regularly tele-

[3] *Swadesa Mitran,* Aug. 24 (*V. of I.,* III, Sept. 1885).
[4] Editorial, *Indian Mirror,* Aug. 25, 1885.

graphic intelligence to the journals as well as to the impartial and
unsectarian public bodies in England; *secondly,* by distributing
printed bills containing a faithful description of the grievances of
India to the public of England; and *thirdly,* by writing letters to
the leading journals of the United Kingdom."[5] He thus emphasized pamphleteering and cooperating with friends of India in England much as "English Elector" had urged, but he foresaw administrative and financial difficulties, and therefore turned to the
associations for support. His was an opportune note; for, although
the Indian press supported the scheme, it would never have come
into existence without action by the associations. In early September, the General Committee of the Bombay Presidency Association,
consisting of P. Mehta, K. Telang and D. E. Wacha, picked up the
reins.

They were immediately confronted with the problem of what
leaflets to use and where to get them printed.[6] They found a ready-
made solution in an announcement in the June report of the Cobden Club, which stated that four Indian leaflets had been sent to the
club and that another eight or nine were in preparation.[7] They
concluded that these leaflets could well serve their purpose and
agreed to adopt them once the committee had reviewed them with
an eye for maximal effect at minimal cost. The cost of such leaflets,
to say nothing of the correct representation of Indian opinions and
grievances, presented major difficulties. The committee, therefore,
"decided that the cooperation of the other presidencies should be
invited in this matter," and hastily drafted letters to the British
Indian Association and the Indian Association of Calcutta, the Sind
Sabha of Karachi, the Mahajana Sabha of Madras, the Poona Sarvajanik Sabha, and the Praja-hita-vardhak Sabha of Surat,[8] requesting
approval for a campaign based upon the leaflets then being reviewed
and soliciting financial support to cover costs of printing, shipping,
and distribution.

The replies to the letters contained "assurances of warm sympathy" and general agreement, but with conditions. Both the
Madras Sabha and the British Indian Association had large member-
ships with grievances of a distinctly regional flavor; moreover, their

[5] Aug. 25 (*V. of I.,* III, Sept. 1885).
[6] See Telang's Report of the General Committee, Bombay Presidency Association,
Sept. 28, in *B.O.G.S.,* Oct. 2, 1885, pp. 8-11
[7] See meetings, Cobden Club, June 13, 27, *Times,* June 15, 29, 1885. It appears that
the four leaflets were those on Indian grievances which had been prepared by M.
Ghose, J. U. Yajnik, Crawley-Boevey and possibly V. Chariar and which Hume in
July had sent to Dufferin (see Chap. VII, p. 164 and n. 31).
[8] Letters were sent only to the major associations of the three presidencies.

respective outlooks on various questions differed considerably not only the one from the other but also from that of the Bombay Presidency Association. Thus the committee of the Madras Sabha, while giving a nodding acceptance to the Bombay plan, stated that it would draft its own leaflets and pay its own campaign expenses.[9] Likewise, the committee of the British Indian Association expressed general concurrence with the Bombay plan and agreed to defray part of the cost, but only after Mehta and Telang had forwarded "positive assurance" that the leaflets would not refer to disputable points, such as land reform or the Bengal Tenancy Act.[10]

It was obvious that such divisive tendencies would render the Bombay plan ineffective. But at the very moment when it was on the verge of collapse for want of funds and a coordinated effort, the committee of the Poona Sarvajanik Sabha, led by K. L. Nulkar, S. H. Chiplonkar, and M. Ranade, agreed not only to make a substantial contribution for the leaflet campaign, but also to pay for an Indian delegation to England consisting of elected representatives from the various associations.[11] If the scheme of "English Elector" was novel for the India of 1885, then the proposal of the Poona Sabha was revolutionary. Except for D. Naoroji, N. Furdunji, and W. C. Bonnerjee during the 1860s and Lal Mohan Ghose in 1879, each of whom had assisted in promoting agitation in Parliament on Indian issues, no Indian group had ever aired Indian grievances during a British election.

Mehta, Telang, and Wacha enthusiastically adopted forthwith the Poona proposal as their plan of action, and sent letters to the associations in Calcutta and Madras requesting them to choose one delegate to cooperate with the other delegates selected and with "the Indian community in London."[12] Problems immediately arose in the selection of delegates, who had to be men representative of the interests and grievances of their respective presidency or provincial communities, possessing an excellent command of English, and willing and able, in terms of caste, family, and occupational obligations, to travel to England.

For Bombay, Narayan Ganesh Chandavarkar[13] was selected,

---

[9] General meetings, Sept. 11, 30, 1885, *M.M.S. Annual Report*, CRO, Tract 634.

[10] See editorial, "The Bombay Presidency Association Leaflets," *Hindoo Patriot*, Nov. 9, 1885.

[11] See n. 6 above.

[12] Letter, undated, to the secretaries of Madras Mahajana Sabha, read at General Meeting, Sept. 11, *M.M.S. Annual Report*. I could find no correspondence of the Bombay Presidency Association with the associations in Calcutta and Poona at the CRO Library or the British Museum.

[13] B. 1885; Elphinstone College, Bombay; B. A., B.L.; editor of *Indu Prakash*, mod-

seemingly by the inner groups of the Sarvajanik Sabha and the Presidency Association alone. *Rast Goftar,* D. Naoroji's paper which was then edited by K. Kabraji, left this insight on record: "If a Parsi gentleman, representing the most advanced community in the Bombay Presidency, had been deputed to England, Bombay would have been adequately represented. Mr. Dadabhai Naoroji is the fittest person for this work . . . if he was not available, Mr. Behramji Malabari or some other competent Parsi would have adequately represented Bombay . . . we do not approve of the clandestine and hasty way in which the appointment from the Bombay side was made."[14] It would appear from this comment that Naoroji and other influential figures had not been consulted about the Bombay delegate. Naoroji, though advanced in age, had received a new burst of energy and wished to stand for Parliament, and in this ambition he was enthusiastically supported by Malabari, who was in touch with Ripon on the matter.[15] As the Bombay delegate to England, his Parliamentary ambitions would have been considerably advanced, but all came to naught when Chandavarkar was selected and when Ripon was unable to obtain the approval of the Liberal party's Credentials Committee for Naoroji. Moreover, as Lord Reay had just appointed Ranade and Naoroji to the Bombay Legislative Council, they would be too preoccupied with their new duties to undertake campaigning in England. Thus, Chandavarkar, a man of unquestioned ability and supported by the two leading associations of Bombay, was an excellent choice.

The Bengali nomination posed problems. Lal Mohan Ghose of Dacca, barrister and member of the Indian Association who in 1879 had presented the All-India Memorial concerning the question of the age limit for the Civil Service to the Secretary of State, and whose brilliant performance had won the acclaim of John Bright and other Liberals in the East India Association, had returned to England in mid-1883 at the invitation of Bright and on behalf of the Indian Association to speak on the Ilbert Bill and the Civil Service question. In early 1885, he had received the nod of the Credentials Committee of the Liberal party to stand for Greenwich.[16] By August, however, the large constituency of Greenwich

---

erate, Anglo-Marathi weekly of Bombay city started by Ranade; member of Poona Sarvajanik Sabha and protégé of its key figure, Ranade; *vakil* in Bombay High Court; interested in social reform.

[14] Sept. 13 *(V. of I.,* III, Sept. 1885, p. 468).

[15] See R. to Malabari, Sept. 10, 1885, RP, BM Add. MSS 43616, pp. 176-178; also selections, *V. of I.,* III, Sept. 1885, pp. 448-458.

[16] See selections, *V. of I.,* III, Jan. 1885. One interesting aspect of the choice of Ghose stems from the treaty ceding Bombay Island to England and from the Royal

had been split by the Redistribution of Seats Act into a number of seats. For one of these, Deptford, Ghose's name was again placed before the Credentials Committee. If Ghose, therefore, became the Bengali delegate, it would mean the involvement of a potential Liberal candidate in what was essentially an Indian delegation, to say nothing of the fact that he would have to devote his efforts to his own election instead of to the delegation.

Hence, instead of L. M. Ghose,[17] the British Indian Association favored the nomination of his brother, Man Mohan Ghose,[18] one of the most competent Indian barristers practising in India. In addition to this qualification, Man Mohan knew London and numerous persons there, having assisted Naoroji and various Englishmen in developing the East India Association in the 1860s while he was competing for the Covenanted Civil Service and studying for the Bar. A Kayastha by caste, he had none of the Brahmanic inhibitions about crossing water to foreign lands. More important still was his position in contemporary Bengali politics. Though closely allied to S. Banerjea and the Indian Association, Man Mohan had earned the respect and support of the British Association by his handling of zemindari cases before the Bar. Unlike his brother, who represented Banerjea's association, Man Mohan was Secretary of the newly formed Indian Union, which took a middle ground between the British Indian Association and Banerjea's Indian Association. Since he was an admirable compromise candidate acceptable to both, he was selected as the Bengali delegate.

The Madras nomination was less difficult. Unlike Bombay and Bengal, where there were a number of associations jealous of each other's political interests and prestige and thus requiring a compromise delegate, Madras had only the Mahajana Sabha, to which by 1885 all the associations of the presidency were appended. A.

Charter whereby the East India Company was to hold Bombay "as of our manor of Greenwich." Ghose was therefore a logical candidate to contest the seat in 1885. See W. Digby, *Indian Politics in England* (Lucknow, 1890), pp. 180-181.

[17] See editorial, "India at the Hustings," *Hindoo Patriot*, Oct. 26, 1885.

[18] B. 1844; Krishnagar Collegiate School and Presidency College, Calcutta; wrote for *Hindoo Patriot* on Indigo Famine, 1861; when *Patriot* became a zemindari paper, he founded fortnightly *Indian Mirror*; left Presidency College, 1862, to go to England as one of the first Indians to stand for I.C.S. examinations; failed 1864, 1865, owing to changes in regulations; wrote pamphlet "'The Open Competition for the Civil Service of India" (1867), describing disadvantages to Indians; Lincoln's Inn, barrister, 1866; assisted D. Naoroji and W. C. Bonnerjee in developing East India Association; Advocate, Calcutta High Court, first Indian barrister, 1867; brilliant career, dealt with all major cases; opened campaign on I.C.S. regulations; pressed for separation of Judicial and Executive functions in districts; advocated female education; Secretary, Bethune College, 1873; worked with N. N. Sen on *Indian Mirror*; close friend of S. Banerjea

Charlu, M. V. Chariar, G. S. Iyer, P. R. Naidu, S. P. Andy—each of
these men would have made an excellent delegate had he been
available for the assignment, but caste or occupational responsibilities prevented their names being put forward. Only S. Ramaswami
Mudaliar,[19] a wealthy landowner and successful *vakil* of the Salem
district, could go, and he was unanimously elected.[20]

These three delegates chosen by the associations received the
approval of the editors of the Indian press,[21] and by mid-September
they had set forth on their pilgrimage to England. Chandavarkar
and Mudaliar were the first to depart, and Ghose and his wife followed later. Their instructions and the leaflets were to be decided
upon and then forwarded to them in England.

Important questions arose as to what claims the delegates should
press and how they should present them to the British public. Soon
after it was known that delegates would be sent to England, these
questions were debated with much gusto by the Indian editors.
S. Banerjea was most comprehensive.[22] Drawing directly upon the
platform of his National Conference of 1883, he devised a program
based "upon the principle that the country should henceforth be
governed by the people and for the people," for the guidance of any
future "Indian party in the new Parliament" as well as for the
delegates. The foremost claim should be "the reconstitution of the
Legislative Councils," "constituted upon a popular basis," with
"functions widened," "control over finances," "right of interpellation," and "newly-created local bodies [to] form constituencies." He
also called for "greater facilities" for Indian admission into the
Covenanted Civil Service by raising the age limit and holding simultaneous examinations in India and England. Modification of the
Arms Act, Indian volunteering, reconstitution of the British Indian
Army to admit Indians to commissioned ranks, and abolition of the
India Council were other claims he wished circulated in Britain.
Other editors recommended parts of Banerjea's scheme.[23] G. S. Iyer,

and member of Indian Association; friend of Hume, for whom he wrote pamphlets;
Secretary, Indian Union, 1885.

[19] B. 1852, son of landowner in Salem District; Madras High School, Pachaiyappa's
and Presidency colleges; B.A., 1871, M.A., 1873, B.L., 1875; *vakil* in High Court, 1876;
District Munsif, but resigned in 1882 and practised in High Court; member of Madras
Mahajana Sabha, interested in Salem and landed grievances; played a central role in
Madras volunteer agitation—being one of the four "native gentlemen" accepted by
Major Branson to join the Volunteer Artillery; close friend of G. S. Iyer, who was
key figure of Madras Sabha and editor of *Hindu, Swadesa Mitran,* and others.

[20] General Meeting, Sept. 11, 1885, *M.M.S. Annual Report.*

[21] See selections, vernacular and English, *V. of I.,* III, Sept. 1885. The only exception
was *Rast Goftar.*

[22] Editorial, *Bengalee,* Sept. 5, 1885.

[23] See selections under "India in Parliament" and "India's Appeal to the British

for instance, like Slagg, viewed the council at the India Office as a reactionary body denying "Young India" its liberal development and called for its abolition.[24] The Ghose brothers wished the iniquities of the judicial system publicly aired with an eye toward reform.[25] N. N. Sen wished attention drawn to the hiatus in the development of local self-government since Ripon's departure and the breach of faith over the Famine Fund.[26] M. Minocher-Homji echoed the refrain of "taxation without representation,"[27] while R. Sarvadhikari and numerous others contended that the foremost claim to be pressed upon the British public was the need for Lord Randolph Churchill to fulfill his promise to hold a Parliamentary inquiry into Indian affairs, but on a broader scale than that which he had announced.[28] The necessity of combining all these grievances into one appeal would be no light task.

Conflicts over the choice of grievances and the method of placing them before the British public proved most divisive. The Madras Sabha was a case in point. Immediately after Mudaliar's selection, the questions of "how" and "with what" he was to appeal to the British electorate were mooted, and by none other than Raja Sir T. Madhava Rao. Maratha Brahmin and wealthy Tanjore landholder, a cousin of the eminent Diwan Bahadur Raghunath Rao, with whom he had founded the Madras Native Association and the journal, *Native Public Opinion,* Diwan successively to the maharajas of Travancore, Indore, and Baroda, and Fellow of Madras University, Madhava Rao was one of the most respected leaders of the Sabha. When he arose to address the Sabha concerning its delegate, his remarks made an instant impression.[29] He suggested that clear instructions be drafted that Mudaliar's main objective should be "to interest the people of Great Britain in the Welfare of India"; he also urged that Mudaliar "not identify himself with anyone of the political parties in England" and instead act the part of the neutral toward both, always remembering that "that party is the best *which does its best* for the welfare of India." He reminded his listeners that Lord Ripon was remembered in India not because he was a Liberal but because he had been "so earnest in promoting India's welfare." Political scrimmaging and liaisons with English

Electorate," in *V. of I.,* III, Sept. and Oct. 1885.

[24] *Hindu,* Sept. 8 *(V. of I.,* III, Sept. 1885).

[25] *Amrita Bazar Patrika,* Sept. 17 *(V. of I.,* III, Sept. 1885).

[26] Editorial, *Indian Mirror,* Sept. 20, 1885.

[27] *Jam-e-Jamshed,* Sept. 26 *(V. of I.,* III, Oct. 1885).

[28] *Hindoo Patriot,* Sept. 21, 1885; also n. 23 above.

[29] Rao's instructions, presented for approval at the Sept. 11 meeting, were reviewed at the Sept. 30 meeting, see *M.M.S. Annual Report.*

parties were to be avoided; Rao wished no tinge of Tory Blue or Liberal Red on India's grievances. He advised close cooperation with the Bengal and Bombay delegates in order to avoid divisive pressures from within and without. As to the substance of Muda-liar's appeal, Rao's chief suggestions were:

Gratefully acknowledge the great good which the British Govern-ment have done in India;

Call for greater interest and sympathy in and for Indian affairs, greater respect and regard for Indian feelings and opinions gen-erally;

Show that India possesses greater political intelligence than ever before;

Plead generally for moderate taxation of the necessaries of life and for greater security of landed tenures;

Dwell on the value of India to England and the value of England to India;

While stating aims and aspirations show reliance on British *wishes, justice* and *benevolences.*

These tentative instructions he proposed for adoption by the Sabha, but their moderate, suppliant tone, their neutralist political method, and their reference to land tenures, which smacked of vested interests, all produced rumbles of disagreement. The in-structions were therefore left for further discussion at the next session at the end of September. The following day, Iyer and Chariar published an editorial in *The Hindu* giving polite support to the proposed instructions but without making specific reference to them or to Rao.[30] The controversy had begun concerning whether or not the delegates should "preserve strict silence as to sympathy with one or other of the English political parties."

Nor was the controversy limited to Madras. The progressive-minded Maharaja of Kolhapur, Rampal Singh, just returned from two years in England where he had worked with members of the Indian Reform Association in support of the Ilbert Bill and a higher age limit for the Covenanted examinations, declared himself pub-licly in favor of Indian political intervention in the British elec-tion.[31] The leading Indian editors of Bombay and Calcutta backed the Poona proposal to have the Indian delegates support Liberal and radical Liberal candidates such as Slagg, Digby, Phear, Keay,

---

[30] Sept. 12, 1885. Also *V. of I.*, III, Sept., 1885, pp. 462-463.
[31] *Indian Mirror,* Sept. 26, 1885.

Bright, and L. Ghose who might stand for Parliament, while a dwindling minority, led by N. N. Gupta of *The Sind Times* and Sarvadhikari of *The Hindoo Patriot,* firmly opposed such action.[32] The storm was gathering force.

The spate of talk and enthusiasm in Indian circles concerning the delegation had immediate repercussions. The partnership of George Allen and Colonel Corry, proprietors and principal editors of *The Pioneer* and *The Civil and Military Gazette* respectively, and their managing editors, H. Hensman, K. Robinson, and Rudyard Kipling, viewed the development with dismay and determined to knock the "Indian grievance-mongering." On September 12, Allen led the attack, aimed both at Churchill and at "Young India" agitators, with a lengthy commentary on an editorial in *The Times* concerning an article on "native aspirations" written by the Bombay correspondent.[33] Stressing the themes in *The Times* editorial on the heterogeneous, nonnational character of India and the impossibility of representative political reform under such circumstances, Allen urged Churchill and his Tory colleagues to read and reread the editorial. His purpose was to discourage the youthful Secretary's inclination to outbid the radical Liberals by "attempting to catch favor in India by giving Indian agitators what even Lord Ripon's government thought prudent to withhold." Churchill's radicalism had been too apparent in the Budget Statement for Allen's liking; he had detected a readiness to expose the Indian government to the inquiries of Radicals and Indophiles, who would "go a long way with those Indian politicians who demand a representative National Council." Allen cautioned the Secretary of State against making Indian reform an English political issue with the slogan of "India for the Indians." "The more closely India is brought within the sphere of party politics, the more liable are we to have new departures thrust on the people in advance of their political capacity." His point was effectively, even bluntly, put: the Conservatives were not to encourage "Young India" in agitating for reform. To underline it, Allen quoted in full the article, "The Black Radical," which had appeared in the *St. James's Gazette,* and emphasized those sections of the article which had argued that India was not a nation, that the Indian government was not despotic, and that the English-educated Indian did not represent the Indian people.[34]

[32] See n. 23 above.

[33] Editorial, "*The Times* on Native Aspirations," *Pioneer,* Sept. 12, 1885. See *Times,* Aug. 19, 1885, for article by Bombay correspondent which reached India by early Sept.

[34] Without giving his source, in "'Native Politicans in England," *Pioneer,* Sept. 12, 1885. *Times of India* published the entire article on Sept. 8 and gave the source. See also above, pp. 192-193.

Allen's shrill note of alarm was uttered not only in anticipation of pending Indian agitation in England but also to forestall renewed action by various Indian editors to promote national organization in India. Daji Adaji Khare, an excellent lawyer, a leading member of the Bombay Presidency Association, and the co-editor with V. Mandlik of the Anglo-Marathi weekly, *Native Opinion,* proposed on September 13 the establishment of a "National Indian Committee" to direct the new political forces of India.[35] This committee, consisting of an "upper house" made up of titled and landed nominees, and a "lower house" made up of representatives elected by the associations and local governments from all the presidencies and provinces, would hold periodic meetings to discuss "national" as opposed to provincial questions and to present them to the Indian government as well as to groups working on India's behalf in England. Khare proposed that the committee sit at Jubbulpore in the Central Provinces, a site accessible and central to all regions of the subcontinent. His plan was virtually a synthesis of Sen's scheme for a National Association and Hume's proposal for the Indian National Union.

Allen, on September 15, hastily framed an editorial in *The Pioneer* designed to wreck Khare's plan, which, he commented, was familiar in content, novel only in form, and impracticable by its pretentiousness. He could see nothing but problems in it because the essential requirements for any such plan were lacking: the trained staff to administer the electoral roles, the police to keep order, the legal overseers to prevent bribery and corruption, the money to pay for these services and also for electoral costs, the bases for electoral franchise, and an elected committee which would represent all sections of the Indian community so as to lend credence to the claim that the committee represented "the voice of India." This was a plan "too obviously beyond the powers of an India still in the long clothes of civilisation and only just learning to mimic the language of European politics without much attention to its meaning. Pleased with the sound, young India babbles about moulding destinies and developing national aspiratons, [but] one must turn a deaf ear to these torrents of ready-made platitudes imported like Calico from England by the yard." Only when the experiments of local self-government and of appointing selected Indians to the provincial councils had been proven successful would it be logical "to develop national aspirations and to discover

---

[35] In *Native Opinion,* Sept. 13, quoted in *Pioneer,* Sept. 15, and *Indian Mirror,* Sept. 17, 1885.

whether an Indian 'Nation' really exists." In the interim, Allen
believed that England could keep for "another century" what she
had fought for and won despite "the fractious threats" of overambitious Indian reformers. Thus wrote Allen with petulant scorn,
betraying the same nervousness which he and other Anglo-Indians
with large vested interests in India had expressed at the zenith of
Ripon's reforms just before the anti-Ilbert Bill agitation exploded.

If Khare's plan was overambitious and vulnerable to criticism,
his spirit and aspirations were not. Iyer and Chariar writing from
Madras expressed much the same aspirations, but, unlike Khare,
they wished to combine the proposals of Hume and Sen with the
Poona Sabha's suggestion of sending a mission to England.[36] In
their opinion, the voice of India had been for too long the voice of
a suppliant to a despot rather than that of a nation to its sovereign.
This lamentable condition resulted from the lack of any means of
organized expression; only once in "the history of modern India"
had this condition been overcome—during the farewell to Ripon.
That occasion had revealed the potential energy and power of joint
expression latent in "the scattered forces of Indian patriotism." The
moment had come for more of the same. "It is now the duty of our
politicians," they declared, "to collect these forces into the centre of
a powerful and widespread organisation and bring to the front that
Native Party which now wastes its resources by working without a
common and well-understood programme and without methods and
appliances chosen after joint deliberation." With such an organized
body, resources for agitation would be conserved instead of wasted
as hitherto, while the public would become educated on questions
of reform. An effective program for redress of grievances, based
solidly upon Indian public opinion, could be drafted and presented
both to the Indian government and to friends of India in England.
But Iyer and Chariar were dubious about the Viceroy's attitude
toward such a development. Would it be reactionary or progressive? Here Sen, who earlier had published their ideas, supplied an
answer.[37] The Viceroy had been the key figure in the policy which
had quashed the future of Arabi Pasha and "the Nationalists of
Egypt." Would he not behave in like fashion toward a similar party
springing up in India? Nevertheless, Sen thought that the editors
of *The Hindu* were right in calling for a national party to rally the
voice of India: "such a party is inevitable in the course of time,
whether in Egypt, India, or Ireland." History was on India's side.
Political organization and agitation, wholly self-interested and inde-

---

[36] *Hindu*, Sept. 19, 20 (quoted in *Indian Mirror*, Sept. 24, 1885).
[37] Editorial, "A National Party in India," *Indian Mirror*, Sept. 24, 1885.

pendent, were now the only logical means for securing political ends.

As he had done in January,[38] Sen incorporated all these suggestions into his own plan:[39] the plea of the Maharaja of Kolhapur for Indian political intervention in the British election, Khare's bid for an Indian national committee, and the call of Iyer and Chariar for an Indian national party. But more important was his firm belief in "national" cooperation and communication. "The leading men of Bengal, Madras, Bombay, the Punjab, the Northwest Provinces, the Central Provinces, and the Native States should take frequent opportunities to see each other, in order to promote and establish a complete harmony of feelings and views," he wrote. The principal holidays would be excellent occasions for an exchange of visits. No time should be lost "to bring about a large conference of all leading Indian gentlemen of different Provinces at some central place, say Jubbulpore or Puna, to discuss and settle measures that should be taken for the welfare and progress of the country." This sounded much like the March decision of Hume and his colleagues of the Bombay Presidency. As India sped into nationhood with its races fast being welded together, Sen believed that such a conference was "a growing necessity." Indeed it should be the foundation upon which the Indian agitation in England, the national committee, and the national party should be constructed if Indian political expression was to be a meaningful force in the future. So S. Banerjea, fully in accord with Sen's views, was moved to action and began to make arrangements for another "Indian National Conference," similar to the one he had staged at Calcutta in 1883.

By the end of September, as ideas for national self-expression exploded in a new blaze of fervor, disagreement over the Indian delegation reached a climax in the Bombay and Madras associations. The controversy left its mark upon the mission, upon the claims of educated Indians to "national" expression, and upon the various plans, including Hume's, for "national" organization. The committee of the Bombay Presidency Association then circulated to the various associations and published in the Indian press a manifesto for the delegates entitled "Appeal on Behalf of the People of India to the Electors of Great Britain and Ireland."[40] This document bore a striking resemblance to an appeal of 1868, which had

[38] See above pp. 40 ff.

[39] Editorial, *Indian Mirror*, Sept. 26, 1885.

[40] A copy of the Appeal, distributed a few days before the plenary session of Sept. 28, is appended to the report of the meeting in *B.G.O.S.*, week ending Oct. 2, 1885, pp. 10-11.

been drafted by D. Naoroji, N. Furdunji, Dr. Bhau Daji, V. F. Sunkersett, and Framji Patel of the old Bombay branch of the East India Association, forwarded to Henry Fawcett and John Bright, then the leading spirits of the East India Association in London, and presented by them, with no results, to the Secretary of State, Sir Stafford Northcote.[41] The manifesto of 1885, although couched in the same moderate tone and including many of the grievances set forth in 1868, contained new grievances and, furthermore, was aimed at the British public, not at the Secretary of State.

The Appeal of 1885 was a direct, temperate, and well-phrased document.[42] It expressed the gratitude of the Indian leaders and people to England for the innumerable blessings bestowed upon India—blessings ranging from a common language, legal system, and educational structure to material advancement and the freedom of the individual. Indians had found that, as time passed, only one boon was lacking, namely, a representative voice in the councils of the Empire; and, as long as this was denied them, they could win no thorough redress of grievances. Fortunately, they possessed, as alternatives to the imperial councils, the enfranchised electors of Great Britain and Ireland and their Parliament, and it was to these alternatives that the Indian people now turned again, fully confident that their voice would be heard and their grievances redressed. Parliament had safeguarded Indian interests against the East India Company and had sponsored the reforms following the Mutiny. Only since then had its concern for Indian affairs waned. The moment had arrived for England again to take stock of its Indian responsibilities. As the events of the past year and a half had well demonstrated, India was the pivot of England's imperial policy. Since the futures of England and India were mutually dependent, Indian policy would necessarily play a central role in the election, and the British electorate would have the opportunity to redress the long-neglected grievances of India.

Parliament had given the Indian people manifold pledges which had been left unredeemed by successive governments. The unfulfilled pledges had turned into grievances: settlement of the land question on a permanent basis, increased employment of qualified Indians in the senior civil and military services, equal distribution of the Home Charges between the British and Indian exchequers, equal participation in the industrial development of India by In-

[41] Similarity pointed out by *Indu Prakash*, Oct. 5 (*V. of I.*, III, Oct. 1885, p. 497). For the appeal of 1868, see *Journal of the East India Association* (London), 4 (1870), 218.

[42] See n. 40 above.

dians and foreigners, representation of Indian interests in the Provincial and Supreme Councils by elected Indians, improved means of famine prevention, modification of the Arms Act, decrease in taxation, and formation of an Indian national army reserve. These pledges Indian people now looked to the British people to redeem. In addition, the Appeal petitioned the British electors, first, that they secure from their respective Parliamentary candidates pledges that, if elected, they would call for the immediate undertaking of the proposed Parliamentary inquiry into Indian administration, and thus, no matter who won, the inquiry would be carried out; and second, that they support candidates who would oppose the forward strategy aimed at Afghanistan with the resulting increase in troops, which, if implemented, would burden the Indian taxpayer with the staggering charge of an extra £2,000,000 to £3,000,000 annually. Had India's present Viceroy followed Ripon's golden maxims—limitation of India's external policy and defense to its own mountainous frontier, trustful acceptance of offers of the Indian princes and people to volunteer their service, light taxation, and internal reforms—no such charges would arise. India wanted Parliamentary candidates who would support an Indian policy dedicated to peace and retrenchment, and who would press for internal reforms giving the Indian people a more representative voice in the councils. To this end, the Appeal called for candidates to support John Bright's original scheme for five presidency governments, each with a governor and a representative advisory council and each responsible solely to the Secretary of State for India and to Parliament, thus eliminating the Viceroy and the Supreme Councils at London and Calcutta.[43] Such governments would be truly representative, acting in India's best interests instead of acting despotically in the civil servants' interests. Finally, casting its net as widely as possible, the Appeal addressed "the working men of England and the other important classes recently enfranchised," urging them to support the Indian people "in avoiding ambitious wars and in developing internal resources."

The Appeal was circulated among the committees of the associations. The response was immediate. Pending final approval by their members, the committees of the Poona Sarvajanik Sabha, the Sind Sabha, the Praja-hita-vardhak Sabha, the Indian Association of Calcutta, and the Mahajana Sabha of Madras gve their tentative assent. Only the committee of the British Indian Association,

---

[43] See J. Bright, June 24, 1885, East India Bill No. 3, Parliamentary Debates, 3 *Hansard,* 151:342-353; also G. M. Trevelyan, *The Life of John Bright* (London, 1913), pp. 265-266.

for reasons seemingly related to the grievance concerning land settlement, withheld support. This indicated that all was not well, and
indeed it proved to be a harbinger of the troubles ahead. Within
the committee of the Bombay Presidency Association, critics mur-
mured about the neutrality, inconclusiveness, and moderation of
the Appeal and threatened modification. When the Association met
in plenary session to approve the Appeal, they made good their
threat.

Before a crowded gathering with the wealthy Parsi textile in-
dustrialist, Dinshaw Petit, in the chair, K. Telang opened the
meeting[44] by reviewing the steps that had been taken to prepare the
leaflets and dispatch the Indian delegates. With the delegates already on their way to England, it remained only for the Association
to get the leaflets to them. This could be done most expeditiously
first, by forwarding some leaflets the following week to reach the
delegates shortly after their arrival in London; second, by having
the delegates themselves draft leaflets for publication in London;
and, third, by having still others prepared before early November
by friends in England. In seeking approval for this schedule, Telang
proposed that every step taken by the Association be in concert
with other Indian associations so as to bring prominently before the
British voter "the Indian view of Indian questions." He then turned
to Badruddin Tyabji to second the resolution.

Plump in stature, in his early forties, with kindly eyes and a
friendly cherubic face nestling behind an unkempt, wispy, greyish-
white beard, Tyabji was one of the most popular men of the "Young
Bombay" movement and of the Muslim leadership. He was sympathetic, understanding, and constructive toward India's grievances
as well as toward British rule. Educated in England and possessing
sound legal training, he had always tried to be fair in his judgments
about British–Indian relations. Having heard the murmurs of discontent raised over the Appeal and anticipating what lay in store
for it that evening, he took occasion not only to second Telang's
resolution but also to urge upon the Association his own ideas on
how the Indian delegation should best utilize the Appeal. The
Indian delegates, he declared, should not look upon the Appeal as
a tool with which they should meddle in British politics and attempt
to tip the scales of the General Election in India's favor. It was sheer
folly for them to believe that they could influence the course or the
result of that election. No, the purpose of the Appeal and the task
of the delegation should be limited to a straightforward presentation
of Indian grievances to all British subjects and politicians and to a

[44] On Sept. 28; for report, see *B.G.O.S.*, week ending Oct. 2, 1885, pp. 8-10.

request for a fair hearing of these grievances. He had much confidence in the fair play and justice of the British—a remark greeted by a sudden burst of applause; and he knew that India had friends in both parties, who would act upon their Appeal. He did not have to remind them that it was a Conservative, Lord Beaconsfield, who had drafted the Queen's Proclamation of 1858 with its generous sweep of Indian rights so dear to each of them, while it was a Liberal, Lord Ripon, who had done so much to make those rights a living reality for them. Set aside meddlesome designs, trust in the leading men of both parties, and appeal to the justice and common sense of the British voter. These, in Tyabji's opinion, were the proper guidelines for the Indian delegation when presenting the Appeal.

Wise, moderate, and moving as were Tyabji's words, it was evident from the remarks that followed that the majority of the Association had different thoughts about India's Appeal. Hormusji Dadabhai and D. Wacha, both younger lieutenants of the Association and Malabari's minions, reviewed the unredeemed pledges of Parliament cited in the Appeal. Dadabhai no longer deemed it wise or right to expect Englishmen to shoulder India's grievances. India must act for herself: "the natives ought now to agitate for constitutional reforms with the ample resources of constitutional ways and maxims." Wacha went further. The delegates should make full use of the existing British political setting and machinery in issuing the Appeal to the glacier-like body of British public opinion and should choose as their allies those who believed "that liberalism is the cause of national liberty." Both speakers received enthusiastic gusts of applause. Dinshaw Pestonji Kanga and Abdulla Meher Ali Dharamsi, a friend of Tyabji and a leader of the Anjuman-i-Islam, in moving the resolution on the Appeal itself, tried to restore the atmosphere of caution and moderation by urging the Association to instruct the delegates to avoid English party entanglements and place the Appeal before both parties. But their exhortations were listened to only out of respect; not even the support of J. E. Modi could retrieve the situation. At this point, Dadabhai Naoroji received acknowledgment from the chair, and, in a shower of shouts and cheers, he rose to speak in favor of the step which Tyabji had refused to countenance.

Where others spoke from hearsay or from theory about Indian affairs and English politics, Naoroji spoke from personal knowledge and experience—from his years of trial and error with the East India Association in England during the sixties and seventies. Here spoke no neophyte, but the seasoned veteran, "the Grand Old Man," whose words were so many rays from the past lighting the dark path into the future. With his bird-like eyes snapping behind his "turn-spin" eyeglasses, with his fine, patriarchal features, wizened and drawn with responsibility, he spoke out in a resonant, clear voice. What he had to say was of utmost seriousness; he wished to take the Appeal a step further. Like "English Elector," he wished the Indian delegates to inform the British public that India supported certain candidates for Parliament and opposed others in proportion to the sympathy and interest in Indian grievances that each would display if elected to the new Parliament. He then moved a resolution consisting of two lists of names, "friends" and "unfriends" of India,[45] remarking that it was high time that the British public realized that "there are Anglo-Indians and Anglo-Indians." For instance, on the basis of past words and deeds, John Bright, John Slagg, and William Digby were to be preferred to Sir Richard Temple, Sir Roper Lethbridge, and James Maclean. He wished the Indian delegates to support or oppose each candidate from the Indian point of view, but not to concern themselves with a particular candidate's opinion on English issues. On the criteria for the delegates' support or opposition, Naoroji made a play for Tyabji's concurrence: a candidate was to be measured by the degree of support which he pledged toward the implementation of the Royal Proclamation of 1858 and the continuance of Lord Ripon's policy. "Whoever are our real friends, be they Liberal or Conservative, we call them our friends."

Thus Naoroji agreed yet disagreed with Tyabji's plan for the Appeal. Like Tyabji, he wished to approach both British parties, but preferred to support only certain candidates, each of whom, with one exception, were Liberals, and oppose others, all Conservative. At no point did he admit that this was a distinctly partisan approach, but he was too clever not to have known it. Neither did he reveal why he preferred this solution—a solution certain to carry the Indian delegation into the crucible of English party warfare. Any possible revelation was lost in the din of applause and cheers which greeted his resolution, and it was not until the next speaker addressed the assembly that the explanation became obvious.

Pherozeshah Mehta, who followed Naoroji, looked like a dainty jeweler. Natty in dress, with a fastidiously close-cropped beard and sideburns, and a bland expression, he had a rather precious, retiring

---

[45] "Friends" were J. Bright, Lord Hartington, J. Slagg, Sir J. Phear, L. M. Ghose, W. Digby, W. S. Blunt, S. Keay, S. Laing, Captain Verney, and W. C. Plowden; "unfriends" were Sir R. Temple, J. M. Maclean, A. S. Ayrton, Sir L. Pelly, and Sir R. Lethbridge.

appearance that was purely deceptive. A Parsi lawyer with much ability and ambition, an energetic Chairman of the Bombay Municipal Corporation, and next to Naoroji the most persuasive speaker in the Presidency Association, Mehta was one of the younger and more forceful leaders of the English-educated class in Bombay. Appreciative of the boons which British rule had brought India, he was one of the more sensitive, positive critics of that rule. He struggled ceaselessly against discriminatory, unjust legislation; he labored incessantly for greater Indian political representation. Less of a gradualist than Tyabji, he was more of an impatient activist when it came to Indian political reform. Nor could he compromise gracefully. This task he left to the more worldly Naoroji, with the result that he and Tyabji often found themselves in opposition and then reached a compromise worked out by "the Grand Old Man." When Mehta spoke that evening, it was evident that he stood poles apart from Tyabji, and that Naoroji's resolution formed the uneasy bridge between the conflicting views of the two younger men.

Mehta frankly admitted that he wished to go considerably beyond Tyabji and somewhat further than Naoroji in their resolutions on the Appeal and the Indian delegation. He wished to introduce both into the fray of English political warfare, and thus to submit Indian questions to the keen, searching criticism characteristic of English party politics, because, in his opinion, until Indian questions were taken up in earnest by an English party, Indian grievances would not be given the airings and sifting sufficient to make an impact on the mind of the British electorate. If they made no impact, how could he or other Indians hope that the Parliamentary candidates elected would dedicate time and energy to redressing India's grievances? He conceded that his recommendation involved certain risks to Indian interests if the particular English party the delegates supported, as a result, lost heavily in the election. But sacrifice had to be made in order to win in the end, and any setback if it came would be transitory and would eventually be wiped out by victory. Finally, Mehta thought that the identification of the Indian delegation with an English party would help unmask the fallacies continually being spread among both English parties by some Anglo-Indians, and which were so harmful to Indian aspirations. He referred to *The Times* article on "native aspirations" as an example, decrying its woeful distortion of the present political status of India and its political future. To counter such misrepresentation, he wished to expand Naoroji's resolution by directing the Indian delegation to associate the Appeal with an English party.

Though Mehta's views were accorded a sympathetic reception, it was Naoroji's resolution that was unanimously adopted. Mehta remained unconvinced of its wisdom; Tyabji was disheartened; and senior ranking members such as Sir Jamsetjee Jeejeebhoy were distressed to the point of openly speaking of resignation. Nevertheless, the die had been cast. The Appeal was to be amended with a provision for support of the friends of India for Parliament, and instructions to this effect were to be forwarded to the delegates. India's Appeal to the British Electors was no longer a neutral, inconclusive document.

The change that Naoroji wrought in the Appeal found ready support elsewhere, particularly among the younger members of the Madras Mahajana Sabha. Meeting on September 30, two days after the Presidency Association, the Sabha in a hard-hitting session[46] followed much the same lines, largely because Telang, on behalf of the Bombay Presidency Association, had written to the Secretaries of the Sabha, A. Charlu and M. V. Chariar, advising them of what had passed at Bombay and requesting them to ascertain the wishes of the Sabha concerning the Appeal and Naoroji's amending resolution. Charlu framed the agenda accordingly. When the Sabha met, supporters of the moderate, neutral course advocated by Sir Madhava Rao in his proposed instructions to Mudaliar found themselves pitted against supporters of Naoroji's resolution. The duel between these conflicting points of view did not occur until the session was well advanced. Until then, the moderates held sway: Pulney Andy, a protagonist for Indian volunteering, G. S. Iyer of *The Hindu,* the Honorable S. Subramania Iyer of the Madras Legislative Council, and W. S. V. Naidu, a wealthy landowner, favored resolutions supporting the Appeal, leaflets, and the Indian delegates as long as they brought Indian grievances impartially before all parties and segments of the British public. It was when P. Theyyaraya Chettiar rose and put Naoroji's amending resolution to the meeting that debate and controversy erupted. Rao was instantly on his feet and spoke against Chettiar's motion. He warned the members that this step would lead the Indian delegation into the jungle of English political strife and undermine the impact of the Appeal and of the leaflets. Opposing Naoroji's resolution, he spoke in support of instructions he had placed before the committee some weeks earlier, but his words were of little avail. "The fiery young patriots" of the Sabha wished more rigorous action. Chettiar's mo-

[46] See *M.M.S. Annual Report.* Neither the *Report* nor *Madras Times, Madras Standard,* and *Madras Mail* gave a complete transcript of the speeches. *Hindu* possibly did, but the CRO Library has no copy for that date. My information is derived from a letter by "Alpha" to *Evening Standard* (London), Dec. 9, 1885.

tion, including the list of English candidates to be actively supported by the Indian delegation, was put to a vote and carried, but
with no overwhelming majority, no unanimity. Nevertheless, Rao,
G. S. Iyer, the Naidus, and other moderates of the landed and official group of the Sabha had been defeated. Numberumal Chetty's
resolution for listing the "unfriends" of India followed and was
carried nem. con by a rubber-stamp vote. Once these resolutions
had been passed, the Sabha acted without hesitation in giving its
support to the delegates and the amended Appeal. The meeting
closed with an attempt by Chariar to heal the breach by moving
that Rao's instructions "be thankfully acknowledged and forwarded
to the Indian delegates for their information." This was duly carried, with C. S. Mudaliar in support, but the fact remained that
Chettiar and the young bloods had won the day and Naoroji's resolution had been adopted.

Elsewhere reactions to Naoroji's resolution varied. Though no
meeting of the Indian Association was held, the principal figures
on its committee—S. Banerjea, Motilal Ghose, A. M. Bose and
N. N. Sen—found little difficulty in supporting the amendment and
wrote editorials in its favor in their respective newspapers. In
Karachi, N. N. Gupta, changing his stand, came out on behalf of
the Sind Sabha in support of the Appeal. The editors and politicians behind *Mahratta, Kesari,* and the Deccan Education Society—
Agarkar, Namjoshi, Apte, and Tilak—also welcomed it, as did Nam-
chandra Moreshwar Sane, the editor of the other leading Poona
vernacular paper.[47] In early October, the Sarvajanik Sabha convened in Joshi Hall at Poona under the chairmanship of Bahadur
Gopalrao Deshmukh. Led by M. Ranade, S. H. Chiplonkar, N. V.
Kelkar, G. Agarkar, and others, the Sabha adopted *in toto* the resolutions passed by the Bombay Presidency Association, and requested
that instructions be forwarded to the delegates to carry out the
Appeal.[48]

But there was one dissenting voice. The committee of the British
Indian Association refused to approve both the Appeal and Naoroji's resolution. Thus the illustrious name of the British Indian
Association was not listed as one of the associations marshalled behind the Appeal to the British electors. This was the first indication
that the influential zemindari group of Bengal would soon withdraw from the entire endeavor. It remained to be seen which of the
two groups within the supporting associations, the "moderates" or

[47] *Sind Times,* Oct. 7, *Mahratta,* Oct. 4, *Dnyan Prakash,* Oct. 5 (*V. of I.,* III, "India
in Parliament," Oct. 1885).
[48] Meeting of Oct. 6, see *B.G.O.S.,* Oct. 16, 1885.

the "radicals," had spoken wisdom and which had spoken folly about the effect of the Appeal upon India's political future. Much of the answer would depend on the Indian delegates and their activities in England. Much would also depend on the support they received from their sponsors in India.

Calls for an Indian parliament, for a national party, and for a national conference, speeches before the associations, the mission to England, and the Appeal to the British electorate—these constituted the idiom of protest which the educated Indian leaders used throughout August and September in reaction to Dufferin's emerging imperial policy. By the Appeal alone, they served public notice upon Dufferin of their awareness of the extremely critical condition of the Indian budget and of their disapproval of the increased taxation that would be required to replenish Indian revenues and to forestall further debt. They were no longer deluded by false hopes and wished him to know it. More important, by the Appeal and the debate on the Appeal, they placed on record for public and official consumption in India and in England their condemnation of his strategic decisions on Afghanistan and the resultant military policy with its costly increase in the manpower of the British Indian Army. By their open discussion of a "national" organization and the future activities of the mission in England, they indicated to the Viceroy their sincere intention to bring about political reform in India which would give them a truly representative and influential voice in the Supreme Council of the Viceroy and the provincial councils of his governors. Only when they had achieved this objective did they foresee an end to unjust imperial taxation and neglect of grievances, and a beginning to just taxation and welfare.

The Appeal had split the associations into opposing camps, with the older, wealthier, and more influential members forming the "moderate" majority and the younger forming the "radical" minority. It had alienated the British Indian Association. It was a long and rapid step forward toward independent, self-interested political action in opposition to the Indian government's policies. It was also a step considerably beyond the line of action which Hume and his friends in England had envisaged to best ensure redress of Indian grievances.

If Dufferin and his officials were aware of these developments, they did not discuss them in their correspondence. Indeed none of the governors and lieutenant-governors seemed to consider them sufficiently noteworthy to call them to Dufferin's attention, partly, in the case of Reay and Grant-Duff, because they were absent from Bombay and Madras, respectively, during the debate on the Appeal, but more probably because of the simple fact that they were absorbed in matters which, from their own point of view, they considered more important than minor Indian political activities. Reay, then at Poona, was engrossed in devising a scheme of technical education as a new outlet for educated Indians[49] and was likewise concerned about outspoken, near seditious publications such as the Gujerati manifesto *Hind and Britannia*.[50] Rivers Thompson, in ill health,[51] was preoccupied with Calcutta municipal sanitation and with the sudden onslaught of damaging floods on the *aus* and *aman* rice crops.[52] Grant-Duff sat in Ootacamund worried about the light rainfall from the southwest monsoon and the existing scarcity of food in Mysore and parts of the Madras Presidency.[53] In short, the Governors were seemingly oblivious of political developments then taking place within educated Indian circles.

But they must have been alive to these developments from what they read in the weekly extracts from the "native" press which crossed their desks and from what they learned in the Anglo-Indian press each morning and evening. Allen's editorials in *The Pioneer* were lashing out at the "national" ideas and activities permeating the Indian associations. Henry Curwen, senior figure behind *The Times of India*, wrote two editorials on the activities of the Bombay Presidency Association: one on the Appeal accompanied by a copy of the Appeal itself,[54] and another on the meeting of the association and Naoroji's resolution, followed by publication of the speeches at the meeting.[55] True, Curwen treated the Appeal as little more than a pinprick in the vast rump of an elephant and dismissed the association's debate on Naoroji's resolution as farcical, ill-judged, and unrepresentative. Nevertheless, Curwen commented on these developments, and by doing so directed public attention to them. The Anglo-Indian editors of Madras, like Curwen, were acidly critical: the Appeal consisted of half-truths; it represented not the aspirations and grievances of the Indian masses, but only those of the small elite of restless, English-educated Indians;[56] Chettiar's

[49] Reay to D., Sept. 16, 1885, and note, undated, DVP, R. 528, nos. 275a, 309.

[50] *Hind and Britannia* was published in *Times of India*, Oct. 1, 1885. See also Reay to D., Oct. 21, 1885, forwarding text, DVP, R. 528, No. 403.

[51] Thompson, after taking sick leave in Aug., returned in mid-Sept. only to resign some time later. See Thompson to D., Aug. 1, 1885, DVP, R. 528, No. 101; Viceroy to Lieutenant-Governor, Bengal, telegram, Aug. 5, 1885, R. 529, No. 33; D. to C., Sept. 4, 1885 (priv.), R. 517, No. 52.

[52] Lieutenant-Governor, Bengal, to Viceroy, telegram, Sept. 27, 1885, DVP, R. 528, No. 305a.

[53] Calcutta telegram, Sept. 27, *Times*, Sept. 28, 1885.

[54] *Times of India*, Sept. 25, 1885, and Appeal, p. 5.

[55] Sept. 30; speeches, Oct. 1, 1885.

[56] Editorial, "India and the General Election," *Madras Mail*, Sept. 30, 1885.

motion was "exceedingly absurd"; and Rao's advice sagacious and far-sighted.[57] In Calcutta, the pattern was much the same. Thus the Anglo-Indian editors placed these developments squarely before the public and officialdom, but with such disparaging, slighting editorials that they distorted the developments and, if anything, lessened their significance in official eyes.

As for Dufferin, he too could have read the Anglo-Indian papers and the official weekly summaries from the "native" press, and thus kept abreast of the drift in Indian politics.[58] But he had little leisure for such pursuits, and what he did read was selected for him by his "Good Man Friday," Mackenzie Wallace. By late September, Wallace was too busy tidying up official affairs before the Viceroy's entourage left Simla on a two-month tour of various Princely States to worry about Indian politics. When not occupied with briefs on the princes for the Viceroy, he was immersed in minutiae, such as working out a scheme with Thomas Cook & Co. for the transport of Indian Muslims to Mecca during the annual pilgrimage.[59] But had Wallace noticed the political events in educated Indian circles, he would have had no reason to become excited or to excite the Viceroy over them, for everyone, and especially Dufferin, thought that the existing policies of his administration were the correct ones. Dufferin, in particular, would have disputed the criticism of his defensive strategy and financial policy in the appeal and the speeches. Were not these remarks, he would have retorted, made by the same misguided, troublesome minority which had sponsored the agitation on Indian volunteering, the Copyright Bill clause, and Calcutta sanitation? Had not he done everything in his power since July to strengthen India's defense yet hold military expenditure down? Had he not promoted a liberal domestic policy with progressive change wherever necessary? Was not Reay's policy in the Bombay Presidency as enlightened as could be found, and had not he as Viceroy encouraged it?[60] Were not Lyall's schemes for a legis-

[57] Editorials, "Nestor's Advice to the Indian Delegates," *Madras Mail*, Oct. 1, "English Sympathy for India," *Madras Times*, Oct. 3, "India and the General Election," *Madras Standard*, Oct. 5, 1885.

[58] Confidential weekly reports to Dufferin on the "native" press for Bengal and Madras during 1885 (Madras only in part), for Bengal, Madras, and Bombay, 1886-1888, are to be found in DP, D.1071H/M12, nos. 1-12; reports for all administrations, including the Northwest Provinces and Punjab Governments, are to be found in Record Section, CRO, India Office Library.

[59] Wallace to Colonel Newmarch, Oct. 5, to A. Mackenzie, Oct. 6, 1885, DVP, R. 529, nos. 83, 85.

[60] See Viceroy to Governor, Bombay, telegram, Aug. 20, supporting Forest Commission, D. to Reay, Aug. 27, 1885, supporting the Machnochie railway discrimination case, DVP, R. 529, nos. 40, 49.

lative council and an amended Tenancy Act progressive steps, and
had not he as Viceroy brought them to the new Secretary of State's
attention? And when Aitchison wished to appoint as a temporary
judge to the Punjab High Court, one Pandit Ram Narain, who was
weak in qualifications, not recommended by the judges of the Punjab Court, and grudgingly endorsed by Ilbert,[61] had not Dufferin
approved the recommendation[62] and thereby given Aitchison untold popular support both in and beyond his province, except with
The Pioneer?[63] By these actions alone, Dufferin would have dismissed the Appeal as inconsequential.

In fact, Dufferin, like his governors, did not take note of the
political developments in Bombay and Madras because he was
attending to more worrisome problems. He was alarmed by the
"terrible floods" in Bengal and Bihar, and worried lest Thompson
should fail either to call upon the Supreme Government for timely
assistance or to give ample publicity to the exertions of the Bengal
Government.[64] He was most concerned about "all the Native Calcutta papers, with the mischievous malice which is their chief
characteristic," whose editors, he felt, were exaggerating the disaster,
creating panic, and depreciating the Bengal Government's efforts.
In Madras, the opposite situation occupied his thoughts. At the very
end of the southwest monsoon, "a few timely days of rain" spelled
the difference in preventing a major drought. But in many areas
the scarcity had continued, and this situation the Indian press
blamed entirely on the costly military and financial policies of his
administration which had retrenched construction of famine railways and absorbed the Famine Fund.[65] He was also worried about
the price of silver. All predictions were that it was on the verge of
tumbling once again.[66] Still more disturbing were Churchill's rapid
decisions at home to bring Indian affairs into line with his electioneering efforts. These decisions related directly to the sharp-
ening of events in Upper Burma. From September onwards
Dufferin had little time to trouble himself about such minor rises
on the Indian political landscape as the activities of the Bombay,
Madras, and Bengal politicians.

[61] Aitchison to Wallace, Aug. 24, Mackenzie to Wallace, Aug. 27, Ilbert to Wallace,
Aug. 28, 31, 1885, DVP, R. 528, nos. 194, 203, 208, 214.
[62] Wallace for Viceroy to Aitchison, Sept. 3, 1885, DVP, R. 529, No. 56; Aitchison
to Wallace, Sept. 4, 1885, R. 528, No. 232.
[63] Editorial, Sept. 17, 1885.
[64] Viceroy to Lieutenant-Governor, Bengal, Sept. 22, 1885, DVP, R. 529, No. 75.
[65] D. to C., Oct. 5, 1885 (priv.), DVP, R. 517, No. 56.
[66] Vienna telegram, Sept. 17, *Times*, Sept. 18, 1885.

X

The Indian Radicals of Cockspur Street

Much had been said at the meetings of the Indian associations about keeping India's Appeal aloof from English party politics. The leaders of the different groups, including Naoroji with his amending resolution, had agreed and voted that a neutral line was to be pursued by the delegates. But none, except Rao and Mehta, recognized the realities of the English political scene; all believed that the Indian grievances and the lists of "friends" and "unfriends" in the Appeal were not political in the English sense, and would be treated as neutral by the English public and politicians. Plausible in theory, such thinking was so much daydreaming in practice. From the outset of the mission, an interesting sequence of events linked the delegates to the radical wing and platform of the Liberal party, and hence cost the delegates their claims to political impartiality.

There were, for instance, the contracts Chandavarkar and Mudaliar made in London soon after they had settled at Cockspur Street.[1] Hume, then trying to obtain Parliamentary representation for the proposed Indian National Union and to establish ties with the London press for the Indian Telegraphic Union, appears to have been one of their initial contacts. More important was William Digby,[2] who, ever since the spring, had been in touch with the

[1] Chandavarkar and Mudaliar reached London in late Sept. or the first week of Oct.; M. M. Ghose arrived about ten days later; headquarters were at 18 Cockspur Street, just off Trafalgar Square. See Chandavarkar, *English Impressions*.

[2] B. May 1, 1849; education, private; journalist in England, 1868, Ceylon, 1871-1876, Madras, 1877-1879; editor, *Madras Times;* Secretary, Famine Insurance Fund, C.I.E.; pamphlet on famine in Madras Deccan; returned to England, 1879; *Western Mercury* and Cobden Club; pamphlet, *Indian Problems for English Consideration* (Plymouth,

Bombay Presidency Association about his candidacy for Parliament.[3] Much younger than Hume, Digby, a radical Liberal, had become concerned in the late 1870s, when serving as editor of *The Madras Times,* with redress of Indian grievances and its importance for the English-educated Indians. Unlike Hume, he realized that the question of Indian reform would be acted upon by the Indian government only when it became a political issue in England; with this tactic in mind, he had entered radical politics in 1880 upon his return to England. A pamphlet of 1881 best summarized his belief;[4] in it, he warned of another strife-torn Ireland if Parliament continued to ignore the aspirations and grievances of educated Indians, and he urged the National Liberal Federation to make Indian reform, especially of the legislative councils, a major feature of the Liberal platform. While his friendship with F. Schnadhorst, Joseph Chamberlain's secretary, and his energetic efforts to establish the National Liberal Club carried him ahead in radical Liberal ranks and secured his candidacy for North Paddington, his labors as Secretary to the British Indian Committee (1883) and the Indian Reform Association (1884-1885) gave him the opportunity to link Indian reform ever more firmly to a coterie of moderate and radical Liberal sympathizers. It was Digby, not Hume, who took the delegates in tow and guided their fortunes. Whereas Hume had planned to leave the entire matter to key political personalities such as Bright, Caird, and Ripon, Digby had every intention of taking the delegates and India's Appeal into the election campaign.

This became apparent when a special meeting was arranged at the National Liberal Club for Chandavarkar and Mudaliar to meet supporters in order to plan India's appeal to the British voter.[5] Although some of those present were Hume's friends, most were Digby's colleagues. All had been members of the British Indian Committee and were then active in the Indian Reform Association; all were Liberals, and most were radical Liberals.[6] Two, Seymour

---

1881); British Indian Committee, 1883; radical Liberal candidate for N. Paddington, 1883-1885. One of Digby's descendants in London advised me that none of his private MSS exist.

[3] Lord Reay was informed confidentially by an unidentified correspondent in the Bombay Association that Digby had requested £1,500 for election expenses and £1,000 a year for five years for arguing India's case in the Commons if elected. See Reay to D., June 4, 1885, DVP, R. 528, No. 377.

[4] Digby, *Indian Problems.*

[5] On Oct. 6, see Chandavarkar, p. 70, *Pall Mall Gazette,* Oct. 7, 1885.

[6] Chandavarkar, p. 70, mentions the following as attending: Dr. G. B. Clark; Major Evans-Bell, formerly Bengal Army, member of East India Association; Martin Wood, formerly editor, *Times of India,* member of East India Association; S. Keay, radical Liberal candidate for Newington; A. Haggard, formerly Bengal Civil Service; J. D.

Keay and Digby himself, were radical Liberal candidates for Parliament. Tories were conspicuously absent. Moreover, none of the key Liberals whom Hume had contacted about Indian affairs was present. Thus, at the outset of their mission, the Indian delegates were taken in hand by a radical fringe group of the Liberal Party who were neither influential nor politically representative of their party, and whose counsels would be most questionable.

This became obvious in the decisions of the meeting when the questions of where and when the delegates should air India's Appeal arose. It was decided to arrange for the delegates to attend various meetings throughout October—one at Paddington, for instance, where Digby was campaigning, another later at Maidstone (Kent). By attending these meetings, which were political rallies for radicals running on the Liberal platform, Chandavakar and Mudaliar could easily find themselves drawn into the swirl of Liberal and radical politics, thus undermining any claim to impartiality they might wish to attach to India's Appeal.

In the matter of the aims of the Appeal, the radical Liberal sympathizers also proved to be unfortunate advisers. Acting on the initial instructions from their respective associations before leaving India, Chandavarkar and Mudaliar listed as the principal aim of their mission the acquisition of public support for the Parliamentary inquiry into the Government of India—an aim excellent in theory, but not in practical politics. By October, the very idea of the Parliamentary inquiry bristled with political controversy. Churchill, when proposing the inquiry in his Indian Budget Statement, gave notice of Tory sponsorship of an idea borrowed from the radical Liberals, and, consequently, he had made the inquiry a controversial subject which all the leading politicians sought to avoid. In the Liberal camp, throughout September, Gladstone, Hartington, Chamberlain, and even Bright preferred to say nothing on the subject, while John Morley, the rising star of the radical Liberals, even went so far as to oppose it on the grounds that Churchill had reduced the idea to a crass political gimmick.[7] On the Tory side, although Churchill had the support of his cabinet colleagues, neither Salisbury, Iddlesleigh, Cranbrook, nor Hicks-Beach chose to say anything in public to support the idea. Thus, should the delegates set forth the idea in their Appeal, it would certainly win no support from politicians who mattered—not even from Church-

---

Digby, W. Dibgy's brother; and W. S. Blunt, the radical Tory. But other statements by Chandavarkar and Blunt's own correspondence in *The Times* (Oct. 15) show that Blunt was not present.

[7] Morley, speech at Cambridge, Sept. 29, *Times,* Sept. 30, 1885.

ill himself. The delegates should have been apprised of this fact and discouraged from focusing their appeal upon such an objective. But, since many in the radical Liberal group intended to campaign partly on Indian issues, of which the inquiry seemed to them one of the most effective, they advised the delegates to make it the principal aim of the Appeal. So indeed it became.

As for the Appeal as a whole, Digby, Keay, and some others suggested that it be drafted to form part of the Liberal platform for the sole use of Liberal candidates.[8] Chandavarkar and Mudaliar, still acting on their original instructions to draft a politically impartial Appeal, and supported by other members of the group, refused this advice.

Thus, the meeting at the National Liberal Club gave full notice how some members of the Indian reform coterie intended to deliver India's Appeal to the British voter. There is reason to believe that Hume was far from satisfied. Thereafter, his name was conspicuously absent in accounts of the activities of the delegates, whereas Digby's stood much to the fore.[9] Certainly, in the eyes of the Tory press, the meeting had linked the delegates to the radical Liberal camp. This identification set the stage for the ultimate failure of the Indian mission, a failure which began almost at once with a sharp setback dealt the Appeal itself both before and upon its publication.

This setback was brought about by political events within the Indian associations and by activities of the Anglo-Indian press in India and the pro-Tory press in London. The approval of Naoroji's amending resolution by the Bombay Presidency Association and the Madras Sabha set the ball rolling.[10] Certain key figures in the associations lost no time in publicly decrying the amendment as politically dangerous. Sir Madhava Rao, disturbed by the revolt of the younger members of the Madras Sabha, in an indignant letter to *The Times of India,* attributed Naoroji's amendment to radical wire-pulling from England and prophesied that it would mean political involvement of the Indian delegates in English politics.[11]

[8] "Occasional Notes," *Pall Mall Gazette,* Oct. 7, 1885.

[9] Chandavarkar after this meeting never mentioned Hume in his memoir; nor did Hume's name appear on any of the committees sponsoring the delegates when they spoke around the country. My search in the numerous London and provincial newspapers has failed to turn up any letters by Hume supporting the delegates or the Appeal. The converse was true of Digby.

[10] See above, pp. 217 ff. Instructions, including Naoroji's motion, were forwarded to the delegates and reached them about Oct. 20.

[11] Letter to the editor by "Native Thinker" (*nom de plume* of Madhava Rao), *Times of India,* Oct. 3, 1885, p. 6.

In the Bombay Presidency Association, the crisis was more serious. Dadabhai Framjee, one of the elder leaders and a Vice-President, resigned and sent to *The Times of India* a copy of his letter of resignation, in which he ridiculed Naoroji's resolution as pointless and condemned it as "highly objectionable."[12] These letters led Henry Curwen, editor of *The Times of India,* to write an editorial supporting Rao and Framjee and calling upon other "moderate" leaders of the Bombay association—Sir J. Jeejeebhoy, B. Tyabji, R. Sayani, N. Haridas, and D. Petit—to join Framjee in resigning.[13] Shortly thereafter, Sir Jamsetjee Jeejeebhoy, the wealthy and influential President of the Association, personal friend of Sir Richard Temple and Sir James Fergusson, and the patron saint of Bombay editors and politicians, resigned,[14] provoking a swirl of indignation and dismay within the Association and among the Bombay editors.[15] Malabari and Agarkar intimated that Jeejeebhoy had been misled by Framjee; Naoroji attributed Jeejeebhoy's action to the outspoken criticism of the British Indian Association of Calcutta and *The Hindoo Patriot;* Sane thought that the baronet had fallen prey to Curwen's devices; Ranade condemned the step as "ill-considered." Sen in Calcutta, lamenting the schism, considered Jeejeebhoy's resignation divisive of the entire Indian political effort.[16] These comments notwithstanding, the fact remained that Rao had spoken out against Naoroji's resolution, and that Jeejeebhoy and Framjee had resigned. No matter what the Indian editors might say, Naoroji's amending resolution had exposed the Indian delegates to charges of political interference in the English election, while the schisms within the leadership of the educated Indian community gravely weakened the claim that the Appeal represented the unanimous expression of the Indian associations, not to mention the Indian people.

These dissensions were eagerly seized upon by certain Anglo-Indian journalists in India. James Wilson, proprietor and editor of *The Indian Daily News* of Calcutta, and a friend of Churchill, followed Curwen's lead and attacked the Indian Appeal in a vitriolic editorial.[17] Denouncing the educated Indians as a micro-

[12] Letter, dated Oct. 6, published, Oct. 7, 1885.
[13] Oct. 7, 1885.
[14] Oct. 12, 1885.
[15] For their comments in *Indian Spectator, Mahratta,* and *Rast Goftar,* Oct. 18, *Dnyan Prakash,* and *Indu Prakash,* Oct. 19, see *V. of I.,* III, Oct. 1885 (section: "The Secession of D. Framjee and Sir J. Jeejeebhoy from the Bombay Presidency Association").
[16] Editorial, *Indian Mirror,* Oct. 16, 1885.
[17] Oct. 12, 1885.

scopic bunch of "pushing young particles" who participated in juvenile political antics, and upbraiding them for "the vile scurrility and disloyalty" that they preached, Wilson dismissed as "preposterous" the claim of their appeal to speak for the people of India. Not only were the Indian leaders divided over the Appeal, but the masses knew nothing about it simply because they possessed "no political feelings or aspirations" but instead basked happily in the kind providence of British law and order. The Appeal he considered merely a lot of "imaginary grievances" dreamed up by vain, conceited, and disgruntled "Young India"; it was, he charged, a disguise for Indian intervention in the General Election in support of the radical Liberal cause.

C. Macgregor, in Calcutta as correspondent for the London *Times,* having read Wilson's editorial and other comments, sent a telegram to *The Times,*[18] attributing the Appeal "to the spirit of restlessness created by Lord Ripon" and dismissing its grievances as fictional and frivolous. Macgregor emphasized the decisions of the Bombay Presidency Association, the Indian Association of Calcutta, and the other three[19] to disregard Madhava Rao's advice and to intervene in the General Election by having the Indian delegates oppose certain Conservatives and support certain Liberals for Parliament. Naming some candidates and noting the curious absence of Churchill's name on either list, Macgregor added that the lists had led to the resignation of Framjee, whose letter he quoted, and that *The Times of India* had urged Jeejeebhoy and other leaders of the Bombay Presidency Association to resign. In conclusion, Macgregor stated that neither the Bombay Association nor the delegates with their Appeal spoke in the name of the Indian people, but were merely agitators whose words were not understood by the dumb millions or by the wealthy landlords—"the real leaders of the people." In much the same fashion as Macgregor, the Bombay correspondent of the London *Evening Standard*, drawing upon the reports and editorials appearing in *The Times of India,* telegraphed a similar report[20] to his journal, giving the lists included in Naoroji's motion.

Developments within the Indian associations and in the Anglo-Indian press were not known by the Indian delegates until too late. They had drafted India's Appeal, and by October 12 had distributed it to the leading newspapers in London. The Appeal itself was a concise, politically neutral, and able statement. Entitled "An Appeal

[18] See *Times,* Oct. 13, 1885.
[19] Madras Mahajana Sabha, Sind Sabha, and Poona Sarvajanik Sabha.
[20] See *Evening Standard,* Oct. 13, 1885.

from the People of India to the Electors of Great Britain and Ireland," it opened with an acknowledgment of the benefits of British rule and then listed the requests which the Indian people wished to address to the British electorate. The first request read: "We pray you to require a pledge from the candidate—whether Liberal or Conservative—who seeks your support that he will press for a Commission of Inquiry into Indian affairs as soon as the new Parliament meets." The following requests were essentially those adopted by the Bombay Presidency Association, Poona Sabha, and Madras Sabha in the Appeal issued in India in early September: a plea for Bright's scheme of 1858, entailing a federal form of government in which some of the powers then held by the Supreme Government would devolve on the provincial governments; a call for "a changed military policy, whereby the extensive costliness of Indian military administration may be reduced"; and a bid for the practical enforcement of equal rights and equal justice for all races, creeds, and classes in India. The fifth and final request, set forth as strongly as the first, asked for reform of the Supreme and provincial legislative councils: "At present we are heavily taxed, but we are denied all voice alike in the imposition of taxes and the expenditure of the money raised by taxation. Our so-called Legislative Councils possess no power of inquiry into or control over, Executive Acts, cannot utter an opinion respecting finance, and possess no representation of native Indian interests, save here and there an Indian gentleman nominated by the Government of the day . . . No opening for honourable and loyal ambition is provided for able Indians." The Appeal concluded by urging British voters to elect those candidates who would support the Parliamentary inquiry into Indian grievances: "We ask simply for reasonable reforms, and for those reforms only after you have satisfied yourselves through your representatives that our requests are just."

Laconic and effective in composition, moderate and loyal in expression, and politically impartial in tone, the Appeal was a judicious statement which should have received a warm welcome from the London press when released for publication on October 13. Such, however, was not the case. *The Times* chose to publish Macgregor's Calcutta telegram first and the Appeal the following day.[21] *The Evening Standard* published the Appeal along with the telegram from its Bombay correspondent summarizing Naoroji's amendment and the troubles within the Indian associations.[22] *The*

[21] Calcutta telegram on Oct. 13, the Appeal on Oct. 14, 1885.
[22] On Oct. 13. The Appeal was also published by the Liberal journals, *Daily News* and *Pall Mall Gazette*, Oct. 13, 1885.

St. James's Gazette printed the Appeal in one column side by side
with another giving the substance of telegrams from India on the
"friends" and "unfriends" of India and the schisms in Indian leadership.[23] The inferences were obvious: either the Indian delegates
did not know what they were talking about, or, in their claims to
political impartiality—claims now laid bare by news from India—
they were trying to disguise a sinister motive. A day later *The Times*
printed a patronizing and damaging editorial based entirely upon
Macgregor's telegram.[24] *The Times* found no discontent with British rule in India such as the Indian delegates alleged. It examined
each of the grievances but refused to concede any. It dismissed the
delegates' claims to represent the Indian people. "India [is] a
congeries of races and religions. . . . Only by a figure of speech can
India be called a country and its population be styled the Indian
people," the editorial maintained. Leading members in Parliament
were fully alive to the problem of contemporary India, and hence
Indians could take heart that their interests were being well looked
after. There was, in short, no need whatsoever for the Indian delegation or the Appeal. But, given the fact that both existed, *The
Times* warned the delegates that they were falling into "a mischievous mistake" by failing to heed Sir Madhava Rao's advice to
steer clear of English party politics. Such was the welcome accorded
the Appeal in Fleet Street. Aided by the Anglo-Indian press, the
London press had cast the Indian delegates in a radical image and
had simultaneously stripped the Appeal of its claim to political
impartiality in the eyes of the English public. The Indian mission
had received a sharp setback at its very inception.

Unfortunately, the delegates could do nothing to counter the
blow delivered to the Appeal or to offset the radical reputation
fastened on their mission. Instead, the reputation grew apace while
all efforts to diminish it—notably, those of W. Scawen Blunt,
Churchill's friend and the radical Conservative candidate for Camberwell—proved ineffective. Having heard a few days before the
Appeal was published that the Indian delegates were in London,
and having read Macgregor's damaging telegram to *The Times*,
Blunt, to ascertain the facts for himself, invited Chandavarkar and
Mudaliar to his house in St. James's Square.[25] Having learned that
they aimed to remain politically neutral, and having convinced
them that Churchill and others in the Tory party were genuinely

[23] Oct. 13, 1885, p. 10.
[24] Oct. 14, 1885.
[25] Afternoon of Oct. 13; see Blunt's letter to the editor, Oct. 14, *Times*, Oct. 15 ,1885,
and Chandavarkar, pp. 43-44.

interested in Indian reform along the lines propounded by Ripon, Blunt set about to remove the radical Liberal tag rapidly becoming attached to their names. He not only agreed to speak at their opening meeting the following evening but also arranged for them to speak before his Camberwell constituency, and he likewise arranged a private meeting with Churchill at the India Office, hoping to enlist the Secretary of State's support for their mission. He also wrote to *The Times* repudiating Macgregor's allegations about the delegates, upholding India's Appeal to the British voter, and emphasizing that the delegates had "nothing whatever to do with party warfare in England," and that their only aim was to enlist the support of candidates "irrespective of party" who would be willing to act upon Indian grievances if elected to the new Parliament.[26] But all of Blunt's promising efforts came to naught when the first public meeting in England for India's Appeal was held.[27] This meeting turned out to be as politically compromising to the delegates as it was embarrassing to Blunt.

The meeting was held at the Westbourne Park Chapel off Porchester Road, in the constituency of South Paddington, which, tagged as Churchill's "safe seat," was adjacent to North Paddington where Digby was standing as a candidate. The meeting place would have mattered little had the chairman and the speakers been of mixed political hues, and the speeches nonpolitical, but such was not the case.[28] Blunt alone among the listed speakers was a Tory, while the others were solidly radical Liberal. Digby, as Chairman, opened the meeting by reading letters from various radical Liberal sympathizers, the most important of whom was Joseph Chamberlain, and then he indulged in a panegyric of Ripon's administration and the Liberal Party's Indian policy. In essence, his speech was a strongly worded plea for the restoration of "Riponism" in Indian policy, and as such it was a sharp rebuke to the Churchill–Dufferin policy. Man Mohan Ghose,[29] who by this time had joined Chandavarkar and Mudaliar in London, followed Digby and went even further in demanding the Liberals' reform policy for India. Repudiating rumors from Anglo-Indian sources that the Indian delegates were representatives of disloyal and revolutionary groups

[26] Letter to the editor, *Times*, Oct. 15, 1885.

[27] Evening of Oct. 14, with an estimated 1,300 persons.

[28] *Evening Standard*, Oct. 15, 1885, gave the most complete coverage. See also *Times*, *Pall Mall Gazette*, and *St. James's Gazette*, Oct. 15, *West London Observer*, week ending Oct. 17, 1885.

[29] The Tory newspapers, *Times* and *Evening Standard*, named L. M. Ghose, while the other Tory journal, *St. James's Gazette*, named (correctly, I believe) M. M. Ghose. Chandavarkar's memoir states that M. M. Ghose was present.

in India, and fully acknowledged the obvious blessings which British rule had bestowed upon all classes in India, Ghose declared that India's Appeal to the British voter aimed at a more just and progressive Indian policy than that currently pursued by the Government of India. He admitted that Indians had been told repeatedly that Indian grievances must not be dragged into English party politics, and that axiom was excellent as long as both English parties emulated each other in seeking liberal reforms, fair taxation, and justice for India. But that axiom had been overthrown during the late seventies when the Tories in England and Lytton in India had launched their costly, reactionary, imperial policy at the expense of the Indian people. Had the Liberals not triumphed in 1879 and Ripon not been appointed Viceroy, Ghose trembled to think where Indian sympathies might have turned and what course British–Indian history might have taken. He would say that once Ripon had made clear that his predecessor had broken the pledges of Parliament to the Indian people, and once it had become evident to the Indian people that the Tory party was working against Ripon's Indian reforms, then most Indians realized that the Tories would never put Indian interests before those of imperial policy and of their own party. Thus the old axiom of political neutrality on Indian issues had long since proved false, and he and his colleagues had come to England to persuade British voters to elect candidates who would work for a policy to extend Ripon's reforms.

Ghose's speech, undisguisedly political, electrified the audience. It startled Blunt. So also did Mudaliar's speech, especially since he had joined Chandavarkar in assuring Blunt that their methods were to be nonpolitical. While more specific, Mudaliar's speech was as able, witty, and damaging as Ghose's. He concentrated upon India's financial grievances, discussing deftly military and administrative expenditures during Dufferin's first year and the financial straits into which the Indian budget had been plunged in recent months. Since entering office, the Tories, he alleged, had made matters worse by doing nothing to decrease administrative costs, through Civil Service reform, for example, and by doing everything to increase expenditure, through higher military estimates. On this basis, he saw no reason why Churchill, in his Budget Statement, had expressed so much surprise that the Famine Fund had been "eaten up." Mudaliar's plea for greater economy and increased employment of qualified Indians in government service was tantamount to a penetrating indictment of Churchill's Budget Statement and Dufferin's policy. Only Chandavarkar, in advocating the reform of the legislative councils, kept to the straight and narrow path of political neutrality; but even he strayed into politics when he reiterated Ghose's plea for a shift in the Government's Indian policy from preoccupation with imperial and external affairs to greater concentration upon internal reform. Seymour Keay, the radical Liberal candidate for Newington, in moving the resolution to support the Appeal and the Parliamentary inquiry, did little to lower the emotional temperature of the meeting by a blistering condemnation of the evils and extravagances of British official administration in India. In the wake of these speeches, Blunt, amidst boos and hisses from the audience because of his Tory affiliation,[30] seconded Keay's resolution and took occasion to encourage the Indian delegates and their British friends to air the Appeal in a nonpartisan manner, so as to rally support from both parties for the Appeal. But his words were overshadowed by what had already been said. On this note the meeting ended with the damage fully done. Digby's speech, to say nothing of his arrangements for the meeting, had carried the Appeal directly into the English political arena, while the speeches by Ghose, Mudaliar, and Keay gave weight to the allegations of political meddling brought by the Anglo-Indian editors against the delegates, made Blunt's nonpartisan plea seem silly, and rendered his further efforts useless.

This was apparent the following day when *The Times* printed Blunt's letter on behalf of the Indian delegates in one column and a résumé of the delegates' speeches in another. *The Evening Standard* gave a more extensive transcript of the speeches, and the *St. James's Gazette* capitalized upon the political aspect of the meeting. Remarking that the Indian speakers had said "a good deal about the wrongs of India and the virtues of Radical candidates," the *Gazette* emphasized that in no circumstances should the delegates be considered as nonpartisan or representative of the Indian people. "To say that this knot of Europeanised pleaders and journalists represents 'the people of India' is ridiculous." Blunt's efforts notwithstanding, the radical Liberal label had been pinned firmly upon the delegates.

Worse still was the effect of the Westbourne Park Chapel meeting upon the interview with Churchill.[31] Introduced to the delegates by Blunt in the Secretary of State's room at the India Office,

---

[30] The hostile reception accorded Blunt astonished Chandavarkar. See Chandavarker, p. 43.

[31] See Chandavarkar, pp. 45-46, for a most interesting account of this meeting and his personal reaction to the dreary, labyrinthine India Office. Blunt's diaries do not record his endeavors on behalf of the Indian delegates or this meeting. His biographers do not mention the meeting, nor did Churchill in his letters to Dufferin.

Churchill was polite and civil, but guarded and unresponsive. When Blunt and subsequently Ghose both stated that the mission did not intend to identify itself with any particular party, Churchill merely nodded slowly and, in Chandavarkar's own words, sought "to convey his meaning by silence." He neither gave warning concerning their mission, nor did he give it his blessing. He never mentioned the Westbourne Chapel meeting, as if it had never occurred. Light pleasantries on his visit to India, remarks about Raja Siva Prasad of Benares, a comment or two on the cabinet's full endorsement of the Parliamentary inquiry and his intention to appoint a committee rather than a commission to conduct it, and an outspoken remark about John Morley's unwholesome political opposition to the in-quiry—these were Churchill's only statements. Rising to conclude the interview, he commented that he would be glad to learn of any issues which troubled the Indian groups in the three presidencies from which the delegates came. Thus subtly saying that he had no intention of recognizing their appeal or their claims to represent the grievances of the Indian people, he withdrew as graciously as he had entered—agreeable but aloof. Blunt's hopes of rallying Tory support for India's Appeal were dashed.[32] Churchill had lumped the delegates with the radical Liberals, and intended to treat them as the political opposition in the contest just beginning.

Thereafter, successive developments identified the Indian dele-gates completely and irrevocably with the radical Liberal camp, and eventually undermined the validity of India's Appeal to the British voter. In India, the most important Indian association, the British Indian Association, publicly withdrew its tentative approval of the Appeal and the delegates upon receiving Naoroji's resolution listing the names of English candidates to be opposed by the delegates in the election. Since Sir Roper Lethbridge, who from England had assisted the Association in its endeavors to block the Bengal Tenancy Bill, was named, the Association naturally declined to support activities designed to thwart the election of Lethbridge, or of other Tories who had, in the past, been advocates of the Association's interests. Sarvadhikhari gave notice in *The Hindoo Patriot* of the Association's decision to withdraw from the Appeal because of the impropriety of Indian intervention in English politics and the impossibility of selecting Indians who could truly represent the different caste, community, and class interests of India.[33] He thus

---

[32] Subsequently, Blunt stopped actively supporting the Appeal, but made good his promise of having the delegates speak from his election platform. See *Times,* Oct. 22, 1885, for meeting in Camberwell on Indian reform.

[33] "India at the Hustings," Oct. 26, 1885.

admitted what the Tory press in London had contended from the start. The defection of the British Indian Association was a serious blow to the Appeal.

In England, Churchill decided to retaliate against Digby's sally into the South Paddington constituency by staging a Tory offensive in Digby's own constituency of North Paddington, designed not only to support the Conservative candidate, Lionel Cohen, one of Churchill's personal friends and a relative of the Rothschilds, but also to refute the charges brought against Tory policy in India by Digby and his Indian friends.[34] Churchill, Lord George Hamilton, the Tory candidate for Ealing,[35] the Honorable Edward Stanhope, the Tory incumbent for Horncastle,[36] and Sir Roper Lethbridge, the Tory candidate for North Kensington,[37] appeared in turn on Cohen's platform to support him against Digby, and to defend Tory policy by pointing to the settlement of the Afghan question, the strengthening of Indian defenses, and the proposed Parliamentary inquiry. In a letter to Digby, Lethbridge went further, asking why, since he and other Tories advocated the Parliamentary inquiry while leading radical Liberals did not, the Indian delegates should not launch their Appeal from Tory, as well as radical Liberal, platforms.[38] Sir Richard Temple, the Conservative candidate for Evesham (South Worcestershire), also supported Cohen's candidacy and was scheduled to speak for him in North Paddington.[39]

Against this brisk and persistent offensive, Digby promptly took action and lashed back at his opponents. In a public letter to Temple, he warned him that, were there any interference in North Paddington, he would retaliate by advising the Evesham electorate of Temple's poor administration while Governor of Bombay during Lytton's viceroyalty. In a hard-hitting, personal letter to the Ealing voters, Digby informed them of Hamilton's role in Lytton's iniquitous and disastrous Indian policy.[40] To the electors of North Kensington, he wrote in the name of the Indian delegates—none of whom was in London at the time—quoting the Bombay Presidency Association's resolution against Lethbridge, and stating that the Indian delegates would not depart from the resolution even

[34] Election intelligence, North Paddington, *West London Observer*, week ending Oct. 31, 1885, pp. 5-6.

[35] Under-Secretary of State for India, 1874–1878.

[36] Under-Secretary of State for India, 1878–1880.

[37] Indian Press Commissioner under Lytton.

[38] Election news, North Kensington, *re* letter, Lethbridge to Digby, Oct. 27, *Times*; Nov. 5, 1885.

[39] See n. 34 above. Governor of Bombay during Lytton's viceroyalty.

[40] Election intelligence, Ealing, *West London Observer*, week ending Nov. 7, 1885, p. 6.

though Lethbridge supported the Parliamentary inquiry.[41] By such petty squabbling, Digby so discredited himself and the Indian mission that Sir George Birdwood, then a ranking member of the India Office who on behalf of Hamilton had replied to Digby's letter, approached Chandavarkar in an attempt to persuade him, his colleagues, and Digby himself that their activities were causing irreparable harm to India's Appeal.[42]

Nor did the Indian delegates themselves help matters in any way. Following the meeting at Westbourne Park Chapel, Man Mohan Ghose shifted his entire effort to helping his brother, Lal Ghose, who, as the radical Liberal candidate for Deptford, was the first Indian to stand for Parliament. No doubt it was most important to secure Lal Ghose's election; an Indian in the new Parliament would be a vital spark in securing Indian reforms. Even Hume's friends had agreed on that. But by his absence from the mission, Man Mohan not only virtually withdrew Bengali representation from the Appeal, but became directly involved on the radical Liberal platform in Deptford. As Man Mohan's radical Liberal prejudices became increasingly apparent, so also did those of Chandavarkar and Mudaliar. As a result of the arrangements made by Digby and his friends both men from mid-October onward spoke only at radical Liberal rallies,[43] except for one meeting at Camberwell held under Blunt's auspices.[44] And with each passing rally, Chandavarkar and Mudaliar fell increasingly under the spell of electioneering and spoke out more openly against Tory policy. From the end of October, after they had received final instructions, including Naoroji's amending resolution listing the "friends" and "unfriends" of India, Chandavarkar, especially, cast restraint to the winds and espoused the radical Liberal cause. At the Maidstone rally for the radical Liberal candidate Major Sharp Hume, Chandavarkar maintained that the extravagant increase in military expenditure of recent months was the wish solely of the Tory cabinet and the Secretary of State for India but not of the Indian people, who, had they possessed genuine representation in the Supreme Legislative Council with

[41] Election News, North Kensington, Digby on behalf of Indian Delegates Committee to Lethbridge, *Times,* Nov. 5, 1885.

[42] Chandavarkar, p. 38.

[43] Maidstone Radical Association, Kent, supporting Major Sharp Hume, Oct. 27; Swansea Liberal Association, Wales, supporting L. Dillwyn, Nov. 2; Newcastle-on-Tyne Liberal Club, Northumberland, supporting J. Morley and J. Cowan, Nov. 7, 1885.

[44] Meeting Oct. 21, chaired by Rev. T. Leary, where Blunt spoke on the reasons for India's appeal and introduced Chandavarkar, Mudaliar, the Honorable A. Bourke, Tory candidate for Kings Lynn and son of the late Lord Mayo, Jemal-al-Din, the Afghan chieftain, and Dr. Yusaf Ali, a Punjab Medical Officer. See *Times,* Oct. 22, 1885.

some voice in budgetary matters, would never have permitted such increases with the inevitable consequences of higher taxes.[45] His speech at Swansea on the same theme was couched in even stronger terms.[46] He would not accept the statement of the Secretary of State or the Viceroy that the increased military strength was required to fend off the Russian threat to Afghanistan and northwest India; this was tantamount to saying that Indian loyalty could not be relied upon in a crisis but British rifles could. He addressed the Newcastle Liberals in similar vein.[47] By such attacks—always accurate and precise, and always specifically anti-Churchill—Chandavarkar contributed as much as Digby and Man Mohan Ghose to identifying India's Appeal with the radical Liberal cause. But, as he admitted some years later, by November he saw no alternative but to become politically involved in the electoral contest.[48] The predictions of Rao, Jeejeebhoy, Tyabji, and other "moderates" of the Indian associations had come to pass.

Adding even more of a radical tint to the Indian mission were the leaflets issued by the delegates in their own, and also Digby's, names. Written to supplement the Appeal, the leaflets consisted of two series. The Bombay series, twelve leaflets in all, prepared by the Bombay Presidency Association and the Poona Sarvajanik Sabha in consultation with other associations and printed in Bombay,[49] reached the delegates in London by early November. Each leaflet was headed "Published and distributed on behalf of the People of India by the British Indian Association and the Indian Association of Calcutta, the Bombay Presidency Association, the Sarvajanik Sabha of Poona, the Mahajana Sabha of Madras, the Sind Sabha of Kurrachee and Praja-hita-vardhak Sabha of Surat," and each treated a particular grievance with relevant statistical data in support.[50] Of particular significance were leaflets 1, 2, 3, and 9, in each of which Dufferin and Churchill were severely criticized for placing the re-

[45] *Tribune,* Dec. 12, 1885.

[46] Nov. 2, *Cambrian,* Nov. 6, 1885.

[47] Nov. 6, *Newcastle Daily Leader,* Nov. 7, 1885.

[48] Chandavarkar, p. 66. M. M. Ghose agreed; see his report to the Bombay Presidency Association, Jan. 14, *Times of India,* Jan. 15, 1886.

[49] See Telang's report, Bombay Presidency Association, *B.G.O.S.,* Oct. 2, 1885.

[50] Twelve leaflets entitled: 1. "India's Appeal to the English Electors—the Reason for It"; 2. "Is India Lightly Taxed?"; 3. "Why Is Lord Ripon Loved by the Indians?"; 4. "The Costliness of British Administration"; 5. "Mistrust of Anglo-Indian Opinion"; 6. "Imperial Stock-taking"; 7. "Is India a Part of the British Empire?"; 8. "Manchester's Interest in India"; 9. "21 Per Cent Growth of Indian Military Expenditure in 20 Years!!"; 10. "Why Do Indians Prefer British to Russian Rule?"; 11. "The Appalling Costliness of the Indian Army!!"; 12. "The Native States of India." Of the two extra, only leaflet 14 has been traced. See enclosures to CRO Tract 658; also editorial, "The Bombay Presidency Association Leaflets," *Hindoo Patriot,* Nov. 9, 1885.

quirements of imperial policy before those of the Indian people, thereby increasing military expenditure and adding to the burden of the Indian taxpayer. The leaflets called for a return to the policy of Ripon and also for a thorough Parliamentary inquiry by Royal Commission into the grievances of the Indian people. It appears that the delegates, acting within their instructions, decided to add two more leaflets to the series. Of these, number 14, "How is India Governed?," discussed the urgent need for election of Indian representatives to the Supreme and provincial councils of India with powers of interpellation and discussion of the Indian budget proposals.

In addition to the Bombay series, there were three Madras leaflets sponsored by the Madras Sabha at its meeting in late September and forwarded to Mudaliar.[51] Possibly these leaflets served as the basis for the two additional leaflets prepared by the delegates in London. Though both series were similar, the Madras series was more moderate and neutral in tone. In addition, Digby wrote a pamphlet of some hundred-odd pages studded with statistics.[52] This political tract was significant for two reasons: first, by its charge that Churchill's Budget Statement had broken the tradition of keeping Indian issues out of English politics; and second, by its bold statement that "Indian reform is altogether impossible, does not come within the range of practical politics, save on the double condition that it becomes a Party question, and is due to the initiation of Liberals." The bulk of the pamphlet was devoted to a forceful argument in support of Indian reform, quoting at length from Colvin's article "If It Be Real—What Does It Mean?,"[53] recapitulating the reformist efforts of Ripon's administration, and weighing the results of British rule in India. Digby concluded that there was a pressing need for the proposed Parliamentary inquiry and for the reform of the legislative councils.

How many Bombay and Madras leaflets were actually printed, and where in London, to whom, and in what quantity they were

[51] Leaflet 1, entitled "Changes in India" and prepared for distribution at conclusion of the Indian mission, discussed the changing condition of India, Indian loyalty, and the need for partnership in administration. Leaflet 2, entitled "The Employment of the Native of India in the Public Service of the Country," discussed the unfulfilled pledges of 1853 and 1858 *re* Indian admission into Covenanted Civil Service. Leaflet 3, entitled "Financial Extravagance," discussed the growth of the Indian debt under Company and Crown and the effect of increased military and civil expenditure in recent years. See *M.M.S. Annual Report,* Appendixes.

[52] W. Digby, *The General Election, 1885: India's Interest in the British Ballot Box* (London [1888]).

[53] See Chap. I, p. 22 and n. 109.

distributed is uncertain.[54] What is known[55] is that the committees of the Bombay Presidency Association and the Poona Sarvajanik Sabha entrusted Digby with the responsibility of having the leaflets reprinted and distributed, and placed at his disposal a joint fund of £200. As for his own pamphlet, Digby kept a faithful record of the facts and figures—for good reason. He had prepared the pamphlet with Ripon's approval and on the understanding that his lordship would defray all costs of publication, which, after Digby had paid £10 from the Indian appeal fund and £20 from his personal election fund, totalled £359/1/0. Of 20,000 copies printed, 19,300 were distributed[56] by late September to newspaper editors in the United Kingdom, Parliamentary candidates, various Liberal organizations, and Digby's own constituents, and 200 had been sent to India. This was indeed extensive coverage. Even Digby could not think of a more complete distribution of this kind ever having been carried out in England on Indian affairs. How did he think the pamphlet would be accepted? "There has not yet been time for people to read the pamphlet," he wrote Ripon, "but such remarks as I have heard from those who have read portions are full of admiration at what they regard as the moral grandeur and material beneficence of your administration." Digby thought that adulation of Ripon's administration would leave an indelible impression upon the minds of British voters as to what could be done to meet Indian grievances.

But Digby's pamphlet and the Indian leaflets did not have the desired effect. None of the key London and provincial journals discussed them, nor did leaders of either party refer to them in their speeches. Given their anti-Churchill, pro-Ripon bias, and their pro-Liberal, anti-Tory sentiments, the tracts could have left no doubts in any reader's mind that the Indian delegates and their erstwhile secretary Digby had every intention of nailing India's Appeal ever more firmly to the radical Liberal masthead, and of carrying it deeper into the political fray.

So, at least, it seemed to certain political circles in India. A major reaction came from the Political Committee of the British Indian Association, which had withdrawn its support from the Appeal and

---

[54] Possibly Bombay Presidency Association records in India, if extant, might disclose more information on the leaflets.

[55] Digby to R., Sept. 26, 1885, RP, BM Add. MSS 43635, pp. 160-163.

[56] Distribution figures were: 200 to India, by Sept. 21; Sept. 24-26, 1 copy each to 2,000 newspaper editors in the U.K. and to 1,000 Parliamentary candidates, 4,300 copies to 800 Liberal associations in packets of 5 to 20 copies each, depending on the importance of the association, 5,000 copies to National Liberal Club members, 6,000 to N. Paddington, and 1,000 to the Liberal conference to be held at Cambridge (Sept. 29) and at Bradford (Oct. 3-4).

now took similar action on the leaflets. In another public statement,[57] the committee reminded the Bombay Presidency Association that the two associations had originally agreed not to touch on controversial issues in the leaflets. It noted that the third leaflet, in praising Ripon's administration, applauded his tenancy reforms, and, since this was contrary to the views of the British Indian Association, and since the leaflets had been prepared without its concurrence, the British Indian Association felt free to disown them and therewith withdrew its support. This action further weakened the Indian mission and the Appeal.

By the outset of November, the delegates had become directly linked to the radical wing of the Liberal Party in the eyes of the interested British voter. Events during the remainder of the month were to strengthen this identification—to the ultimate undoing of India's Appeal.

[57] Editorial, "The Bombay Presidency Association Leaflets," *Hindoo Patriot*, Nov. 9, 1885.

XI

"A Military Adventure up the Irrawaddy"

By early October, Dufferin had completely thrown over his cautious approach of July and, though well aware that the Indian taxpayer could not afford a war, was fully in step with Churchill's forward policy toward Upper Burma. Once again, imperial politics were to prevail over Indian finance.

Throughout September, Charles F. Bernard, the Chief Commissioner of British Burma, and H. M. Durand, the Foreign Secretary, had been advocating action against Ava.[1] The mercantile interests in Rangoon and Calcutta had been renewing their clamor, urging "immediate action" on the part of the Government of India;[2] and Wallace Brothers had obtained from "friends" in Paris what was alleged to be an official Franco-Burmese agreement signed in April for the formation of a bank and a copy of a prospectus submitted to French firms, and had sent these documents on to Durand for Dufferin's attention.[3] This news, coupled with the mounting pressures for action, made Dufferin conclude that the time had come to act.[4]

In London, during Churchill's brief pre-election holiday in late

---

[1] Bernard to Durand, telegrams, Sept. 23, 24, 1885, DVP, R. 528, nos. 295, 299; Durand to Wallace, Sept. 25, 1885, R. 528, No. 302.

[2] Rangoon Chamber of Commerce to Bernard, Sept. 24, Bernard's Secretary to Durand, Sept. 24, 1885, *P.P.*, 1886, Vol. 50, Com. 4614, pp. 216-217, 215; Secretary, Bengal Chamber of Commerce, to Viceroy's Private Secretary, Sept. 25, 1885, DVP, R. 528, No. 303.

[3] Jones to Bernard, Sept. 23, 1885, with enclosures, *P.P.*, 1886, Vol. 50, Com. 4614, pp. 217-219.

[4] Viceroy to Secretary of State, telegram, Sept. 28, 1885, DVP, R. 519, No. 258.

September, both press and commercial circles also began to call for action in Upper Burma. *The Times* published news telegrams from their Rangoon and Calcutta correspondents, covering more or less the same ground as Wallace Brothers and giving prominence to the alleged secret Franco-Burmese agreement.[5] The London Chamber of Commerce declared that the Franco-Burmese transactions could no longer be glossed over and called upon the Indian government to end Thibaw's rule and annex the country. *The Times* agreed, and thought that the forthcoming speech before the chamber of Archibald Colquhoun, *The Times* expert on affairs in the Indo-Chinese peninsula, would provide convincing arguments for such action.[6] Indeed Colquhoun did just that. Addressing the chamber on September 29, he spoke of alleviating industrial depression in England by opening new markets in the highly populated Indo-Chinese peninsula and in southwestern China. He stated bluntly that King Thibaw and his Court were the principal impediments to opening these markets, and that, because of Thibaw's misman-agement of his kingdom, his involvement with the French, and his anti-English prejudice, the Kingdom of Ava should be annexed out-right and brought within the British Indian Empire. The chamber applauded these recommendations, and *The Times* thereafter picked up the agitation, referring to Colquhoun's arguments as "unimpeachable" and calling upon the Home Government to act against Thibaw.[7] The Manchester Chamber of Commerce followed suit and declared itself in full support of Colquhoun's bold policy;[8] even the liberal *Pall Mall Gazette* succumbed and joined this rising clamor.[9]

Within the India Office, A. Moore, Churchill's private secretary and formerly the expert on Burma in the Political and Secret De-partment, and Owen Tudor Burne, then head of the Political and Secret Department, joined hands with the pro-war group. Signifi-cantly as pressure for action increased in India and England, M. de Freycinet, the French Premier, acting on Salisbury's earlier warn-ings against French involvement in the Burmese question, advised Salisbury privately that he had ordered an official repudiation of the alleged secret Franco-Burmese agreement and that the French Government "disavowed" Haas and his reckless dealings at Man-

[5] *Times,* Sept. 21, 24, 26, 28, 1885.
[6] Editorial, *Times,* Sept. 28, 1885.
[7] Speech on "A National Policy in the East," and editorial, Sept. 30, 1885.
[8] Resolution, Sept. 30, *Times,* Oct. 3, 1885.
[9] Oct. 1, 1885, p. 4, "Occasional Notes."

dalay.[10] Going even further, de Freycinet made a private bid "for a division of influence in the Indo-Chinese peninsula," and Salisbury, in turn, expressed much interest in exploring this idea.[11] By October 2, Haas had been recalled and was packing his bags to leave Mandalay at once.[12] Had Dufferin and his Council been informed of these developments and of the possibility of negotiations to eliminate French influence at Mandalay, they would certainly have encouraged it. Such a solution would have been in keeping with Ilbert's "Monroe Doctrine" for Upper Burma.[13] But Moore and Burne, though it is unclear whether they acted at Churchill's behest, never informed Dufferin of the French gesture. Instead, Burne, who in Lytton's time had advocated a forward policy against Thibaw, counseled his friends at the Foreign Office to reject the French overtures, and declared "we should now get *any* pretext to annex or make Burmah into a protected State."[14]

Thus, by October 4, when Churchill returned to London, a small but influential "lobby" had sprung up within and without the Government which advocated a forward solution, and Churchill, quite naturally, responded favorably to its pressure. The election campaign was about to begin; if ever there was a time for a bold policy to further English interests, it was then. Following Burne's advice, Churchill began to look for a pretext for action against Thibaw. The pretext was soon forthcoming. On October 13, Bernard notified Durand that a letter from King Thibaw and his ministers in the Hlutdaw had arrived.[15] The letter stated tersely that Bernard's analysis of the log dispute was fallacious and biased, and that the decree against the corporation, suspended at Bernard's behest, was to be reenacted at once; it made no mention of Bernard's proposals for arbitration and adjudication of the dispute.

Dufferin lost no time in calling his Executive Council to decide upon an answer. Acting on a decision made at the previous Council session on Burma in August that, if Thibaw replied in the negative to Bernard's proposals, the next step would be to issue an ultimatum, the Council drew up a series of demands: Thibaw must receive an envoy from the Indian government who was not to be subjected to any form of "humiliating ceremony" or diplomatic

[10] Walsham to S. with enclosures, Sept. 24, S. to Walsham, Sept. 26, 1885, *P.P.*, 1886, Vol. 50, Com. 4614, pp. 220-221, 210; Secretary of State to Viceroy, telegram, Oct. 3, 1885 (priv.), DVP, R. 519, No. 335.

[11] See S. to Walsham, Sept. 28, 1885, CRO, Home Corr. 1885, Vol. 80.

[12] Simla telegram, Oct. 2, *Times*, Oct. 3, 1885.

[13] See above, p. 145.

[14] Memorandum, Oct. 3, 1885, CRO, Home Corr. 1885, Vol. 80.

[15] Bernard to Durand, telegram, Oct. 13, 1885, DVP, R. 528, No. 378.

etiquette unfamiliar to Western courts and who would arrange for a settlement of the log dispute; the Court of Ava must not proceed with the decree or any other threatening action against the corporation; following any settlement of the log dispute, Thibaw must accept an English agent in permanent residence at Mandalay with adequate provision for his protection; the King and the Hlutdaw must regulate Burmese external affairs in accordance with the advice of the English Agent and must grant "proper facilities for opening up British trade with China via Bhamo." But the Council did not decide what action would follow if Thibaw rejected the demands. With the "unanimous consent" of the Council, Dufferin drafted the ultimatum and telegraphed extracts to Churchill for his approval.[16]

Churchill, for various reasons, wished to go beyond an ultimatum. Since, through the activities of the Burma lobby and *The Times,* the Burmese question had become an electoral issue in recent weeks, he aimed at turning the question to his political advantage. Immediate preparation for intervention was Churchill's plan of action, and he so informed the Viceroy. As for an objective, Churchill had no doubt that it should be annexation. Why? Because it would be a "very popular" step in England and Scotland "on account of the prospects of good trade." Moreover, "the press prefers annexation."[17] With the election campaign already begun, he could not, and did not wish to, ignore this drift of opinion; to do so would be contrary to the spirit of the speeches that he had made during the past two years in defense of British imperial interests. To his friend, George Buckle, the editor of *The Times,* he handed the first three clauses of the ultimatum and the substance of his telegram to Dufferin, and *The Times* came out with an editorial in support of annexation, which left the reader with the leading inference that Salisbury, Churchill, and Dufferin were in complete agreement on this policy.[18] This was just the impression Churchill wished to convey to the electorate, and he now began to force the pace, while Dufferin did the running.

Without entering into any exchange of telegrams over the pros and cons of intervention and annexation, Dufferin responded to

[16] Viceroy to Secretary of State, telegram, Oct. 16, 1885 (secret), DVP, R. 519, No. 273.
[17] Secretary of State of Viceroy, telegram, Oct. 17, 1885 (secret), DVP, R. 519, No. 356; C. to D., Oct. 16, 1885, R. 517, No. 76. A check of the press shows that in London the *Times, Evening Standard, Pall Mall Gazette, Globe, Army and Navy Gazette,* but not the *Daily News* and *Echo,* and in the provinces, the major journals, *Manchester Guardian, Leeds Mercury, Glasgow Obesrver,* and *Birmingham Daily Post,* though liberal, supported the cabinet's Burmese policy.
[18] Oct. 17, 1885.

Churchill's exhortations and acted. He named General Harry Prendergast of the Madras army as Commandant of the Burma Expeditionary Force and directed General Thomas F. Wilson, the Military Member of the Viceroy's Council, to mobilize three of the best British regiments in the Bengal army and a large contingent of Madrassi troops. "I propose," he telegraphed Churchill, "to start them off at once, as I am convinced that no settlement will prove permanent or satisfactory unless our troops are seen at Mandalay."[19] When Bernard informed him that the ultimatum would be sent on October 22 to reach Mandalay by October 30 and that a reply could be expected by November 10,[20] he sent instructions to General Wilson for immediate embarkation.[21] By the end of October, the Irrawaddy expeditionary force was embarking for Rangoon, which it expected to reach by November 10.[22]

Nor did Dufferin disagree with Churchill on the objective of the expedition. Reversing the position taken by the Council in early August,[23] he advised Churchill that he and his Council were agreed that "annexation pure and simple" was preferable to placing another prince on the throne of Ava.[24] He had no wish to attempt another "buffer" policy on the eastern flank of India which might prove as troublesome as the "buffer" policy he was conducting on the western flank in Afghanistan. While he had no fear of possible Chinese influence on any future Burmese ruler, he was worried about French influence emanating from Annam and Tongking. When a Reuter's telegram from Paris with news that the Burmese envoy in Paris was proposing a Burmese mission to either Calcutta or London to settle the current difficulties reached the Viceroy, he telegraphed Churchill "not to countenance the idea."[25] Only briefly and fleetingly did he consider the probable costs of intervention and annexation. He estimated that, if an expedition up the Irrawaddy proved necessary, it would require five lacs of rupees, that is, £42,515 per month, or about £127,545 for three months. This was

---

[19] Viceroy to Secretary of State, telegram, Oct. 20, 1885 (priv.), DVP, R. 519, No. 278; Wilson to Viceroy, telegram, Oct. 22, 1885, R. 528, No. 405a.

[20] Bernard to Durand, telegram, Oct. 21, 1885, *P.P.*, 1886, Vol. 50, Com. 4614, pp. 252-253.

[21] Viceroy to Secretary of State, telegram, Oct. 25, 1885 (priv.), DVP, R. 519, No. 284.

[22] Viceroy to Secretary of State, telegram, Oct. 27, 1885, DVP, R. 519, No. 284a; Diary of Movements and Operations of the Burma Expeditionary Force, Oct. 21, 1885, enclosed in Dispatch of Governor-General-in-Council, No. 17, Milit, Feb. 2, 1886, CRO, Bengal Milit. Let., 1886, Vol. 489.

[23] See above, p. 145.

[24] Viceroy to Secretary of State, telegram, Oct. 18, 1885 (priv.), DVP, R. 519, No. 275; D. to C., Oct. 19, 1885 (priv.), R. 517, No. 58.

[25] Viceroy to Secretary of State, telegram, Oct. 21, 1885 (priv.), DVP, R. 519, No. 279.

"an over-sanguine estimate" in all likelihood, he consoled himself. Nevertheless, the prospect of more extraordinary expenditure made him take another look at Colvin's marginal budget planning. For the first time, he grasped what Churchill meant when he had talked about making provision for unforeseen developments. Although Dufferin had formerly supported Colvin, he shifted over to Churchill's proposal of a large sterling loan to cover strategic preparations and famine railways, in spite of Colvin's warnings that to borrow in sterling was to add permanently to India's sterling debt.[26] But, in addition, he also proposed the remedy, already put forward by Colvin and Ilbert in a dissenting Minute of August,[27] and agitated by the Indian editors and politicians. "Would it be any good," he queried Churchill half-heartedly, by letter, not by telegram, "asking you if there was any chance of inducing the British Parliament to undertake a portion of the extra expenditure occasioned to India by the advance of Russia eastwards?" Having raised the question, he buried it by suggesting that it might be "a proper subject of enquiry on the part of the [Parliamentary] Commission you propose to constitute."[28]

Churchill was gratified by Dufferin's espousal of annexation because it brought the Viceroy into harmony with the prevailing mood in influential circles in England.[29] When Salisbury placed the facts of the Burmese question before the Queen, she readily agreed that war with Thibaw and annexation of his Kingdom were "quite inevitable and necessary."[30] Churchill advised Dufferin not to worry about any diplomatic bid by the Burmese envoy at Paris, for Lord Lyons, acting on instructions from Salisbury and Churchill, had politely turned down a Burmese bid already made on October 18.[31] With the fever of annexation running strong in the cabinet, the chambers of commerce, and the press, it only remained for Churchill to stimulate greater popular support in his electoral campaign. This task he skillfully executed in his opening speech at Birmingham. Pointing to the costly failure of the Gladstone cabinet to relate foreign policy to commerce for the benefit of depressed British markets, industries, and wages, Churchill spoke about the success of the Tory

[26] Colvin to Wallace, Oct. 12, 1885, DVP, R. 528, No. 370.
[27] Minute enclosed in Dispatch of Governor-General-in-Council, No. 135, Milit., Aug. 14, 1885, CRO, Bengal Milit. Let., 1885, Vol. 485.
[28] D. to C., Oct. 19, 1885 (priv.), DVP, R. 517, No. 58.
[29] Secretary of State to Viceroy, telegram, Oct. 19, 1885 (priv.), DVP, R. 519, No. 360.
[30] Queen to D., Oct. 20, 1885, DVP, R. 516, No. 20.
[31] Secretary of State to Viceroy, telegram, Oct. 22, 1885 (priv.), DVP, R. 519, No. 364; Lyons to S., Oct. 22 with enclosure, and Oct. 23, 1885, *P.P.*, 1886, Vol. 50, Com. 4614, pp. 223, 234.

cabinet in restoring this relationship. "We are threatened with a war with the King of Burmah," he announced. "The result of that war," he continued, "unless the King of Burmah yields in time, will probably be the annexation of Burmah," because "a great industry supported by British capital and employing numbers of British subjects" had been "plundered and persecuted." "A firm and resolute policy applied to Burmah," he concluded, "will not only protect existing British interests, but may, if wisely guided, offer an extraordinary development to British manufacturers."[32] The public now knew that Salisbury's cabinet was bent on annexation of Upper Burma; and more important, that annexation meant employment. Churchill's speech was greeted with so much enthusiasm that he could write with reason: "I believe the policy will be popular here."[33]

To pay for this forward policy in Burma, Churchill placed Colvin's budget plan and scheme for railway priority before the India Council. With the rigor and determination that he could display when he so wished, he called for immediate action, and, after stormy sessions with General Strachey and Bertram Currie, he forced through the scheme for railway sales and secured Colvin's other requests.[34] Significantly, Churchill relied upon the deepening Burmese crisis to foster support within the Council for Colvin's planning. But with all this said and done, he thought the Indian budget could only be rescued by bolder solutions. "I suppose," he wrote privately to Dufferin, "the Burmah business will a little upset your calculations. . . . You can increase the next year's loan by yet another million if you think proper . . . I find I have now borrowing powers to the extent of thirteen millions without having recourse to Parliament." A facile solution from Churchill's point of view, it ignored the fact that borrowing for wars and other unremunerative undertakings in a depreciated currency would only add to the Indian debt and place heavier burdens on the Indian taxpayer. This did not trouble Churchill, who was less worried about how the annexation of Upper Burma was to be paid for and by whom, than he was about the rapid execution of the annexation itself. He was chiefly concerned with the political implications of annexation. Time and timing were important, and it was but a few weeks until mid-November and the General Election.

[32] Speech, Oct. 23, *Times*, Oct. 24, 1885.
[33] C. to D., Oct. 27, 1885, DVP, R. 517, No. 77.
[34] C. to D., Oct. 16, 27, 1885, DVP, R. 517, nos. 76, 77; Secretary of State to Viceroy, two telegrams, Oct. 22, 1885 (priv.) and (Fin.), R. 519, nos. 365, 366. Railway sales restored £510,000 to the budget for military and famine railway expenditure.

But now at the very moment when Churchill's determination to annex Burma had crystallized, Dufferin, although completely committed, began to have some doubts, stirred by warnings from senior officials outside the Council, who had each been Chief Commissioner of British Burma. Crosthwaite, Aitchison, Thompson, and even Bernard now counseled replacing Thibaw by a prince, who would be guided by an English Resident, rather than embarking on a "difficult and costly" attempt to annex Burma.[35] Bernard's sudden conversion to the antiannexationist point of view bothered Dufferin, and he stated Bernard's view to Churchill.[36] Although it was too late in the game to reconsider military intervention, Dufferin began to reassess the consequences of annexation.[37]

As might have been expected, the rumors and newspaper reports of early October about the Government's intentions in Upper Burma, followed by the ultimatum to Thibaw and the embarkation of the expeditionary force, evoked expressions of intense disillusionment and bitter protests from Indian editors and politicians. With the exception of three or four editors, the majority were unanimous in denouncing Dufferin's Burmese policy.[38] They took issue with the Government's entire rationale for its forceful handling of Thibaw. The Government claimed that it was acting to safeguard British–Indian interests and to uphold British prestige, but the editors requested the Government to specify what Indian interests were being endangered by Thibaw and to designate the particular threat to British prestige. As for the Bombay Burma Trading Corporation's dispute with Thibaw, the facts were most unclear. Surely, the editors argued, it was a private matter between the two parties which did not involve the interests of either the Indian government or the Indian people. Indeed, the Indian people possessed neither knowledge nor interest in Upper Burma and bore no grudge against Thibaw. As for the Government's charges of misrule and maladministration in Upper Burma, the editors were of the opinion that Thibaw was within his rights to rule his Kingdom as he pleased; as long

[35] Crosswaite and Aitchison to Wallace, Oct. 12, 22, Thompson to D., Oct. 22, 1885, DVP, R. 528, nos. 374, 404, 405.

[36] D. to C., Oct. 26, 1885 (priv.), enclosing Bernard's letter, DVP, R. 517, No. 59.

[37] See below, p. 256.

[38] The following analysis of the Indian press reaction, Oct. 30–Nov. 11, to the government's Burmese policy is based on a study of selections from Indian newspapers, originally in English or translated from the vernacular, in CRO, *V. of I.*, III, Nov. 1885 (sections: "The War with Burmah" and "Misc."), on Selections from the Native Press 1885, separate volumes per province re vernacular press in CRO, on translations from the vernacular published in *The Englishman* (Calcutta) and *The Bombay Gazette,* and on newspapers in English in CRO newspaper collection under separate volumes for 1885.

as he did not disturb the administration of British Burma, the Indian government was bound to treat him as an independent sovereign. His sovereignty, of course, raised the issue of his relations with the French. Even on this point, the editors found no justification for the Government's policy: not only did they think that Thibaw could enter into relations of any sort with any nation, but they also noted that the French had disclaimed officially and publicly any political and commercial intentions toward Upper Burma.

If, therefore, none of the reasons set forth by the Government for its policy stood up on close examination, the Indian editors questioned why it had acted so hastily and decisively. Their facts were accurate, their statements penetrating, and their questions embarrassing. Was not the ultimatum to Mandalay a mere pretext for action? Were not the real reasons to be found in the Home Government's wish to expand the Empire and create new markets, and to use the political significance of this commercial expansion to influence the General Election? N. N. Sen declared that "the gods of the English nation—the manufacturing classes of Glasgow and Manchester, London, Leeds, Birmingham and Sheffield" were thirsting after new markets in Asia to succor their depressed industries, and that the Home and Indian governments had responded to their "insatiable craving" by producing a pretext for the expansion of the British Indian Empire.[39] "King cotton is ever anxious to extend his territories, and his power is irresistible. . . . Neither Conservatives nor Liberals dare to go against his commands," wrote Sarvadhikari.[40] They only had to quote the staunch Anglo-Indian press— *The Indian Daily News* and *The Englishman* of Calcutta, *The Pioneer* of Allahabad, *The Civil and Military Gazette* of Lahore, and *The Times of India* of Bombay, with their ties to the Anglo-Indian business communities and the chambers of commerce—to back up their arguments.[41] Finally, asked the Indian editors, were not the interests of the depressed industries of England closely linked with the political ambitions of Lord Randolph Churchill? Did not his outspoken speech in favor of annexation reveal the essential reason behind the Government's Burma policy? Sarvadhikari thought it did.[42] Malabari also thought so; he condemned Churchill for taking

[39] Editorial, "The Threatened Military Expedition to Mandalay," *Indian Mirror*, Oct. 21, 1885.

[40] Editorial, *Hindoo Patriot*, Oct. 12, 1885.

[41] See Anglo-Indian declarations for annexation, Oct. 30-31, especially the rabidly pro-annexationist editorials of Churchill's friend, James Wilson, in *The Indian Daily News*. For comments by Indian editors, see editorials, *Indian Mirror*, Oct. 17, 21, 23, 31, *Indian Spectator*, Oct. 25, *Hindoo Patriot*, Oct. 26, 1885.

[42] Editorial, *Hindoo Patriot*, Oct. 26, 1885.

advantage of a confused English public "on the eve of a great election to bid for power publicly by announcing his intention of annexing the other half of the Burmese Empire!"[43]

Of most concern to the Indian editors was the cost of the impending expedition. They knew that the charges for the Third Burmese War and its aftermath would be fixed squarely on the shoulders of the Indian taxpayer, as had been the case in the previous Burmese wars. The conspiracy against Thibaw was also a conspiracy against the Indian people. The Burmese policy added fuel to the press agitation[44] already in progress against the costs of the Afghan policy. The editors were irate over the recklessness, callousness, and high-handedness with which the government was plunging into a new war with the obvious intent of making India pay for it. Intervention was bound to provoke Burmese and tribal resistance, and many British and Indian troops would be required to subjugate the new territory; annexation was certain to follow with unlimited administrative and military charges not to be paid by Burma itself for some years to come. These prospects led Motilal Ghose, S. Mukherji, S. Chatterjee, and B. Malabari to oppose in blunt and emphatic terms the Government's policy, and to state flatly that the Indian taxpayer could not and should not shoulder what would obviously be imperial charges. Except for a few minor Gujerati editors in Bombay, Surat, and Broach, who were possibly linked with Parsi and Gujerati textile interests which hoped to acquire increased markets in a British-dominated Upper Burma,[45] their sentiments were shared by all the other Indian editors writing in English or the vernacular. Whether expressed in Tamil, Telugu, Marathi, Gujerati, Punjabi, Bihari, or Bengali, the verdict was the same.

Furthermore, they turned upon Dufferin. In agitating against the Afghan strategy, they had directed their criticism at the government as a whole and not specifically at the Viceroy. But now, led by N. N. Sen, they fired their volleys at Dufferin personally. In his widely circulated *Indian Mirror,* Sen initiated what eventually became a sustained campaign of blistering denunciation of Dufferin as a liberal Viceroy.[46] Dufferin's "perfectly unjust, inequitable and

[43] Editorial, *Indian Spectator,* Nov. 1, 1885.

[44] See selections under "New Army Expenditure" and "Misc.," *V. of I.,* III, Oct., Nov. 1885. See also editorials, "Threatened Revival of the Income Tax in India," "Jingoism and Our Impending Dangers on All Sides," "Retrenchment or Additional Taxation," *Indian Mirror,* Sept. 30, Oct. 3, 9, 1885.

[45] See *Broach Samachar,* Oct. 29, *Gujerati Mitra,* Nov. 1, *Akhbar-e-Soudagar,* Nov. 10, *Surya Prakash,* Nov. 17, *Satya Mitra,* Nov. 15 (*V. of I.,* III, Nov. 1885, "The War with Burmah").

aggressive" step of annexation would wreck not only the Indian Exchequer but also what remained of Dufferin's reputation and popularity with the Indian community. Sen warned Dufferin not to fly in the face of "educated and independent Native public opinion" which so opposed intervention and war. Views similar to Sen's were expressed by Chariar, Sarvadhikari, Chatterjee, Daji Khare, Malabari, and other leading editors. Malabari summed up the censure of Dufferin: "It is painful to us to find that the first year of Lord Dufferin's viceroyalty should be signalised by that policy of aggression which discredited the administration of Lord Lytton, wrought manifold disasters in India, and generally shook the confidence of the people in the righteousness of British rule."[47] All the Marathi editors were of the same opinion. Gangaprasad Varma, writing from Lucknow, went further and thought that the Burmese policy was as much as could be expected from a Viceroy who had paid not the slightest attention to the Indian press throughout the year and who had already been found wanting in ability.[48] Defective policy was shaped by a defective Viceroy!

So went the strictures, growing in acerbity and casting Dufferin in a reactionary image. Some critics still held out hopes that Dufferin would step back from war and encouraged him to do so. Sen and Malabari, Ranade and Chandarvarkar, Kabraji and Naoroji— all implored Dufferin to pay attention to Indian public opinion and revert to a peaceful solution while there was still time.[49] But others —among them, N. N. Gupta, V. Chariar, Sarvadhikari, G. S. Iyer— no longer saw reason to hope; they were resigned to the fact that imperial wars and increased expenditure would occur and recur as long as representatives of the Indian people had no control over the Indian revenues in the senior councils of the Empire.[50] Hopes and pleas were no acceptable substitute for political rights and responsibility.

The latter were correct in their assessment. Dufferin neither listened to the Indian editors' advice, heeded their pleas, nor apprised Churchill of their agitation. Moreover, he acquiesced, when Churchill, in the early days of November, slammed the door on all pro-

---

[46] Editorials, "The Threatened Military Expedition to Mandalay," "A War Sought to be Forced on Upper Burmah," "Native Opinion and the Pending War in Upper Burmah," *Indian Mirror*, Oct. 21, 23, 29, 1885.

[47] Editorial, *Indian Spectator*, Nov. 1, 1885.

[48] Editorial, *Hindustani*, Nov. 11 (*V. of I.*, III, Nov. 1885, "The War with Burmah").

[49] Editorials, *Indian Mirror*, Oct. 29, 31, *Indian Spectator*, Nov. 1, 1885, *Indu Prakash*, Nov. 2, *Rast Goftar*, Nov. 8 (*V. of I.*, III, Nov. 1885, "The War with Burmah").

[50] *Sind Times*, and *Hindu*, Oct. 24, *Hindoo Patriot*, Oct. 26 (*V. of I.*, III, Nov. 1885, "New Army Expenditure"); *Swadesa Mitran*, Nov. 2, *Indian*, Nov. 8 (*V. of I.*, III, Nov. 1885, "The War with Burmah").

posals for a diplomatic settlement—a bid by the Chinese in London,[51] a renewed bid by the Burmese envoy in Paris,[52] and a final bid by the French ambassador to replace Thibaw by a prince then in exile in Pondicherry.[53] In fact, Dufferin's main concern by November was how to carry out a successful campaign against Thibaw. "Half the battle will be to strike quick and hard and to go with a force sufficient to render opposition hopeless," he wrote Churchill.[54]

On November 8, the river boat "Ashley Eden" steamed into Rangoon harbor bearing the official answer of Thibaw and his Hlutdaw to the Indian government's ultimatum. A British courier handed it to Bernard. The reply was restrained, although polite. The Court of Ava declined arbitration of the log dispute by a British envoy; it agreed to the reestablishment of a British Resident at Mandalay, but did not mention whether he would be received with Western diplomatic etiquette or be permitted a military guard; it declined the demand for British paramountcy over Burmese foreign affairs; and it refused to give British traders any exceptional advantages in the Bhamo trade with China.[55] Bernard telegraphed Dufferin that the reply "is practically [a] refusal or evasion on all points . . . clearly not satisfactory within terms of [the] ultimatum," and sent an abstract of the translated document.[56] Dufferin immediately telegraphed Bernard's conclusion to Churchill, adding: "I propose, with your approval to instruct General Prendergast to advance upon Mandalay at once."[57]

Dufferin's cable arrived at the India Office at a propitious moment. The previous evening Salisbury, speaking at the Lord Mayor's Day dinner to a large audience, had announced that in Burma a British expeditionary force was "going forward to reduce a somewhat eccentric potentate" and to ensure England "a large increase in the opportunities of commerce" in Upper Burma.[58] Now a Cabinet Council was convened to discuss among other questions Duf-

[51] Secretary of State to Viceroy, telegrams, Nov. 5 and 10 (secret), Nov. 9, 1885 (priv.), DVP, R. 519, nos. 379, 387, 386; Viceroy to Secretary of State, telegrams, Nov. 8, 1885 (secret), R. 519, No. 292. See also Y. K. So, "Anglo-Chinese Diplomacy Regarding Burma 1885-1897" (unpublished Ph.D. thesis, University of London, 1960), Ch. I.

[52] Burmese envoy to Lyons, Nov. 3, Lyons to S., Nov. 3, 1885, *P.P.*, 1886, Vol. 50, Com. 4614, pp. 228-229, 227; Secretary of State of Viceroy, two telegrams, Nov. 8, 1885 (priv.) and (secret), DVP, R. 519, nos. 384, 385.

[53] Secretary of State to Viceroy, telegram, Nov. 10, 1885 (priv.), DVP, R. 519, No. 388.

[54] D. to C., Nov. 1, 1885 (priv.), DVP, R. 517, No. 60.

[55] For the Burmese reply, see Viceroy to Secretary of State, telegram, Nov. 11, 1885. DVP, R. 519, No. 297.

[56] Bernard to Viceroy, two telegrams, Nov. 9, 1885, DVP, R. 528, nos. 455, 456.

[57] Viceroy to Secretary of State, telegram, Nov. 10, 1885 (secret), DVP, R. 519, No. 293.

[58] Nov. 9, *Times*, Nov. 10, 1885.

ferin's telegram. The cabinet members, none of whom discounted the beneficial political effects which a military success might have upon the election, were content to leave the entire matter of intervention to Dufferin. As for the future political status of Upper Burma, they were in favor of "annexation pure and simple."[59] Upon the termination of the Cabinet Council and without waiting to receive and study the text of the Burmese reply being telegraphed by Dufferin, Churchill instructed Dufferin to have Prendergast advance upon Mandalay "at once" and to have a Viceregal Proclamation issued as Prendergast crossed the British frontier into Thibaw's Kingdom, much as Lytton had done at the commencement of the Afghan campaign in 1879.[60] The moment had come for "a military adventure up the Irrawaddy."[61]

On November 15, General Harry Prendergast and his force of some 5,000 men sailed into Upper Burmese waters and the Viceregal Proclamation of War was issued. The Third Anglo-Burmese War had begun. Its outcome was never in doubt. Within less than a month, after rapid victories at Minhla and Myingyan which led King Thibaw to sue for peace, Prendergast's fleet dropped anchor off Mandalay.[62] Thibaw, whom the Rangoon correspondent of *The Times* learned was not the ruthless tyrant and drunkard the English press and Chamber of Commerce had made him out to be,[63] was deposed and sent quietly out of the pages of history into exile on the west coast of India. Arrangements were made to administer the new territory "provisionally in Her Majesty's name" without any reference to incorporation in the British Indian Empire, pending final legal and political decisions about Upper Burma's status and administration.[64] Honors, medals, jewels, contracts, eulogistic editorials, and congratulations—all flowed freely. These were the toys and trinkets of victory, the spoils of a war that had been sparked by a combination of personal political ambition, English commer-

[59] C. to D., Nov. 10, 1885, DVP, R. 517, No. 78; Godley to Wallace, Oct. 30, 1885, R. 525, No. 93a. Also editorial, *Times*, Nov. 11, 1885, on Cabinet Council.

[60] Secretary of State to Viceroy, two telegrams, Nov. 11, 1885 (secret), DVP, R. 519, nos. 389, 390.

[61] Phrase coined by Dufferin when writing Kimberley earlier in the year opposing a forward policy toward Upper Burma at that time. See D. to K., Jan. 12, 1885 (priv.), DVP, R. 517, No. 6.

[62] Bernard to Viceroy, telegram, Nov. 15, 1885, DVP, R. 528, No. 465; Diary of Movements and Operations of the Burma Expeditionary Force, Nov. 15-29, enclosed in Dispatch of Governor-General-in-Council, No. 17, Milit., Feb. 2, 1886, CRO, Bengal Milit. Let., 1886, Vol. 489.

[63] Mandalay telegram, Nov. 29, *Times*, Dec. 5, 1885.

[64] Secretary of State to Viceroy, telegram, Dec. 1, 1885 (secret), DVP, R. 519, No. 428; Viceroy to Secretary of State, telegrams, Dec. 1, Dec. 2, 1885 (priv.), R. 519, nos. 323, 324; Viceroy to Prendergast, telegram, Dec. 4, 1885, R. 529, No. 188.

cial expansion, and a yearning for national self-assertion. Beneath
these sparkling superficialities, the harsh realities were soon apparent. The war only partially achieved Churchill's ambitions, and it
left its arch-critics, the Indian editors, with a deep sense of failure
and resentment. Worse for Dufferin, it proved to be a grave administrative and financial blunder, the reverberations of which were
felt throughout the remainder of his viceroyalty and even extended
into that of his successor, Lord Lansdowne.

The victory at Mandalay came too late to be of real assistance to
Churchill's or the Tories' electoral fortunes. Polling began on
November 24 and 25, but it was not until December 1, with polling
all but completed and victory in Liberal hands, that the official
announcement of the capture of Mandalay was made. Churchill
had managed to carry his "safe seat" in the Paddington borough but
had lost to John Bright by 733 votes in Birmingham.[65] Writing just
as the election was ending, Churchill confided to Dufferin: "I wish
the Burmese business could have taken place a month earlier; we
should have been much strengthened by it."[66]

It is very doubtful, however, whether the Burmese victory would
have made a substantial difference in the outcome of the election.
The boroughs and divisions, in which the issues of Free Trade versus Protection, the depression in trade and industry, the expansion
of British trade in Asian markets, and a well-defended Empire had
been aired by the Tories, were the only seats likely to be affected by
an issue like the conquest of Burma. Indeed, those seats had by and
large returned Tory candidates. But generally speaking, the majority of the electorate were not interested in such issues; in the county
divisions of England, Wales, and Scotland,[67] which proved decisive,
the issues which counted were the Irish question, land and agricultural policy, the disestablishment of the Church, and local self-
government. J. A. Godley wrote just before the polling began: "The
mass of the electors, not having to pay for the war, cannot be got to
take any interest in it one way or the other."[68] Thus, even had the
Mandalay victory come earlier, it is most unlikely that the Tory
chances of victory would have been greatly enhanced. By January
1886, it was clear that the Tory party would once again be in oppo-

[65] Electoral returns, *Times*, Nov. 25, 26, 1885.
[66] C. to D., Dec. 4, 1885, DVP, R. 517, No. 81.
[67] Wales went solidly Liberal; Scotland did also, with the exception of one seat; see
Times, Nov. 28, 1885.
[68] Godley (Permanent Under-Secretary of State for India) to D., Nov. 13, 1885, DVP,
R. 525, No. 96.

sition, unless of course it had the support of the Irish Nationalists.[69]

Dufferin had planned for a brief Burmese expedition with a minimal expenditure in money and lives. This he nearly achieved when Prendergast's forces reached Mandalay within one month instead of the allotted three, and with small cost in lives and money. Dufferin soon learned, however, that Thibaw's dethronement did not mean the end of the war. Churchill's imperial ambition, coupled with unforeseen circumstances, was to force his hand.

Dufferin had from the beginning preferred to disregard the Shan tribal feudatories, living in a vast territory stretching east from the Irrawaddy valley toward Yunnan, and to postpone occupation of the port of Bhamo and its surrounding region northeast of Mandalay. He was prepared to accept the suggestion of Sir Robert Hart, Inspector-General of the Chinese Imperial Maritime Customs, to make Bhamo a treaty port between China and British-conquered Upper Burma—the site at which future border negotiations between the two countries could take place.[70] But Churchill, backed by Sir Ashley Eden, the oracle on Burma at the India Office, had very different ideas. As soon as Thibaw's government had been toppled, Churchill informed the Viceroy that the British–Indian forces should bring the Shan States under direct British influence and occupy Bhamo and the vicinity so that the Salween River, which flowed some 110 miles east of Bhamo, would be the British boundary in any future negotiations with the Chinese.[71] Dufferin accepted these instructions,[72] and thereby expanded the scale and scope of the war. Worse still, as his senior officials with experience in Burma had predicted, Burmese reaction to the British occupation of Mandalay was by no means peaceful. Various scions of the royal line, mobilizing whatever armed forces they could muster, began to press their claims to the Crown of Ava; and tribal leaders and dacoits rose in guerrilla activity against foreign domination.[73] The pacification of Burma eventually became an unfinished task which Dufferin handed on to Lansdowne.[74]

[69] Final count: Liberal 333, Conservative 255, Irish Nationalists 86, *Times*, Dec. 10, 1885; C. to D., Dec. 11, 17, 1885, DVP, R. 517, nos. 82, 83.

[70] Viceroy to Secretary of State, telegram, Nov. 20, 1885 (priv.), DVP, R. 519, No. 314.

[71] Secretary of State to Viceroy, telegrams, Nov. 18 (secret), Nov. 25 and Dec. 7, 1885 (priv.), DVP, R. 519, nos. 403, 418, 437.

[72] Viceroy to Secretary of State, telegrams, Dec. 8 and 15, 1885 (priv.), DVP, R. 519, nos. 336, 340; Viceroy to Prendergast, telegram, Dec. 18, 1885, R. 529, No. 219.

[73] G. Geary, *Burma, After the Conquest* (London, 1886), pp. 70-79, 83; Nisbet, I, 109-110.

[74] The Burmese regions of Upper Burma alone took five years, with 34,712 British–Indian troops involved by 1888, with 1,000 casualties per year, and with cost over

The decision regarding the future administration of Upper Burma was also taken out of Dufferin's hands. By the time Prender-gast had achieved his victory, Dufferin had reversed his original view that annexation was the best administrative solution. There was Peking's attitude and tributary claims to worry about,[75] the reaction of the Indian princes to consider,[76] the uncertainty of the political situation at home, and the certainty of the antiannexation-ist attitude of Ripon, Northbrook, Chamberlain, Dilke, and Bright, when the Liberals returned to power.[77] To crown it all, the financial aspect weighed heaviest against annexation. Dufferin realized that Upper Burma would be more nearly self-supporting under the rule of a native prince and thus would not be so dependent upon the revenue surplus from Lower, or British, Burma which the govern-ment of India was counting upon to meet the extraordinary military expenditure during the next three years.[78] But direct annexation would mean that the British Burma surplus would have to cover the large estimated deficit of the new territory for some years to come.[79] In effect, the Indian taxpayer would be paying for Upper Burma's deficit.

Churchill, on the other hand, seeking to make good his own and his Tory colleagues' campaign pledges, was determined on annexa-tion. After the Law Officers of the Crown had informed him that a formal and public notification announcing the inclusion of Upper Burma within the Empire had to be made in order to negate exist-ing treaties, Churchill at once secured Salisbury's approval, and tele-graphed Dufferin to submit a draft proclamation which would authorize the Viceroy "to proclaim Upper Burma part of Her Maj-esty's dominions and to administer [the] country during pleasure of Crown, Government of India having financial control and responsi-bility."[80] The proclamation was to be issued on January 1, 1886, as a "New Year's gift to the Empress and her subjects."[81] A supple-

£5,000,000, or ten and a half times Dufferin's original estimate. See J. G. Scott, *Gazet-teer of Upper Burma and the Shan States* (Rangoon, 1900; CRO 6606), Vol. I, Pt. I; Nisbet, I.

[75] D. to C., Nov. 9 and 17 (priv.), Dec. 22, 1885, DVP, R. 517, nos. 61, 62, 66; Viceroy to Bernard, telegram, Nov. 29, 1885 (priv. and confid.), R. 529, No. 165.

[76] Speeches at Mayo College, Ajmir, Nov. 7, at Gwalior, Dec. 1, 1885, Wallace, pp. 53-57, 57-61.

[77] R. to D., Dec. 4, received *ca.* Dec. 22, Northbrook to D., Dec. 17 (priv. and confid.), Lord Harris to D., Nov. 24, received *ca.* Dec. 15, 1885, DVP, R. 525, nos. 108, 116, 103.

[78] Viceroy to Secretary of State, telegrams, Nov. 8 and 20, 1885 (secret), DVP, R. 519, nos. 292, 314; D. to C., Nov. 9 and 17, 1885 (priv.), R. 517, nos. 61, 62.

[79] D. to C., Dec. 22, 1885 (priv), DVP, R. 517, No. 66.

[80] Secretary of State to Viceroy, telegram, Dec. 24, 1885 (secret), DVP, R. 519, No. 456.

[81] Secretary of State to Viceroy, telegram, Dec. 24, 1885 (priv.), DVP, R. 519, No. 458.

mentary document, giving financial control of Upper Burma to the Indian government, was to be published simultaneously.[82] Churchill was forcing Dufferin's hand.

After but a momentary hesitation, Dufferin acted on Churchill's instructions, and forwarded to the latter a draft proclamation worded in such a way that the question of Upper Burma's future administration could and would still be kept open.[83] Churchill, however, was quick to strike out any words smacking of "indecision" about Upper Burma's future. Only in the matter of "financial control" of the country did he concede Dufferin's suggestion that the Indian government announce it by a less obtrusive method, such as a dispatch from the Secretary of State for India in Council.[84] Churchill concluded his work with a terse official dispatch to the Viceroy reviewing the Burmese question: first, "the annexation of Burmah to the dominions of Her Majesty was the inevitable result of the deportation of King Thibaw"; second, the Viceroy and his officers had full responsibility for the finances, administration, and pacification of the newly conquered territory.[85] The proclamation awaited publication. Vast new responsibilities and extensive new charges were about to accrue to the Government of India, the Indian budget, and the Indian taxpayer.

[82] Secretary of State to Viceroy, telegram, Dec. 25, 1885 (priv.), DVP, R. 519, No. 461.
[83] Viceroy to Secretary of State, telegram, Dec. 27, 1885 (secret), DVP, R. 519, No. 352.
[84] Secretary of State to Viceroy, two telegrams, Dec. 28, 1885 (priv.), DVP, R. 519, nos. 467, 468.
[85] Dispatch of Foreign Secretary of State in Council, No. 34, Dec. 31, 1885, *P.P.*, 1886, Vol. 50, Com. 4614, pp. 263-266, paras. 11, 12, 13.

XII

The End of the Appeal

Whatever disappointment or frustration at the outcome of the Burmese question Churchill and Dufferin may have felt could hardly compare with that of the Indian leaders. With as much force, conviction, and logic as they could muster, they had mounted their plea against intervention in Upper Burma—but to no avail. In spite of all they had written, Dufferin had sent Prendergast to Mandalay to snuff out Thibaw. "The good sense" and the avowed respect from Dufferin for the opinions of the Indian press which they had hoped would tip the scales toward nonintervention had not been forthcoming; instead, traits different, completely unexpected, and more characteristic of Lytton had been revealed. Dufferin's decision irritated some, frustrated others, and dismayed all.[1] "War against Upper Burma," wrote N. N. Sen on the day that Minhla was seized, "has been declared against the strongest remonstrances of the whole Native population expressed through the Native Press with a unanimity of opinion, which we have never witnessed before; never was Native public opinion disregarded with such unmistakable marks of contempt."[2] Yet Dufferin had told the Oudh Press Association in May that he held in profound respect the views of the Indian press![3] The editors, one and all,[4] denounced his decision.

[1] Except for *Tribune, Indian Mirror, Indian Spectator, Bengalee,* and *Hindoo Patriot,* the following selections from the Indian Press are in *V. of I.,* III, Dec. 1885, "The Future of Burmah," pp. 622-634, and CRO, Selections from the Native Press, Bombay, Madras, Bengal, Northwest Provinces and Oudh, and the Punjab, Nov.-Dec. 1885.

[2] Editorial, *Indian Mirror,* Nov. 17, 1885.

[3] See above, p. 179.

[4] Except for the editor of *Gujerati Mitra* of Bombay and its Gujerati affiliates.

Some were disappointed because Dufferin had not chosen to follow Ripon's course of patient negotiation with the Court of Ava to settle the dispute and to make an acceptable arrangement for a British Resident;[5] a number were disturbed by Dufferin's willingness to play host to the noisy demands of self-interested business and commercial circles;[6] still others were distressed that he had never responded to Thibaw's overtures for peace and conditional surrender.[7] Sen, going further, charged Dufferin with being a mere puppet who played to the tugs and pulls of designing forces—the London press, which had fostered the cause of war and had applauded Dufferin's performance,[8] or Churchill, who had leagued himself with the depression-ridden English industrialists in his political campaign and had opted for war against Thibaw.[9]

Behind these criticisms lurked the fear that Dufferin planned to hand the bill for the war and the probable annexation of Upper Burma to the Indian taxpayer. Dufferin's references to the need of fresh taxation for the war in a speech at Agra soon after the conquest of Mandalay were certainly open to this interpretation. On annexation and how to pay for it, he had been ominously evasive in his speech at Lucknow, and had caused most Indian editors to fear the worst.[10] S. Mukherji noted that Dufferin had been "characteristically, yet beautifully, vague" on this point, the more so because it was an "open secret" in government circles that annexation was official policy.[11] Despondently aware that Dufferin would not listen to them, the editors nevertheless decided on new and more forceful protests.

V. Chariar best expressed the attitude of the Indian leaders when he stated frankly that there was no possible basis upon which Indians could justify annexation or its costs. "Neither the political nor the commercial needs of our country require the annexation of Burmah. . . . Why, then, should India be forced to contribute the necessary cost in money, as well as in blood, of an undertaking intended solely to conciliate the powerful mercantile interests of Eng-

[5] *Behar Herald,* Nov. 24, *Bodhasudhakar,* Nov. 25, *Advocate of the Agriculturists,* Nov. 27.

[6] *Shivaji,* Nov. 20, *Ananda Bazar Patrika,* Nov. 23, *Bharat Mihir,* Dec. 3, *Hindu,* Dec. 8, *East,* Dec. 12, *Poona Vaibhav,* Dec. 13, *Swadesa Mitran, Dec.* 14.

[7] Editorial, "King Thebaw a Captive," *Indian Mirror,* Dec. 5, 1885; also *Native Opinion* and *Arundaya,* Dec. 6, *Subodh Patrika,* Dec. 13.

[8] Editorial, "The London Press and the War," *Indian Mirror,* Nov. 22, 1885.

[9] Editorials, "Lord Randolph Churchill and India," *Indian Mirror,* Nov. 27, "Lord Randolph Churchill and the Election," *Hindoo Patriot,* Dec. 7, 1885.

[10] Dufferin visited Agra Nov. 25-29, Lucknow Dec. 4-7; for speeches, see *Suryodaya,* Dec. 7, 1885, Wallace, pp. 62-64.

[11] Editorial, *Tribune,* Dec. 12, 1885.

land?"[12] The Marathi and Bengali vernacular editors couched their opposition in even stronger terms. Naoroji and Kabraji added the somber fact that the unknown costs of annexation would be limitless, given the probability of endless border conflicts on the new northeast frontier;[13] Parsi and Gujerati editors, some of whom had originally supported the war, agreed. Thus, the Indian editors to a man recommended to Dufferin Ripon's proposal to administer the conquered area as a British protectorate ruled by a new king of the Alaungpaya Dynasty under the guidance of a British Resident.[14] Some were still hopeful that when the Liberals returned to office, Dufferin might put this proposal into effect; others thought that they could no longer depend upon Dufferin but instead had better look to Gladstone and Ripon, who would act in Parliament to ensure the proposal.

Nevertheless, the majority placed their plea directly before Dufferin. If he had not listened to them about the war, they hoped that he would listen to them about annexation. "The Native Press has emphatically declared itself against annexation," asserted N. Moreshwar Sane, the editor of the influential Anglo-Marathi newspaper, *Dnyan Prakash.* "We hope that Lord Dufferin will not revive the annexation policy, which was the vogue during the administration of Lord Dalhousie. . . . The present emergency will show to us what the real character of Lord Dufferin is."[15] Sarvadhikari in Calcutta and Malabari in Bombay struck a similar note.[16] "The question of the future of Upper Burmah is left to the decision of Lord Dufferin," wrote Malabari, "and that decision will demonstrate how far his Lordship can penetrate beneath the surface, or resist the clamour of aggressive opinion." Would they succeed this time? Would Dufferin listen to their pleas? Few editors were optimistic.

Aggravating the frustration and bitterness engendered in their minds by Dufferin's Burmese policy were the results of the General Election, news of which reached them in the first two weks of December.[17] Virtually every Parliamentary candidate whom they and their delegates in England supported had been defeated, while those whom they opposed had been elected. Slagg had been dropped at Manchester; Keay had gone down in the Newington contest; Blunt had been defeated for Camberwell; Digby had fallen in North

[12] Editorial, *Hindu,* Dec. 8, 1885.
[13] *Rast Goftar,* Dec. 12, 1885.
[14] For one of the few against the proposal, see *Muslim Herald,* Dec. 12, 1885.
[15] *Dnyan Prakash,* Dec. 7.
[16] Editorials, *Hindoo Patriot,* Dec. 14, *Indian Spectator,* Dec. 20, 1885.
[17] Telegraphed to *The Times of India.* See n. 33 below.

Paddington; Phear had been turned down at Honiton; Plowden had lost Wolverhampton West; and Samuel Laing, too old and tired, had not stood for Orkney and Shetland. Most discouraging of all was the defeat at Deptford of Lal Mohan Ghose by John Evelyn. Only Lord Hartington, John Bright, and Captain Verney among the "friends of India" had managed to survive. The "unfriends" had produced notable victories; except for A. S. Ayrton, every one of the Anglo-Indian candidates had been elected to the new Parliament: Sir Richard Temple for Evesham (Wolverhampton South), Sir James Fergusson for Manchester (Northeast), J. M. Maclean for Oldham, Major-General Pelly for Hackney, and Sir Roper Lethbridge for North Kensington. All along the line, the advocates of Indian reform and spokesmen of educated India had been defeated by the Anglo-Indian representatives. India's Appeal to the British voter had failed ignominiously; with this failure was lost any hope of either checking Dufferin's policy or building upon Ripon's legacy. The despondency of the Indian editors reached a new low, but it would have sunk to even greater depths had they but known why and how this failure had come to pass.

As it happened, the final blows to the Appeal were dealt by the delegates themselves just before the polling for the General Election took place. Throughout November, they intervened outright in a number of electoral contests, and actively supported radical Liberal candidates against their Tory opponents. The spirit of political impartiality proclaimed in the Appeal was cast to the winds and in most instances the Appeal itself lost sight of. As a result, the delegates' efforts reaped no rewards either for the Appeal or for the Liberal candidates whom they supported.

Certainly the delegates' decision to support J. B. Firth, the radical Liberal incumbent, against Sir Roper Lethbridge in the North Kensington contest proved an ill-judged and detrimental step for all concerned. By early November, this contest had taken a bitter, personal turn: Lethbridge was dropping insidious hints about Firth's Quaker irreligion, while Firth was countering by denigrating Lethbridge's record in India and by citing the Indian delegates' opposition to Lethbridge's candidacy.[18] Firth arranged with Digby for the delegates to attend a rally in North Kensington ostensibly to air the Indian Appeal but actually to support his own candidacy.[19] Addressing some 2,000-odd constituents, Firth charged Lethbridge

[18] For comments on speeches of Lethbridge and Firth, see *West London Observer*, week ending Nov. 7, 1885, pp. 5-6.
[19] Notting Hill, Nov. 9, 10, see *West London Observer*, week ending Nov. 14, 1885.

with having a hand in Lytton's disastrous Afghan policy and the iniquitous Vernacular Press Act, and declared that the Indian people had no desire for the restoration of such a policy or for representation by reactionaries such as Lethbridge. Each delegate in turn, when speaking on a particular Indian grievance, echoed Firth's remarks, attacked Lethbridge's Indian service record, and advocated Firth's election. Sir Charles Dilke and Lal Mohan Ghose, who had both momentarily forsaken their campaigning in Chelsea and Deptford, also spoke for Firth. But Lethbridge, undaunted by this attack, had the last word. The following evening, armed with copies of the latest *Madras Weekly Mail* and with leaflets on his record in India, and supported by A. P. Sinnett, the former editor of *The Pioneer* and a friend of Hume, and by Manekji Bigramji Dadabhoy, a Parsi lawyer from Bombay, Lethbridge parried each of Firth's wild allegations anent his complicity in Lytton's Afghan policy and the Press Act, and effectively demolished the charges of the delegates and their claims to represent the Indian people. Reading out the news of the resignations of Jeejeebhoy and the others from the Bombay Presidency Association and of the British Indian Association's withdrawal from the Appeal, and pointing out that the resignations were sparked by opposition to Indian political intervention in the General Election, Lethbridge concluded that the so-called Indian delegates spoke for nobody but themselves and their small, unrepresentative segment of Indian society. More effective still, he read from memorials, written in 1880 and signed by Chandavarkar, Man Mohan Ghose, and Lal Ghose, lauding his work as Press Commissioner and calling for his reappointment. Sinnett followed in similar vein, and Dadabhoy threw more cold water on the claims of the delegates by dismissing them as little more than the puppets of radical Liberal "wire-pullers." As a result of this encounter, Lethbridge emerged unscathed and stronger, Firth suffered a serious setback, and the Indian delegates and their Appeal were made to look ridiculous.

Subsequent interventions proved equally damaging to the Indian cause. Manchester was a case in point. John Slagg, the radical Liberal M.P., who considered liberal reform of Indian administration the true safeguard for Manchester's investment in India, was standing for his seat in the northwestern division of the city, and his colleagues, H. L. Blennerhassett and C. E. Schwann, were pitted against the Tories, Sir James Fergusson, former Governor of Bombay, and J. F. Hutton, in the northeastern and central divisions respectively. The Indian delegates' decision to intervene seemed straightforward; in Naoroji's amendment, Slagg had been listed as a "friend" and Fergusson as an "unfriend" of India; moreover, Churchill had just visited the city in support of the Tory cause and had censured Gladstone's Indian policy, blaming its weakness upon "the blind and foolish policy of Lord Ripon."[20] Until Churchill's visit, there had been little discussion of Indian affairs, and no personal attacks, in the Manchester campaign. To all intents and purposes, the radical Liberal candidates were assured of victory. But once the Indian delegates, particularly Chandavarkar, appeared on the scene, this changed. On two occasions—at a rally for Blennerhassett and the following evening at a major radical Liberal gathering for Slagg—Chandavarkar attacked Fergusson personally for being hostile to Indian interests and challenged the veracity of the ex-Governor's statements on the low incidence of Indian taxation and the high percentage of Indians serving in the Indian Civil Service. He even accused Fergusson of intentionally confusing the Manchester voter about Indian affairs and of attempting to discredit Slagg when all the statistics and facts clearly supported Slagg's criticisms of Tory Indian policy. These remarks, delivered after Man Mohn Ghose had specifically stated in the opening address that the delegates had no intention of indulging in politics in furthering India's Appeal, did little to improve, and possibly much to harm, the political fortunes of Slagg and Blennerhassett.[21] In like manner at Deptford, the Indian delegates rallied around Lal Mohan Ghose in his contest with the Tory, John Evelyn. At three successive meetings,[22] the delegates denounced Churchill's decision to approve the Indian government's financial and military proposals and called for a speedy return to Ripon's India policy by the ouster of the Tories from office. At the largest of these meetings, Mudaliar declared that the Liberal program and its candidates were more suited to the needs and aspirations of contemporary India than were their Tory counterparts.[23]

So outspoken and clearly pro-Liberal had the activities of the delegates become that they attracted even official Tory concern. At a meeting of the East India Association, Lord Harris, Churchill's aide and Parliamentary Under-Secretary of State for India, took it upon himself to speak to Chandavarkar and Mudaliar about their activities. Writing a few days later to Dufferin, Harris commented: "The electioneering campaign has been recently enlivened by the presence on Liberal platforms *only* of some young Native gentlemen who profess to represent India and its peoples. . . . At a meet-

[20] Speech, Nov. 6, *Manchester Guardian*, Nov. 7, 1885.
[21] Speeches, Nov. 10, 11, *Manchester Guardian*, Nov. 11, 12, 1885.
[22] Chandavarkar, p. 72.
[23] Nov. 16, *Times*, Nov. 17, 1885.

ing of the East Indian Association, [I] took the liberty of telling them I thought they couldn't make a greater mistake than to attempt to establish an idea that the welfare of India rested on the presence in power of *one* of the two political parties, the Liberal."[24] But this warning had little effect.

On November 21, all three delegates travelled to Birmingham where Schnadhorst, a friend of Digby and the moving force behind the Birmingham Caucus, had hastily arranged for the delegates to join Chamberlain and Bright in their electoral activities.[25] This was a most serious step. To support Chamberlain was one thing, but to support Bright was quite another, for he was running against Churchill in the central division of the city. For some weeks previous, Bright and Churchill had been engaged all over England in a running skirmish on Indian policy, in which Churchill needled Bright for his refusal to support the Government's policy in Upper Burma, designed to safeguard the Empire and expand trade, and for his silence on the Parliamentary inquiry,[26] while Bright, directly encouraged by Ripon,[27] censured the cabinet's "jingo" policy in Upper Burma on the grounds of its cost to the Indian people and of its reversal of Ripon's policy.[28] Thus, with Indian policy a pertinent issue for both men in the final stages of the Birmingham campaign, intervention of the Indian delegates might seem to be all to the advantage of Bright.

Upon arrival at noon, the delegates went directly to the Bordesley division of Birmingham and joined Chamberlain in supporting the candidacy of Broadhurst.[29] In his address, Chamberlain saw fit to ridicule Churchill's claims of reducing Indian expenditure: the British Indian Army was being increased by 10,000 men, and a new war had just started in Upper Burma "ostensibly" in the best interests of India. This was no economy, in Chamberlain's opinion; if the audience did not believe him, perhaps they would believe "some distinguished representatives of the natives of India" who would speak for themselves. Chandavarkar was only too glad to do so. Although he said nothing on the Burmese war and made no direct mention of Churchill, Chandavarkar decried recent criticism of Ripon and his administration as blatant vilification of one of the

[24] Harris to D., Nov. 24, 1885, DVP, R. 525, No. 103. Meeting the week of Nov. 16.
[25] Chandavarkar, p. 47.
[26] Speeches, Birmingham, Oct. 23, 30, *Times,* Oct. 24, 31; Nov. 20, *Birmingham Daily Post,* Nov. 21, 1885.
[27] R. to Bright, Oct. 24, 1885, RP, BM Add. MSS 43635.
[28] Speeches, Birmingham, Nov. 5, 18, *Times,* Nov. 6, 19, 1885.
[29] For speeches, Nov. 21, see *Birmingham Daily Post,* Nov. 23, 1885. Also Chandavarkar, p. 49.

finest Viceroys who had ever ruled India, and declared that such criticism could only have been made by one whose self-interest over-rode the best interests of the Indian people. The Government's decision to increase the annual Indian military expenditure of £17.5 millions by another £2.5 millions per year, in spite of the advice of Canning, Lawrence, the Royal Army Commission, and Ripon to keep this expenditure at £12,000,000 to £15,000,000 per year, was indicative of this self-interest. He hoped that Chamberlain and other Liberals, if elected, would use their influence in the new Parliament to knock this decision on the head.

By evening a full report of the afternoon meeting had reached Churchill. He had also learned that the delegates were to appear with Bright that same evening. He had been patient long enough with the delegates' little games, and now he decided that the time had come when he must put an end to their frolic. In his speech that evening on behalf of the Tory candidate for the Bordesley division, while noting the dissension within the radical Liberal camp on all aspects of government affairs, he remarked quite casually that "the Radicals," in seeking a remedy to their ills, had, as a last resort, brought to Birmingham to support Bright three Indian gentlemen, who claimed to represent the Indian people. Very worthy and interesting the Indian gentlemen might be, he added, but they no more represented the opinions of the Indian public than they did those of the inhabitants of Kamchatka (howls of laughter). He would not be surprised, he said, if the Indians went to Midlothian to give Gladstone a helping hand (more laughter). Then in a more serious, patronizing tone, he commented that radical Liberals were making utter fools of these poor Indians by taking advantage of their credulity and ignorance of English politics and using them unfairly. What desperate anxiety must have seized them to bring three "Bengali Baboos" to Birmingham to assist "Mr. Bright" (roars of laughter and cheers). In his witty, seemingly casual, but deadly effective manner, Churchill had written off the Indian delegates. By no word did he betray the anger he truly felt at their intervention.[30]

What Chandavarkar had not had time to say earlier in the day was fully said that evening by Mudaliar at the large Birmingham Town Hall. At a meeting for Bright and other radical Liberal candidates, Mudaliar rose to support the resolution "to promote the return of Liberal candidates for the Central, Edgbaston and South divisions" of the city, and amid loud applause stated that he and his colleagues had come there to support John Bright, the best friend

[30] See below, p. 272 for his real attitude.

that India ever had, and that they represented the wishes of the Indian people for the policy advocated by Bright, namely, that India be given a fair share in its own administration and a voice in legislation and finance. Such a voice was badly needed. He referred to the war in Upper Burma. The Indian people could see no justification for it, only added expense and suffering from it. But, Mudaliar charged, the Indian people had never been consulted. He implored the audience, and the British voters in general, to come out firmly against the war, and, turning to Bright, Mudaliar asked him to speak for India and to restore the liberal policy for which he and Ripon had stood. Bright spoke, not once, but twice, and on the second occasion dealt exclusively with Indian grievances. After acknowledging the delegates as representative of "a considerable and important opinion" in the three major cities of the Indian Empire and speaking of the urgent need to develop a group of responsible and truly loyal educated Indians to carry on the Empire after the "temporary superiority" of the British had ceased, Bright demanded that Indian grievances be aired and removed. The welfare of India and the honor of England were bound up in this task, and he looked to successive Liberal governments to accomplish it, so as to leave with the Indian people a genuine appreciation for what had been done for them under British rule. The applause which greeted this generous and extemporaneous outburst was deafening; the delegates were thrilled. It was the highpoint of their mission. They had spoken in support of their key Parliamentary figure, who in turn had spoken for them.

The final touch came just before the delegates returned to London. Having read Churchill's remarks on their visit, they sent identical letters to the editors of *The Birmingham Daily Post* and *The Times*, in which they took issue with Churchill's critical comments.[31] Declaring that they had come to Birmingham of their own accord for nonpolitical reasons and with "no device to oppose any particular candidate" but to do homage to Bright on behalf of the Indian people, the delegates reminded one and all that they had been "deputed by the leading associations in different parts of India, acting in concert with one another," and that undoubtedly it was this representative character that had prompted Churchill to give them a long, cordial interview shortly after their arrival. In conclusion, they took issue with Churchill for referring to them as "Bengali Baboos." Someone in his position who had visited India should have known better than to have made such a mistake. On this caus-

31 Published Nov. 24, 1885.

tic note, the delegates left Birmingham. Man Mohan Ghose rushed back to London to assist his brother Lal at Deptford, while the others moved off for a final round of visits in support of Liberal candidates.[32] At the time, their intervention appeared to have been a political success, but subsequent events proved otherwise.

After the Birmingham visit, which virtually ended the Indian mission in Britain, it only remained to be seen how the British voters would react to India's Appeal as presented by the delegates. By December 5, with all the polling completed and the figures tallied, this reaction was known;[33] and subsequently, when read in the light of the Indian Appeal, it was decidedly negative.

The majority of the radical Liberal candidates, as well as Blunt, the radical Tory whom the Indian delegates supported and from whose platform they delivered India's Appeal, had been defeated—heavily, in most cases. Paddington North, Kensington, and Manchester, the seats with direct relevance to the Indian Appeal, were major defeats. The exceptions were Dillwyn at Swansea and Bright, Chamberlain, and their satellites at Birmingham, all of whom triumphed as expected; Lal Mohan Ghose lost by so slight a margin to Evelyn that Man Mohan Ghose called for a recount, which was never granted.[34] On the other hand, many moderate and radical Liberals interested in Indian reform on whose behalf the delegates had not intervened were successful.

The conclusion to be drawn from these results was that the British voters had voted against the "friends" listed in the Indian Appeal and by so doing had voted down the Appeal. But just how many voters actually took an interest in Indian reform and the Parliamentary inquiry as aired by the delegates and just how much influence the delegates' presentation of the Appeal had upon the voters' final decision will never be accurately known. It appears that even voters who were fully exposed to India's Appeal, such as the newly enfranchised working class in Paddington North, Deptford, and Manchester, were more concerned with employment, wages, and the depression than with Indian reform. They therefore voted for the candidate who could best safeguard England's economic future, and this more often than not meant the Tory representative. The radical Liberal label, which had become indelibly imprinted upon the Indian delegates, undoubtedly did the Indian

[32] Sir John Phear for Honington (Devon) and Dr. W. A. Hunter for Aberdeen; see Chandavarkar, pp. 72-73.

[33] Polling, Nov. 25-Dec. 1; results known by Dec. 5; and tabulation official by Dec. 19. See *Times*, Dec. 5, 7, 10, 19, 1885.

[34] Election intelligence, *Times*, Nov. 28, Dec. 1, 1885, pp. 6, 12.

cause much harm, because the Appeal was voted upon as part and parcel of the Liberal platform. Worse still, the schisms within the Indian political associations lent valuable support to the Anglo-Indian contention that the delegates did not represent either national or popular Indian grievances, and thus cast doubt in the average voter's mind on the delegates' claims. With a great deal less partisan identification, with more judicious planning and influential support, with less Digby and more Hume, with less naiveté and more political sophistication on the part of the delegates themselves, and, above all, with stronger all-India credentials, India's Appeal to the British voter could have been a brilliant success. As matters stood by December 5, the mission had been a conspicuous failure.

W. Stead, writing in *The Pall Mall Gazette,* admitted as much when he noted that "the severest loss" resulting from the election was suffered by neither the Liberals nor the Tories but by the Indian people and their delegates.[35] The editors of *The Times, The Evening Standard,* and *St. James's Gazette* by their silence concurred.[36] The scoffing Mr. "M," however, in a letter to the editor of *The Evening Standard,* did not mince words. "Whatever may be the final result of the Election," he wrote, "it has at least made one thing clear, that the voice of the self-elected Indian Association is as little regarded by English electors as it is representative of the Indian people at large."[37] The mysterious "Alpha" in a letter to *The Times,* citing as his source an Indian in the Madras Sabha, laid the failure of the mission at the feet of the younger Indians in the associations and their fateful decision to support political intervention in England. He also criticized Lal Mohan Ghose's unfortunate decision to join the radical Liberal fringe instead of the Independents. "The failure of the delegates' mission," "Alpha" concluded, "so far as influencing the election of certain candidates was concerned, will not excite much surprise or regret in India."[38]

But John Bright foresaw what effect the election results would have upon the educated Indian leaders. In Birmingham, at a crowded farewell for the Indian delegates given by friends and sympathizers, Bright did all in his power to offset any sense of failure. He commended the delegates for overcoming the humiliation of having to come all the way to England to appeal for millions of their countrymen and praised them for their worthy representa-

---

[35] Dec. 5, 1885, "Occasional Notes."

[36] Later in the month, *St. James's Gazette* wrote that the delegates' failure and Lal M. Ghose's defeat were all that could have been expected from such frivolity.

[37] Dec. 7, 1885.

[38] Dec. 9, 1885.

tion of Indian grievances before the English public.[39] He said nothing of the setbacks at Paddington North, Deptford, or Manchester, nor did he refer to India's Appeal or the fate of the Parliamentary inquiry. He said only what he had said before, but this time rather as a tribute to the Indian leaders and as a warning to the Anglo-Indian bureaucrats that they had better reconstitute their policy in order to accept the educated Indian class and its claims.

In their farewell remarks, the delegates also tried to salvage victory from defeat.[40] They had discovered who India's friends and sympathizers in England were, and they had aired Indian grievances before the English public. These, they claimed, were the chief aims of the mission. They disclaimed any intention of seeking to influence the course of the election or to achieve a particular political objective, although they did not review their electoral activities, or mention Naoroji's resolution in the Appeal or the Parliamentary inquiry. Only fleetingly did they allude to defeat, then only to comment how impressed all educated Indians would be by the poll in support of Lal Mohan Ghose and by the number of true British friends who were willing to support "Young India" and Indian reform. Comforting as these statements might be to the delegates in the face of the snide remarks emanating from Tory and Anglo-Indian circles, the fact remained that the mission had failed.

That the majority of Indian editors and politicians had from its very inception expected the mission to succeed was evident from their earlier writings.[41] They had considered the period prior to the General Election as an extraordinary opportunity for themselves and the delegates to air India's case.[42] Completely convinced of the justice and wisdom of appealing for a Parliamentary inquiry, they had had no doubts that their Appeal would be warmly received by the rational British voter once he possessed the facts.[43] They had also been heartened by the news received during October and early

---

[39] Birmingham Liberal Association meeting for the Indian delegates, Dec. 7, *Times* and *Birmingham Daily Post*, Dec. 8, 1885. The delegates met privately with Chamberlain and secured his support for reform of the Indian legislative councils; see *Pall Mall Gazette*, also *Times* and *Evening Standard*, Dec. 9, 1885.

[40] Speeches by M. M. Ghose and Mudaliar at farewell breakfast in honor of Indian delegates at National Liberal Club, Dec. 16, *Times*, Dec. 17, 1885. Chandavarkar had left for India, see "Occasional Notes," *Pall Mall Gazette*, Dec. 17, 1885.

[41] Except for *Hindoo Patriot*, all references to editorials in the Indian press, nn. 42-48 below, and from *V. of I.*, III, Oct., Nov. 1885, "India in Parliament," pp. 520-526, 562-573.

[42] *Indian Mirror*, Oct. 21, *Bengalee*, Nov. 14.

[43] *Tribune*, Oct. 10, *Jam-e-Jamshed*, Oct. 15, *Sind Times*, Oct. 21, *Subodh Patrika*, Oct. 25, *Hindu*, Nov. 7, *Behar Herald*, Nov. 10, *Indian Courier*, Nov. 14.

November of the warm reception accorded the delegates in London and elsewhere.[44] All indicators had pointed to the success of the mission;[45] no other outcome was ever seriously considered.

Their certainty, however, was entirely delusive. At no point did they fully understand what was actually happening to the mission in England. The random telegraphic summaries and the few, brief reports received from London supplied them with only partial, and essentially misleading, information, which led them in turn into misinterpretations and raised great expectations. Only one editor predicted what damage Naoroji's resolution and the resulting schisms in the Bombay Presidency Association would do to the Appeal;[46] only a few editors expressed concern at the danger of the radical Liberal bias of the delegates;[47] only one realized that the delegates would fail to air the real grievances that plagued both educated and uneducated India.[48] The majority of the editors believed implicitly that the mission was going smoothly and would succeed in convincing the British voters to elect the "friends" of India to Parliament, who would represent Indian grievances and fulfill the Parliamentary inquiry.

It was this misguided expectation that made the electoral results all the more stunning a blow to the Indian editors and politicians.[49] However much Dufferin and his advisers might have ignored their pleas for curtailing imperialist ventures, cutting military expenditure, and pressing domestic reform, and however much they might have smarted under this slight, from September onward they had rested assured that the British voter would assist them in bringing their Appeal before the new Parliament. But now this alternative had failed. "Election news from England is as bad as it can be to us," wrote Agarkar; "whether the results finally show a majority for the Liberals or the Conservatives, the misfortunes cannot be less severely felt."[50] "Whatever the measure of success the Indian delegates have achieved," noted another editor, "they have not, as it was fondly hoped, been able to influence the course of the General

[44] *Indian Spectator*, Oct. 18, *Bombay Samachar*, Oct. 23, *Subodh Patrika*, Oct. 25, *Suryodaya*, Oct. 26, *Rast Goftar*, Nov. 8, *Swadesa Mitran*, Nov. 9, *Hindustani*, Nov. 11, *Tribune*, Nov. 14.

[45] *Shivaji*, Oct. 30, *Indu Prakash*, Nov. 2, *Swadesa Mitran*, Nov. 9.

[46] "India at the Hustings," *Hindoo Patriot*, Oct. 26, 1885.

[47] *Sind Times*, Oct. 21, *Gujerati Mitra* and *Subodh Patrika*, Oct. 25, *Akhbar-e-Soudagar*, Nov. 6, *Liberal*, Nov. 8, *Dacca Prakash*, Nov. 15.

[48] *Amrita Bazar Patrika*, Nov. 12.

[49] All references to editorials in the Indian press, nn. 50-57 below, are from *V. of I.*, III, Dec. 1885, "Results of the General Election," pp. 605-622.

[50] *Mahratta*, Nov. 29.

Election."[51] V. Chariar and G. S. Iyer commented: "The defeat of almost all our particular friends, including Mr. Lal Mohan Ghose, who were candidates for Parliamentary election, as well as the success of men like Mr. Maclean, the inveterate enemy of the Indian people, and of Sir Lewis Pelly, a fiery imperialist, will be learnt with regret in India."[52] The mood in Calcutta was even more despondent. N. N. Sen, referring to Ghose's defeat at Deptford, admitted that the news had been received "with very great disappointment and sorrow by every eduated Native;"[53] and Motilal Ghose wrote cryptically that "India is in a bad way . . . India wanted a closer intimacy with England, and England rejected the advance."[54] S. Banerjea, reviewing the mission, concluded dejectedly: "We have been defeated along the entire line. The candidates whom we had named have been defeated [while] the candidates, to whom we had taken exception, have all been returned. Such is our influence over the British electors."[55]

Other editors of the English and vernacular press expressed the same sentiments.[56] The British voter had not heard the delegates' appeal. Parliament could no longer be considered an immediate court of appeal. They felt isolated. The conclusion seemed inescapable: they would have to rely upon their own efforts if they were to protest effectively against Dufferin's imperial policy and secure their rights. The stage was set for Hume and the Indian National Union, but it was set in a very different atmosphere from that in which he and his Bombay colleagues had originally brought forward their scheme. What solace the Indian leaders could glean from the mission's failure centered upon the Parliamentary inquiry. As Agarkar noted, "There is one consolation. Whoever goes in and whatever party clears a majority, we shall have an inquiry into the Government of India."[57]

But on this point the Indian mission had failed more seriously than the editors and politicians then realized. The price of the delegates' Birmingham intervention was high indeed, for it provoked Churchill's wrath and caused him to retract his interest in

[51] *Indian Echo,* Nov. 30.
[52] *Hindu,* Dec. 1.
[53] *Indian Mirror,* Dec. 1.
[54] *Amrita Bazar Patrika,* Dec. 3.
[55] *Bengalee* and *Indian Courier,* Dec. 5.
[56] G. Varma, B. Malabari, D. H. Khare, S. K. Chatterjee, S. Mukherji, A. Ali, G. C. Mukhopadhyaya, N. N. Gupta, D. Naoroji, and G. M. Ranade; see *Hindustani, Indian Spectator,* and *Native Opinion,* Nov. 29, *Tribune* and *Mahomedan Observer,* Dec. 5, *Sangabad Pravarkar,* Dec. 7, *Sind Times,* Dec. 12, *Rast Goftar,* Dec. 13, *Indu Prakash,* Dec. 14.
[57] *Mahratta,* Nov. 29.

the English-educated Indian class and his sympathy for the Parliamentary inquiry. Lytton, having seen Churchill not long before the final results of the General Election were known, referred to his changed attitude in a letter to Dufferin.[58] Commenting that Dufferin would probably have no regrets about the defeats of Lal Mohan Ghose and Scawen Blunt, and expressing the hope that the "impudent" Indian mission had cured Churchill of his *"lubees"* about the educated Indian, Lytton added: "Churchill does not forgive these gentlemen their pilgrimage to the shrine of Bright, and he now calls 'the highly educated Native'—'a beastly impostor.'" Churchill, never one to conceal the truth from himself, confirmed Lytton's words.[59] "Fancy the impudence of those Indian delegates going down to Birmingham to speak against me," he wrote Dufferin. "They are making great fools of themselves, and their special protégés, Digby and Lalmohan Ghose, have been defeated, I am thankful to say." To show clearly his change of attitude, he rejected outright the Bombay Government's tentative suggestion to appoint Sir William Wedderburn to the High Court of Bombay when Judge Pinkey stepped down. In addition to finding Wedderburn "crochetty" and incompetent, Churchill charged him with being "a political incendiary." "He had a great deal to do with sending over to England this absurd Indian deputation, and never loses an opportunity of associating himself with native political movements," Churchill declared. He had no intention of advancing him unless Dufferin strongly advocated the appointment. "The natives are sure to raise an angry cry if one of their idols is set aside, but for my own part I should attach little importance to their views," Churchill concluded. He might have added—but did not until a few months later—that what applied to Wedderburn's appointment also applied to Indian reform in general and the Parliamentary inquiry in particular. He was finished once and for all with English-educated Indians, their sympathizers, and their grievances. No longer a friend, he had become a foe.

Just as the Indians had no way of judging the effect of the delegates' intervention at Birmingham, so also Dufferin had no means of fathoming Churchill's mind until mid-December when Churchill's letter reached him. Even then Dufferin did not realize that Churchill's anger would affect the proposed Parliamentary inquiry. This lack of comprehension was most serious because of the importance which Dufferin attached to the inquiry and to the retrenchment in Indian expenditures which would follow. These

[58] L. to D., undated, but filed under letters, Nov. 27-29, 1885, DVP, R. 525, No. 105b.
[59] C. to D., Nov. 27, 1885, DVP, R. 517, No. 80.

were the remedies which he had in mind for falling revenues and rising criticism of his administration. Both his and Colvin's efforts to cut expenses had yielded minimal results in meeting the rising costs of the Afghan strategy during the preceding six months. Now with added Burmese expenditure, he was convinced that more extensive and systematic retrenchment of civil and military expenses would be required to avoid further taxation, but this could only be done by official inquiry and recommendations. So anxious was he to make the inquiry succeed that he had decided to appoint a special committee composed of officials and civilians to select areas for retrenchment, upon which the Parliamentary inquiry could concentrate when it began its work. That he expected solid results from the inquiry was revealed by a letter to Northbrook.[60] By the end of December, the plan for a Committee for Reduction of Expenditure had been drawn up by Colvin and the council.[61]

At the moment when the proclamation announcing the annexation of Upper Burma was about to be issued and Colvin was putting the final touches on the License-Income Tax Bill,[62] Dufferin looked to this committee and to Churchill's Parliamentary inquiry as political counterchecks which would mollify the rising dissatisfaction with himself and his administration of the Indian editors and politicians.[63] He, like the educated Indian leaders, did not realize that, given Churchill's touchy reaction to the Indian Radicals of Cockspur Street, the Parliamentary inquiry would never materialize. In the space of six short weeks, all had changed.

[60] D. to Northbrook, Dec. 21, 1885 (priv.), DVP, R. 525, No. 73.

[61] Minute drafted by Colvin and council, Dec. 24, 1885, DVP, R. 529, No. 606. The committee was to consist of a number of officials and five civilians, three from Bengal and one each from Madras and Bombay (none Indian), with Colvin's colleague, J. Westland, as Chairman.

[62] Colvin to Wallace, Dec. 29, 1885, DVP, R. 529, No. 628.

[63] Dufferin's sensitivity to their attitude by late December is partly evidenced by his agreeing with, and sending to Churchill, Ilbert's advice that "the leading natives at Bombay and Poona, [then] so capable of becoming formidable enemies or valuable friends," should not be alienated by making official or public the decision to pass over Wedderburn's appointment to the Bombay High Court. See Ilbert to D., Dec. 20, 1885, DVP, R. 529, No. 592; D to C., Dec. 22, 1885 (priv), R. 517, No. 67.

XIII

"New India" Unveiled

The utter inability of the Indian editors and political leaders to influence the Viceroy's policy on Burma and the dismal failure of the Indian mission made the Indian leaders realize that their role and interests were being purposefully thwarted not only by the Anglo-Indian community in India and in England but also by the Viceroy himself and his lieutenants. At the beginning of 1885, the Indians were confident they had a role to play in forming Indian policy; by December they knew that such was not the case, but rather that they would be opposed skillfully and steadfastly, as in the days before Ripon. N. N. Sen best expressed the prevailing sentiment when he wrote apprehensively: "The opposition to Native interests is growing more and more in intensity from day to day."[1]

The words of certain Englishmen, highly respected in Indian circles, powerfully supported this conclusion. Henry John Stedman Cotton, a scion of two generations of eminent civil servants in India, himself a member for twenty years of the Bengal Civil Service, and a liberal, was a constructive critic of the administration in which he served. In advocating lighter taxation, noninterference by the Supreme Government in provincial administration, and decentralization of its functions, he was a proponent of Ripon's entire policy. Cotton wished the Indian government to recognize the movement of educated Indians as a "national movement" beneficial to British rule and to grant their requests for increased employment of qualified Indians in the Indian Civil Service and for greater Indian

[1] Editorial, *Indian Mirror*, Dec. 8, 1885.

274

representation in the provincial and Supreme legislative councils. These ideas, largely elaborated in articles prior to 1885,[2] combined with reflections on the farewell to Ripon, the Volunteer question, and the views of Blunt, Colvin, and Harrison on educated India, he set forth in a short, lucid, and controversial book entitled *New India, or India in Transition*. Written during the summer of 1885, published in London just before the General Election, read by Tories and Liberals alike, and referred to publicly by Bright during the Birmingham campaign as a rebuff to Churchill,[3] Cotton's book reached India by December. It was eagerly seized upon by the Indian editors, especially in Bengal where Cotton was standing for election as Calcutta Municipal Commissioner. After arguing the case for Indian reform, Cotton considered whether Ripon's policy of "systematic encouragement of the aspirations and spontaneous tendencies of the Indian people" should be acted upon and, if so, how.[4] Replying in the affirmative and calling for the policy of official guidance and control of Indian national development without undue interference, advocated by Ripon and Hume, Cotton warned Indian sympathizers, and educated Indians themselves, of the obstacles which lay in their path:

The members of the Anglo-Indian community have shown themselves incapable of appreciating these new political forces, and their bitterness of dislike towards the members of the subject races has been aggravated by their incapacity. No help, therefore is to be expected from them. Even the majority of the officials employed under Government are in complete accord with non-officials in this respect, and are as directly opposed as non-officials can be in giving effect to that policy of general sympathy and encouragement of all national and popular aspirations with which the late Viceroy of India [Ripon] has permanently identified himself.[5]

Cotton's warning substantiated what Sen and his colleagues already sensed.

Ripon's comments, which reached India by mid-December, did likewise. His speech at Edinburgh during the electoral campaign had been more than just another political address or a rebuff to

[2] "Has India Food for Its People?" and "The Prospects of Moral Progress in India," *Fortnightly Review*, New Series, 22 (1877), 867-877, and 24 (1878), 387-398. Also "India's Need and England's Duty," *New Quarterly Magazine*, New Series, 2 (1879), 237-254.

[3] On Nov. 21, Bright discussed the English-educated Indian class in Cotton's terms, whereas on Dec. 7, just after the election campaign closed, he publicly acknowledged the significance of Cotton's book and his advocacy of a federalized India (Bright's own proposal in 1858); see *Birmingham Daily Post*, Nov. 23, Dec. 8, 1885.

[4] H. J. S. Cotton, *New India, or India in Transition* (London, 1885), p. 9.

[5] Cotton, p. 29.

Churchill's criticism of his Indian policy.[6] It was a statesmanlike bid to British electors and politicians to take cognizance of "the silent revolution" then occurring in India, which was producing a new class of English-educated Indians with aims and aspirations for political and social change. This was "a progressive movement" sparked by English education, law, modern communications, and the press. Educated Indians might well be limited in number and geographic distribution, but this, he pointed out, in no wise detracted from their ability to lead other Indians lower on the social and educational scale along the path of reform and agitation. "Theirs is a growing power," he declared; and, in answering the question which Baring, Colvin, Harrison, and Cotton had each asked as to how this power could be harnessed for the good of India and British rule, Ripon urged the Indian government to recognize the movement and "guide and control it" into a path of steady development so as to "fertilize and not destroy, enrich and not uproot." That this would be difficult to do, he was fully aware: his own bitter experience was witness to the fact. Like Cotton, Ripon frankly acknowledged the opposition to the Indian movement that existed in official and nonofficial circles in England and India, and identified the quarters whence it was most likely to continue. In conclusion, he called for perseverance in pursuit of reform as the only practical policy to match the progressive spirit abroad in India. Widely printed in the Indian press, Ripon's speech fired the self-respect and budding national consciousness of the Indian leaders. His comments on the opposition highlighted a reality which they had already come to accept.[7]

In their view, the Anglo-Indians in England had completely undermined the Appeal and the claims of the delegates to represent India by playing up the disagreements among the Indian associations, and, as a result, had defeated the candidates who had espoused the Appeal and who had been supported by the delegates.[8] Henceforth, the Indian editors expected the Anglo-Indian bloc in the Commons to prevent the presentation of even so much as a motion which might hint at Indian reform. They realized that Churchill was against them. Originally, many of them, because of his appreciative remarks on the Indian reform movement and his announce-

[6] Nov. 10, see *Times*, Nov. 11, 1885, for an abstract; *V. of I.*, III, Dec. 1885, pp. 1-11, for full text.

[7] See *V. of I.*, III, Dec. 1885, section "Some Aspects of the India of Today"; also editorial, "The Growing National Unity in India," *Indian Mirror*, Dec. 13, 1885.

[8] *Satya Mitra*, Nov. 29, *Poona Vaibhav*, Dec. 13 (*V. of I.*, III, Dec. 1885); also editorial, *Indian Mirror*, Dec. 8, 1885.

ment of the Parliamentary inquiry in his August Budget Statement, had been hopeful of his support, but, by late December, when the news of his curt rebuff to the Indian delegates at Birmingham reached them, most of the editors realized that their confidence had been misplaced, and that he would oppose the Indian cause to the end with all his political cunning and influence.[9]

The editors were aware that in India even more intensified opposition stood in their way. Any confidence they had once placed in the Viceroy had all but evaporated. By December, looking back on Dufferin's record during the year, they could say that at no point had he shown the slightest regard for Indian opinion on any major issues. The Burmese war had been the final blow. As S. Mukherji noted caustically, "Lord Dufferin was enjoying lavish dinners and parties and making nice postprandial speeches, whilst the native public was in one voice crying hoarse over the unrighteousness and the inexpediency of the enterprise against Burmah."[10] To make matters worse, the Viceroy had not limited the intervention to the Mandalay region but had extended it as far north as Bhamo at a time when guerrilla operations had begun among the Burmese "for the preservation of national independence," which eventually would require all available British–Indian troops to suppress them.[11] Thus, the more outspoken Indian editors thought the Burmese question revealed Dufferin's basic opposition to Indian financial and domestic reform. Indeed, the year had been one "of all but complete inaction" on the reform program that Ripon had initiated.[12] They recalled that in December 1884 Dufferin had said that he would develop Ripon's principle of local self-government, but his support of Thompson on the Calcutta Municipality Bill and the sanitation question had been contrary in word and in spirit. In May, he had said that he would act on the Indian Volunteer question, but again he had done nothing. Clearly, he was paying lip service to domestic reform while acting on imperial questions. His inaction indicated but one thing to them: that he had fallen prey to the climate of opinion within the community of Anglo-Indian residents and administrators which was so hostile to Indian reform.

The threats of heavy taxation and of the annexation of Upper

[9] *Amrita Bazar Patrika,* Dec. 17, *Indian Courier,* Dec. 19, *Mahratta,* Dec. 20 (*V. of I.,* IV, Jan. 1886, "The Work of the Indian Delegates").

[10] Editorial, *Tribune,* Dec. 19; see also editorial, *Hindoo Patriot,* Dec. 21, *Bharatbasi, Sahachar, Bangabasi, Sanjibani, Sangabad Pravakar,* and *Englishman's Overland Mail,* Dec. 22, 1885.

[11] Editorial, *re* Upper Burma resistance, *Hindoo Patriot,* Dec. 23, 1885.

[12] Editorial, *Bengalee,* Dec. 19; also editorial, "Lord Dufferin's Novitiate," *Tribune,* Dec. 26, 1885.

Burma, an awareness of disunity, of provincialism in political outlook, and of inaction, coupled with the news of the failure of the
Indian delegates' mission, and a growing sense of strong opposition
from official quarters—these developments made the leading Indian
editors and politicians again think seriously about national political
activity as they had done briefly in September, before India's Appeal
and the Indian mission to England had seemed a possible solution
to their problems. But, whereas in September they had merely
talked about possibilities such as G. S. Iyer's plan for a national
party or Sen's idea for a national conference,[13] in order to bring
Indian grievances to the attention of the Viceroy, by December they
ceased referring to their grievances and instead spoke out about
their rights and their entire disagreement with Dufferin's imperial
policy. They were ready to act. Whereas at the beginning of the
year, they had looked upon national political activity as no more
than extending Ripon's reforms, they now considered it an instrument of opposition to Dufferin's administration.

Hume, who had left England in mid-November, arrived at Bombay by early December and contacted his friends in the Poona
Sarvajanik Sabha and Bombay Presidency Association, with every
intention of pushing ahead with his scheme for the Indian National
Union. Hume's views, like those of the educated Indian leaders,
appear to have undergone considerable change—a change in all
probability reflected in an editorial published by Malabari in the
Indian Spectator.[14] This bore unmistakably the flavor of Hume's
style, expressing ideas he had formerly held and was to continue to
hold in subsequent years. It called for the immediate formation of
a national organization modelled on the Indian Reform League,
embracing within it the existing provincial associations and any
future regionally organized bodies. The national organization thus
envisaged would meet annually to draft a platform of reforms and
to plan activities designed to redress Indian grievances and achieve
Indian rights. The platform would be acted upon during the ensuing year at both national and provincial levels by the constitutional
method of political agitation used in England formerly by the Anti-
Corn Law League and currently by the Cobden Club[15]—namely,
meetings, speeches, and leaflets. There would also be Parliamentary
representation of Indian claims and rights. This scheme was identi-

[13] See above, p. 199.
[14] Dec. 6, 1885.
[15] Hume was always proud of the fact that his father, Joseph Hume, the Radical
M.P., had joined the Cobden Club and given much support to it. He was consequently familiar with its organization and methods and its associations in England
and Scotland.

cal with the proposed Indian National Union, save that it laid special emphasis upon political agitation in India and incorporated a link with Parliament. In the spring, Hume had already developed plans for the Union;[16] while in England, he had worked on the other scheme, with the result that when he returned to India, he was more convinced than ever of the need for both. Given the frustration of the educated Indian leaders, he too realized the need for action. The editorial in *The Indian Spectator* was seemingly Hume's opening call to arms for the Indian National Union.

In Calcutta, S. N. Banerjea had, throughout September, been working for another "national" conference. Although G. S. Iyer's idea for a national party interested him.[17] Banerjea had by early December begun to make arrangements for the second National Conference. By means of a circular letter, he sounded colleagues in Calcutta and friends in other cities, including Lahore and Bombay.[18] He proposed that a second truly national conference be held at Calcutta during Christmas week when it would be convenient for delegates from other associations to attend a three-day session. An agenda covering five grievances was to serve as the basis for discussion and also as a common Indian program if the Parliamentary inquiry requested opinions from Indian associations.

N. N. Sen, in response to Banerjea's letter,[19] was not unenthusiastic about national action: "The necessity for more united action among the educated people of the different Provinces of India to protect Native interests and to acquire larger rights and concessions for ourselves is becoming more and more apparent." Yet he did not declare himself in favor of the conference. He wanted something more than a repetition of the first National Conference with its distinct Bengali overtones. Like the writer "A.B.," who had addressed *The Indian Mirror* earlier in the year[20] and was doing so once again with proposals for a national assembly, Sen favored "something like a National Congress to be held periodically in India at some important centre in India, convenient to the people of different Provinces." This was a more grandiose scheme than that which Banerjea had in mind. With an organization such as that of the Congress of the United States of America, the congress plan

[16] See above, pp. 76 ff.

[17] Editorial, *Bengalee*, Nov. 7, 1885.

[18] See editorials, *Indu Prakash*, Dec. 7 (quoted in *Indian Mirror*, Dec. 16), and *Tribune*, Dec. 8, 1885, announcing conference at Calcutta under Banerjea's sponsorship. Circular letter was published in *Bengalee* and *Tribune*, Dec. 12, 1885.

[19] Editorial, "The Need for a National Congress in India," *Indian Mirror*, Dec. 8, 1885.

[20] See above, p. 44.

would be more in line with the proposals for a federated, decentralized government of India, which Bright had elucidated in 1858 and had recently brought forward again at Birmingham, which Cotton had set forth in his book, and which the delegates had included in India's Appeal to the British electorate. Sen valued this plan as a logical outgrowth of the Appeal. Furthermore, a conference in Calcutta held under Bengali auspices, which would inevitably be regarded as primarily provincial, not national, in character, would be unable to produce what in his opinion was now so urgently needed by "New India," namely, a truly representative spirit and unified voice. The delegates had failed bcause they could not substantiate their claims to represent all India. On these grounds, Sen withheld his support from Banerjea's scheme.[21]

Just when replies were coming in to Banerjea's letter, Hume and his group, quite independently of Banerjea, set in motion their plans for a conference at Poona of the Indian National Union.[22] Initially they considered Calcutta as the most likely spot for the conference,[23] but later they decided upon Poona, because it was more centrally located, and more especially because the Excutive Committee of the Poona Sarvajanik Sabha stood ready to undertake all arrangements for a session at Poona and, furthermore, possessed greater financial resources than any of the other associations involved.[24] Consequently, with the assistance of the committee of the Bombay Presidency Association, the Poona Executive Committee set up a reception fund and began to make the necessary arrangements for the meeting. To ascertain how many persons would attend, telegrams were sent to individuals and associations, advising them of the conference to be held at Poona, December 27-29, and requesting their participation.[25]

Upon receipt of the telegrams, G. S. Iyer announced the particulars in an editorial in *The Hindu*.[26] The Executive Committee of the Madras Sabha convened a small meeting to consider the telegram.[27] Since arrangements had already been made for the second

[21] As did the mysterious writer "A.B.," see letter to the editor, undated, "A National Assembly for India VI," *Indian Mirror*, Dec. 10, 1885.

[22] Hume and his colleagues probably met at Poona or Bombay (see n. 27 below), rather than at Madras as Banerjea seemed to think (Banerjea, pp. 98-99).

[23] See Agarkar's editorial in *Mahratta*, Dec. 12, 1885, as quoted in *Source Material for a History of the Freedom Movement in India* (Bombay, 1958), II, 7.

[24] "Origin and Composition of the Congress," *I.N.C. Report 1885*, p. 3.

[25] Sent probably Dec. 8, see nn. 26, 27 below.

[26] Announcement, Dec. 9, in tri-weekly *Hindu*, quoted in *Indian Mirror*, Dec. 12, 1885.

[27] Telegram, Bombay Presidency Association to Madras Sabha, undated, reviewed on Dec. 12 by Madras Sabha, see *M.M.S. Annual Report*, pp. 5-6.

Madras Conference,[28] the meeting decided to advance their date, and to notify the Bombay Presidency Association that they were sending delegates to the Union Conference at Poona. In Calcutta, when word of the conference reached W. C. Bonnerjee, Hume's friend and a leading figure at the Calcutta Bar, he invited S. Banerjea, whom he had known for years and had defended in the contempt case in 1883, to attend the Poona meeting. The latter declined with the excuse that his responsibilities at the Calcutta Conference, which could not be called off, virtually precluded his attendance at Poona.[29] But in fact, Banerjea had not even announced the dates for the Calcutta Conference. Whether pique and Bengali pride were involved in his refusal seems doubtful in the light of his dedicated response to the Poona ideal from 1886 onward. More likely his refusal was prompted by the Political Committee of the British Indian Association, which had agreed to participate in and finance the second Calcutta Conference, and which, after the misunderstanding over the Appeal and the leaflets of the Indian mission to England, was chary of joining in hastily conceived political activities with the Bombay Presidency Association. On December 12, Banerjea published a circular letter, which announced that the second National Conference would be held during Christmas week, with exact dates to be specified later.[30]

Damaging as Banerjea's decision against any strong Bengali representation at Poona was, it was more than compensated for by the hearty welcome and tentative acceptances which greeted the Bombay committee's telegrams from editors and politicians in Sind, Madras, the Northwest Provinces, Oudh, and the Punjab. All told, 75 to 100 persons were expected to attend. Planning began in earnest. By mid-December, a circular[31] was distributed to the delegates, advising them on expenses, transportation, and accommodations, and stating that the conference's aim was primarily to enable all those persons laboring for "national progress" to meet for discussion and to decide on political operations for the ensuing year and, indirectly, to serve as the germ of a "National Parliament," which, if properly conducted, would in a few years' time demonstrate that India was most suited for representative institutions.

The response to the idea of the Indian National Union Conference was excellent and virtually instantaneous. "Instead of the Na-

[28] Circular issued to associations in Madras Presidency in Oct., see *M.M.S. Annual Report, Appendixes,* pp. 37-40.

[29] Banerjea, p. 98, gives no date for the meeting with Bonnerjee.

[30] *Bengalee* and *Tribune,* Dec. 12; also *Times,* Dec. 14, 1885.

[31] Undated in *I.N.C. Report 1885,* pp. 3-4. No record of it can be found in the contemporary press, though studies on the Congress make much of it.

tional Conference at Calcutta, which we announced last week,"
declared the *Indu Prakash*, "a Conference is to be held at Poona
[over] Christmas when representatives of different cities throughout
the country will meet and discuss certain questions of national importance," and, it continued, since invitations had been sent to
Calcutta, Madras, Benares, Ahmedabad, Surat, and elsewhere and
all preliminaries had been settled, the conference was a certainty.[32]
More important, N. N. Sen gave the conference the full support he
had withheld from Banerjea's scheme:

We believe that the gathering at Poona will be a large, and, in the
strictest sense, a national one, representing all classes of the educated
Native community of the great Empire . . . on one common platform
for the purpose of considering and discussing in a perfectly loyal spirit,
and, according to constitutional forms, the great political questions
which affect them separately and collectively . . . In a few days more, we
will find that the long cherished dream of an Indian patriot—namely a
National Assembly or Congress—will be realized.[33]

"National Assembly," "Congress," these were terms that had not
been used in the telegrams or the circular announcing the Poona
meeting. Sen did not name the "Indian patriot"; nor did he refer
to any personal exchange of ideas with members of the Poona Sabha
or the Bombay Committee, and he did not discuss the objectives proposed. He accepted the Indian National Union as the closest expression of the plan that he had been advocating throughout the year,
and continued: "We have seen the utter valuelessness of mere *talking* and begun to feel the necessity of *doing*." Referring to Ripon's
farewell, the Volunteer agitation, Cotton's book, and Ripon's Edinburgh speech, he concluded: "New India . . . with its new ideas,
aspirations, hopes and fears, must be administered on new principles
altogether." The Poona meeting of the Indian National Union
would be the first step in fostering this new administration.[34]

The Anglo-Indian editors entirely ignored this sudden spate of
circulars and editorials calling for national conferences, assemblies,
and Parliaments, with the exception of Grattan Geary, the proprie-
tor-editor of *The Bombay Gazette*.[35] Of the two conferences then
being organized, Geary thought that the one at Calcutta would be
the more important, but he did not think the time had yet arrived

[32] Editorial, *Indu Prakash*, Dec. 14 (quoted in *Indian Mirror*, Dec. 16, 1885).
[33] Editorial, "The Proposed National Congress at Poona," *Indian Mirror*, Dec. 16,
1885. Sen probably learned of it either from his friend, W. C. Bonnerjee, or from
Hindu (n. 26 above) and his Theosophist colleagues in Madras.
[34] Editorial, "The Proposed Conferences at Calcutta, Allahabad, and Madras and
the National Congress at Poona," *Indian Mirror*, Dec. 18, 1885.
[35] Editorial, "Native Politicians in Conference," Dec. 18, 1885.

for a "national conference," since much preliminary political spade-
work remained to be done at the provincial level to create a "national" spirit or opinion, and so prevent official and nonofficial
antagonists of Indian reform from shouting that "a race of Indian
Schnadhorsts had come to life" in Calcutta, whose dangerous activities were aimed at subverting British rule. He would have preferred
a more limited conference without the flourish of national overtones, but he felt that if, with all its weaknesses, the conference was
conducted responsibly like the senior political associations, it would
help educate and give "genuine form and expression to such opinion
as exists" in India. Moreover, whatever conclusions it might reach
would be valuable for the pending Parliamentary inquiry and for
possible reform of the legislative councils.

On December 19, S. Banerjea announced that the National Conference would be held at Calcutta from December 25 to 29 (about
the same time as the Poona Conference), and that delegates from all
the leading Bengali associations, including the British Indian Association, as well as from other associations outside Bengal would
attend.[36] Significantly, the leading spirit behind the Central National Mahommedan Association, Syed Ameer Ali, gave his support
to Banerjea. "We hope for the best results from this Conference and
trust Mahommedan public bodies throughout India will respond to
the circular by sending delegates to represent them," he declared.[37]
Banerjea had rallied strong support, but there was no more talk of
the Poona and the Calcutta conferences merging forces. Each conference went its own way and thereby weakened the impact of the
other.

During the latter half of December, five conferences were held.
Both a conference at Jubbulpore, concerned with the rights and
interests of a specific class in India, and a small provincial meeting
at Allahabad of editors and politicians concerned with the Northwest Provinces and Oudh, though of considerable interest at the
time and of much significance later because of their eventual representation at the Indian National Union, were overshadowed by the
other three conferences. These three, despite distinct differences,
reached similar conclusions.

The first of the three, namely the second Madras Conference, met
under the auspices of the Madras Mahajana Sabha, December 23-25,
at Pacheappa Hall, Madras City. It followed the first Madras Conference, held at the end of 1884 to unite the proliferating Madras

[36] Editorial, *Bengalee,* Dec. 19, 1885.
[37] *Mahomedan Observer,* Dec. 19, 1885 (*V. of I.,* IV, Jan. 1886, p. 56).

political groups in a common cause and action.[38] Both in inspiration and organization, the Conference, being the work of the Madras Sabha, reflected it in character. The Sabha was composed of thirty-six members from Madras City and forty-one from the mofussil,[39] the majority of whom were Hindu, with a few Theosophists and Christian converts; of the Hindus, the majority were Brahmins.[40] The Brahmins and the urban members dominated the Executive Committee and the Secretariat.[41] Over half of the Executive Committee held university degrees,[42] although the figure was lower for those from the mofussil.[43] Most of the members were lawyers,[44] with a number of merchants and bankers,[45] and very few teachers and journalists;[46] most, also, were landholders. Four Brahmins and two Christians were the driving spirit behind the Sabha,[47] with two large landholders—one Brahmin and one Kshatriya[48]— and three wealthy merchants, also landholders,[49] showing keen interest and lending sound support. While not all members attended the Conference, it, for the most part, reflected the composition of the Sabha,[50] though with some distortions. More Brahmins,[51] more outsiders—from the Tanjore People's Association, the Triplicane Literary Society, and the Coconnada Literary Association—more landholders, and, at the second Conference especially, delegates from ryoti associations at Tinnevelly, Trichinopoly, Coimbatore, and Vellore, who had been urged to come, changed the distribution.[52] Regionally and occupationally, the conference cast a wider net than the Sabha.

Control of the Conference rested firmly with the Sabha, whose

[38] Speech, P. A. Charlu, Dec. 29, 1884. *The Report of the First Madras Conference* (Madras, 1885; CRO, Tract 658), p. 3.

[39] See *M.M.S. Annual Report,* flyleaf.

[40] Approximately 34 Brahmins, 5 Kshatriyas, 13 Vellalas (11 Mudaliars, 2 Pillais), 8 Chettiars, and 1 Reddi.

[41] Approximately 13 Brahmins, 4 Kshatriyas, 7 Vellalas, 6 Chettiars, 1 Nair, 1 Menon, 1 Naicker, 1 Christian, 1 Deva, and 1 Muslim merchant (Gulam Dostagir).

[42] Out of 36 members, 22 had B.A. or B.L. degrees.

[43] Out of 41 from the Mofussil, 18 had B.A. or B.L. degrees.

[44] There were 14 out of 36; 24 out of 41.

[45] Approximately 12 out of 36; 10 out of 41.

[46] There were 2 editors out of 36; 2 editors, 3 teachers out of 41.

[47] Brahmins: G. S. Iyer, the Honorable S. Subramania Iyer, P. A. Charlu, V. Chariar; Christians: Dr. S. P. Andy, Paul Peter Pillai.

[48] The Brahmin was a Maratha Brahmin, Diwan Raghunath Rao, the Kshatriya was P. Rungiah Naidu. The Naidu caste in Telingana was classified Sudra, but Naidu and his relations claimed to be Kshatriya; see Blunt, *India under Ripon,* p. 50.

[49] C. S. Mudaliar, S. Rungia Chetti, Numberumal Chetty.

[50] *Report, First Madras Conference,* pp. 1, 2; references to the Second Madras Conference, except where otherwise noted, are based on *Madras Mail,* Dec. 24, 25, 26, 1885.

[51] At first conference, 46 out of 68 members were Brahmin.

[52] *M.M.S. Annual Report,* p. 3; also *Hindu,* Jan. 7 (*V. of I.,* IV, Jan. 1886, pp. 58-59).

President and Secretariat served the Conference in the same capacities. The latter's Executive Committee, also, consisted largely of members of the Sabha Executive, from which were drawn the principal speakers. The agenda, drafted and distributed in October, was based on resolutions and committee reports initiated at the first Conference by the Sabha's Executive. It was not surprising, therefore, that the proceedings of the second Conference reflected the occupational interests of the Sabha Executive—the law and the land.

Conducted with strict adherence to Parliamentary procedure, the Conference reached, after moderate discussion, moderate solutions. Much attention was given to the memorial of G. S. Iyer calling for the separation of revenue from judicial functions in the district administration of the Madras Presidency. Speeches in Tamil and Telugu supported the resolution. A discussion lasting for a day and a half dealt with the hardships inflicted on the ryots and the damage done to agricultural productivity and the land by the Forest and Salt laws. V. Chariar and Paul Peter Pillai quoted from ryoti protests written in the vernaculars, while Kasava Pillai and T. Numberumal Chetty successfully moved commissions of inquiry with a view to reducing or rescinding the taxes levied under the Forest and Salt acts. These were essentially provincial matters, appraised in terms of provincial facts and figures.

The most notable step taken by the Conference was the adoption of a memorial, calling for the reform of the legislative councils, to be submitted to the Home and Indian governments. The memorial was based on recommendations for the councils, presented by V. Chariar at the first Conference in 1884, and subsequently revised by a subcommittee headed by P. A. Charlu during 1885.[53] Since the Supreme and provincial councils were ineffective in legislating for the true needs of Indian society, because the nonofficial members added under the Act of 1861 were appointed by the official executive segments of the councils and hence controlled by them for their own legislative ends, Chariar had recommended that the nonofficial seats be filled by strictly nonofficial members, elected from specified electorates—representatives to the Supreme Council by the municipal corporations, and to the provincial councils by the district boards—and that advance publicity be given by the councils on all proposed legislation. Charlu's subcommittee added that members of municipalities, district local boards, universities, chambers of commerce, and "other representative bodies" should serve as elec-

---

[53] *Report, First Madras Conference*, pp. 1-19.

tors for the provincial councils, and nonofficials elected to the provincial councils, as electors for the Supreme Council. Moved by Charlu, and seconded by S. A. Swaminatha Iyer of the Tanjore People's Association, the memorial, after brief discussion by the Conference, was unanimously approved for submission to the Secretary of State for India. This action marked the most nationally minded phase of the Conference. Solidly Madrassi in membership and concerned primarily with grievances which affected the members' own interests and livelihood, the Madras Conference was provincial in character, constitutional in method, and moderate in reform.

On December 25 as the Madras Conference ended, the second National Conference in Calcutta got under way with much fanfare and publicity at the headquarters of the British Indian Association.[54] Of the initial session, S. Banerjea wrote: "It was attended by men of rank, wealth and culture, the representatives of every section of the Hindu community, and by delegates from different parts of the country," and thus gave the false impression that the Conference was truly national. Among the forty-odd members were delegates from zemindari associations in Assam and Tripura, from groups at Meerut, Allahabad, and Benares in the Northwest Provinces, and from the Orissa People's Association.[55] One member, the Honorable V. N. Mandlik, came from Bombay City; an original member of "Young Bombay" of the 1870s and a successful barrister, he had been appointed by Ripon to the Supreme Legislative Council. One Englishman, H. J. S. Cotton, author of *New India*, was present. Telegrams of support came from Pandit Ramnarain, Secretary of the Lahore Indian Association, and from Raja Kunwar Harnam Singh of Kapurthala, Secretary of the British Indian Association of Talukhdars of Oudh. But that was all the interest in the Conference manifested in regions beyond the borders of Bengal, from which province came more than half the participants, with the largest number from Calcutta and the rest from the mofussil. Four major associations, with headquarters in Calcutta, accounted for the bulk of the gathering and provided leadership for the Conference.

First and foremost was the Indian Association, organized and led

---

[54] The following account of the conference, except where otherwise noted, is based on Banerjea's reports and editorials in *Bengalee,* Dec. 26, 1885, Jan. 2, 1886.

[55] Banerjea stated in an editorial, Jan. 2, that "not less than forty members" attended, but from the rest of his account and his book (pp. 98-99), one receives the impression that considerably more were present. A. C. Mazumdar's statement, in *Indian National Evolution,* 2nd ed. (Madras, 1917), p. 59, that there were "nearly 200 delegates" at the conference seems erroneous.

by Surendranath Banerjea himself, with subassociations throughout
Bengal and in the Northwest Provinces.[56] Its widespread influence
was enhanced by the writings of Banerjea in *The Bengalee* and of
Mukherji and Chatterjee in *The Tribune* at Lahore. From the
Association's largest following, in Calcutta, came its delegates to the
conference—a delegation which accounted for at least 25 per cent
of the Bengalis present. All Hindus—either Brahmins or Kayasthas
—with the exception of a few Brahmo Samajists, Theosophists, and
Christians, they were largely university-educated lawyers, civil servants, journalists, or teachers. Most belonged to the middle- or lower-
income groups, few were wealthy. Banerjea's colleagues at the Conference were Ananda Mohan Bose,[57] co-founder and Secretary of
the Indian Association, the Ghose brothers,[58] owners and editors of
Amrita Bazar Patrika, Ashutosh Biswas,[59] who had assisted Banerjea
in developing *The Bengalee* and was his keen legal adviser, Dwarka-
nath Ganguli,[60] a Brahmo Samajist and a founder of the Association,
and Dr. Gurudass Banerjea[61] and Dr. Trailaknath Mitra,[62] both
members of the faculty at Calcutta University.

Different in composition and influence was the British Indian
Association, the senior political association at the time not only in
Bengal but also in India, in whose hall the conference was held.
With its roots firmly established in the Bengal history of the fifties
and linked with the rise of *The Hindoo Patriot,* this association had
always worked for Indian reform, even after the sixties when its
membership came to represent the wealthier segment of the Bengali
community. By 1885, a smaller, more select group than the Indian
Association, it was solidly Hindu, with a broad representation of the
higher castes—Brahmin, Kshatriya, Rajput, Kayastha—and a sprinkling of Suvarnabanik and Sudra members. Though most were educated to the college level, there were fewer university men than in
the Indian Association. With members' interests centered on land—
some princely, mostly zemindari estates—and to a lesser extent upon
banking and commerce, it had close ties with the British Indian
Association of Talukhdars of Oudh. In short, the British Indian
Association was backed by great wealth, and numerous titles, inherited over the years or granted by the Government, and positions
in the Supreme and Bengal Legislative Councils increased its influ-

[56] At Lahore, Meerut, Allahabad, Cawnpore, and Lucknow.
[57] Kayastha.
[58] Shishir and Motilal; Kayastha.
[59] Vaisya.
[60] Brahmin.
[61] Brahmin.
[62] Kayastha.

ence. Chief among its delegates to the Conference were: Maharaja Sir Jotindra Mohan Tagore,[63] Maharaja Narendra Krishna Deb,[64] Dr. Raja Rajendra Lal Mitra,[65] Maharaja Durga Churn Laha,[66] Raja Purna Chandra Singh Bahadur and his brother, Kumar Surrat Chandra Singh;[67] and Joy Kissen Mukherji and his son, Raja Piari Mohan.[68]

The Indian Union, more recently founded, with a small membership of educated Hindus—Brahmin and Kayastha—mostly lawyers and landowners, advocated a more independent line, especially concerning the Government's land policy, than the other two associations. Its importance stemmed from the fact that it was founded by the Maharaja of Durbhanga, Sir Lachmeswar Singh, the owner of one of the oldest and largest landed estates in India, and was supported by a number of competent barristers and politicians, such as Man Mohan Ghose. Durbhanga's lieutenants at the Conference were Kunjolal Banerji Rai Bahadur, Parbutti Sanker Roy, and Rai Jotendra Nath Chowdhry.[69]

Finally, there was the Central National Mahommedan Association, the major Muslim political and social organization at the time. Founded in 1876 by Syed Ameer Ali[70] to promote progressive re-

[63] B. 1831; Brahmin; private education; related to founder of British Indian Association; Honorable Secretary, British Indian Association; wealthy zemindar; former member, Bengal Legislative and Supreme Legislative Councils.

[64] B. 1822; Kayastha; great-great grandson of Raja Naba Krishna Bahadur of Sovabazar (Diwan to Lord Clive); Hindu College; wealthy zemindar; Vice-President, British Indian Association; former member, Supreme Legislative Council, member, Bengal Legislative Council; Fellow, Calcutta University.

[65] B. 1824; Sudra; English schools and Calcutta Medical School; learned in Sanskrit and archaeology; President, Asiatic Society of Bengal; Vice-President, British Association and influential member of Political Committee; from 1884 wrote numerous editorials for *Hindoo Patriot;* D.L., Calcutta University.

[66] B. 1832; Suvarnabanik; Hindu College; partner of one of oldest Bengali mercantile houses, founded by father; wealthy landowner, banker; appointed Commissioner for Reduction of Public Debt, 1882; former member, Bengal Provincial and Supreme Councils; President, British Indian Association, 1885; Fellow, Calcutta University.

[67] Members of large landholding family, Paikparah District, Bengal.

[68] J. K. Mukherji, b. 1808, Kulin Brahmin; educated as regimental clerk, became record keeper of Hugli Collectorate and acquired large landed estates; a founder of British Indian Association; doyen of Bengali zemindars. Son, Piari, b. 1840; Calcutta University and B.L.; made Raja by Government in 1877 in recognition of father's services; Supreme Legislative Council, 1885-1886; Honorable Secretary, British Indian Association.

[69] All Brahmin; Durbhanga was Maithili Brahmin.

[70] B. 1849; Hugli College; Calcutta University, M.A., B.L., barrister; Fellow, Calcutta University; Chief Magistrate, Calcutta, 1878-1881; Bengal Legislative Council, 1878-1883; Supreme Legislative Council, 1883-1885; founder, Central National Mahommedan Association and its Secretary, 1876-1890. See also *Rules and Objects of the Central National Mahommedan Association and Its Branch Associations with the Quinquennial and Annual Reports and List of Members* (Calcutta, 1885), CRO, Tract 634.

form in the Muslim community, and supported by certain princely and landed Muslim families in Bengal, the Association had developed links throughout the Muslim community of India, even in Madras. Ali had called for Muslim support of the Conference;[71] to what degree the Muslim community heeded his call remains unclear. Years later Banerjea mentioned the participation of the Association;[72] but in 1885 he mentioned the activities of only the three Hindu associations; in fact, the roll of the Conference includes no Muslim names and none of the resolutions was moved by Muslims.

These associations had come together, then, to form the second Calcutta Conference. Their leaders, all Bengali and predominantly Hindu, controlled the entire proceedings of the Conference; they constituted the secretariat and the executive committee; and each resolution was moved by a member of one of the three Hindu associations. Any representatives from beyond Bengal proper were neither seen nor heard.[73] Thus, like the Madras Conference, this conference, representing only special landed and educated groups, had a provincial rather than a national tint. Yet the Madras Conference, as a "regional"[74] conference, was representative of a wider range of opinion than the Calcutta Conference.

Yet in aim and spirit, the Calcutta meeting, by the form and content of its resolutions, was more national than the Madras Conference. Before the opening of the Conference, the associations had agreed not to bring up the question of land reform, for the Indian Association had supported, and the British Indian Association and the Indian Union had opposed, the Bengal Tenancy Act.[75] The only strictly provincial resolution passed concerned the reorganization of the Bengal police to enable qualified, educated Bengalis to enter this service.[76] All other resolutions had a national ring, to some extent weakened by the fact that each was moved by a Bengali, who, while doing his best to speak for all of India, spoke really for Bengal. In adopting a resolution, moved by Ashutosh Biswas, to remove the discriminatory clauses of the Arms Act—which had been largely instrumental in keeping Indians out of the Volunteer Corps—the conference called for a thorough inquiry into the working of the act and for the full application of Canning's interpretation there-

[71] See above, p. 283.

[72] Banerjea, p. 98.

[73] Except for letters of best wishes from Raja Kunwar Harnam Singh of Kapurthala, Secretary, Oudh Talukhdar's Association, and a large landholder, and Pandit Ram Narain, Secretary, Lahore Indian Association, and the presence of H. J. S. Cotton.

[74] See above, pp. 283 ff.

[75] See *Indian Union*, Jan. 11 (*V. of I*, IV, Jan. 1886, "The Calcutta Conference," p. 58).

[76] Fifth resolution moved by Kunjolal Banerjea, third day of conference.

of.[77] A resolution moved by Joy Kissen Mukherji decrying the rapid and excessive rise in civil and military expenditure evoked unanimous disapproval of Dufferin's external and financial policies. Mukherji also won the Conference's support for greater employment of Indians in the Civil Service and in the British Indian Army and for extensive retrenchment instead of additional land and income taxes. Kali Charan Banerjea set forth the Indian Association's demands for reform of the requirements for entrance into the Civil Service roundly censured Kimberley's handling of the question of the age limit, and called for a total reorganization of the entire Civil Service, starting with the elimination of lieutenant-governorships. Like the Madras Conference, this conference passed a resolution calling for separation of judicial from executive functions in mofussil administration.[78] The Conference supported closer consultation on grievances with the mofussil centers, and gave full support to the Parliamentary inquiry with the qualification that a subcommittee be sent to India to take evidence.

The most important resolution, with the widest national scope, adopted by the Conference concerned reform of the legislative councils. Here its action bore a striking resemblance to that of the Madras Conference. In moving the resolution, S. Banerjea, like Chariar, proposed a curb on the official, executive segment of the councils by increasing, in both the Supreme and provincial councils, the number of nonofficial seats to two-thirds; nonofficial members were to be elected by electoral bodies of much the same composition as recommended in the Madras scheme, except that Banerjea omitted any provision for regional electors or for communal representation other than Hindu. Also in contrast to the Madras plan, in order to give greater control over finance to the legislative councils, nonofficial members were to have the right of interpellation concerning any and all budget proposals and modifications. True representation and financial responsibility were the ends Banerjea sought in his plan for reform of the councils.

It received a mixed welcome. Members of the Indian Association and various reformers in the British Indian Association were for it; and Henry Cotton, in praising it, stated that a similar scheme drawn up by himself had won the support of Lord Ripon. But some of the larger landholders were hesitant; they were naturally reluctant to discard nominated nonofficial seats which clearly worked to their political advantage and self-interest. As Banerjea reported, "a some-

---

[77] Second and third days of conference. See also above p. 104.

[78] Moved by Babu Dwarka Nath Chuckerbutti, Assistant Secretary, British Indian Association.

what animated discussion" took place on the principles and details of his scheme, but in the final analysis there was only general, not unanimous, approval. The Conference adopted a resolution, stating that the question of the reconstitution of the councils was "one of the utmost importance" and appointing a large committee from the leaders of the three associations "to consider what steps should be taken to bring about the satisfactory settlement of this question." Banerjea's scheme was to serve merely as a basis for further discussion. Thus the Calcutta Conference failed to go as far as the Madras Conference, but its resolution on reform of the councils derived some slight significance from the participation of the Maharajas—Durbhanga, Tagore, Deb, and Laha—on the same committee with S. Banerjea and Ananda Mohan Bose.

After passing resolutions extending best wishes to the forthcoming conference in the Bombay Presidency, and after agreeing to meet at Calcutta for a third conference at the end of 1886, the Calcutta Conference closed. Moderate in tone, with the possible exception of Kali Charan Banerjea's speech, constitutional in procedure, and loyal in spirit, the Conference presented a more mature image than its predecessor of 1883. It was notable primarily for the illustrious personalities of the Bengal community who attended and for the specific criticisms they leveled at Dufferin's administration.

Only the conference of the Indian National Union remained to be held. Between December 16 and 25, however, important changes had taken place regarding its title and the place of meeting. A decision was made to call the conference the Indian National Congress, a title in keeping with the ideas of N. N. Sen and others in Bengal, that the meeting be chaired by a "president" and that those attending be called "representatives."[79] Though the reasons for the change cannot be established with certainty, there are a number of likely explanations. Hume had much admiration for the American system of government, and cetrainly the terms "Congress" and "representative" had more of an American halo about them than did the terms "conference" and "delegates." Then, too, Hume had visited Bright in England during the election campaign when Bright was again propounding his ideas for a federalized India. If the time came for such federalization, a representative congress would make a more substantial contribution to it than would a mere conference. Moreover, the name "Congress" would distinguish this meeting on the west coast from the earlier conferences held in India, particularly

[79] "Origin and Composition of the Congress," *I.N.C. Report 1885* p. 3. Except where otherwise noted, the following account of the Congress is based on this report.

Banerjea's. Finally, Sen's exhortation for a "National Congress" cannot be disregarded.

Furthermore, when cholera appeared at Poona on December 25, the meeting was shifted to Bombay. Hume and the executives of the Bombay Presidency Association and the Poona Sabha made frantic rearrangements, so that by the 27th the representatives began to arrive in Bombay. Hume, working with Telang, Mehta, and Chiplonkar, and consulting Sir William Wedderburn, Justice Jardine, Professor Wordsworth, and other notables in Bombay sympathizing with Indian reform, appointed a Platform Committee, arranged the agenda, listed the speakers against resolutions, and proposed for President, W. C. Bonnerjee from Calcutta.[80] On December 28, with the recorder of the minutes present,[81] and with Bonnerjee voted unanimously into the chair as President, the first Indian National Congress commenced its deliberations in the large hall of Gokuldas Tejpal Sanskrit College.[82]

"Historic," "unique," "momentous," "colourful," "national," "thoroughly representative"—such were the adjectives used to describe the first Congress. Viewed with hindsight, they seem justified; indeed the intervening eighty-three years have done little to diminish their original lustre. If the Madras Conference had been singular, and the second Calcutta Conference eventful, then the Congress was historic for India much as the first sitting of the Continental Congress at Philadelphia in 1774 was for the United States. Nothing can dim its fame. Perspective and detail can be added, yet these are but qualifications which in no wise detract from the importance of the event.

Of some eighty-odd participants in the Congress, seventy-three were officially registered as representatives.[83] Between ten and fifteen persons, including D. S. White,[84] Diwan Raghunath Rao,[85] Govind

[80] P. 4.

[81] T. Allen Reid, President of the Phonetic Society of Great Britain and an expert in shorthand, took down the proceedings verbatim at the Congresses (until 1892). Hume edited, redacted, and formulated the transcript into the *Congress Report* for the particular year. See *Source Material*, II, 11.

[82] The first Congress has been described in numerous studies, none of which does more than summarize the *I.N.C. Report 1885*. See Wedderburn, Mody, Mazumdar, Besant, S. K. Ratcliffe, *Sir William Wedderburn and the Indian Reform Movement* (London, 1923), H. V. Lovett, *A History of the Indian Nationalist Movement* (London, 1920), B. P. Sitaramayya, *The History of the Indian National Congress 1885-1935* (Madras, 1935), and C. F. Andrews and G. Mukerji, *The Rise and Growth of the Congress in India* (London, 1938). All these studies say the same thing; few are critical, and none has given a more thorough analysis than the *Report* itself.

[83] P. 4. Hume's figures for distribution do not tally with the names he listed. One name should be added to the eight registered for Poona, and one dropped for the three for Ahmedabad; thus total registration was seventy-three.

Mahadev Ranade,[86] Lala Baijnath,[87] Professor A. V. Kattawath,[88] Dr. Sundara Raman,[89] R. G. Bhandarkar,[90] Professor Wordsworth,[91] and Sir William Wedderburn[92] attended as *"amici curiae* to listen and to advise,"* because they were employed by the Government of India, and Hume had agreed with Dufferin that no senior officials would be invited to participate. Yet eventually a number of them did speak. Thus the Congress was just slightly larger than the Madras Conference and considerably larger than the Calcutta Conference. By contemporary standards, seventy-three may seem a small number, but for the period it was a large gathering, especially as half of the representatives travelled from the far corners of the subcontinent to attend the session at a time when such a journey was no light undertaking. For 1885 it was a most impressive gathering.

Hume claimed that the gathering bore a truly national composition.[93] Certainly, with geographical distribution covering a wide sweep—the key centers of Bombay, Madras, Bengal, the Northwest Provinces and Oudh, and the Punjab—the Congress wore the ambitious adjective "national" more comfortably than did the Calcutta Conference, but even Hume would have admitted that it did not fit as well as he had hoped. He and his colleagues had estimated from the responses to their telegrams that, excluding Poona, twenty representatives would come from the Bombay Presidency including the Berars and Sind, twenty from Madras, twenty from Lower Bengal, and ten in all from the Northwest Provinces and the Punjab. Actual distribution at the Congress proved quite different and by no means gave equal representation to all regions. Of the seventy-three, thirty-nine came from the Bombay Presidency, with eighteen from Bombay City, eight from Poona, and the rest from the Kon-

[84] Eurasian; Assistant to Director of Public Instruction, Madras; Life President, Eurasian and Anglo-Indian Association of South India.

[85] Maratha Brahmin; formerly Diwan to Maharaja Holkar of Indore; large landowner in Tanjore; Madras Collector.

[86] Maratha Brahmin; member, Bombay Legislative Council; Judge, Small Cause Court, Poona, Judicial Department; Brahmo, Prarthana Samaj; Poona Sarvajanik Sabha.

[87] Kayastha; Statutory Civil Service, Agra.

[88] Bombay Educational Department; Elphinstone College.

[89] M.A.; Madras Educational Department; Madras University.

[90] Brahmin; M.A.; Bombay Educational Department; Fellow, Bombay University, Professor of Sanskrit, Deccan College.

[91] Professor and Head, Elphinstone College; Bombay Educational Department; Sheriff, Bombay.

[92] Fourth Baronet; Bombay Civil Service; Secretary, Judicial-Political Department, Bombay.

[93] Pp. 3-5.

kan, Berars, Gujerat, and Sind regions; twenty-one came from Madras, with eight from the city and the rest from the mofussil. Of the remaining thirteen, seven came from the Northwest Provinces and Oudh, three from the Punjab (but none for Multan, Rawalpindi, or Delhi), and three from Calcutta. With the significant omissions of mofussil Bengal, Bihar, Orissa, Assam, Tipperah, and the Central Provinces, Hume's claim that "all parts of India were represented" at the Congress was rather an exaggeration.

Political representation tended to follow the geographic distribution, although on a more limited scale. Madras was well represented with one delegate from the Tanjore People's Association, and the rest, for both city and mofussil, coming from the Madras Mahajana Sabha. Bombay was equally well represented with delegates from the Bombay Presidency Association from Bombay City, the Praja-hita-vardhak Sabha of Surat, the Gujerat Sabha of Ahmedabad, and the Poona Sarvajanik Sabha. D. S. White, the leader of the Eurasian Association of India, was present, but not officially registered. These were the only associations represented as such, though persons active in political associations in Karachi, Calcutta, Benares, Allahabad, Agra, Lahore, and Lucknow came as individual representatives to the Congress. Thus, far from covering all the political associations, it was oriented towards the Madras and Bombay associations.

Nor was the Congress quite so "thoroughly representative" of communities and classes as Hume claimed.[94] He admitted that it was dominated by Hindus,[95] and that there were present only two Muslims, both members of the Municipal Corporation and the Anjuman-i-Islam of Bombay City. True, two of the leading figures of the Anjuman, Badruddin and Cumruddin Tyabji, were slated to attend as representatives for the Bombay Presidency Association, but shortly before the meeting they had been called away to deal with affairs in the state of Cambay where they held land and were close friends of the Nawab.[96] But had the Tyabjis been able to attend, they would have done little to rectify the imbalance of Muslim representation, for there were no Muslim delegates from Bengal, the Punjab, the Northwest Provinces, or Madras. There was a scattering of representatives from the Parsi and Jain communities in the Bombay Presidency,[97] one Brahmo missionary, and one Chris-

[94] For the following analysis, see names and occupations of representatives, pp. 4-5. In addition, for J. Ghosal, *vakil,* Allahabad, Rao Saheb V. Pantulu, landowner, Masulipatam, and one unkown for Ahmedabad, see *I.N.C. Report 1886,* Appendix.
[95] Of 73 representatives, 54 were Hindu.
[96] Tyabji, pp. 175-176.
[97] Surat, 2 Jain, 2 Parsi; Ahmedabad, 1 Jain, 1 Parsi; Bombay City, 7 Parsi.

tian, Hume. A few of the Hindus were active theosophists.[98] Among the Hindus, caste representation followed much the same pattern as at the Madras and Calcutta conferences with a high incidence of Brahmins,[99] largely from Madras[100] and Bombay[101] Presidencies, with two from Calcutta and one each from Agra, Benares, Allahabad, and Lucknow. The rest were Kshatriyas,[102] Kayasthas,[103] Vellalas,[104] and Banias,[105] with one Marwari and one Lohana.[106] This religious and caste distribution did not mean necessarily that specific religious or caste interests were given political representation or expression. There was, in fact, a distinct absence of any political representation of specific religious or caste interests. Yet sociologically it was significant that the distribution of caste and religion within the associations represented at the Congress was reflected in the leadership of the Congress. Eighty per cent of the Madras Sabha delegates[107] and 100 per cent of the Poona Sabha delegates were Brahmin; the largest number of delegates from the Bombay Presidency Association were Parsi, and the next largest, Brahmin;[108] while the Surat Praja-hita-vardhak Sabha and the Gujerat Sabha were mostly Jain and Parsi.[109] Thus Brahmins and Parsis predominated in the leadership of the associations, and likewise in that of the Congress. Yet the figures as a whole revealed that individuals from the most varied religious and caste backgrounds were willing to come together to work at a national level for a common cause. This had been demonstrated, to a lesser extent, at the preceding two conferences. But, as at those meetings, so too at the Congress, education, occupation, and income proved to be the real magnets that generally brought the seemingly disparate representatives together.

These magnets were very strong within the Congress. At least 80 per cent of the representatives spoke English; forty-five delegates had attended colleges and twenty-five at least had taken higher

[98] N. N. Sen, P. A. Charlu, S. S. Iyer, and others from Madras.
[99] There were 36 Brahmins. This and the following figures are approximate.
[100] There were 15 Brahmins from Madras Presidency, 6 from Madras City and balance from mofussil.
[101] There were 9 Brahmins from Poona, 5 Bombay City, 1 Surat.
[102] Two, the Naidus of Madras.
[103] Six, 2 from Lucknow, 1 each from Calcutta, Agra, Amballa, and Bombay.
[104] Four, a Vaisya caste from the agrarian groups in north and south Madras, Mudaliar, and Pillai.
[105] One from Viragram, 1 Surat, 3 Bombay.
[106] Jethmal and Moolchand from Karachi.
[107] Six Brahmins, 1 Kshatriya, 1 Vellala.
[108] Seven Parsi, 5 Brahmin, 3 Bania, 2 Muslim, 1 Chandrasena Kayastha.
[109] Surat Sabha: 2 Jain, 1 Brahmin, 1 Bania, 1 Parsi; Gujerat Sabha: 1 Parsi, 1 Jain.

degrees.[110] Over half were lawyers,[111] of whom most were Brahmins and Parsis,[112] one a Kshatriya, and the rest Kayastha, Bania, Jain, Muslim, or a Vaisya subcaste.[113] Others were journalists, business men, and landholders, with a very few teachers.[114] In some instances, no clear distinctions between categories can be drawn, for landholding went hand in hand with law, law with journalism, or trade with landholding.[115] In contrast to the conferences at Madras and Calcutta, journalists figured strongly at the Congress, with fifteen newspapers directly or indirectly represented.[116] With the addition of certain Bengal and Bombay newspapers, both English and vernacular, the Congress would have been fully representative of the Indian press. The Congress representatives included, as at Madras, a small proportion of merchants and bankers, but, unlike the other two conferences, few landholders, and most of these came from Madras. The overwhelming majority of the Congress belonged to the middle- or lower-income groups.[117] What financial strength the Congress had came from a few larger landowners and wealthy

[110] *I.N.C. Report 1885,* pp. 4-5, does not give complete coverage of educational qualifications. Only 23 cases can be evaluated as follows: 11 B.A. (3 became M.A.); 10 B.L.; 2 M.D. From Madras City, 3 B.A., 3 B.L.; Bombay, 4 B.A.: (1 became M.A.), 1 B.L.; Poona, 2 B.A. (both became M.A.); Surat, 3 B.A., 3 B.L.

[111] Forty engaged in law: 30 *vakil*-pleaders, 4 barristers, 4 solicitors, 1 sub-judge, 1 law professor.

[112] Brahmin: Surat, 1; Poona, 3; Calcutta, 2; Agra, Allahabad, Benares, 1 each; Bombay City, 5; Madras City, 3; Madras mofussil, 4 (two were barristers). Parsi: Surat, 1; Ahmedabad, 1; Bombay City, 3 (two barristers, 1 solicitor).

[113] Kayastha: Agra, Amballa, Lucknow, 1 each; Bania: Viragram, Surat, Bombay City, 1 each (one solicitor); Jain: Surat, Ahmedabad, 1 each; Muslim: Bombay, 2, both solicitors. Vaisya subcaste: Karachi, 1 Marwari, 1 Lohana; Madras mofussil, 1 Vellala. One Kshatriya, P. R. Naidu from Madras City.

[114] Forty law, 9 journalism, 7 mercantile, 6 landholding, 3 professors, 3 secretaries to political associations, 2 medicine, 1 unknown, 1 ex-I.C.S. (Hume).

[115] P. R. Naidu, registered as a *vakil,* was also a large landholder in Coimbatore; D. E. Wacha, registered as Secretary, Bombay Presidency Association, was also a leading editor for *Kaiser-i-Hind;* Murlidhar, Jamandas, and G. B. Mookherji, registered as pleaders, also represented *Tribune, Nassim,* and *Nababibhakar;* A. S. Moodeliyar, registered as a merchant, was also a large landholder in Bellary.

[116] Poona: *Dnyan Prakash, Mahratta, Kesari;* Calcutta: *Indian Mirror, Nababibhakar;* Agra: *Nassim;* Lucknow: *Hindustani;* Lahore: *Tribune;* Bombay City: *Kaiser-i-Hind, Rast Goftar, Indian Spectator, Indu Prakash;* Madras City: *Hindu, Swadesa Mitran;* Coimbatore: *Crescent.*

[117] Hume included no data on income distribution. It is thought that the income scale of the majority, excluding the wealthy landlords and merchants, ranged from Rs. 25,000 per year at the top for an Indian barrister, small court judge, or collector to Rs. 2,400 to Rs. 1,000, or about £68 per year at the bottom for a munsif. *Vakils* in private legal practice, professors, and editor-proprietors made about the same as munsifs. G. P. Sen estimated for the third Congress that only 10 per cent of the members had incomes of less than Rs. 1,000; see *I.N.C. Report 1887.*

merchants,[118] but its members possessed none of the princely and zemindari fortunes, the titles, or the influential offices[119] with which the Calcutta Conference had glittered. With fewer social and economic distinctions, the Congress constituted a more cohesive body, the majority of whose members, because of their Western education, their training in the law or in journalism, and their middling incomes, could cut across differences of religion, caste, title, and wealth to meet and act on common ground as a new class in the social and political spectrum of British India.

Although the Congress did not warrant Hume's claim that it was "thoroughly representative of the entire nation," it was representative of this new, small, and important class whose members held similar interests, values, and aspirations. As Grattan Geary remarked following the first session, "They all appeared to have agreed in the opinion that they had some political aspiration . . . and that for the promotion of their common object there was a necessity for concerted action."[120] By acting together for their own ends, the representatives believed that they were representing the best interests of the Indian people, Hindu or non-Hindu, high or low caste, rich or poor, even though they were not directly elected to do so. W. C. Bonnerjee said as much when he called the Congress truly representative because its participants shared "a community of sentiments, a community of feelings, and a community of wants" with the people of India and hence knew the people's needs and aspirations.[121] Bonnerjee's speech was valid up to a point. The representatives undoubtedly had the best interests of all India at heart, but actually they represented the aspirations of their own class, "New India," for a greater share in the government that ruled them.

No aspiration was more warmly felt or keenly expressed during the Congress than that for Indian national unity. It was a thread woven through the addresses of the key speakers and giving brilliant color to the proceedings from start to finish. In opening the Congress, Bonnerjee spoke of the central mission of the Congress to replace divisive elements such as race, creed, and provincial prejudices with a sense of national unity. G. S. Iyer, in moving the first

[118] W. C. Bonnerjee and P. Mehta were successful practitioners before the Calcutta and Bombay Bar; Nulkar, Nadkarni, the Naidus, N. N. Aiyar, V. S. Pantulu, and A. S. Moodeliyar, large landholders; J. Wacha and C. S. Moodeliyar, prosperous merchants; T. M. Nathuboy, a philanthropist and scion of a great banking family; G. S. Iyer, a successful journalist and business man.

[119] K. L. Nulkar and P. R. Naidu were Rao Bahadur; D. Naoroji and K. Telang, members, Bombay Legislative Council; S. S. Iyer, member, Madras Legislative Council.

[120] Editorial, *Bombay Gazette*, Dec. 29, 1885.

[121] Inaugural speech, p. 7.

resolution, thought this mission already well started. "From today forward," he declared, "we can with greater propensity than heretofore speak of an Indian nation, of national opinion and national aspirations." V. Chariar, in a speech on the third resolution, called for a more sensitive awareness of nationality. "We now begin to perceive that notwithstanding the existing differences in our mother tongue, social habits and manners, we possess the true elements of nationality about us." D. S. White, speaking on behalf of the Eurasian community, echoed these sentiments.

National unity was a positive, not a negative, aspiration, in which antipathy toward British rule and disparagement of the British Crown were not to be found. Bonnerjee pointed to the blessings of British rule—law and order, the railways, the telegraph, and the post—and P. Rangiah Naidu emphasized the boons of English education and Western civilization. Both concluded that without these there would have existed no unity in India, no feeling of progress, no common ground for them to meet and interchange their thoughts, and, above all, no sense of nationality. Iyer went so far as to say that a sense of national unity was a unique British characteristic, which it was the British mission to foster. "For the first time" in Indian history, he emphasized, "the phenomenon of national unity [and] a sense of national existence" were at work within the divided, fissile Indian population thanks to British rule. Dadabhai Naoroji was still more emphatic. "What attaches us to this foreign rule with deeper loyalty than even our own past Native rule, is the fact that Britain is the parent of free and representative Government and that we, as her subjects and children, are entitled to inherit the great blessing of freedom and representation." Rao Saheb Venkata S. Pantalu drove home these points by reading excerpts from Ransome's book, *India and How We Keep It,* describing what would happen to both countries—and India in particular—if the Empire were dissolved. Hume perhaps best summarized the feeling among the assemblage when at the end of the three-day session he led them in three resounding cheers for Her Majesty the Queen. Loyalty and gratitude to Britain and the Crown for the inheritance they had received through British rule were the positive notes motivating the nationalist aspirations of the first Congress.

So great a premium did they place upon this inheritance that they wished to ensure its stability and continuity by reforming the existing government to give Indians more responsibility for the material and moral progress of their country. W. C. Bonnerjee gave the keynote to these aspirations for reform, and D. Naoroji was their liveliest exponent. Political reform was their primary concern.

They called for implementation of the pledges given to the Indian people in the Queen's Proclamation of 1858 and the Act of 1858—pledges which the Congress speakers held to be inalienable rights, and which, left unfulfilled, had hardened into grievances. Fundamentally, the Congress speakers were calling for a redistribution of administrative and legislative power; they were talking politics. The resolutions moved and discussed, whether relating to the usefulness of the Secretary of State's Council for India, the condition of the Indian Civil Service, or the burden of military expenditure, were all political, demanding a redistribution of administrative and legislative power with greater Indian participation in and responsibility for government. Social reform, for the Congress as for Hume earlier in the year, was but a secondary concern, although listed by Bonnerjee as one of the Congress's aims. Hume and the Managing Committee agreed that the thorny problems of social reform should be reserved for a separate meeting of the Congress at the conclusion of the deliberations on political reform.[122]

The resolutions adopted by the Congress dealt essentially with the grievances listed by the Bombay Presidency Association, the Poona Sabha, and the Madras Sabha in India's Appeal to the British voter. Thus the Congress deliberations were an extension of the work of the Indian delegates' mission in England,[123] and were intended to counter the criticism that the Appeal was unrepresentative of any Indian national voice by providing that voice.

Of utmost significance were the two distinct aims proposed in the resolutions and debates: first, to protest and oppose both the spirit and results of Dufferin's administration; and second, to activate a political movement on a national scale in India and on the Parliamentary front in England in order to revive the political reforms begun under Ripon. Dutiful supplication to Government House and reliance on the good intentions of the Viceroy were to be replaced by independent action and appeal over the head of the Viceroy and the Government of India to the highest court for all British people, the Parliament. These were not the methods for reform which Ripon envisaged or which Hume and his colleagues in Bombay political circles had originally planned to launch. But Hume's ideas, and, more important, those of the educated Indian leaders, had changed during the course of 1885, when Dufferin

[122] Held Dec. 31, with Diwan R. Rao, M. Ranade, B. Malabari, N. N. Sen, and others present. See K. T. Telang to editor of *Times*, Mar. 9, 1886, and C. Y. Chintamani, ed., *Indian Social Reform* (Madras, 1901), pp. 365-376.

[123] Vote of thanks to N. G. Chandavarkar and the other delegates for services rendered to India while in England, moved and unanimously carried; Chandavarkar's reply, p. 33.

shifted from a middle-of-the-road to an extreme imperial policy, to the detriment of all financial and domestic reform. Hence the resolutions of the Congress represented the disenchantment of the educated leaders with the new Viceroy and their realization that responsible political opposition to Dufferin's policies was the only feasible method to secure official recognition of the rights of educated Indians.

The resolutions comprised three programs: a key political program to change the framework of government, another on civil rights, and a third on finance. The core of the first program was embodied in three resolutions. The first resolution[124] called for the appointment by Parliament of a Royal Commission of Inquiry to collect evidence on Indian administration and affairs from Anglo-Indians in England and, in addition, from qualified Indians in India, so as to place before the English public and Parliament "the correct facts" too long withheld from public knowledge by Anglo-Indian bureaucrats in India and England. In this, the Congress representatives aimed at the restoration of full responsibility for Indian administration to the House of Commons, as in the days of the East India Company when detailed, regular, and systematic Parliamentary review and supervision of Indian affairs were the prevailing practices. Only by these methods could the English and Indian governments understand, and act upon, the grievances of "New India." To guarantee the effectiveness of this resolution, the representatives adopted a second resolution[125] calling for the abolition of the Council of the Secretary of State for India. Like John Slagg,[126] they traced to the Council some of the principal evils then plaguing Indian administration: its meddlesome interference between the Secretary of State and the Indian government, with the deleterious result that India was governed from England rather than from India; its lack of comprehension of Indian affairs and its prejudiced advice, since it was composed of old men, products of pre-Mutiny India, and therefore out of touch with contemporary India; and its high cost to Indian taxpayers, who, in effect, were paying for double government. These evils would disappear only when the Council disappeared and the Secretary of State became directly responsible to Parliament on the one hand and to the Indian government on the other, as was the case of the Colonial Secretary in his relations with the Ceylon government. This reform related directly

[124] Speeches, G. S. Iyer (Madras), N. N. Sen (Calcutta), pp. 1, 8-12 *passim.*

[125] Speeches, S. H. Chiplonkar (Poona), P. A. Charlu (Madras), J. Ghosal (Allahabad), P. Mehta (Bombay), pp. 1, 17-23 *passim.*

[126] See above, p. 43

to the reconstitution of the provincial and Supreme legislative councils, the subject of the third resolution.[127] This resolution reproduced the scheme of elected nonofficials and of electorates approved by the Madras Conference, but it stated more definitely than did the Madras resolution that elected nonofficials were to be empowered to review all budget proposals, including taxation, and to interpellate the executive on its policies. It called for extension of these reforms to councils, which it proposed for the Northwest Provinces and Oudh and the Punjab, and recommended the formation of a Standing Committee in the House of Commons to decide any conflict over policy between the executive and legislative segments of the councils, in which the former had overruled the latter. This third resolution aimed at making the councils truly representative and effective, at giving the taxpayer a voice in the management of Indian finance, and at increasing the control of Parliament over Indian policy. These three political resolutions formed the basis for the Congress's future efforts and activities.

The second program, concerned with civil rights, was embodied in the fourth resolution,[128] demanding the right, as stipulated in the Royal Proclamation of 1858, for qualified Indians to enter fairly, freely, and fully into the Indian Covenanted Civil Service. Various speakers charged that the existing requirements were unjustly advantageous to British candidates and alarmingly disadvantageous to Indian candidates, and called for the changes that the India Office Committee of 1860 had advocated: that examinations be held simultaneously in England and India and that the maximum age for entrance be raised to not less than 23 years. They also asked that successful Indian candidates be allowed to complete their education in England. All these changes aimed at removing the necessity for Indians to enter the Civil Service via the "native" or Statutory Civil Service. The Indian government, by selecting poorly qualified Indians, had failed to make a success of the Statutory Service, and the speakers claimed that educated Indians had come to look on it as inferior since it was noncompetitive, based on official appointment, set apart from the Covenanted Service, and hence discriminatory.

The third program concentrated on financial reform. Well aware that Indian finance had been for some time in a most unsatisfactory state, the representatives sought for causes and found one in the double expense of government arising from the existence of the In-

---

[127] Speeches, K. T. Telang (Bombay), S. S. Iyer (Madras), D. Naoroji (Bombay), pp. 1, 23-32 *passim*.

[128] Speeches, D. Naoroji, V. Chariar (Madras), D. S. White, pp. 1, 33-40 *passim*.

dia Council,[129] where costs fell on the Home Charges and had to be paid in sterling against the Indian Treasury at a loss of exchange. Another cause arose from the employment of a foreign-recruited, high-salaried, sterling-paid, British-dominated Civil Service—another case of sterling charges on the Home accounts paid against the Indian Treasury with a loss of exchange—which, Naoroji alleged, was "the sole cause of India's extreme poverty and wretchedness."[130] These ills had been dealt with in the second and fourth resolutions, but various speakers maintained that the chief cause for India's financial dilemma was the soaring rate of military expenditure. So serious did they consider this development that they passed a special resolution resolving unanimously that the increase of £2,000,000 to pay for the 30,000 additional British and Indian troops proposed by the Indian government was "unnecessary, and regard being had to the revenues of the empire and the existing circumstances of the country, excessive."[131] Nor were facts and figures wanting to support their resolution. It was pointed out that in recent years the annual increase in military expenditure had been at least twice the annual increase in Indian revenue; that the most rapid increase in military expenditure was still taking place in the War Office segment of the Home Military Charges; that in 1884-85 total military expenditure amounted to £17,000,000, or 39.5 per cent of India's total revenues of £43,000,000, and that of this expenditure £4,000,000 had to cover Home Military Charges, and hence was paid in gold at an annual loss of £100,000 to Indian revenues. Against this dismal picture, the speakers pointed out that Lord Dufferin had secured the Secretary of State's approval for a vast new increase in military expenditure. They could find no justification for such a decision: the Russian threat during the spring had passed. If a crisis was still pending, then the Viceroy should have accepted the existing offers of Indian princes to lend troops and of Indian gentlemen to volunteer before bringing out any new troops from England. Further, it was declared that the Indian expenditure of the War Office should be effectively curbed by Parliament, while in England and in India the entire British–Indian military establishment should be reduced.

Yet the Congress representatives knew that no matter how strong their cry of opposition might be, the Viceroy had every intention of increasing military expenditures, even though Colvin's budget had been seriously unbalanced by the Afghan crisis, the trade depres-

---

[129] S. Mudeliar (Bellary), p. 22.
[130] D. Naoroji, p. 34.
[131] Speeches, P. R. Naidu (Madras), D. E. Wacha (Bombay), pp. 2, 41-48 *passim.*

sion, and the Burma campaign.[132] New revenues would have to be found, and the Congress representatives were alarmed and worried about another income tax. Beginning in 1870, taxes had been levied on middle and upper-middle incomes from Rs. 250; in 1872 the minimum taxable income had been raised to Rs. 500. If more taxes on either scale were levied in 1886, most of the Congress representatives would be directly affected, and such taxes would constitute a more thorough, costly form of taxation for them than either the license tax of 1.5 to 2 per cent on annual incomes of Rs. 500 or over, then being paid by merchants, traders, bankers, and moneylenders only, or the indirect taxes, chiefly on salt, liquor, and imported English cloth, which fell more heavily on the ryoti millions than on themselves.

To deal with this situation, they adopted a sixth resolution. The budget was to be restored to health by severe retrenchment starting with top official salaries. To obtain increased revenues to meet military expenditure, they approved two measures—customs duties on imports and a broader-based license tax. Reimposition of import duties, which had been removed at various stages from 1873 to 1883, would not be protective but would be solely a measure to strengthen Indian finances in the one way which least touched the pockets of the people. Moreover, since England supplied such duties to Indian goods, in justice to India the rule should work both ways. The incidence of the license tax should be broadened to fall more evenly on all classes, urban and regional. Such a tax would end discrimination against the Indian trading community and, further, would avoid the need for an income tax, certain to be higher and more oppressive. While recommending the extension of the license tax to include the incomes of classes previously untaxed, such as the official and professional classes, at the same time they called for the exemption of all incomes of Rs. 1,000 or under. This would cover the middle income, professional, mercantile, and artisan groups of the educated class, some of whose representatives were at the Congress, and whose support would be vital to the growth of the Congress. The exemption of landed incomes bore striking evidence to the influence of landed groups behind the Congress. Thus the weight of the proposed taxation was to fall upon the wealthy, largely members of the Anglo-Indian official and nonofficial class who in the past had shaped the Indian tax structure to its own fancy. The representatives

[132] Speeches, J. U. Yajnik (Bombay), D. E. Wacha, S. A. Swaminatha Iyer (Tanjore), D. Jethmal (Karachi), pp. 2, 48-57 passim.

unanimously voted down an income tax and a rise in the salt duty.[133] Their financial program also called for an Imperial guarantee for India's mounting debt,[134] so as to make the English public and Parliament more aware of India's financial plight. The logic was simple; if the Indian debt continued to soar, it would soon consume so much of the Indian revenues that Parliament would have to pay for Indian administration and military forces if England wished to retain its hold on India. Finally, the Congress condemned the war in Upper Burma, opposed annexation, given India's financial plight, and demanded that the Government keep the new territory separate from India as a Crown Colony "in all matters" should annexation become official policy.[135]

In the opinion of the representatives, the three programs of reform were not new: the Civil Service question and proposed councils reforms dated back to the fifties, while the financial reforms had come to the fore during Lytton's viceroyalty. Nor did they consider their proposals extreme in demand or radical in solution: each had been soundly conceived. G. S. Iyer and S. H. Chiplonkar proposed the Parliamentary Commission of Inquiry and the abolition of the India Council respectively, on the grounds of utility: Parliament had successfully supervised the East India Company in its day and should do the same with the Indian government, while the India Council was an outmoded, vestigial organ of the Company's day. K. Telang and S. S. Iyer drafted the provincial and Supreme councils reforms on the basis of their personal experience as members of the Bombay and Madras Legislative Councils respectively; moreover, Telang pointed out that the proposed reforms had been framed to allow for the exercise of the executive responsibilities of the Government as well as for the satisfaction of Indian aspirations. D. Naoroji, D. E. Wacha, and J. U. Yajnik based their respective proposals for the Indian Civil Service, military expenditure, and Indian finance solely upon official reports, opinions, and statistics. Utility, experience, and the test of official opinions and figures were the standards which the representatives applied to their reforms and invoked in their speeches. On the basis of such standards, they concluded that their reforms were moderate, justifiable, and essential for the task of correcting the abuses in Indian administration.

[133] Proposed by Yajnik, seconded by S. A. S. Iyer, supported by Rao Saheb V. S. Pantalu, carried by a majority after motion by Jethmal opposing extension of license tax was voted down; pp. 50-57.

[134] Chiplonkar, Telang, pp. 5-7.

[135] Resolution VII, moved by P. Mehta, seconded by K. L. Nulkar (Poona), unanimously carried, p. 58.

With the benefit of hindsight, one cannot but agree with the representatives that their proposed reforms were both just and necessary. But had they not become oblivious to the essentially revolutionary implications of their reforms, because of the persistent reiteration of such proposals in the preceding years? It was scarcely likely that the Viceroy and his officials, the chief targets of the reforms, would take the same view as the Congress of the proposals for the abolition of the India Council, the extension of the elective principle to the councils in India, and the reduction of all official salaries, to say nothing of the reimposition of import duties. Furthermore, the reforms might not seem so essential or justifiable to other Indian politicians who had not attended the Congress, but from whom the Congress hoped for support in the year ahead. The Congress had scarcely touched on the Volunteer question and Government policies on the Arms Act and district administration, given high priority at the Calcutta Conference, or on the impoverished condition of the ryots, a matter of great concern at the Madras Conference. Yet, however much friends and foes might differ on the importance and character of the resolutions passed by the Congress, one conclusion was inescapable: the Congress had carefully weighed and unanimously promulgated a reform program which neither their colleagues in other parts of India nor the Viceroy and his advisers could discount or ignore. They had, in short, initiated unified political action.

Notable also was the orderly and efficient manner in which the Congress was conducted. What might have turned into a wild sophomoric rally, was, on the contrary, a distinctly professional affair, which would have been the envy of any comparable political meeting held in England or the United States at that time. For this, much credit must go to Hume, his Managing Committee, and to the first President, W. C. Bonnerjee. Hume and his committee prepared the agenda, made the schedule, and arranged for the drafting of the resolutions. Their selection of the representatives who were to move, second, and support the resolutions in accordance with strict Parliamentary procedure gave a truly national character to the resolutions. Although all the resolutions except the eighth were moved by a speaker allied with either the Bombay Presidency Association or the Madras Sabha, the first, second, fifth, and eighth resolutions were voted upon by representatives from other regions and associations. Hume watched over the entire proceedings like a hawk, checking the minutes, scrutinizing procedure, and intervening in the debate only where necessary to keep the momentum going and to add some concluding remarks at the final session.[136] His was the guiding hand at work at all times behind the scenes, and it was with good reason that the representatives gave him three loud cheers at the end of the final session. W. C. Bonerjee made a similar but more direct contribution as President. He held the three sessions to the allotted schedules and maintained effective control over the debates. When these tended to drag on indefinitely, he intervened and added lucid statements of his own to terminate them.[137] With Hume and his committee guiding and Bonnerjee controlling, the Congress was an efficient, orderly instrument of political discussion.

But much credit for this result must also go to the representatives themselves. One often gets the impression when reading about the first Congress that the representatives were in complete accord on the reform program and that the resolutions were approved in perfect harmony. Such was not the case, for, although the representatives were unanimously agreed that reforms were needed, they differed considerably on the substance and scope of the reforms, and on the tone and the wording of the resolutions. From this resulted three roughly defined camps of opinion within the Congress. The most influential of the three were the moderates, represented by such key speakers as G. S. Iyer, K. T. Telang, S. Subramania Iyer, D. Naoroji, P. A. Charlu, B. M. Malabari, V. Chariar, J. U. Yajnik, P. R. Naidu, Dr. S. Raman, and D. E. Wacha, and including Hume, the Managing Committee, and W. C. Bonnerjee. The conservatives, consisting of registered and unregistered speakers such as Rahimtulla Sayani, Diwan R. Rao, M. Ranade, D. S. White, S. A. Swaminatha Iyer, Rao Saheb V. S. Pantalu, and other Madras landholders, formed an influential minority. The radicals, who included such forceful personalities as P. Mehta, N. N. Sen, D. Jethmal, S. H. Chiplonkar, J. Ghosal, A. Subapathi Moodeliyar, Peter Pillai, and Rao Bahadur K. L. Nulkar, constituted another minority group. The resolutions for the most part were framed by the moderates, with the conservatives agreeing to the financial resolutions, while only the second resolution on the abolition of the India Council and the seventh on Upper Burma were framed by the radicals. Thus, throughout the debates the moderates were constantly being challenged by one or the other of the two minority groups.

On the first resolution, for example, the radicals challenged the moderates by amending the resolution to specify that the Parliamentary inquiry should be a "Royal Commission fairly consti-

[136] See first and third resolutions and conclusion, pp. 13, 28, 59.
[137] See first and third resolutions, pp. 15, 32.

tuted." This was contested by the conservatives, who, preferring a vaguer resolution, alleged that such an amendment was dictating to Parliament. Hume, supported by various moderates, produced a compromise which retained the words "Royal Commission" but deleted "fairly constituted"; the radicals agreed; and the amended resolution was duly voted.[138] The conservative camp made its most formidable stand on the rest of the political program, claiming that the abolition of the India Council in the second resolution was inadequately compensated for by a Standing Committee of Parliament as proposed in the third resolution. The radicals, who had successfully carried the second resolution, also joined the attack on the third resolution by calling for the removal of all official members from the legislative councils in India; they also took issue with the conservative opposition to a Standing Committee of Parliament. The moderate position was sustained, however, once Hume, G. S. Iyer, D. Naoroji, S. Raman, and A. Charlu had entered the lists and after K. Telang had delivered a withering attack on both the conservative and radical points of view. With strong support from W. C. Bonnerjee, the third resolution was moved as drafted by the moderates and voted unanimously.[139] The sixth resolution on financial policy, introduced by the moderate J. U. Yajnik and supported by two conservatives, was contested by the radicals, who unsuccessfully moved an amendment opposing any additional taxation whatsoever to meet increased military expenditure. The radicals' seventh resolution, on the other hand, which was moved by Mehta and the Poona landholder, Nulkar, was disputed by the moderates, S. S. Iyer and S. Raman, and the conservative S. A. Swaminatha Iyer, all of whom wished the deletion of the first portion of the resolution condemning the possible annexation of Upper Burma, but the radicals carried the resolution.[140]

These and other differences of opinion among the Congress representatives were thrashed out in the forum provided by the Congress. In crossing out their disagreements in an orderly and efficient manner, the representatives contributed as much as did Hume and Bonnerjee in making the Congress the law-abiding and democratic assembly that it was designed to be.

After deciding to disseminate the resolutions among the various Indian political associations for discussion and action,[141] and to hold

[138] See pp. 8, 13, 14-15.
[139] See pp. 18-22, 27-33.
[140] See pp. 52-58.
[141] Resolution VIII, Murlidhar (Punjab), Dhruva (Surat), pp. 2, 5.

the next Congress in Calcutta,[142] the first Congress closed its doors. From all points of view, it had been a unique and historic occasion. Though it had not spoken for the multitudes, it had successfully represented the class that formed Cotton's "New India." It had also provided a focus of opposition to Dufferin's imperial policy. Like the Madras and the Calcutta conferences but on a more national scale, the Congress had demonstrated that educated Indians from different backgrounds and regions were capable of united organization, mature debate, and legitimate and responsible political action.

The Anglo-Indian press, with some exceptions, showed little interest either in the conferences or in the Congress. The editor of *The Madras Mail* gave some coverage to the Madras Conference; Robert Knight, editor and owner of *The Statesman* in Calcutta, and for some years past a staunch supporter of Indian political reform, reported the second Calcutta Conference; and Grattan Geary, proprietor and editor of *The Bombay Gazette,* commented upon the first Congress. The other Anglo-Indian newspapers remained silent. Of the implacable foes of educated India—Henry Curwen of *The Times of India* in Bombay, George Allen, Colonel Corry, and their editors on *The Pioneer* and *The Civil and Military Gazette,* and Saunders of *The Englishman* of Calcutta—not one of them contributed an editorial or gave space for a report about these assemblies. James Wilson, the proprietor and editor of *The Indian Daily News* of Calcutta, withheld his comments until the new year. Only the Bombay correspondent of the London *Times* took note of this further phase of Indian political development and reported to London on the Congress.[143] Forwarding the eight principal resolutions of the Congress, and giving credit where credit was due in his brief summary, the reporter acknowledged the capacity for organization of the Bombay leaders and their colleagues who had brought together such a national and representative gathering of individuals drawn from such diverse religions, castes, occupations, and political associations. He lauded the tone of loyalty to the Crown and the spirit of gratitude for British rule that had pervaded the proceedings. Quick to seize upon the weaknesses of the Congress, he provided his own explanation: the conspicuous absence of representatives from the Muslim community, arising from the Muslims' utter disdain for the Hindus and Parsis, whom they had once ruled; the preponderance of "lawyers, school-masters, and newspaper editors," who "fairly" represented "the education and intellectual power of

[142] Resolution IX, Hume, S. S. Iyer, pp. 2, 58-59.
[143] "Political Progress in India," Dec. 31, 1885, Bombay *Times,* Feb. 1, 1886, p. 13.

India" but nothing more; the total absorption in political, not social, reform, designed to increase at one jump educated India's share
in the Government; the failure to question their own ability to
govern; and their undue emphasis upon a Royal Commission of
Inquiry and the councils reform. "Though there was much crude
talk, much of that haste which only makes delay, and of that ignorance which demands premature concessions," he wrote, "there was
also much of most noble aspiration and sense of patriotism and
national unity which is a new departure in the races of the East."
What he failed to add was that this new departure would henceforth
command the earnest attention of the Viceroy.

The Viceroy, as supreme executive of a despotic government ruling and administering the millions of the Indian subcontinent,
could well afford to disregard criticisms directed at him by individual editors in different parts of the country. Not that all viceroys
in the past had done so; nor did Dufferin make a point of doing so
during his first year. But from the spring onward, with herculean
tasks before him and with little time to spare for seemingly lesser
matters, he had come to accept the advice of those around him and
had dismissed the words of the editors as mere variations on a theme,
the carping of disgruntled, opportunistic individuals who had to
make a living and who represented little more in this world than
their own opinions. He had kept an ear cocked to their murmurs
in recent months more out of concern for what might be said in
Parliament than for what the editors themselves were saying. He
could afford to do so, because, in his view, they comprised merely
a knot of individuals who were of little consequence to British rule.
But by the end of December, this picture had changed. In three
corners of India, two conferences and a Congress, totalling over 200
persons, had been held at which the editors present had been well
out-numbered by men from other walks of life. These men had not
only reiterated what the editors had long been saying, but had also
translated their words into formal criticism and demands directed
at the Viceroy and his administration. This was something to be
reckoned with. Dufferin, at least, was beginning to think so.

On the last day of the old year, he scribbled a minute to the Home
Department, in which he called attention to Lal Mohan Ghose's
candidacy for Deptford and to the Indian delegates' mission to
England.[144] As these developments constituted "a new feature in
the relations between Great Britain and the Indian Empire," he

---

[144] Minute by D., Dec. 31, 1885, DVP, R. 521, No. 23.

thought it desirable that a "careful and impartial" memorandum should be prepared for the Secretary of State concerning the status of these gentlemen and "the degree to which they may be considered as representatives of any section of the Indian people or of any Indian interest." This request was chiefly in response to the letters he had just received from Harris, Lytton, and Churchill on the appearance of the delegates at Birmingham. Such a memorandum, Dufferin believed, would prove in the case of the delegates what he had long thought about the Indian editors, namely, that they prattled empty words and made ridiculous claims for themselves. But he also added another request in his minute: "It would be as well to give an account of what passed at the meeting which was held the other day in Calcutta by certain Indian associations, together with a description of the nature of these societies, and of the extent to which they influence public opinion or command the support of any portion of the community."

It was Banerjea's conference, with its seemingly novel alliance of the "nimble-witted Babus" with the titled nobility and wealthy zemindars of Bengal, Bihar, and Oudh, which worried Dufferin. While he seems not to have heard of the Madras Conference, and while Hume's Congress for the moment escaped his notice, he did not know what this new expression of political action at Calcutta meant for British administration.

Numbers command respect in any political system; organization of numbers under a despotic government commands even more. National and regional political organizations led by intelligent, able men and ranging from the titled and the wealthy to village leaders, from Brahmin to Sudra, were of utmost novelty and signifiance for British rule in India. They represented a new element outside the existing social and political structure of a despotically controlled and administered state. They presented the prospect of a coalition of groups and classes which British rule out of self-preservation consciously or unconsciously tried to keep separate, and of political agitation which could reach and stir the uneducated, impoverished millions into such violence that the handful of British troops in India would be like so many straws in a summer's wind. They presaged the likelihood of ties with Parliamentary groups and of far-reaching Parliamentary interference in Indian administration. However much Dufferin had been able to disregard the individual Indian editors and politicians in the past, neither he nor his advisers could afford to do the same with the conferences and the Congress in the future. They represented unknown and unpredictable quantities.

At the beginning of 1885 the educated Indian leaders were still searching for their role and purpose in British Indian society. By the end of the year they had found both. "New India" stood forth unveiled. It stood in opposition to official policy.

Epilogue

At the end of 1884 and throughout 1885, Ripon, Colvin, Justice West, Harrison, and Cotton had, both in their speeches and writings, stressed their belief that during the next few years the Government of India would have a unique opportunity to come to grips with the problem of the English-educated Indians. Each pointed out that this new class was entering into a period of significant political development which would hold serious implications for British rule in India; it was thus up to the Home and Indian governments to recognize the claims of this class to a role in Indian political affairs. None dismissed this class as inconsequential or its leaders as a handful of troublesome wire-pullers; all respected them for their abilities demonstrated in the courts, in the colleges, in the press, and in their political activities. Each was fully aware that these leaders could influence both the higher and lower classes in such a way as to do great good or harm to the British Raj. Ripon and his disciples wished to link the new class to the Government of India—to make it the interpreter between the rulers and the ruled much as Macaulay had originally intended, and to provide it with sufficient opportunities and responsibilities within the Government to serve as outlets for its political energies and to achieve its political ambitions. To guide, to shape, to contain—underlying these official objectives was the hope that this class would be a source of infinite strength to British rule, if officially recognized and given a role to play in the British–Indian social and political framework. 1885 was the decisive year in which to lay the ground work for a positive, far-sighted policy toward this class.

Dufferin, however, arriving in India with Kimberley's prejudices that these English-educated Indians represented little more than an uninfluential, meddlesome minority consisting largely of "Bengali Baboos," acted upon Kimberley's instructions to shelve reforms of the grievances of the educated Indians in order to avoid additional dissatisfaction within official and nonofficial Anglo-Indian circles. Except for the Bengal Tenancy Act, he concentrated exclusively upon external and financial policy. Domestic policy, as in Lytton's viceroyalty, played second fiddle to imperial concerns, a point clearly demonstrated by Dufferin's attitude on the Indian Volunteer question. His conclusions on this subject colored his entire thinking on what Hume was trying to tell him about Indian political reform and the proposed Indian National Union. By August 1885, he, like Lytton, accepted the thesis that Indian internal security rested upon British troops and contented princely and landed classes. These groups, not the educated Bengalis or Maratha Brahmins, needed support; hence his decision in favor of the proposal for Indian officers, his silence on Indian volunteering, and his willingness to tax the educated "middle class" in order to avoid taxing the more influential landed classes. Constrained further by his dutiful acceptance of Churchill's decisions on heavy military expenditure and the Burmese war, Dufferin moved in one direction while Hume and the educated Indian leaders moved in the opposite direction. By the end of the year, they had withdrawn their confidence in him and had ceased to look to him or Government House for sympathetic interest and counsel; through their conferences and Congress they had organized to oppose his wanton sacrifice of Indian financial stability and domestic reform to imperial interests. Thus the variables at the outset of 1885 had been transformed by the end of the year, and the Government's opportunity for molding "New India," which Ripon, Colvin, Cotton, and others envisaged, had disappeared. Nor was this opportunity to recur.

Throughout 1886 the gap between Dufferin and the educated leaders widened. Persistent and caustic opposition arose—to Dufferin as a person and to the policies that his name had come to represent.[1] The themes of this opposition were varied: the annexation of Upper Burma with the costly war of pacification, censured ever more bitterly each week as the toll of lives and money rose; the amended license tax, hurried through the Supreme Legislative Council early in 1886, with no consideration given to the imposition of import duties on British goods as an alternative; once again, the sharp fall, as predicted, in the price of silver; the appointment of a Retrenchment Committee with only one Indian, Mahadev Ranade; and the costs of the Simla exodus. With Dufferin's own pronouncement at Madras in early March that Indian volunteering had not received official approval,[2] with the decision of his Council later in the year to apply the annual allocation of the famine fund toward payment of Burmese charges, and with the depreciation of the rupee, opposition rose to a peak. It was aggravated by the news from

[1] See selections from the Indian press in *V. of I.*, IV, 1886, V, 1887.
[2] Speech, *Madras Mail*, Mar. 2, 1886; Wallace, pp. 112-117.

England that Gladstone and his new cabinet refused to accept any part of the military costs of the Burmese war and that the Parliamentary inquiry into Indian affairs, owing to Churchill's hostility, had collapsed.[3] The Indian editors, especially in Madras and Bengal, led the opposition. In Bengal, the chief protagonists were Jogendra Bose, G. Mukhopadhyaya, Shishir Ghose, and S. Banerjea, with N. N. Sen setting the pace. His bitter editorials against Dufferin stimulated the entire Bengali vernacular press to action. It was Sen who, upon Dufferin's return from Burma and Madras, staged such a successful boycott[4] that the public welcome for the Viceroy passed off as "distinctly a failure" with no Bengali demonstrations.[5]

Other opposition took the form of political action. New associations sprang up[6] which supported the aims of the Congress, particularly the demands for elected representation in the councils and the right of interpellation. Ryot meetings also started in early March and continued intermittently into June throughout lower Bengal, Assam, and Bihar and subsequently in the Madras mofussil.[7] Like the meeting organized the previous year at Jhinkergatchi,[8] these meetings were organized by the Indian Association led by S. Banerjea and its mofussil associations, financed by the Maharaja of Durbhanga and other large landholders, and given strong press support by N. N. Sen, the Ghose brothers, and the more influential vernacular editors. Banerjea, impressed with the political success of the Irish Land League, sought to take the issues of councils reform, taxation, and the anti-Burmese policy to the villages.[9] On another level, the Bengal National League brought together for the first time the leaders, the wealth, and the talents of the British Indian Association, the Indian Union, and the Indian Association to oppose Dufferin's administration and support the Congress resolutions for councils reform and the Parliamentary inquiry.[10] Hume was the genius behind this political arrangement.[11] He was also the author, under the nom de plume "Union," of two pamphlets, *The*

[3] K. to D., Mar. 25 and Apr. 16 (priv.), Apr. 28, 1886, DVP, R. 517, nos. 13, 18, 21.

[4] Editorial, *Indian Mirror*, Mar. 7; also *Bengalee*, Mar. 13, 1886.

[5] *Times*, Mar. 9, 1886.

[6] See *Indian Mirror*, Feb. 9, 12, Mar. 5, 1886, *re* spread of associations in Madras, Bombay, Northwest Provinces, and Punjab.

[7] See *Indian Mirror*, Mar. 6, 21, 24, Apr. 11, *Statesmen and Friend of India*, Apr. 6, 13, 17, 20, 27, 28, May 4, 5, 7, 11, 12, 16, 21, 26; for Assam and Madras, see *Indian Mirror*, May 5, 6, 7, 8, 12, 18, 21, June 4, 1886.

[8] See above, pp. 140-141.

[9] Editorials, *Bengalee*, Jan. 30, May 15, 1886.

[10] See "Prospectus and Appeal of the Bengal National League," *Indian Mirror*, Apr. 8, also *Bengalee*, Mar. 6, Apr. 10, *Hindoo Patriot*, Apr. 12, 1886.

[11] *Tribune*, Mar. 13, 1886.

Old Man's Hope and *The Rising Tide*,[12] which were widely distributed to editors and association secretaries in India, and to the
Cobden Club and radical Liberal spokesmen on Indian policy in
England. In the former pamphlet, Hume denounced Dufferin's
lamentable failure to act on the Volunteer question, and his policy
on the Burmese war and annexation; he warned the Indian princes,
merchants, professional men, and even the ryots that their interests
were directly threatened by the Viceroy's imperial administration;
and, to secure their rights, he called for each of these classes to enter
into concerted political agitation modelled after Cobden's Anti-
Corn Law League. *The Rising Tide,* issued to mark the inauguration of the Bengal National League, consisted of editorials previously published in *The Indian Mirror* in rebuttal to an editorial in
The Pioneer advocating sterner official measures to deal with the
press and the political agitation of "Young India."[13] In the preface
Hume stated that this editorial had been inspired by the Viceroy
just as Lytton had done in his day; he referred to proposals which
had been privately discussed between Whitehall and Fort William
for checking the aspirations of educated Indians. Both the editorials
in *The Indian Mirror* and the pamphlet set off a wave of rumors
throughout the Indian press, even in the more moderate journals
of the Bombay Presidency, that Dufferin was about to invoke
Lytton's Press Act and to repress Indian political agitation at all
levels.[14] By late spring, the opposition of the educated Indian leaders and Hume to the Viceroy had grown stronger than ever with
little prospect of rapprochement unless Dufferin did a complete
volte-face.

This, however, became less likely with each passing week as
Dufferin grew increasingly angry at the criticism directed at him by
his Indian adversaries and by Hume. Already troubled by the news
of blunders in the British pacification of Upper Burma reaching the
House of Commons via *The Times* correspondent at Mandalay,
Dufferin feared that similar reports would be made about the de-
terioration of Indian finances and his growing unpopularity. Indeed, by March, *Times* telegrams in this vein were already arriving
in London,[15] and no information was more cleverly used than this
by the radical Liberals in the Commons. Furthermore, Samuel

---

[12] *The Old Man's Hope: A Tract for the Times* (Calcutta, 1886); *The Rising Tide:
Or the Progress of Political Activity in India* (Calcutta, 1886).

[13] Editorial, *Pioneer,* Mar. 31; "Political Agitation in India," and "The Progress
of Political Activity in India, I, II, III, *Indian Mirror,* Apr. 2, 7, 8, 9, 1886.

[14] Translation from Bombay "native" press enclosed in T. Bennett, editor, *Bombay
Gazette,* to Wallace, May 3, 4, 1886, DVP, R. 529, nos. 453, 459.

[15] *Times,* Mar. 9, 15, 22, 29, 1886.

Smith, a most perceptive radical Liberal, then M.P. for Liverpool, visiting Calcutta, witnessed the growing opposition to Dufferin and attended the inaugural session of the Bengal National League.[16] Meanwhile, the Indian Telegraphic Union, under arrangements made by Hume,[17] was sending to the London press news of the opposition to Dufferin instigated by his severest critics. The Viceroy felt uneasy about the prospect of radical Liberals drawing upon such sources of information—characterized by him as the "more violent and less respectable party, headed by Mr. Surendro Nath Banerjea [sic], who is connected with a cleverly-conducted but vicious paper called the *Mirror*"—for Banerjea and his colleagues, in Dufferin's opinion, were tarnishing his name in the Indian press, in the associations, and in ryot meetings.[18] Although he admitted that this censure was not politically dangerous at the moment, he disliked being so unpopular and cast in the role of a reactionary. In this vein, he wrote to Kimberley, who had returned with Gladstone as Secretary of State for India: "For a long time, even after the Income Tax Bill was passed and the Burmese war begun, I was not personally very much found fault with; but from the moment that I announced at Madras that the Government would not support the Native Volunteer movement, I have been more or less denounced as a very unworthy successor to Lord Ripon, and, various evil designs similar to those conceived by the Satanic imagination of Lytton have been attributed to me."[19] It was the misrepresentation of his policies and of the actions of his colleagues, Grant-Duff, Rivers Thompson, and others, and particularly the identification of himself with Lytton which Dufferin so disliked and for which he never forgave the Indian—particularly the Calcutta—editors. Tied as they were to the educated class and to the Congress, his antipathy toward the one, as to the other, deepened.

Since there was no hope of a rapprochement between himself and the educated Indian leaders, there was need for a new policy, Dufferin thought.[20] He wished to temper "the foul torrent of abuse" against his administration and senior officials emanating from the pens of the Indian editors "from one end of India to the other," especially in Calcutta; he also wished to nip in the bud an agitation that was, in his opinion, being skillfully developed along

[16] See *Bengalee*, Aug. 7, 1886.

[17] See above, p. 195; also Telang, Secretary, Bombay Committee, to the editor, Jan. 30, *Times of India (Overland)*, Feb. 5, 1886.

[18] D. to K., Apt. 26, 1886 (priv.), DVP, R. 517, No. 17.

[19] D. to K., May 17, 1886 (priv.), DVP, R. 517, No. 20.

[20] This discussion of Dufferin's ideas about policy is based on D. to K., Mar. 21, Apr. 26, May 17, June 11, 1886 (all priv.), DVP, R. 517, nos. 12, 17, 20, 23.

the lines of the Irish Home Rule movement, with every possibility of erupting into the same pattern of demands for repeal of the union, a land league, and a powerful nationalist bloc in Parliament, all of which in recent years had contributed so much to the dire state of Anglo-Irish relations. He had read carefully A. Mackenzie's brief memoranda on the educated class, its delegates to England, and S. Banerjea's Calcutta Conference, and he had reached the conclusion that the educated class, though very small when compared to India's millions, could make its influence felt far beyond its own circle by its monopoly over the Indian press and its knowledge of Western political methods. He was convinced that the "extremist" group of leaders was not only forming links with radical Members of Parliament in both parties, but was also enlisting the cooperation of the "moderate," wealthy, and influential Indian leaders in molding a program of Indian political rights—"the Indian Bill of Rights," as he called it. While he discerned these designs in the Indian mission to England and the Calcutta Conference, he thought they were even more evident in the formation of the Bengal National League, which bound together important "moderates" and radicals. Maharaja Jotindro Tagore, his colleagues, and others in the British Indian Association were now meeting with S. Banerjea, N. N. Sen, the Ghose brothers, and other radicals who had attended the ryot meetings in which the Maharaja of Durbhanga and other zemindars had teamed together with the "Baboo" lawyers and editors of the Indian Association and its mofussil branches. Thus, whether considering the tone of the press or the tendencies of "the associations, sub-associations . . . and caucuses," Dufferin assessed their opposition in terms of Irish nationalism, with Indian leadership passing rapidly into the hands of the radicals. "My fear," he admitted to Kimberley, "is that the moderate men have already lost a great deal of their original influence, and that they will be eventually overpowered and dominated by the more violent and extravagant section of their fellow-countrymen, who in their turn will join hands with a certain number of enthusiasts in the British Parliament." He wished the Home and Indian governments to determine as soon as possible the policy to be pursued toward the radicals.

Dufferin hoped to kill two birds with one stone—to render ineffective the leadership of the radicals in the educated Indian movement and to control their political and journalistic activities. He had no intention of using outright repression, which would only strengthen the radical threat; he preferred to combine reform with control. Referring to the ryot meetings and the Indian press, he wrote: "My own inclination would be to examine carefully and seriously the demands which are the outcome of these movements, to give quickly and with good grace whatever it may be possible or desirable to accord, to announce that these concessions must be accepted as a final settlement of the Indian system for the next ten or fifteen years, and to forbid mass meetings and incendiary speechifying."[21] Unless the radicals, in a critical situation, propagated blatantly seditious propaganda against British rule, he preferred not to interfere in or to restrict their activities until he had carried out a reform calculated to counter their misrepresentations and to influence Indian public opinion. A reform should be selected to aim at the moderate leaders, to strengthen them at the expense of the radicals both within and without the associations, and to turn them away from Parliament and back to Government House. Sifting the demands of the moderates set forth at the conferences and in the associations, he considered the Parliamentary inquiry a reasonable and timely demand, and accepted "the introduction of a large admixture of elected natives into the Legislative Councils" at the provincial, if not the Supreme, level in addition to the right of interpellation as "the most important of all." The latter would be an excellent method of "correcting misstatements and of disabusing the public mind of many of the hallucinations" then circulating in the Indian press and at the ryot meetings.

While in 1885 Dufferin had failed to recognize and to come to grips with the educated Indian leaders, he now, in 1886, was willing to do so. The far-sighted, timely reform he might have given gradually during the previous year to encourage and guide the educated Indian leaders he now intended to hand down as a defensive measure, to manipulate and counteract the radical segment, which he alleged was without question extremist in its criticism of his administration.

Dufferin's plans, however, did not work out as he had hoped. Churchill, one of the central figures of the Tory opposition in the Commons, because of his dislike of the educated Indians and "Indian reformers," opposed the Parliamentary inquiry and single-handedly blocked it during Gladstone's brief stay in office.[22] Although Kimberley, in an abrupt about-face, consulted Northbrook and Ripon on Dufferin's anxiety concerning the Indian agitation and finally recognized its seriousness, he concluded that it stemmed, not from the impact of the Irish question, but rather from educational and technological change in India itself. He warned Dufferin,

---

[21] No. 17.
[22] K. to D., May 21 and June 4, 1886 (priv.), DVP, R. 517, nos. 25, 29.

as gently as possible, against dubious Irish analogies and, above all, against allowing the criticisms of the Indian editors to sway his judgment for the sake of mere popularity. Kimberley agreed that something had to be done, yet he viewed interpellation as "a serious innovation" fraught with uncertainty, and shunned elective reform of the councils since it entailed Parliamentary legislation at a time when Gladstone's ministry faced another General Election.[23] He therefore rejected Dufferin's recommendations and instructed him to appoint an Indian government commission with members selected from all communities, including the educated Indian, to investigate the defects of the Statutory Service and make recommendations to the Home Government for improving Indian entrance into the Covenanted Service.[24]

Though Dufferin dutifully accepted Kimberley's decision and agreed that Civil Service reform would go far to compensate the disappointment of the educated leaders over the collapse of the Parliamentary inquiry,[25] he was still convinced of the wisdom of his own plans. As an alternative to interpellation, he proposed an official gazette, like the Russian *Journal de St. Petersbourg*, which would disseminate official news,[26] and accepted the advice that more official recognition and encouragement should be given to the influential, elderly, and moderate leaders, especially in Bengal and in both Hindu and Muslim communities.[27] He took great interest in the discussion between Justice Cunningham of the Bengal High Court and his Bengali friend, Protap Chunder Mazumdar, the leader of the Brahmo Samaj, concerning the formation of a new, moderate Indian party, which would receive full official endorsement and cooperation.[28] Following the General Election of August, in which Salisbury and the Conservatives were victorious, Dufferin placed before the new Secretary of State, Viscount Cross, suggestions for councils reform and gained Cross's approval for the Public Service Commission.[29] In October, the commission, headed by Sir Charles Aitchison and including some moderate leaders, both Hindu and Muslim, representing the educated Indians, was duly

[23] On the Irish Home Rule Bill.

[24] K. to D., Apr. 22, May 21, 27, June 11, (and telegram) June 11, 1886 (all priv.), DVP, R. 517, nos. 20, 25, 27, 30.

[25] D. to K., June 11, July 2, 9, 1886 (all priv.), DVP, R. 517, nos. 23, 26, 27.

[26] D. to K., May 17, 1886 (priv.), DVP, R. 517, No. 20.

[27] Bayley to Wallace, May 9, Bayley to D., June 20, 1886, DVP, R. 529, nos. 482, 705.

[28] Cunningham to Wallace, July 21, Mazumdar to Wallace, July 26, 1886, DVP, R. 530, nos. 111, 136.

[29] D. to Cross with enclosure, Aug. 13, and Sept. 3 (priv.); Cross to D., Sept. 8, 1886, DVP, R. 517, nos. 32, 39, 51.

constituted.[30] However, when N. N. Sen and other editors attacked the commission because of the small number and poor selection of Indian representatives, and when, at Poona, Dufferin, in reply, cast restraint to the winds and struck out against the irresponsibility and childishness of the Indian editors, his charge brought a welcome response from the moderate leaders in Bombay and Poona, and began what Dufferin believed was a division of opinion within educated Indian ranks.[31] This incident helped to clear the air and define the issue between himself and the educated Indian community, but it made him realize that he would have to pursue to the end his policy to isolate the radicals. By the end of 1886, however, his major concern with the radicals centered less upon the Indian leaders and more upon Hume and his activities.

During 1886, Hume played a most critical yet unfortunate role in worsening relations between Dufferin and the educated Indian leaders. The viceregal correspondence shows that there was little fact and much fiction behind the allegations in *The Indian Mirror* and *The Rising Tide* concerning Dufferin's bid to Whitehall for a repressive policy.[32] After issuing a firm denial of such intentions,[33] Dufferin and Wallace set in motion a private inquiry to track down the author of the allegations, and by late April their endeavors led them to Hume.[34] In a private interview with the Viceroy,[35] Hume admitted his authorship, and said that the statements were based on information from England, where, he claimed, there was decided opposition in the senior Liberal ranks to Dufferin's entire policy. When visiting Bright, Hume added, he had learned that Ripon's disagreement with Dufferin's policy was so strong that Ripon would refuse to serve as Secretary of State for India, if offered the post when the Liberals returned to office. Deeply wounded by this statement and angered by such prevarications and by the damage done to his name in India and England,[36] Duffer-

[30] Resolutions nos. 34/1573-98 (Oct. 4), 42/1859-98 (Nov. 4), Governor-General-in-Council, Oct. 19, Nov. 23, 1886, CRO, Pub. Let., 1886, Vol. VII, nos. 53, 60.

[31] Speech, Nov. 19, 1886, Wallace, pp. 133-137; D. to Cross, Dec. 21, 1886 (priv.), Jan. 18, 1887 (priv.), DVP, R. 518, nos. 59, 3.

[32] See above, p. 315.

[33] Wallace to the editor, *Indian Mirror*, Apr. 27, 1886, DVP, R. 529, No. 211.

[34] Wallace to Godley, Apr. 26, 1886, DVP, R. 525, No. 88.

[35] Except where otherwise noted, *The Rising Tide* incident is based on: D. to K., June 11, 1886 (priv.), DVP, R. 517, No. 23; D. to R., July 8, 1886 (strictly personal), R. 525, No. 145; D. to Geary, Oct. 27, 1888 (priv. and confid.), R. 534, No. 329a. Significantly, Hume in his letter to Ripon on his break with Dufferin never mentioned *The Rising Tide*, which sparked the bitter disagreement; see H. to R., Jan. 13, 1889, RP, BM Add. MSS 43616, No. 33.

[36] D. to Northbrook, June 23, 1886 (priv. and confid.), DVP, R. 525, No. 132.

in wrote two drafts of a letter rebuking Hume,[37] but, on the advice of Bayley and Aitchison, both of whom thought this would play into Hume's hands,[38] Dufferin sent neither letter and let Wallace deal with the matter in a tame, impersonal note.[39] Subsequently, Kimberley, Maine, and Ripon verified that Hume's information did not come from London: there had been no leak from the India Office (in terms of time, this would have been virtually impossible).[40] Ripon, mortified by what Hume had said to Dufferin, firmly denied Hume's statement.[41] In another interview with the Viceroy, Hume, embarrassed and uneasy, told Dufferin that what he had meant was that the documents had come from "outside of India"—by theosophic, supernatural transmission. When he expressed his regret over what had happened, Dufferin showed him the relevant sections of his letters of March and April to Kimberley in which he had outlined his program of reform, whereupon Hume admitted that his information had been wrong.[42] Dufferin attributed Hume's animus to the Government's inability to meet Indian wishes on the volunteer question,[43] and Wallace thought that Hume aimed at becoming "the Indian Parnell."[44]

Hume offered to make amends by writing a public letter setting forth their conversation, but Dufferin refused, saying that it would be ill-advised for the Viceroy to enter into print in such a manner.[45] Hume then wrote another pamphlet, *The Star in the East*, which he submitted to Dufferin.[46] After pointing out how the desire for popular representation had found expression, formally in the National Congress and forcibly in the Bengal National League, Hume went on to say that "something, we fear, very akin to mutual misunderstanding, distrust and dislike" had suddenly come to pass between ruler and ruled principally because Lord Dufferin and his policies were looked upon by Indian editors as inimical to Indian interests and rights. "Had India enjoyed some such modified form of representative institutions" as the educated Indian leaders were

[37] D. to H., June 18, (priv.), undated, June 1886, DVP, R. 529, No. 341 and enclosure.
[38] D. to Bayley, June 20 (strictly personal and confid.), Bayley to D., June 20; D. to Aitchison, June 21 (strictly priv. and confid.), Aitchison to D., June 22, 1886 (priv. and confid.), DVP, R. 529, nos. 343, 705, 348, 715.
[39] Wallace to H., June 26, 1886 (priv.), DVP, R. 529, No. 360.
[40] K. to D., July 9, 1886 (priv.), DVP, R. 517, No. 37.
[41] R. to D., Aug. 2, 1886 (priv.), DVP, R. 525, No. 150.
[42] See minute by D., Aug. 7, 1886 (confid.), DVP, R. 521, No. 34.
[43] D. to Maine, May 9 (priv. and confid.), D. to R., July 8, 1886 (strictly personal), DVP, R. 525, nos. 92, 145.
[44] Wallace to Mackenzie, May 11, 1886, DVP, R. 525, No. 101.
[45] H. to D., undated, June, D. to H., June 29, 1886, DVP, R. 529, nos. 740, 364.
[46] *The Star in the East: Or the Bengal National League* (Calcutta, 1886); H. to D. Aug. 7 and 13 (priv.), Aug. 27, 1886 (strictly priv.), DVP, R. 530, nos. 176, 190, 232.

then seeking, this misunderstanding would never have arisen, because the better qualities of the Viceroy himself, to say nothing of the more worthy objectives of his policies, would have been fully understood by the Indian people and their leaders. Although the pamphlet gave Dufferin more than his fair share of praise, he was careful not to give it his sanction, even though he read it and suggested changes, which Hume accepted.[47] On the tacit understanding that no one was to know the reasons for writing the pamphlet, by mid-September it had been published and distributed by Hume. Though it failed to dispel distrust of Dufferin's intentions on the part of the educated leaders, it did, momentarily, restore harmony between them and Hume on the one hand and the Viceroy on the other. Hume wrote several letters, under a pseudonym, to support Dufferin's efforts, notably on the Public Service Commission, which in October 1886 got underway to investigate reform of the Covenanted Civil Service. Dufferin did a number of favors for Hume and, had it not been for Ilbert's opposition, would have appointed him to the Public Service Commission,[48] where indeed Hume himself thought he belonged. Superficially, there ensued a respite from controversy and disagreement.

But bitterness rankled in Dufferin's breast.[49] Sometime in October 1886, in a private conversation with P. C. Mazumdar on Indian politics, Dufferin disclosed Hume's authorship of *The Star in the East,* denounced his political activities, and informed Mazumdar that as Viceroy he had no intention of being "drawn" by giving Hume's pamphlet official sanction. When the Congress met at Calcutta in late December, Dufferin made a point not to accord it any recognition.[50] Even when he invited some of its leading members to a garden party, he made it clear that he was inviting distinguished men from various parts of India who were visiting Calcutta on private business. Any disappointment at this which Hume may have felt, he refused to acknowledge,[51] but the news of Dufferin's disclosure to Mazumdar angered him deeply. Man Mohan Ghose queried Hume, upon his arrival in Calcutta for the Congress session, about the veracity of Mazumdar's information, which had

[47] D. to H., Aug. 28 (priv. and confid.), H. to D., undated, Aug. 1886, DVP, R. 530, nos. 109, 243; also H. to R., Jan. 13, 1889, RP, BM Add. MSS 43616, No. 33, p. 153.

[48] Viceroy to Peile, telegram, Nov. 3, Peile to D., Nov. 3, Home Secretary to Private Secretary of Viceroy, telegram, Nov. 3, Ilbert to D., Nov. 4 (priv.), D. to Peile, Nov. 6, 1886 (priv.), DVP, R. 530, nos. 304, 595, 596, 601, 313.

[49] Except where otherwise noted, *The Star in the East* incident is based on: H. to D., Sept. 26 (priv. and confid), D. to H., Oct. 8, 1887 (priv. and confid.), DVP, R. 532, nos. 351, 206; H. to R., Jan. 13, 1889, RP, BM Add. MSS 43616, No. 33, pp. 153-154.

[50] See H. to D., Dec. 21, 1886, DVP, R. 530, No. 797.

[51] See D. to Connemara, Jan. 2, 1888, DVP, R. 533, No. 8.

become common knowledge among all the leading editors and politicians of Bengal. Hume felt betrayed and discredited; he never got over Dufferin's "breach of confidence."

A year later, in early autumn 1887, Hume, having recovered from an illness during the summer when he had brooded over Dufferin's action, took the occasion of a protest to Dufferin over the Public Service Commission's mishandling of his own evidence to comment acidly that his letter was not to be construed as an attempt "to draw" the Viceroy.[52] When Dufferin, attributing Hume's outburst to ill health, replied that he had neither felt nor told anyone that Hume had ever tried to "draw" him,[53] Hume reproached the Viceroy for the Mazumdar incident and his lack of appreciation of the efforts and good intentions behind *The Star in the East,* which had regained for the Viceroy much public goodwill and understanding.[54] Dufferin, in an equally frank and caustic reply, wrote Hume that his chat with Mazumdar had occurred in October, after *The Star in the East* had been circulated; he angrily reviewed the reasons for its publication, the "malicious misrepresentations" in *The Rising Tide,* its encouragement of the "dishonest and malignant tactics" berating his viceroyalty of the Bengali editors, and its wide circulation in England and India. Dufferin reminded Hume that *The Star in the East* was Hume's own token offering of remorse—"an honourable, though imperfect endeavour to counteract the effects" of Hume's grievous mistake—in no wise solicited by Dufferin. The Viceroy concluded: "No reparation is ever commensurate with the original wrong. . . . Indeed the balance of the debt still remains very much the other way."[55] In a final reply, cordial but cool, Hume wrote: "I regret very much that your view is different, but I simply *cannot* alter what to my mind seem facts."[56] On this note, the correspondence between Hume and Dufferin ceased, and likewise Hume's role as intermediary between the educated Indian leaders and the Viceroy. In Hume's own words, "I never wrote to him or saw him again."[57]

This bitter contretemps had grave repercussions on official policy toward the Congress. Dufferin became disgruntled with the whole Congress movement, and refused any longer to acknowledge the claims of the moderate leaders or "advanced party" to represent Indians in their demands for reform of the councils. This was un-

---

[52] H. to D., Sept. 20, 1887 (priv.), DVP R. 532, No. 322.
[53] D. to H., Sept. 25, 1887 (priv. and confid.), DVP, R. 532, No. 177.
[54] H. to D., Sept. 26, 1887 (priv. and confid.), DVP, R. 532, No. 351.
[55] D. to H., Oct. 8, 1887 (priv. and confid.), DVP, R. 532, No. 206.
[56] H. to D., Oct. 9, 1887 (priv.), DVP, R. 532, No. 396.
[57] H. to R., Jan. 13, 1889, RP, BM Add. MSS 43616, No. 33, p. 155.

fortunate, because Cross, aware that Churchill would never yield on the Parliamentary inquiry, had privately authorized Dufferin to draft a tentative scheme for reform of the provincial councils to meet the wishes of the moderates, even though it did not concede the elective principle.[58] Dufferin had started on the project,[59] before the fracas with Hume brought a change of heart. Now, upset by the incident, he received word from J. B. Peile, then an Acting Member of his Council, advising him not to treat "the advanced party" of the Congress "as supplying the motive or occasion of anything the Government may resolve to do" in connection with reforms. In Peile's view, the Congress could never be connected with such reforms, since it did not represent the important interests of British–Indian society, "the Native Princes and Nobles, the agricultural and landed interests, the Army, Commerce," each of which would have to be represented to make any reform meaningful.[60] Dufferin admitted wholeheartedly that he had been taking an overly Congress view of the problem, and began to recast the entire project of reform along much broader lines than those conceived of by the Congress, and which would minimize any probable representation of the "advanced party."[61]

From the moment that Hume ceased to act as an intermediary between the Viceroy and the educated Indians, he directed all his efforts toward making the Congress a political success. The Third Congress held at Madras[62] marked an important turning point in the development of the organization and refuted the numerous criticisms which the Anglo-Indian editors and officials had levelled at the First and Second Congresses. Preparations began in the spring, and 604 delegates from different parts of India, duly "elected" to represent particular associations or groups, attended. Support came from ranking maharajas, rajas, and zemindars of Madras, Mysore, Bengal, and Bihar, from artisan and ryoti groups, chiefly from the Madras Mahajana Sabha, from legal and other professional groups, and from the mercantile community. Eighty-three Muslims, mostly from Bombay and Madras presidencies, and led by Tyabji, were present to refute charges of Muslim apathy

[58] Cross to D., Jan. 27, Feb. 3, 17, 25, Mar. 25, Apr. 14, 22, 1887, DVP, R. 518, nos. 4, 5, 7, 8, 12, 15, 16.

[59] D. to Cross, Mar. 20 (priv.), May 9, 1887, DVP, R. 518, nos. 13, 22; replies to D's inquiry: H. J. S. Cotton, Mar. 24, June 9, Raja P. Mookherjee, June 1, Maharaja Sir J. Tagore, June 6, A. P. MacDonnell, June 14, 1887, R. 531, nos. 481a, 760, 734, 745, 784.

[60] Peile to D., Oct. 2, 1887, DVP, R. 532, No. 369.

[61] D. to Peile, Oct. 5, 1887 (priv.), DVP. R. 532, No. 198; D. to Cross, Feb. 26, 1888 (priv.), R. 518, No. 9.

[62] This account is based on *I.N.C. Report 1887*, especially pp. 6, 10-13, 57, Appendixes II, III.

toward the Congress. Sir Madhava Rao spoke for the elderly "moderates," Eardley Norton for the liberal Anglo-Indians, and W. Gantz for the Eurasians. For the first time, the Congress presented the spectacle of a growing force which had the potential of drawing together all-India interests, classes, and religions.

The sponsors also demonstrated their ability to raise funds not only from the wealthy upper classes, but also from shopkeepers, artisans, and ryots. Much credit for this rested with the Madras Sabha which stimulated interest in Indian grievances and the Congress at the town and village level. V. Chariar's concise leaflet, *The Tamil Congress Catechism*, explaining in simple language the aims of the Congress, its demand for representative councils, and the need for organizing affiliates in town and village and for contributing funds to the Congress, was distributed in a Tamil edition numbering 30,000 throughout southern India and British Burma, and raised Rs. 5,000 (or one-sixth of the costs of the Third Congress) from 8,000 persons, lower-middle class and ryots. Hume wrote a pamphlet of similar purport, based on an actual conversation and entitled *A Conversation Between Moulvi Farid-ud-Din, M.A., B.L. and Rambaksh, One of the Mukkudams of Kambakhtpur,* in which an educated Indian explained to an intelligent village headman the need for representative, as opposed to despotic, government, and the aim of the Congress to achieve this goal. Written in late 1886 and approved by the maharaja of Durbhanga, W. C. Bonnerjee, Man Mohan Ghose, Justice Romesh Mitter, and various persons in England, Hume submitted the pamphlet to Dufferin, and, when he received no official objection by the time the Congress met, he distributed 20,000 copies in Hindi and Urdu in northern India.[63]

The proceedings, speeches, and resolutions of the Madras Congress expressed loyalty to the Crown, but were critical of Dufferin's administration, in a constructive spirit. Hume's report, distributed widely in the spring of 1888, with some 10,000 copies going to England, was moderate in tone and just and fair to the Viceroy, except for one sour note when he blamed "the chief features of Lord Dufferin's administration," the resumption of an annexationist policy and the resultant increased taxation, for the poverty decimating the lower classes. Whatever bitterness Hume may have felt toward Dufferin did not find expression in his Congress activities; Hume buried himself in his work and helped to bring the Congress to a stage which confounded its critics.

Even Dufferin, who had seen fit to dismiss the Calcutta Congress of 1886 as "very childish . . . rather of an Eton or Harrow Debating

[63] H. to R., Jan. 13, 1889, RP, BM Add. MSS 43616, No. 33, p. 162.

Society than even of the Oxford or Cambridge Union,"[64] took the session of 1887 far more seriously than he was willing to admit. He was genuinely disturbed by Sir Madhava Rao's participation and attempted to recover his allegiance by offering him a seat in the Supreme Legislative Council[65]—an offer which Rao politely declined.[66] Dufferin was deeply troubled by its financial support from the princely and landed classes, especially from the Maharaja of Mysore, and personally warned the Maharaja's Diwan against similar action in the future.[67] The only bright spots for Dufferin were the continued abstention of Muslim leaders in Bengal and the Northwest Provinces and Lord Connemara's care not to extend any official recognition to the Congress.[68] Dufferin realized that the Congress had taken on new dimensions which could no longer be treated lightly. The stage was set for the final act of the drama and the emergence of an official policy toward the Congress. Developments in England as well as in India precipitated matters.

At the outset of 1888, Lord Cross had become rattled by the radical Liberal motions on Indian questions being tabled in the Commons, which, he feared, might provoke a sudden, embarrassing defeat for the government, with its slim majority. Tracing the source of the motions to the Indian "radicals," he wrote Dufferin: "I must, I am afraid, trouble you for your opinions as to the question of these congresses or conferences, or whatever they call themselves. Will they grow or lessen? What weight is to be attached to their deliberations? Is it wise to take action in any way?"[69] For the first time, questions of policy had been raised. Dufferin, who had just increased the salt duty to offset the heavy charges for the Burmese pacification and the sharp depreciation of the rupee,[70] and who had dispatched a British–Indian military force to Sikkim to counter an alleged Tibetan incursion, was being sharply criticized in the Bengali press, led by N. N. Sen and his colleagues. When it was officially announced that Dufferin's viceroyalty would terminate at year's end and arrangements were thereupon made for a farewell demonstration before his departure for Simla, Sen began a fierce, personal agitation against Dufferin as a most unworthy successor to Ripon

---

[64] D. to Cross, Jan. 4, 1887, DVP, R. 518, No. 1.

[65] D. to Rao, Dec. 26, 1887, DVP, R. 532, No. 367.

[66] Rao to D., Jan. 4, 1888, DVP, R. 532, No. 19.

[67] See enclosure, Prendergast to W. J. Cunningham, Jan. 11, 1888, DVP, R. 532, No. 41a; Wallace to Cunningham, Jan. 26, 1888, R. 533, No. 74.

[68] See D. to Connemara, Jan. 2, 1888, DVP, R. 533, No. 8.

[69] Cross to D., Feb. 10, 17, 1888, DVP, R. 518, nos. 7, 8.

[70] Burmese charges of $1,700,000 after British Burma revenues had been applied; depreciation of rupee from 1s. 7d. in 1885 to 1s. 4d. in 1888.

and, assisted by the Ghose brothers, fomented a partially disruptive boycott of the farewell, news of which was telegraphed to *The Pall Mall Gazette* and other papers in London.[71] Only the attendance of some important "moderates" and the Muslim leaders of Bengal and Bihar saved the occasion from being a starkly Anglo-Indian affair; for Dufferin, who had witnessed the incredible farewell to Ripon and who had hankered after similar popular honors, it was a bitter disappointment.[72] Unfortunately and most unfairly, the ambitious, self-seeking Robert Knight, then editor and owner of *The Statesman and Friend of India,* who espoused the educated Indian cause but who disliked Hume, laid the blame on Hume.[73] But it was Colvin, then Lieutenant-Governor of the Northwest Provinces and Oudh, who cast Dufferin's bitterness against Hume and the Bengali editors into bold relief and directed it against the entire Congress movement just when Cross's questions on the Congress reached Dufferin.

Word of Hume's activities and samples of his speeches and writings began to reach Colvin during April. In a speech at Jubbulpore, Hume had advocated for the Central Provinces a central organization with subcommittees like the Madras Sabha to carry the Congress gospel to the people.[74] At Allahabad, he called for "quiet teachings and preachings" on Indian rights and duties under beneficent British rule and the need for organization in the Northwest Provinces and Oudh before the Congress met at Allahabad at year's end.[75] By late April, copies of Hume's report of the Third Congress, which noted that the growing rapport between the English-educated and less educated Indians was adding thousands of supporters to the Congress annually, and to which were appended copies of Chariar's *Catechism* and Hume's *Conversation,* were circulating in the Northwest Provinces. All this activity led Colvin to warn Dufferin that such Western political gimmicks unleashed by an Englishman on the loose were wholly inadvisable in the upper provinces of India with their volatile social and religious mixture.[76] He found the pamphlets disloyal in certain parts and so written as to create in even educated minds distrust of, and animosity toward, British rule. He looked ahead apprehensively to the Allahabad Con-

[71] See D. to Cross, Feb. 20, Mar. 19, 26, 1888, DVP, R. 518, nos. 8, 12, 13.

[72] D. to Connemara, Mar. 27, 1888, DVP, R. 533, No. 306.

[73] Knight to Wallace, Mar. 16, 1888, DVP, R. 533, No. 349.

[74] Hume's speech, *Morning Post,* Apr. 23, enclosed in Colvin to Dufferin, Apr. 25, 1888, DVP, R. 533, No. 483.

[75] *A Speech on the Indian National Congress: Its Origins, Aims and Objects, Delivered at Allahabad, 30 April 1888* (Calcutta [1888]).

[76] Colvin to D., Apr. 27, 1888, DVP, R. 533, No. 496.

gress; he feared clashes between Muslim and Hindu groups and suggested sound police surveillance of Congress activities. He was convinced that the Muslim leaders, looking upon the Congress as synonymous with Hindu supremacy, and the taluqhdars of Oudh, seeing it as a threat to landed interests, were preparing stern opposition to the Congress.[77] Colvin's view was not unreasonable.

Sir Syed Ahmad Khan, the elderly founder of Aligarh College who had long been uneasy at the inability of Muslims on the one hand, and the ability of Hindus, especially Bengalis, on the other, to adapt themselves to English education and public service, regarded the Congress from its inception as a tool for Bengali hegemony.[78] Ably assisted by his young Cambridge-educated, Islamophile principal, Theodore Beck, Sir Syed staged the Mohammedan Educational Conferences of 1886 and 1887, which drew together all interests in the upper provinces and at which Sir Syed declared himself opposed to Muslim participation in the Congress or to Muslim support for any changes in the councils unless communal interests were duly recognized.[79] Early in 1888, Beck contributed articles to *The Pioneer* defending Muslim interests against the rising tide of the Congress,[80] and urging formation of a Muslim organization. A formal call for such an organization was issued in March at Meerut by Sir Syed.[81] The taluqhdars, supporting Sir Syed's anti-Congress stand in letters to *The Pioneer*,[82] were also on the move. "They are powerful, conservative, landed proprietors, and they don't like 'Young India,'" concluded Colvin.[83]

With a conflagration threatening, Colvin urged Dufferin to consider checking the incendiary pamphleteering and speechifying in towns and villages without in any way interfering with the annual Congress. When Dufferin replied that such action was unnecessary in light of the growing opposition to the Congress of the "conservative and non-Hindu minorities" and that repression of any sort should be postponed until moderate Indian leaders had been given a greater voice in their own affairs through possible council re-

[77] Colvin to D., May 24, 1888, DVP, R. 533, No. 612.

[78] J. M. S. Baljon, *The Reforms and Religious Ideas of Sir Sayyid Ahmad Khan* (Leiden, 1949); G. F. I. Graham, *The Life and Work of Syed Ahmed Khan* (Edinburgh, 1885); W. C. Smith, *Modern Islam in India* (Lahore, 1943); A. K. Sherwani, "The Political Thought of Sir Syed Ahmad Khan," *Islamic Culture*, 18 (July 1944), 236-253.

[79] Sherwani, p. 249.

[80] Reprinted, pp. 93-127, in *Essays on Indian Topics* (Allahabad, 1888).

[81] Mar. 16, 1888, Sherwani, pp. 250-251.

[82] Letters from Rana Shankar Buksh and T. Hussein to editor, *Pioneer*, Apr. 23, 1888.

[83] See n. 77 above.

forms,[84] Colvin exhorted him to reconsider and pointed out that, since the Congress leaders had skilfully created the impression that the Government sanctioned the new movement, and by this adroit move had virtually paralyzed the formation of any strong opposition, official silence, far from encouraging, was rather preventing opposition to the Congress. Colvin predicted that, since the educated Indian leaders had fostered so great popular expectations for councils reform, all groups would conclude that organized agitation against the Government was the most productive course.[85] While George Chesney, the Military Member of Council, somewhat astounded by Colvin's arch-conservative attitude, concurred with Dufferin that councils reform must precede action to put the Congress quietly into limbo and to restrict the Indian press,[86] he agreed with Colvin that something be done immediately lest the Congress agitation arouse in the Indian officer and cadre ranks of the army a discontent which might erupt into another 1857.[87]

Dufferin realized the time had come to act. He answered Cross's questions on policy by forwarding Chesney's and Colvin's minutes,[88] and requested Cross's permission to make formal proposals for reform of the provincial councils, which would provide "a legitimate opportunity of getting rid of the Congress as well as restricting the abuses of the Native Press." He thought it "a great pity that these Congresses should have only occupied themselves with political questions . . . instead of the great social and economic problems which are now pressing for solution in India."[89] He had forgotten the gist of his remarks to Hume in the spring of 1885 on the scheme of the Indian National Union.[90] Whereas, in 1886, he had looked to reform coupled with repression to deal with what he loosely called the Indian "radicals," now, in the summer of 1888, smarting under his treatment by Hume and the "Bengali Babus" and pressed by influential advisers, he was advocating a similar policy to do away with the Congress.

He did not have long to wait for the green light to proceed. Chesney's and Colvin's minutes made a favorable impression on Cross,[91] and the political climate in Parliament precipitated mat-

[84] D. to Colvin, June 6, 1888 (priv.), DVP, R. 533, No. 488.
[85] Colvin to D., June 10, 1888, DVP, R. 533, No. 668.
[86] Chesney to D., July 1, 1888 (priv.), DVP, R. 533, No. 1.
[87] Confidential minute by Chesney, June 22, 1888, enclosed in Chesney to Temple, Oct. 29, 1888 (confid.), Temple MSS, CRO, Eur. F. 86, Sec. III, Box 5, No. 263.
[88] D. to Cross, June 29, 1888 (priv.), DVP, R. 518, No. 30.
[89] D. to Cross, Aug. 17, 1888 (priv.), DVP, R. 518, No. 38.
[90] See above, pp. 117-118.
[91] Cross to D., July 27, 1888, DVP, R. 518, No. 31.

ters. In early August in debates in the Commons on the Indian Budget Statement, Charles Bradlaugh, a leading radical Liberal who had begun to take a serious interest in Indian affairs, attacked the Home Government's fiscal and frontier policies in India in a manner which corresponded closely with the views of the Indian Congress. This, coupled with the news that Bradlaugh and other radical M.P.s intended to visit India during 1889, prompted Cross to urge Dufferin to consider action on Indian grievances which "really exist and ought to be removed."[92] Dufferin seized the opportunity to press Cross for a final decision on councils reform.[93] At the same time, he showed the direction toward which his policy was tending by heeding Mackenzie's warning on the lines developing between the Congress and the subordinate civil servants, and by instructing the local governments to tolerate no official support of, or participation in, political associations of any kind.[94]

During August and September, opposition to the Congress in the Northwest Provinces intensified with the formation of the United Indian Patriotic Association under the auspices of Sir Syed Ahmad Khan and Beck.[95] *The Pioneer, The Civil and Military Gazette,* and many noble and influential Muslims and taluqhdars gave it their support, and a propaganda campaign was launched. A collection of essays,[96] ostensibly written by noted members of the association but with a preface by Beck, charged the Congress with sedition and warned that Hume was fomenting another Mutiny. These essays were followed by a pamphlet by the Raja of Bhinga,[97] and by the collected *Speeches by Sir Syed Ahmed* against the Congress, both of which received wide distribution. This sudden buildup represented just the sort of counteragitation which Hume, Tyabji, Sayani, Telang, and other Congress leaders, both Hindu and Muslim, wished to avoid. When rumors reached Hume that official support, meaning Sir Auckland Colvin's, lay behind the movement, Hume wrote frankly asking Colvin to put a stop to the rumors by coming out into the open.[98] Hume genuinely wished to

[92] Cross to D., Aug. 10, 16, Sept. 11, 1888, DVP, R. 518, nos. 33, 34, 39.
[93] D. to Cross, Aug. 30, 1888 (priv.), DVP, R. 518, No. 40.
[94] Mackenzie to Wallace, Sept. 5, 1888, DVP, R. 533, No. 219; D. to Cross, Sept. 24, 1888 (priv.), R. 518, No. 43.
[95] For details, see editorials in *Pioneer* and the appendix of pamphlet, n. 96 below.
[96] *Showing the Seditious Character of the Indian National Congress and the Opinions Held by Eminent Natives of India Who Are Opposed to the Movement* (Allahabad, 1888). Beck included his earlier articles in *Pioneer*, see n. 80 above.
[97] *Democracy Not Suited to India* (Allahabad, 1888), which Colvin credited to Arthur Strachey, an Allahabad barrister, see Colvin to D., Aug. 27, 1888, DVP, R. 533, No. 186.
[98] H. to Colvin, Sept. 19, 1888, enclosed in D. to Cross, Cross MSS, CRO, Eur. E. 243/25/Let. Bk. 5, No. 116.

avoid the dangers of communalism and hoped that Colvin would declare either his neutrality or his friendship for the Congress in its struggle with the Patriotic Association.

Colvin, following the very advice he had given Dufferin, took the occasion, in his reply to Hume, to make a public declaration of opposition to the Congress.[99] He stated straightforwardly that he had approved of the Congress at the time of its first two meetings, but his opinion had changed after the Madras meeting in 1887, when it turned to forceful agitation and began to split India into two hostile camps. Its pamphlets, tinged with disloyalty, were hideous caricatures of British rule. The Congress represented just "a very small and peculiar class," created by British rule, with aspirations representative only of itself; the Muslim opposition, of which he did not necessarily approve, proved the hollowness of the Congress's claim to represent all India. It could neither claim nor dictate councils reform; it offered no solution for the problems of educated Indians. "New India" would do better to drop the organization, to take its rightful place in British–Indian society, and to enter "one of the many mansions" provided by British rule. This was still the policy he had advocated, under Ripon's inspiration, in 1884 and 1885.

Hume, disappointed, yet appreciative of this forthright opposition, produced a lengthy rebuttal.[100] The Congress had not split India, because active opposition to the Congress was nonexistent. Although Sir Syed, the Maharaja of Benares, Raja Siva Prasad, the Raja of Bhinga, and the Anglo-Indian editors might lead official circles to think that a Muslim opposition to the Congress existed, they were merely a small clique. The pamphlets were neither disloyal nor exaggerated, for the ills and injustices of India still remained after thirty years under the Crown. The Congress did represent a political force, for it reached beyond the English-educated class to some ten million souls in the lower class, with no English education, yet intelligent and interested in political reform. The Congress would provide an excellent crosssection for any representation in reformed, elected councils. In spite of Hume's efforts, the cards lay heavily stacked for Colvin. His official statement against the Congress pointed out the existence of the Muslim opposition and classified the English-educated class as only a minor spoke in the wheel of Indian society.

[99] Colvin to H., Oct. 8, 1888, enclosed in D. to Cross, Eur. E. 243/25/Let. Bk. 5, No. 116.

[100] H. to Colvin, Oct. 30, 1888, *Audi Alteram Partem: Being Two Letters on Certain Aspects of the Indian National Congress Movement* (Simla [1888]), pp. 21-69.

While Colvin and Hume locked horns, Dufferin was shaping his policy toward the Congress.[101] Upon receiving Cross's authorization, Dufferin constituted a committee, composed of Westland, Chesney, Aitchison, and MacDonnell as secretary, which speedily prepared a scheme for reform of the provincial councils, and he confided to Colvin that once the scheme was officially accepted, he would act against the Indian press and, particularly, the Congress.[102] "We cannot allow the Congress to continue its existence." True, it had no roots in the influential classes and indeed was provoking their wrath. True, its agitations were "factitious." Nevertheless, like Colvin, Dufferin feared that, if the Congress's radical tactics and "seditious pamphlets" continued to spread among the high-spirited, martial tribes of the Northwest Provinces and the Punjab, there would be serious trouble. By mid-October 1888, the councils proposals were submitted privately to Cross.[103] The existing provincial councils, as constituted by Wood's Act of 1861, were to be made bicameral, composed partly of elected members, with property and income qualifications, and partly of nominated members, and were to have rights of interpellation and budgetary debate; communal representation, whether Muslim, Parsi, or Christian, as well as European planter and commercial interest, was to be recognized and safeguarded by nomination; the Government was to be assured of a majority in each division in order to carry any critical vote. This modest reply to the demand of the Congress, Chesney, who was instrumental in drafting the proposals, considered not strong enough to placate the Congress, and he feared that, though Dufferin fully recognized the dangers of the Congress, he might waver and fail to act, because of Cross's apprehensions of Parliamentary repercussions.[104] Chesney was in for a surprise.

Soon after the dispatch of the proposals to Cross, word reached Dufferin of a virulent campaign against him personally,[105] just begun in the Bengali press and spreading to other sectors of the Indian press. He was charged with fostering support for the Muslim opposition in the Northwest Provinces in an attempt to create Hindu–Muslim antagonism which would check the Congress. Two of the letters between Hume and Colvin, published at this time in pam-

---

[101] D. to Cross, Oct. 8, 1888 (priv.), DVP, R. 518, No. 45.

[102] D. to Colvin, Oct. 9, 1888 (priv. and confid.), DVP, R. 534, No. 263.

[103] Report on the Subject of Provincial Councils, enclosed in D. to Cross, Oct. 20, 1888 (priv.), DVP. R. 518, No. 47. For minute by D. and committee papers, see Dispatch of Governor-General-in-Council, Nov. 6, 1888, CRO, Pub. Let., 1888, Vol. IX.

[104] See n. 87 above.

[105] D. to Cross, Oct. 29, 1888 (priv.), DVP, R. 518, No. 48.

phlet form,[106] gave weight to the charge. Dufferin, recently honored
by the Queen with a marquisate, was in no mood for slurs and was
deeply angered by the accusation. He pointed the guilty finger at
Sen, whose editorials in *The Indian Mirror* had extensively ex-
ploited the theme. Recalling the incident of *The Rising Tide*[107]
and Hume's disappointments at failing to obtain official recognition
for the Congress, Dufferin also blamed Hume.[108] Thus, while Dufferin was unjustly accused of playing communal politics—a charge
which both his speeches and activities convincingly refute—he was
unfairly arraigning Hume on charges also nonexistent. When, at
this moment, copies of Colvin's correspondence with Hume reached
the Viceroy, he was so pleased with Colvin's public statement that
he at once sent copies to Cross and urged Colvin to have extra copies
printed for distribution in Parliament. "The only remarks I have
to make," Dufferin wrote Colvin, "is that you have treated that silly
imposter with too great courtesy and indulgence."[109] Indeed, Colvin's handling of Hume and the Congress gave Dufferin the answer
on how to deal with the Congress.

With time running out on his viceroyalty and with little chance
of securing the approval of the India Office and the cabinet for reform of the councils before his departure, Dufferin decided to act
on his own. Following Colvin's lead, he would declare the official
view on the Congress in a public statement. In Calcutta, the attacks
in the Bengali press had reached such a white heat that even Hume,
to the detriment of his own reputation, in a letter to *The Indian
Mirror,* asked the editor to give Dufferin his due and moderate the
severity of the attack.[110] Hume's action failed to move Dufferin,
who thought this "extraordinary circumstance" was dictated by
fear that he would take the opportunity of a farewell speech "to
cut up the silly programme to which he [Hume] has been idiot
enough to commit himself in a letter addressed to Sir Auckland
Colvin."[111] After consultation with both Bayley and Colvin, Dufferin decided to speak out against the Congress at the St. Andrew's
Day dinner in Calcutta.[112]

Dufferin's long, discursive speech before the crowded dinner
ranged from the problem of the educated Indian with all its rami-

[106] *Audi Alteram Partem;* it does not contain Hume's first letter of Sept. 19 to Colvin,
see n. 98 above.
[107] See above, pp. 315, 320 ff.
[108] D. to Geary, Oct. 27, 1888 (priv. and confid.), DVP, R. 534, No. 329a.
[109] D. to Colvin, Oct. 28, 1888 (priv.), DVP, R. 534, No. 342; also n. 105 above.
[110] Nov. 11, 1888, in DVP, R. 534, No. 522.
[111] D. to Cross, Nov. 18, 1888 (priv.), DVP, R. 518, No. 51.
[112] D. to Bayley, D. to Colvin, Nov. 22 (both secret and confid.), Colvin to D., Nov. 26,
1888, DVP, R. 534, nos. 454, 457, 590.

fications to the work of the Congress.[113] His remarks partly echoed his own conclusions, sent earlier to Cross, but largely reflected the view of Colvin. Since the English-educated class comprised "only a very few thousands" out of a population of "200 millions," he asked "how any reasonable man could imagine that the British Government would be content to allow this microscopic minority to control their administration of that majestic and multiform empire for whose safety and welfare they are responsible in the eyes of God and before the face of civilization?" Willing to admit that the new class was growing, he pointed out that it was "a groundless contention that it represents the people of India." Without mentioning the Muslim and taluqhdari opposition, he noted that "large sections of the community are already becoming alarmed at such self-constituted bodies interposing between themselves and the august impartiality of English rule." There could be "no real or effective representation of the people" of India, given their enormous numbers and varied nationalities. At this point he mentioned the Congress and expressed his disappointment that it had chosen mistakably to pursue political reform, in its own interest, rather than social reform—the one area, touching the welfare of the millions, where Government could never tread. That the Congress had turned to pamphleteering among the ignorant, credulous thousands with the "manifest aim to excite the hatred of the people against the public servants of the Crown in this country" was "still a greater matter of regret." Cheers greeted his remark on "the microscopic minority," and sustained applause his comment on the Congress; but the loudest applause was reserved for his handling of Hume, when he commented slightingly: "Nor is the silly threat of one of the chief officers—the principal secretary, I believe—of the Congress, that he and his Congress friends hold in their hands the keys not only of a popular insurrection but of a military revolt, calculated to restore our confidence in their discretion. . . ." Unrepresentative, misguided, and disloyal—such was Dufferin's image of the Congress, its leaders, and its principal mentor.

Having demolished the Congress, Dufferin skillfully returned to the essential purpose of his remarks. "I do not wish to imply that I view with anything but favour and sympathy the desire of the educated classes of India to be more largely associated with us in the conduct of the affairs of their country." Although he said nothing on the scheme for reform of the provincial councils, he read from part of his Jubilee speech in 1887, where he had stated his wish to reform Wood's original plan, adding that he hoped that "the

[113] Nov. 30, 1888, Wallace, pp. 229-248.

legitimate and reasonable aspirations of the responsible heads of native society, whether Hindu or Mahomedan," would in due time receive legitimate satisfaction. During his tour of duty, he had come to gauge and admire the good sense, practical wisdom, and experience of "the leading men of India, both among the great nobles . . . and amongst the leisured and professional classes," and it was such educated, intelligent opinion as theirs that the Government now needed increasingly to take into consideration and which he had advised the Home Government to recognize. Ignoring the Congress and its claim to represent educated India, Dufferin had beckoned to the enlightened nobility and the elderly, wealthy "moderates" of the educated class to accept the boons which he sought to bestow on India. "New India" was to be kept waiting in the wings.

The speech made a deep impression. Anglo-Indian opponents of the Congress regarded it as a victory, while Congress supporters accepted it as a stunning setback.[114] Only the few who knew his intentions in advance were not surprised at his frankness. Dufferin told Cross that he "thought it would clear the atmosphere and render Lansdowne's position easier and pleasanter," but his references to "the 'bastard' disloyalty" of Sen and *The Indian Mirror* and to "the insubordinate proceedings of the Congress-Wallahs, such as Mr. Hume . . ." showed that the events of 1885 and their aftermath still rankled.[115] In his final hour Dufferin struck down those who had struck at him. Hume might attempt to write off Dufferin as "an ass, and a touchy ass to boot" and to dismiss the speech as inconsequential,[116] but he and the members of the Congress knew, when they met at Allahabad not long after Dufferin's departure, that "New India" and the Congress had been cast adrift. They were "misunderstood, misrepresented, and maligned."[117]

The years intervening between the viceroyalties of Dufferin and Curzon saw virtually no change in the pattern of relations between Government House and the Congress movement which Dufferin had established—a studied, official aloofness, a ban on official participation, yet a watchful, covert eye on all the proceedings through the Intelligence Department which Dufferin had set up at Cross's suggestion. Both Lansdowne and Elgin showed a fleeting interest in the annual sessions, especially when the resolutions were brought

[114] See letters to D. from Colvin, Dec. 3, G. P. Evans, Dec. 7, Bayley, Dec. 8, J. B. Lyall, Dec. 11, 1888, DVP, R. 534, nos. 613, 641, 648, 669.

[115] D. to Cross, Dec. 3, 1888 (priv.), DVP, R. 518, No. 52.

[116] H. to R., Jan. 13, 1889, RP, BM Add. MSS 43616, No. 33, pp. 159-160.

[117] See Telang's speech at Allahabad Congress and Hume's report, *I.N.C. Report 1888*, pp. 15-20, 1.

before them; and both became more alert whenever Parliament was involved in a particular issue. Beyond this, they did not venture. Under "the official umbrella," like Dufferin, they found no room for the Congress.

Dufferin's scheme to reform the councils was deferred, largely as a result of the blow struck in his own St. Andrew's Day speech against Indian reform, or so it seemed to Cross and Salisbury, and to the Indian editors, all of whom were left with the impression that Dufferin considered reform of the councils unsuitable, under existing circumstances, to India. Salisbury, always hypersensitive to any reform smacking of Home Rule, took Dufferin at his word and opposed the proposals as too advanced and politically dangerous. Cross followed suit, and the reforms were shelved throughout most of Lord Lansdowne's viceroyalty, even though Lansdowne was aware of their timeliness and urged the India Office to carry them out.[118] Finally, Bradlaugh's threat in 1890 to introduce a bill reforming the Indian councils along the lines advocated by the Congress compelled Cross and Salisbury to move, but Salisbury delayed until potential Liberal opposition had been reduced and the Parnellite party had entered its decline. In 1892, not long before Lansdowne left India, an Amendment to the Indian Councils Act of 1861 was successfully carried in both Houses of Parliament which gave effect to most of Dufferin's original scheme, except for the "elective principle" which Salisbury had carefully deleted.

Dufferin's answer to the problem of the educated Indian—his bid to the "moderates" and his blow to the Congress—arrived four years too late. By then, the problem had changed and had developed new variables within the educated class, to say nothing of the Congress itself. The difficulties of outlets and occupations for the educated elite had become more severe than in 1885. The so-called Indian "radicals" of Dufferin's day had become "moderates" by Elgin's time. A new wave of leaders had emerged—Bal Gangadhar Tilak, Lala Lajpat Rai, and the Bengali extremists—and these and other men were destined to give to the terms "radical" and "extremist" their true meaning for the Congress and for the Government of India.

These and other developments could not have been foreseen in the halcyon days of the 1880s. But their roots were struck firmly in 1885 and the years that immediately followed. During those years, the interplay between the leading actors with their ambitions, prej-

---

[118] Dufferin's timetable had been to reform the councils and then suppress the Congress and stifle the press, but, without reforms, there was no basis for the "suppression" of the Congress.

udices, and misunderstandings on the one hand, and the circumstances of uncertainty, change, and complexity on the other, had
led to the emergence of "New India" and its Congress and to an
unresolved official policy toward these novel forces.

Bibliography

ORIGINAL SOURCES

PRIVATE PAPERS

I. INDIA OFFICE LIBRARY, COMMONWEALTH RELATIONS OFFICE.

A. *Papers of the Marquis of Dufferin and Ava,* Viceroy and Governor-General of India, Dec. 1884 to Dec. 1888. These papers were microfilmed by permission of the Marchioness of Dufferin and made available at the India Office Library in 1958. The following microfilm reels contain the pertinent volumes of printed correspondence used in this study.

Reel 516, Vol. 26: Correspondence with the Queen, 1884-1888.

Reel 517, Vol. 19: Correspondence from the Secretary of State for India, Dec. 1884 to Dec. 1886; and to the Secretary of State, Dec. 1884 to Oct. 25, 1886.

Reel 518, Vol. 19: Correspondence to the Secretary of State, Oct. 25 to Dec. 1886; Vol. 20: Correspondence to and from the Secretary of State, Jan. to Dec. 1887; Vol. 21: Correspondence to and from the Secretary of State, Jan. to Dec. 1888.

Reel 519, Vol. 22: Telegraphic Correspondence to and from the Secretary of State, Dec. 1884 to Mar. 1885; Vol. 25; Telegraphic Correspondence to and from the Secretary of State, Mar. 1885 to June 1886. The telegrams are in chronological order without a break, despite the gap in the numbers of the two volumes. A gap does occur in the correspondence June to Aug. 1886, when there was a change in the Home Government. Thereafter for telegraphic correspondence, one must refer to the Cross Papers at the India Office Library or to the Dufferin and Ava Papers, Public Record Office, Northern Ireland, listed below.

Reel 521, Vol. 27: Notes and Minutes by the Viceroy, 1884-1888.

Reel 525, Vol. 36: Correspondence to and from Persons in England, Nov. 1884 to Dec. 1885; Vol. 37: Jan. to Dec. 1886.

Reel 526, Vol. 38: Correspondence to and from Persons in England, Jan. to Dec. 1887; Vol. 39: Jan. to Apr. 1888.

Reel 527, Vol. 39: Correspondence to and from Persons in England, Apr. to Dec. 1885.

Reel 528, Vols. 47, 48 (part): Correspondence to and from Persons in India, Dec. 1884 to Dec. 4, 1885; Reel 529, Vols. 48 (part), 49; Dec. 5, 1885 to June 1886; Reel 530, Vols. 50, 51 (part): July 1886 to Jan. 13, 1887; Reel 531, Vol. 51 (part): Jan. 14, 1887, to June 30, 1887; Reel 532, Vols. 52, 53 (part): July

1887 to Feb. 19, 1888; Reel 533, Vols. 53 (part), 54 (part): Feb. 19, 1887, to Oct. 13, 1888; Reel 534, Vol. 54: Oct. 14 to Dec. 1888.

B. *Papers of Lord Cross,* Secretary of State for India, Aug. 4, 1886, to Aug. 14, 1892, MSS Eur. E. 243.

Through the endeavors of the Librarian of the India Office (Mr. Stanley C. Sutton) and his senior assistant, the present Lord Cross very kindly made available these papers. Though the Dufferin–Cross correspondence is identical in these and the Dufferin papers, the Cross papers contain numerous enclosures sent by Dufferin, not in the Dufferin papers, and are invaluable for the correspondence with the governors of Madras and Bombay.

Vol. 17, Letter Book I: Letters to the Viceroy and the Governors of Madras and Bombay, Aug. 6, 1886, to Dec. 29, 1887; Vol. 18, Letter Book II. Jan. 5 to Dec. 21, 1888.

Vol. 19, Letter Book III: Letters to the Viceroy (Lansdowne) and the Governors of Bombay and Madras, Nov. 22, 1888, to Oct. 9, 1890; Vol. 20, Letter Book IV: Oct. 16, 1890, to Aug. 12, 1892.

Vol. 21, I: Letters from the Earl of Dufferin, Aug. 6 to Dec. 21, 1886; Vol. 22, II: Jan. 4 to June 24, 1887; Vol. 23, III: July 1 to Dec. 27, 1887; Vol. 24, IV: Jan. 2 to June 29, 1888; Vol. 25, V: July 6 to Nov. 4, 1888.

Vol. 26, I: Letters from the Marquis of Lansdowne, Dec. 11, 1888, to June 28, 1889; Vol. 27, II: July 5 to Dec. 31, 1889; Vol. 28, III: Jan. 7 to July 14, 1890; Vol. 29, IV: July 21 to Dec. 31, 1890; Vol. 30, V: Jan. 7 to June 30, 1891; Vol. 31, VI: June 7 to Dec. 30, 1891; Vol. 32, VII: Jan. 6 to Aug. 16, 1892 (incorrectly marked VI).

Vol. 33: Telegraphic Correspondence to and from India, Aug. 1886 to Dec. 1887; Vol. 34: 1888. Vol. 35: 1889. Vol. 36: 1890. Vol. 37: 1891. Vol. 38: Jan. 1 to Aug. 18, 1892.

Vols. 39-47: Letters from Governors of Madras, Sir M. E. Grant-Duff, Aug. to Dec. 1886; Lord Connemara, Dec. 1886 to Nov. 1890; Lord Wenlock, Dec. 9, 1890, to Aug. 16, 1892.

Vols. 48-57: Letters from Governors of Bombay, Lord Reay, Aug. 9, 1886, to Apr. 11, 1890; Lord Harris, Mar. 30, 1890, to Sept. 18, 1892.

C. *Papers of Sir John Arthur Godley,* first Baron Kilbracken, Permanent Under-Secretary of State for India, 1883-1909. MSS Eur. F. 102.

Important for correspondence between Godley and the Secretary of State for India and others at the India Office, not duplicated in the Dufferin papers.

Bundle 3: Correspondence, Lord Kimberley, 1883-1886; Bundle 4: Correspondence, Lord Cross, 1886-1892; Bundle 10: Correspondence, Lord Dufferin, 1885-1888; Bundle 27: Correspondence, Mackenzie Wallace, 1885-1888.

D. *Papers of Sir Courtenay Peregrine Ilbert,* Legal Member of the Viceroy's Executive Council, 1882-1886. MSS Eur. D. 594.

Packet 4: Diaries, 1885-1886; Packet 13: Letters from Lord Dufferin, 1885-1888; Packet 16: Letters from A. C. Lyall and others, 1885-1886; Packet 18: Letters from D. Naoroji and others, 1885-1886.

E. *Papers of Sir Alfred Lyall,* Lieutenant-Governor of the Northwest Provinces and Oudh, 1882-1887. Formerly in the private possession of Mrs. R. A. Lyall, who most generously permitted me to use Sir Alfred's correspondence with his sisters, Mrs. Barbara Lyall Webb and Mrs. Sibylla Lyall Holland, as well as his official, private correspondence and miscellaneous papers; in particular, Letter Books 1885-1888, Letters to England.

F. *Papers of the Earl of Lytton,* Viceroy and Governor-General of India, Apr. 1876 to June 1880. MSS Eur. E. 218.

Vols. 13, 14: Printed Papers and Correspondence *re* the Vernacular Press Act, 1878; Vol. 23, I, II: Printed Papers *re* Rules of 1879 for the Indian Civil Service.

Vol. 516, No. 1: Letters from the Secretary of State for India, 1876; No. 2: 1877; No. 3: 1878; No. 4: 1879; No. 5: 1880.

Vol. 518, No. 1: Letters Dispatched to the Secretary of State, 1876; No. 2: 1877; No. 3: 1878; No. 4: 1879; No. 5: 1880.

Vol. 519, Nos. 1, 2, 3: Correspondence to and from Persons in India, 1876; Nos. 4, 5, 6: 1877; Nos. 7, 8, 9: 1878; Nos. 10, 11, 12: 1879; No. 13: 1880.

Vol. 520, No. 1: Notes and Minutes, 1876-1877; No. 2: 1878.

Vol. 522, No. 1: Notes and Minutes, 1879; No. 2: 1880.

G. *Papers of Sir Richard Temple,* I.C.S., 1847-1880; Governor of Bombay, 1877-1880; M.P., Evesham Division of Worcestershire, 1885-1892. MSS Eur. F. 86.

Section III, Box 5, No. 263: Papers *re* Native Agitation in India, 1888.

Vol. 5: Letters to Lytton, 1877-1880; Vols. 193-194: Minutes of the Governor of Bombay, 1877-1880.

H. *Papers of Sir Charles Wood* (Lord Halifax), Secretary of State for India, 1859-1866. MSS Eur. F. 78.

Letter Books, Vol. 3: to Lord Canning, Viceroy, Jan. to Apr. 1860; Vol. 4: May to Sept. 1860; Vol. 5: Oct. to Dec. 1860; Vol. 6: Jan. to Mar. 1861; Vol. 7: Mar. to May 1861; Vol. 8: May to Sept. 1861; Vol. 9: Oct.-Dec. 1861 to Feb. 1862.

Correspondence, India, Box 2, (A), (B) from Canning.

India Board Papers, No. 35, Legislative Council Papers. Printed Material, No. 52, Government of India Bill, 1854.

II. PUBLIC RECORD OFFICE OF NORTHERN IRELAND, BELFAST: THE MARQUIS OF DUFFERIN AND AVA COLLECTION.

All the private papers relating to the official life of the Marquis of Dufferin and Ava were deposited between 1958 and 1960 and catalogued by 1961. Those relating to India (D.1071H/M) consist largely of original copies of letters and telegrams (to 1888) upon which the printed volumes of the Dufferin viceregal correspondence were based.

M1/1-5: Copies of Original Letters from the Viceroy to the Secretary of State, Nov. 1884 to July 27, 1887; M2/1-4: Copies of Original Letters from the Secretary of State to the Viceroy, Feb. 20, 1885, to July 12, 1888.

M6A/1-3: Copy Letters out from Europe, 1885-1887; M7A/1-3: Copy Letters in from India and Burma, 1885-1887; M8A/1-3: Copy Letters out from India and Burma, 1885-1887.

M10/1, 6: Miscellaneous Papers *re* Indian Military Affairs, 1885-1888, 1886-1888.

M12/1-6: Report of the Native Papers, Bengal, Jan 1885 to Dec. 1888; M12/7: Report of the Native Papers, Madras, Jan. 1885 to Dec. 1887; M12/8-10, 12: Report of the Native Papers, Bombay, July 1886 to Dec. 1887.

M13/2: Confidential Report on the Reorganization of the Provincial Legislative Councils, 1889.
M13/9: Notes and Minutes by Lord Dufferin in India, 1885-1888.

III. BRITISH MUSEUM.

A. *Dilke Papers.* Add. MSS 43883, Correspondence with Lord Dufferin.

B. *Gladstone Papers.* Add. MSS 44102, Correspondence with Duke of Argyll especially 1872; Add. MSS 44147, with Lord Hartington, 1884-1885; Add. MSS 44148, with Lord Hartington, 1885-1896; Add. MSS 44151, with Lord Dufferin, 1870-1889; Add. MSS 44177, with Lord Granville, 1884-1885; Add. MSS 44223, with Sir Arthur Godley; Add. MSS 44228, with Lord Kimberley, 1882-1886; Add. MSS 44267, with Lord Northbrook, 1883-1885; Add. MSS 44286, 44287, with Lord Ripon, 1883-1887.

C. *Ripon Papers.* Add. MSS 43515, Correspondence with Gladstone; Add. MSS 43525, 43526, with Lord Kimberley, Mar.-Nov. 1884, 1885-1894; Add. MSS 43569, with Lord Hartington, 1882-1904; Add. MSS 43573, with Lord Northbrook, 1881-1904; Add. MSS 43601, with Sir Courtenay Ilbert, 1880-1886; Add. MSS 43606, with Major General George Chesney, 1883-1889; Add. MSS 43611, with Sir James Gibbs, 1880-1885; Add. MSS 43616, with A. O. Hume and B. Malabari, 1882-1904; Add. MSS 43617, with Sir W. W. Hunter, 1880-1885; Add. MSS 43618, with H. J. S. Cotton, Sir William Wedderburn, 1881-1904; Add. MSS 43635, 43636, General Correspondence, 1884-1885, 1886-1892.

D. *Theosophical Correspondence of A. P. Sinnett, The Mahatma Letters.* Add. MSS 45284-45289, especially 45287, Vol. IV, 45288, Vol. V, 45289A, Vol. VI.

E. *Ripon Viceregal Papers.*
Printed correspondence, in State Paper Room, which in some instances differs significantly from the manuscript correspondence.
I.S. 290/5, 1880, 1881, 1882, 1883, 1884: Correspondence to and from the Secretary of State for India.
I.S. 290/6, Vol. I: Telegraphic Correspondence to and from the Secretary of State, 1880 to July 1884; Vol. II: July 1884 to Dec. 1884.
I.S. 290/7, 1880, 1881, 1882, 1883, 1884: Correspondence to and from Persons in England; I.S. 290/8, two volumes per year, 1880, 1881, 1882, 1883, 1884: Correspondence to and from Persons in India.
I.S. 290/13: Notes on the Principal Measures of Lord Ripon's Viceroyalty.

IV. UNIVERSITY LIBRARY, CAMBRIDGE.

A. *Papers of the Earl of Mayo,* Viceroy and Governor-General, Jan. 1869 to Feb. 1872. Add. MSS 7490, Bundle 14, Sections I-IV, Finance; Correspondence 10, Bundle 60, XXIV, Mayo–J. Strachey Correspondence in India; Correspondence 11, Bundle 61, XLVI, Mayo–Temple Correspondence.

B. *Papers of Sir D. Mackenzie Wallace.* These are uncatalogued, and none of them pertains to his years in India; many of his papers were destroyed in a fire shortly after his death.

V. MISCELLANEOUS.

A. *Papers of Lord Kimberley.* These were closed for research in 1959 in accordance with the personal wishes of the present Lord Kimberley but Dr. Sarvepalli Gopal very kindly permitted me to use his notes. Most of the Kimberley–Dufferin correspondence is to be found in the Dufferin papers.
Box D/22b: Kimberley to Dufferin, Nov. 21, 1884, to July 1885; Box D/22d: Dufferin to Kimberley, Feb. 14 to Sept. 20, 1886.
Box D/26a: Kimberley to Lord Reay, 1885-1886; Box D/26b: from Lord Reay, 1885-1886.
Box D/30, 31: Parliamentary Inquiry into Indian Administration, 1886.
Box D/34: Miscellaneous Correspondence, 1885-1886.

B. *From members of their families I learned that the families now possess no papers of: Allan Octavian Hume; William Digby; Sir William Wedderburn (destroyed); Sir Auckland Colvin (destroyed 1954); Sir George Allen (destroyed 1958); Theodore Beck and Sir Theodore Morison (no private correspondence between them or their colleagues).*

OFFICIAL RECORDS

I. INDIA OFFICE LIBRARY, COMMONWEALTH RELATIONS OFFICE.

Abstract of the Proceedings of the Council of the Governor-General of India for making Laws and Regulations, 1869, 1878, 1885, 1887, 1888, 1889.
Abstract of the Proceedings of the Council of the Lieutenant-Governor of Bengal for Making Laws and Regulations, 1885.
Bengal Military Letters and Enclosures, 1885, Vols. 482, 483, 484, 485, 486, 487; 1886, Vols. 489, 490, 491.
Government of India Legislative Department Proceedings, 1885, Vol. 2572.
Government of India Military Proceedings, Abstracts Part A, Part B, 1885, Vols. 2553, 2554, 2555, 2557, 2559.
Indian Financial Letters and Enclosures, 1885, Vol. 147 and enclosures Vol. 149; 1886, Vol. 148 and enclosures Vol. 150.
Judicial and Public Copies of Dispatches to India, Madras, and Bombay, Vols. 1883, 1885, 1886, 1887, 1888, 1889, 1892.
Political and Secret Records (Home Correspondence), 1885, Vol. 80.
Public Letters from India and General Letters from Bengal, Judicial and Public, 1884, Vol. V; 1885, Vol. VI; 1886, Vol. VII; 1887, Vol. VIII; 1888, Vol. IX; 1889, Vol. X.
Selections from Dispatches Addressed to the Several Governments in India by the Secretary of State in Council, 1876, Series 19, Vol. 9, Part I, 1884; Series 27, Vol. 25, Part I, Vol. 26, Part II; 1885, Series 28, Vol. 27, Part I, Vol 28, Part II, 1886, Series 29, Vol. 29, Part I, Vol. 30, Part II; 1888, Series 31 Vol. 33, Part I, Vol. 34, Part II; 1889, Series 32, Vol. 35, Part I, Vol. 36, Part II.
Selections from the Native Press, Vols. Bombay, Madras, Bengal, Northwest Provinces and Oudh, Punjab for 1885, 1886, 1887, 1888.
The Calcutta Gazette, 1884-1885.
A Collection of Statutes Relating to India (Calcutta, 1881), Vol. I.

The Gazette of India, 1885-1888.
The Report of the Administration of Bengal, 1885-86 (Calcutta, 1887).
The Report of the Indian Education Commission (Calcutta, 1883).
The Report of the Public Service Commission, 1886-87 (Calcutta, 1888).

II. PARLIAMENTARY PAPERS.

Burma, *P.P.,* 1883, Vol. 50, Com. 3501; 1886, Vol. 50, Com. 4614, Com. 4690.
Central Asia and Afghanistan, *P.P.,* 1880, Vol. 78, Com. 2470; 1881, Vol. 70, Com. 2852; 1881, Vol. 98, Com. 2798, Com. 2802, Com. 2844; 1884-85, Vol. 87, Com. 4309; 1885, Vol. 87, Com. 4387.
Egypt, *P.P.,* 1883, Vol. 83, Com. 3529.
Employment of Indians in public service and Civil Service reform: *P.P.,* 1847-48, Vol. 48, Ret. 20; 1857-58, Vol. 42, Ret. 201-VI; 1867-68, Vol. 50, Ret. 178, Vol. 51, Ret. 108; 1878-79, Vol. 55, Com. 2376; 1894, Vol. 60, Com. 7378. Repeal of Vernacular Press Act, *P.P.,* 1881, Vol. 68, Ret. 160. Local self-government reform, *P.P.,* 1883, Vol. 51, Ret. 931. Criminal Jurisdiction Bill, *P.P.,* Vol. 51, Com. 3512.
Sanitation, *P.P.,* 1884, Vol. 54, Com. 4116; 1887, Vol. 63, Com. 5209.

III. PARLIAMENTARY DEBATES.

3 *Hansard,* 18, 19 (1832) ; 151 (1858) ; 246, 247 (1879) ; 292 (1884) ; 295, 297, 298, 299, 300 (1885).

NEWSPAPERS

Collections at India Office Library and Newspaper Room, British Museum Annex.

I. INDIA: ANGLO-INDIAN (1884-1888).
The Bombay Gazette, The Bombay Gazette Overland Summary, The Civil and Military Gazette (Lahore), *The Englishman* (Calcutta), *The Englishman's Overland Mail* (Calcutta), *Indian Daily News* (Calcutta) *The Madras Mail,* 1883-1888, *The Madras Times,* 1883-1888, *The Madras Standard,* 1883-1888, *The Pioneer* (Allahabad), *The Pioneer Mail* (Overland), *The Statesman and Friend of India* (Calcutta), *The Times of India* (Bombay).

II. INDIA: INDIAN (1884-1888).

The Voice of India, selections from the Indian press published in English and in vernacular. Proprietor, D. Naoroji; editor, B. M. Malabari; published, Bombay. Vols. II, June-Dec. 1884; III, 1885; IV, 1886; V, 1887; VI, 1888, VII, 1889.
The Bengalee (Calcutta), *The Hindoo Patriot* (Calcutta), *The Indian Mirror* (Calcutta), *The Indian Spectator* (Bombay), *The Tribune* (Lahore).

III. ENGLAND.

The Birmingham Daily Post, Sept.-Dec. 1885; *The Cambrian* (Swansea), Sept.-Dec. 1885; *The Christian World* (London), Sept.-Dec. 1885; *The Daily News* (London), July-Dec. 1885, Jan. 1886; *The Echo* (London), Sept.-Dec. 1885; *The Evening Standard* (London), July-Dec. 1885, Jan. 1886; *The*

Manchester Guardian, July-Dec. 1885, Jan. 1886: *The Newcastle Daily Lead-er* (Newcastle-on-Tyne), Sept.-Dec. 1885; *The Pall Mall Gazette* (London), Jan.-Dec. 1885, Jan.-Feb. 1886; *St. James's Gazette* (London), Jan.-Dec. 1885, Jan.-Feb. 1886; *The Times* (London), 1884-1888; *The West London Observer,* Sept.-Dec. 1885.

CONTEMPORARY ARTICLES, SPEECHES, JOURNALS, PAMPHLETS, REPORTS.

Audi Alteram Partem: Being two letters [by Sir A. Colvin and A. O. Hume, respectively] *on certain Aspects of the Indian National Congress Movement. With an Appendix Containing a Letter* [by A. O. Hume] *to the Indian Mirror.* Simla [1888].

Baring, Evelyn. "Recent Events in India," *The Nineteenth Century,* 14 (Oct. 1883), 569-584.

Beck, Theodore. *Essays on Indian Topics.* Allahabad, 1888.

Bhinga, Raja of. *Democracy Not Suited to India.* Allahabad, 1888.

Chandavarkar, Narayana G. *English Impressions, Gathered in Connection with the Indian Delegation to England during the General Election of 1885.* Bombay, 1887.

Collen, H. H. "The Volunteer Force of India," *Journal of the United Service Institution of India,* 12:58 (1883).

Cotton, Henry J. S. "Has India Food for Its People?" *The Fortnightly Review,* new series, 22 (1877), 867-877.

———. "India's Need and England's Duty," *The New Quarterly Magazine,* new series, 2 (1879), 237-254.

———. *New India, or India in Transition.* London, 1885.

———. "The Prospects of Moral Progress in India," *The Fortnightly Review,* new series, 24 (1878), 387-398.

Curzon, George N. "Our True Policy in India: A Rejoinder," *The National Review,* 13 (Mar. 1889), 118-124.

"Data for History," *The Theosophist,* 10, Supplement (Sept. 1889), 169-170.

Digby, William. *The General Election, 1885: India's Interest in the British Ballot Box.* London (1888).

———. *Indian Politics in England: The Story of An Indian Reform Bill in Parliament.* Lucknow, 1890.

———. *Indian Problems for English Consideration: A Letter to the Council of the National Liberal Federation.* Plymouth, 1881.

Dufferin and Ava, Hariot Georgina Blackwood, Marchioness of. *Our Viceregal Life in India: Selections from My Journal, 1884-1888.* 2 vols. London, 1889.

Hume, Allan O. *Agricultural Reform in India.* London, 1879.

———. *The Old Man's Hope: A Tract for the Times.* Calcutta, 1886.

———. *The Rising Tide: Or the Progress of Political Activity in India.* Calcutta, 1886.

———. *A Speech on the Indian National Congress: Its Origins, Aims and Objects, Delivered at Allahabad, 30 April 1888.* Calcutta [1888].

———. *The Star in the East: Or the Bengal National League.* Calcutta, 1886.

"India under the Marquis of Dufferin," *The Edinburgh Review,* 169 (Jan. 1889), 1-43. [Attributed to Sir A. Lyall.]

The Indian National Congress: Session at Allahabad, December 1888. Impressions of Two English Visitors. London, 1889.

Jennings, Louis J., ed. *Speeches of the Right Honourable Lord Randolph*

Churchill, M.P., 1880-1888. 2 vols. London, 1889.

Journal of the East India Association. Vols. 4, 15-21. London, 1870, 1883-1889.

Keay, J. Seymour. "The Spoliation of India," *The Nineteenth Century,* 14 (July 1883), 1-22; 15 (Apr. 1884), 559-582; 15 (May 1884), 721-740.

The Madras Mahajana Sabha: Annual Report for 1885-1886. Madras, 1886.

"Marquis of Salisbury, K. G.," *The Fortnightly Review,* new series, 36 (1884), 149-163.

Mr. A. O. Hume's Farewell to India. As Reported for the Bombay Presidency Association. London, 1894.

Pal, Bipin C. *The Basis of Political Reform: The Substance of a Lecture* [Mar. 18, 1889]. Calcutta, 1889.

———. *The National Congress.* [Lecture, Nov. 20, 1887]. Lahore, 1887.

Palit, Ram C., ed. *Speeches of Babu Surendra Nath Banerjea.* 2 vols. Calcutta, 1885.

Pincott, Frederic. "Indian National Congress," *The National Review,* 13 (June 1889), 526-538.

The Poona Sarvajanik Sabha Quarterly Journal. Vols. 7-11. Poona, 1884-1888.

Pullen, J., ed. *The Journal of Miss Adelaide M. Shuckburgh, 1885.* [Reprinted in *The Missionary Times,* London, Mar.-Apr. 1948.]

Report of the First Indian National Congress Held in Bombay on the 28th, 29th, 30th December 1885. Lucknow, 1886.

Report of the Second Indian National Congress Held at Calcutta on the 27th, 28th, 29th, 30th December 1886, Calcutta, 1887.

Report of the Third Indian National Congress Held at Madras on the 27th, 28th, 29th, and 30th December 1887. London, 1888.

Report of the Fourth Indian National Congress Held at Allahabad on the 26th, 27th, 28th and 29th of December 1888. [N.p.], 1889.

The Report of the First Madras Conference, 1884-1885. Madras, 1885.

Rules and Objects of the Central National Mahommedan Association and Its Branch Associations with the Quinquennial and Annual Reports and List of Members. Calcutta, 1885.

Showing the Seditious Character of the Indian National Congress and the Opinions Held by Eminent Natives of India Who Are Opposed to the Movement. Allahabad, 1888.

Slagg, John. "The National Indian Congress," *The Nineteenth Century,* 19 (May 1886), 710-721.

Smith, G. Leslie. "The Congress and Modern India," *The National Review,* 13 (Apr. 1889), 202-219.

Speeches by Sir Syed Ahmed. Allahabad, 1888.

"Trust and Fear Not" [Harrison, Sir Henry]. *Ought Natives to Be Welcomed as Volunteers?* Calcutta, 1885.

Wallace, Donald MacKenzie, ed. *Speeches Delivered in India, 1884-8, by the Marquis of Dufferin and Ava.* London, 1890.

Watson, Robert S. "Indian National Congresses," *The Contemporary Review,* 54 (July 1888), 89-104.

SECONDARY WORKS

ARTICLES

Ballhatchet, Kenneth A. "The Home Government and Bentinck's Educational

Policy," *The Cambridge Historical Journal,* 10 (1951), 224-229.

Cowling, Maurice. "Lytton, the Cabinet, and the Russians, August to November 1878," *The English Historical Review,* 76 (1961), 59-79.

Cumpston, Mary. "Some Early Indian Nationalists and Their Allies in the British Parliament, 1851-1906," *The English Historical Review,* 76 (1961), 279-297.

Hambly, G. R. G. "Richard Temple and the Punjab Tenancy Act of 1868," *The English Historical Review,* 79 (1964), 47-66.

Martin, Briton Jr. "The Viceroyalty of Lord Dufferin," *History Today,* 10 (Dec. 1960), 821-830, and 11 (Jan. 1961), 56-64.

Metcalf, Thomas R. "The Influence of the Mutiny of 1857 on Land Policy in India," *The Historical Journal,* 4 (1961), 152-163.

Penson, Dame Lillian M. "The Principles and Methods of Lord Salisbury's Foreign Policy," *The Cambridge Historical Journal,* 5 (1935), 87-106.

Sherwani, A. K. "The Political Thought of Sir Syed Ahmad Khan," *Islamic Culture,* 18 (July 1944), 236-253.

Spear, Percival. "Bentinck and Education," *The Cambridge Historical Journal,* 6 (1938), 78-101.

Trench, Frederic C. "The Late Russian Campaign Against Khiva," *Journal of Royal United Service Institution,* 17:73 (1875), 212-226.

BOOKS

Andrews, Charles F., and Girija Mukerji. *The Rise and Growth of the Congress in India.* London, 1938.

Argov, Daniel. *Moderates and Extremists in the Indian Nationalist Movement,* 1883-1920. Bombay, 1967.

Argyll, George Douglas Campbell, eighth Duke of. *The Eastern Question.* 2 vols. London, 1879.

Ashworth, William. *An Economic History of England: 1870-1939.* London, 1960.

Baljon, Johannes M. S. *The Reforms and Religious Ideas of Sir Sayyid Ahmad Khan.* Leiden, 1949.

Banerjea, Surendranath. *A Nation in Making: Being the Reminiscences of Fifty Years of Public Life.* London, 1925.

Banerjee, Anil C. *The Annexation of Burma.* Calcutta, 1944.

Barns, Margarita. *The Indian Press: A History of the Growth of Public Opinion in India.* London, 1940.

Bell, Evans. *The Oxus and the Indus.* 1st and 2nd eds. London, 1869, 1874.

Bell, John Hyslop. *British Folks and British India Fifty Years Ago: Joseph Pease and His Contemporaries.* London, 1891.

Besant, Annie. *How India Wrought for Freedom.* Madras, 1915.

———. *India: A Nation.* London, 1915.

Blavatsky, Helene P. *From the Caves and Jungles of Hindostan.* London, 1892.

Blunt, Wilfrid Scawen. *Ideas about India.* London, 1885.

———. *India under Ripon: A Private Diary.* London, 1909.

———. *My Diaries, Being a Personal Narrative of Events, 1888-1914.* 2 pts. London, 1919, 1920.

Bonnerjee, Womesh C., ed. *Indian Politics.* Madras, 1898.

Buckland, Charles E. *Dictionary of Indian Biography.* London, 1906.

Buckle, George E., ed. *The Letters of Queen Victoria.* 2nd series. Vol. III, *1879-1885.* London, 1928.

Cady, John F. *A History of Modern Burma.* New York, 1958.

Campbell, Sir George. *The British Empire.* London, 1886.

———. *India As It May Be: An Outline of a Proposed Government and Policy.* London, 1853.

Cecil, Lady Gwendolen. *The Life of Robert, Marquis of Salisbury.* 4 vols. London, 1921-1932.

Charlu, P. Ananda. *On Indian Politics: Letters (1886-1899).* Madras, 1899.

Chintamani, Chirravuri Y. *Indian Politics since the Mutiny.* Allahabad, 1947.

———. *Indian Social Reform.* Madras, 1901.

Churchill, Winston S. *Lord Randolph Churchill.* 2 vols. London, 1906.

Colquhoun, Archibald R. *Across Chryse.* London, 1883.

———. *Burma and the Burmans: "Best Unopened Market in the World."* London, 1885.

———. *English Policy in the Far East,* London, 1885.

Cory, Arthur. *Shadows of Coming Events or the Eastern Menace.* London, 1876.

Cotton, Sydney J. *The Central Asian Question.* Manchester, 1873.

Cromer, Evelyn Baring, first Earl. *Modern Egypt.* 2 vols. London, 1908.

Cross, Cecil M. P. *The Development of Self-Government in India 1858-1914.* Chicago, 1922.

Cumming, Sir John, ed. *Political India 1832-1932:A Co-operative Survey of a Century.* London, 1932.

Das Gupta, Hemendra N. *The Indian National Congress.* Vol. I. Calcutta, 1946.

De Mello, Frederick M. *The Indian National Congress: An Historical Sketch.* Bombay, 1934.

Desai, Aksayakumar R. *Social Background of Indian Nationalism.* Oxford, 1948.

Dodwell, Henry H., ed. *The Cambridge History of India.* Vol. V. *British India 1497-1858.* Vol. VI, *The Indian Empire 1858-1918.* Cambridge, 1929, 1932.

Finch, Edith. *Wilfrid Scawen Blunt 1840-1922.* London, 1938.

Furnivall, John S. *Colonial Policy and Practice.* Cambridge, 1948.

Fytche, Albert. *Burma Past and Present.* 2 vols. London, 1878.

Geary, Grattan. *Burma, After the Conquest.* London, 1886.

Ghosh, Pansy Chaya. *The Development of the Indian National Congress 1892-1909.* Calcutta, 1960.

Gopal, Ram. *Indian Muslims: A Political History (1858-1947).* Bombay, 1959.

Gopal, Sarvepalli. *The Viceroyalty of Lord Ripon 1880-1884.* London, 1953.

Graham, George F. I. *The Life and Work of Syed Ahmed Khan.* Edinburgh, 1885.

Griffiths, Sir Percival. *The British Impact on India.* London, 1952.

Gwynn, Stephen, and Gertrude M. Tuckwell. *The Life of the Rt. Hon. Sir Charles W. Dilke, Bart., M.P.* 2 vols. London, 1917.

Halévy, Elie. *Imperialism and the Rise of Labour.* 2nd ed. Vol. V. London, 1951.

Hamilton, Lord George: *Parliamentary Reminiscences and Reflections 1868 to 1885.* London, 1917. [Reprinted in 1922 as Vol. I of a two-volume edition; Vol. II, *1886-1906.*]

Hammond, John L. *Gladstone and the Irish Nation.* London, 1938.

Holland, Bernard. *The Life of Spencer Compton, Eighth Duke of Devonshire.* 2 vols. London, 1911.

Ilbert, Courtenay. *The Government of India: Being a Digest of the Statute Law Relating Thereto.* 2nd ed. Oxford, 1907.

James, Robert R. *Lord Randolph Churchill.* London, 1959.

Kaye, John W. *The Administration of the East India Company.* 2nd ed. London, 1853.

Kennedy, Aubrey L. *Salisbury 1830-1903: Portrait of a Statesman.* London, 1953.

Kilbracken, Sir Arthur Godley, first Baron. *Reminiscences of Lord Kilbracken.* London, 1931.

Laurie, William F. B. *Our Burmese Wars and Relations with Burma.* 2nd ed. London, 1885.

Lecky, William E. H. *Leaders of Public Opinion in Ireland.* 2 vols. New ed. London, 1903.

Lovett, H. Verney. *A History of the Indian Nationalist Movement.* London, 1920.

Lucy, Henry W. *A Diary of Two Parliaments.* 2 vols, London, 1885-1886.

Lyall, Alfred C. *The Life of the Marquis of Dufferin and Ava.* 2 vols. London, 1905.

McCully, Bruce T. *English Education and the Origins of Indian Nationalism.* New York, 1940.

Maclagan, Michael. *"Clemency" Canning: Charles John, 1st Earl Canning, Governor-General and Viceroy of India 1856-1862.* London, 1962.

Mallet, Bernard. *Thomas George Earl of Northbrook G.C.S.I.: A Memoir.* London, 1908.

Marvin, Charles. *The Russians at Merv and Herat, and Their Power of Invading India.* London, 1883.

Masani, Rustom P. *Dadabhai Naoroji: The Grand Old Man of India.* London, 1939.

Mayhew, Arthur. *The Education of India.* London, 1926.

Mazumdar, Amvika C. *Indian National Evolution: A Brief Survey of the Origin and Progress of the Indian National Congress and the Growth of Indian Nationalism.* 2nd ed. Madras, 1917.

Misra, Bankey B. *The Indian Middle Classes: Their Growth in Modern Times.* London, 1961.

Mody, Hormasji P. *Sir Pherozeshah Mehta: A Political Biography.* Bombay, 1921.

Morley, John Morley, Viscount. *The Life of William Ewart Gladstone.* 3 vols. London, 1903.

Mukherjee, Maniklal. *W. C. Bonnerjee: Snapshots from His Life and His London Letters.* Calcutta, 1944.

Natarajan, J. *History of Indian Journalism.* Republic of India, Report of the Press Commission, Pt. II. New Delhi, 1954.

Newton, Thomas Wodehouse Legh, second Baron. *Lord Lansdowne: A Biography.* London, 1929.

Nicolson, Harold. *Helen's Tower.* London, 1937.

Nisbet, John. *Burma under British Rule—and Before.* 2 vols. London, 1901.

Olcott, Henry S. *Old Diary Leaves: The True Story of the Theosophical Society.* 3 vols. I, *1874-78.* New York, 1895. II, *1878-83,* and III, *1883-87.* London, 1900, 1904.

O'Malley, Lewis S. S., ed. *Modern India and the West.* London, 1941.

Pal, Dharm. *The Administration of Sir John Lawrence in India 1864-1869*. Simla, 1952.

Panikkar, Kavalam M. *Nationalism: Its Origin, History and Ideals*, by K. M. Panikkar and an Englishman. London, 1920.

Pillai, Govinda P. *Representative Indians*. London, 1897.

Raghuvanshi, V. P. S. *Indian Nationalist Movement and Thought*. Agra, 1951.

Rai, Lala Lajpat. *Young India: An Interpretation and a History of the Nationalist Movement from Within*. New York, 1916.

Ratcliffe, Samuel K. *Sir William Wedderburn and the Indian Reform Movement*. London, 1923.

Rawlinson, Henry C. *England and Russia in the East*. London, 1875.

Robinson, Ronald, and John Gallagher, with Alice Denny. *Africa and the Victorians: The Official Mind of Imperialism*. London, 1961.

Rosebery, Archibald Philip Primrose, fifth Earl of. *Lord Randolph Churchill*. London, 1906.

Scott, James G. *Gazetteer of Upper Burma and the Shan States*. Vol. I, Pt. I. Rangoon, 1900.

Singh, Hira Lal. *Problems and Policies of the British in India 1885-1898*. London, 1963.

Sinnett, Alfred P. *The Occult World*. 2nd ed. London, 1881.

Sitaramayya, B. Pattabhi. *The History of the Indian National Congress 1885-1935*. Madras, 1935. [Reprinted in Bombay in 1946 as Vol. I of a two-volume edition; Vol. II, *1935-1947*, Bombay, 1947.]

Smith, Wilfred C. *Modern Islam in India*. Lahore, 1943.

Source Materials for a History of the Freedom Movement in India (Collected from Bombay Government Records). Vol. II, *1885-1920*. Bombay, 1958.

Strachey, Sir John. *India*. London, 1888.

Strachey, Sir John, and Lieutenant-General Richard Strachey. *The Finances and Public Works of India from 1869 to 1881*. London, 1882.

Symonds, John. *Madame Blavatsky: Medium and Magician*. London 1959.

Temple, Sir Richard. *India in 1880*. London, 1880.

———. *Men and Events of My Time in India*. London, 1882.

Thornton, Archibald P. *The Imperial Idea and Its Enemies: A Study in British Power*. London, 1959.

Trench, Frederic C. *The Russo-Indian Question*. London, 1869.

Trevelyan, Sir Charles Edward. *On the Education of the People of India*. London, 1838.

Trevelyan, George M. *The Life of John Bright*. London, 1913.

Tyabji, Husain B. *Badruddin Tyabji: A Biography*. Bombay, 1952.

Wedderburn, Sir William. *Allan Octavian Hume, C.B.: "Father of the Indian National Congress." 1829 to 1912*. London, 1913.

Wolpert, Stanley A. *Tilak and Gokhale: Revolution and Reform in the Making of Modern India*. Berkeley, 1962.

Woodman, Dorothy. *The Making of Burma*. London, 1962.

Woodward, Ernest L. *The Age of Reform 1815-1870*. 7th ed. London, 1958.

Wyllie, John W. S. *Essays on the External Policy of India*. London, 1875.

Young, George M., ed. *Speeches by Lord Macaulay, with His Minute on Indian Education*. London, 1935.

UNPUBLISHED THESES

Chakvravarty, S. "The Evolution of Representative Government in India,

1884-1909, with Reference to Central and Provincial Legislative Councils." University of London, Ph.D., 1954.

So, Y. K. "Anglo-Chinese Diplomacy Regarding Burma 1885-1897." University of London, Ph.D., 1960.

Jones, I. M. "The Origins and Development to 1892 of the Indian National Congress." University of London, M.A., 1947.

Index

In compiling the index the following abbreviations have been used:
I.N.C.: Indian National Congress; I.N.U.: Indian National Union